COLONIALISM, WORLD LITERATURE, AND THE MAKING OF THE MODERN CULTURE OF LETTERS

In a radical and ambitious reconceptualization of the field, this book argues that global literary culture since the eighteenth century was fundamentally shaped by colonial histories. It offers a comprehensive account of the colonial inception of the literary sovereign – how the realm of literature was thought to be separate from history and politics – and then follows that narrative through a wide array of different cultures, multilingual archives, and geographical locations. Providing close studies of colonial archives, German philosophy of aesthetics, French realist novels, and English literary history, this book shows how colonialism shaped and reshaped modern literary cultures in decisive ways. It breaks fresh grounds across disciplines such as literary studies, anthropology, history, and philosophy, and invites one to rethink the history of literature in a new light.

BAIDIK BHATTACHARYA is Associate Professor at the Centre for the Study of Developing Societies. He is the author of the much-acclaimed book *Postcolonial Writing in the Era of World Literature: Texts, Territories, Globalizations* (2018). His works have appeared in some of the leading journals of our times: *Critical Inquiry*, *New Literary History*, *Boundary 2*, *Modern Philology*, *Interventions*, and *Postcolonial Studies*, among others.

CAMBRIDGE STUDIES IN WORLD LITERATURE

Editors
Debjani Ganguly, University of Virginia
Francesca Orsini, SOAS University of London

World Literature is a vital part of twenty-first-century critical studies. Globalization and unprecedented levels of connectivity through communication technologies force literary scholars to rethink the scale of literary production and their own critical practices. As an exciting field that engages seriously with the place and function of literary studies in our global era, the study of world literature requires new approaches. Cambridge Studies in World Literature is founded on the assumption that world literature is not all literatures of the world nor a canonical set of globally successful literary works. The series will highlight scholarship on literary works that focus on the logics of circulation drawn from multiple literary cultures and technologies of the textual. While not rejecting the nation as a site of analysis, the series will offer insights into new cartographies – the hemispheric, the oceanic, the transregional, the archipelagic, the multilingual local – that better reflect the multiscalar and spatially dispersed nature of literary production. It will highlight the creative coexistence, flashpoints, and intersections of language worlds from both the Global South and the Global North, and multiworld models of literary production and literary criticism that these have generated. It will push against existing historical, methodological, and cartographic boundaries and showcase humanistic and literary endeavors in the face of world-scale environmental and humanitarian catastrophes.

In This Series
SAMUEL HODGKIN
Persianate Verse and the Poetics of Eastern Internationalism

DUNCAN M. YOON
China in Twentieth- and Twenty-First-Century African Literature

LEVI THOMPSON
Re-Orienting Modernism: Mapping a Modernist Geography Across Arabic and Persian Poetry

SARAH QUESADA
The African Heritage of Latinx and Caribbean Literature

ROANNE L. KANTOR
South Asian Writers, Latin American Literature, and the Rise of Global English

COLONIALISM, WORLD LITERATURE, AND THE MAKING OF THE MODERN CULTURE OF LETTERS

BAIDIK BHATTACHARYA
Centre for the Study of Developing Societies

Shaftesbury Road, Cambridge CB2 8EA, United Kingdom

One Liberty Plaza, 20th Floor, New York, NY 10006, USA

477 Williamstown Road, Port Melbourne, VIC 3207, Australia

314–321, 3rd Floor, Plot 3, Splendor Forum, Jasola District Centre, New Delhi – 110025, India

103 Penang Road, #05–06/07, Visioncrest Commercial, Singapore 238467

Cambridge University Press is part of Cambridge University Press & Assessment, a department of the University of Cambridge.

We share the University's mission to contribute to society through the pursuit of education, learning and research at the highest international levels of excellence.

www.cambridge.org
Information on this title: www.cambridge.org/9781009422642

DOI: 10.1017/9781009422635

© Baidik Bhattacharya 2024

This publication is in copyright. Subject to statutory exception and to the provisions of relevant collective licensing agreements, no reproduction of any part may take place without the written permission of Cambridge University Press & Assessment.

First published 2024

Printed in the United Kingdom by TJ Books Limited, Padstow, Cornwall, 2024

A catalogue record for this publication is available from the British Library

A Cataloging-in-Publication data record for this book is available from the Library of Congress

ISBN 978-1-009-42264-2 Hardback

Cambridge University Press & Assessment has no responsibility for the persistence or accuracy of URLs for external or third-party internet websites referred to in this publication and does not guarantee that any content on such websites is, or will remain, accurate or appropriate.

*For
Mallarika
The comrade in arms*

Contents

List of Figures	*page* viii
Preface and Acknowledgments	ix
Introduction: Formations of the Literary Sovereign	1

PART I   EPISTEMIC HABITS

1	Ethnographic Recension	53
2	Colonial Untranslatables	82
3	Comparatism in the Colony	117

PART II   AESTHETIC CONVENTIONS

4	Impure Aesthetics	149
5	Sanskrit on Shagreen	174
6	National Enframing	201
Coda: Decolonization after World Literature		239

Notes	243
Bibliography	272
Index	286

Figures

3.1 Jones's table showing parallels between Christian, Islamic, and Hindu chronologies. William Jones, "On the Chronology of the Hindus," in *The Works of Sir William Jones*, 13 Vols. (London: John Stockdale and John Walker, 1807), 4: 47. *page* 125
3.2 A list of comparative vocabulary. B. H. Hodgson, "Comparative Vocabulary of the Languages of the Broken Tribes of Népál," *Journal of the Asiatic Society*, Vol. 26, No. 5 (1857), 320. 133
3.3 Table from W. W. Hunter, *A Comparative Dictionary of the Languages of India and High Asia, with a Dissertation* (London: Trübner, 1868), 82. 135
3.4 George Abraham Grierson, "Map Showing the Localities in Which the Eastern Group of the Indo-Aryan Languages Is Spoken," in *Linguistic Survey of India*, 11 Vols. (Calcutta: Government of India Central Publication Branch, 1903–28), vol. v, Part 1, frontispiece. 141
5.1 Honoré de Balzac, *La Peau de chagrin* (Paris: Charpentier, 1839), 40. 185
5.2 "La Rue du Caire," Delort de Gléon, *La Rue du Caire: L'Architecture Arabe des Khalifes d'Égypte à l'Exposition Universelle de Paris en 1889* (Paris: Librairie Plon, 1889), 21, 25. 198
6.1 John Beddoe, *The Races of Britain* (Bristol: J. W. Arrowsmith 1885), 150. 226

Preface and Acknowledgments

This book has two different yet related genealogies. The first one is concerned with the origins of the modern idea of the literary in the late eighteenth century. I trace this history through the dusty colonial archives of British India and suggest that it had a close and reciprocal connection with the new idea of colonial sovereignty. The second genealogy is concerned with the circulation of this colonial moment into the wider world, and how this specific history created the modern culture of letters across continents and languages. I first track this circulation through the idea of world literature and then show how colonialism made important inroads into modern literary cultures in Europe. Through related studies of eighteenth-century German philosophy of aesthetic judgment, through French novels, and eventually through the rise of the new discipline of literary history in Britain I demonstrate how the colonial moment constituted the bedrock of modern literary cultures.

This book also stands at the crossroad between postcolonial studies and world literature studies, and attempts to reimagine both. It is in conversation with recent works in both fields, and, as such, is an endeavor to redraw the boundaries between the two. My suggestion is that by revisiting the vital question of the historicity of the literary, and by placing it within imperial networks and colonial governance, we can get a new and historically accurate perspective on the connection between postcolonial and world literature studies. Modern literary culture, after all, is not a clear bequest of any one culture or civilization – whether European or otherwise – but a complex legacy of global connections and transactions. From the eighteenth century onward the behemoth of these interactions has been modern European empires and their vast networks of overseas colonies. It is only by attending to these multilingual and multicultural contexts of modern empires, and their political and social institutions, that one can get a glimpse into the historicity of literature.

In other words, this book challenges some of the accepted tenets of literary studies, and reopens its foundational principles for fresh and innovative reinvestigation. The framework within which this operation takes place is the broad idea of decolonization both as a political orientation and as a working method. Decolonization as a method is intended to function as the subtext for the intellectual inquiry I undertake in this book, guiding its minute details and conventions. But, at the same time, it is also meant to gesture at a political horizon or an ethical limit that informs my argument. In essence, it is a position born out of my location in a postcolonial academic world and out of my attempts to reimagine the vast field of literary studies in all its myriad minutiae. Decolonization as a principle, thus, is both a signal for locational politics and a method to reimagine literary studies for our present times. This book is offered in terms of this dual strategy, in its essential contingency and ambition.

This book was conceived and written over a period of time, and I have incurred debts of various kinds along the way. I am most grateful to a group of friends and colleagues who read various sections of the book and gave me invaluable feedback: Emily Apter, Prathama Banerjee, David Damrosch, Debjani Ganguly, Udaya Kumar, Premesh Lalu, Aamir R. Mufti, Aditya Nigam, Francesca Orsini, V. Sanil, Sambudha Sen, Mallarika Sinha Roy, Ravi Sundaram, and Rajeswari Sunder Rajan. Their suggestions, queries, and support have been critical in clarifying my thoughts and arguments. While I have benefited from their scholarship and generosity, all the shortcomings are strictly mine.

I have presented parts of this book at various fora during the last few years, including Ambedkar University, Ashoka University, the University of California, Los Angeles, the University of Cape Town, the Centre for the Study of Social Sciences, Calcutta, the University of Chicago, Columbia University, Delhi University, Jawaharlal Nehru University, Jindal Global University, New York University, Shiv Nadar University, SNDT University, the University of Virginia, the University of the Western Cape, and the University of Wisconsin-Madison. I would like to thank my hosts and different interlocutors at these venues for their generosity, discussions, suggestions, and questions, all of which have been crucial for the book: Radha Chakravarty, Sayandeb Chowdhury, Saikat Majumdar, Muhsin al-Musawi, B. Venkat Mani, Ato Quayson, Bodhisattva Kar, Rosinka Chaudhuri, Prachi Deshpande, Josephine McDonagh, Rochona Majumdar, Gayatri Chakravorty Spivak, Bruno G. Bosteels, Brent Hayes

Edwards, Sonali Perera, Mark Sanders, Priya Kumar, Rita Banerjee, Kanupriya Dhingra, Toral Gajarawala, the late Aniket Jaaware, Debjani Ganguly, Mrinalini Chakravorty, Patricia Hayes, Premesh Lalu, John Mowitt, and Sunny Yudkoff.

I am thankful to David Damrosch for his invitation to teach at the Harvard summer school at the Institute for World Literature (IWL) in 2020 and 2022. While trying out some of the material offered here in my seminars, and interacting with a diverse group of participants of the IWL, I became keenly aware of a possible international audience for my arguments. And this has played a decisive role in the final writing process. I would also like to thank the participants of my seminars for their patience with unfamiliar material and also for their enthusiasm for debate and discussion.

My sincere thanks are also due to my colleagues at the Centre for the Study of Developing Societies (CSDS), Delhi, for their intellectual camaraderie and enthusiasm for a project like this: Hilal Ahmed, Sanjeer Alam, Prathama Banerjee, Rajeev Bhargava, Abhay Dubey, Nishikant Kolge, Prabhat Kumar, Sanjay Kumar, Shail Mayaram, Rakesh Pandey, Ravikant, Awadhendra Sharan, Ravi Sundaram, Ananya Vajpeyi, and Ravi Vasudevan. I have benefited from many discussions – both formal and informal – with my colleagues over the last few years since I joined the CSDS.

I am extremely fortunate to have Debjani Ganguly and Francesca Orsini as my series editors. Their enthusiasm for the project from the beginning and their sound advice at various stages of writing and editing have sustained the book in important ways. I am also grateful to the two anonymous readers for Cambridge University Press for their careful reading of the manuscript and their constructive suggestions on certain sections. I am equally grateful to my Cambridge University Press editor Ray Ryan, whose support and professional help have been absolutely exemplary. I would also like to thank the staff at Cambridge University Press, who have been extremely helpful during the production of the book: Edgar Mendez, Nicola Chapman, and Thirumangai Thamizhmani. I am also grateful to Steven Holt for his careful copy-editing of the manuscript.

I do not have enough words to express my gratitude to my family, who remain the central bedrock of my intellectual life. Apart from my parents Swapna and Banabir Bhattacharya, I would like to take this opportunity to record my gratefulness and love for all my extended family members in Jalpaiguri, Kolkata, and elsewhere. During the pandemic and after, my pet cat Bullet was absolutely essential in maintaining my mental sanity. And finally, this book would not have been possible without Mallarika, without her presence in my life. And this book is dedicated to her.

Earlier versions of Chapters 3 and 5 were published in *Critical Inquiry* (Vol. 42, No. 3, Spring 2016. Published with permission by The University of Chicago Press. Copyright © 2016 by the University of Chicago Press. 000931-1896/16/4203-0002S10.00. All rights reserved), and *New Literary History* (Vol. 48, No. 3, Summer 2017. Published with permission by Johns Hopkins University Press. Copyright © 2017 The University of Virginia), respectively. Material from Chapter 1 was published in a different form in Debjani Ganguly (ed.), *The Cambridge History of World Literature* (Cambridge University Press, 2021). Copyright Cambridge University Press. Reprinted with permission.

Introduction: Formations of the Literary Sovereign

On January 15, 1784, as part of his inaugural address as the first president of the Asiatic Society of Bengal in Calcutta, Sir William Jones outlined the primary research program to be undertaken by the members of the Society.[1] The meeting was carefully planned. Following an invitation from Robert Chambers – the acting chief justice of the Supreme Court of Judicature of Bengal and Jones's acquaintance from his Oxford days – twenty-nine men assembled that evening in the Grand Jury Room of the court to constitute a learned society. No doubt, many of those prominent merchants and administrators of the English East India Company were attracted by Jones's reputation as a polymath and a literary celebrity in England. Described by the preeminent eighteenth-century critic and lexicographer Samuel Johnson as "one of the most enlightened of the sons of men," Jones was part of a circle that included, apart from Johnson, some of the most illustrious men and women of his contemporary London: Joshua Reynolds, Edmund Burke, Hannah More, Edward Gibbon, Elizabeth Carter, and James Boswell.[2] Even before he reached Calcutta on September 25, 1783, at the age of thirty-six, Jones was the celebrated author of a French (and later English) translation of a Persian biography of the Afsharid monarch Nader Shah, a popular Persian grammar in English, translations of poems from various Asian and European languages, treatises on ways to suppress political riots and the principles of governance, legal tracts on the laws of bailments, and numerous poems, pamphlets, and essays in English, French, and Latin that displayed his classical education at Oxford as well as his remarkable talent for language learning. In addition to this fame, he had received his knighthood just a year earlier – at the king's levee of March 20, 1783 – in recognition of his administrative acumen as the Commissioner for Bankruptcy. With a curious mix of legal and literary fame, Jones was an unusual addition to the colonial settlement in Calcutta.[3]

What probably intrigued the gathering even more was the charismatic prodigy's dramatic vision of a sea voyage from Europe, entering the "amphitheatre" of Asia, where "*India* lay before us, and *Persia* on our left, whilst a breeze from *Arabia* blew nearly on our stern." While this almost epiphanic experience of being "encircled by the vast regions of *Asia*" triggers "a train of reflections" with "inexpressible pleasure" for him, Jones cannot but lament that, with the current paucity of reliable knowledge about those regions, "how important and extensive a field was yet unexplored, and how many solid advantages unimproved." But he has a hope – despite his apprehension that "it might have [an] appearance of flattery" to the congregation of men that evening, he nevertheless tells them that he harbors the belief that if any serious inquiry "into the history and antiquities, the natural productions, arts, sciences, and literature of *Asia*" were to be made, and if a group of capable men were to be assembled to accomplish this arduous mission, he had his best chances among his own "countrymen in *Bengal*." He raises the stakes even higher by comparing the new Society with the Royal Society of England – he reminds his audience that the venerable English society, just like the one being proposed in front of them, also had a humble origin in "a meeting of a few literary friends at *Oxford*," but it "rose gradually to that splendid zenith, at which a *Halley* was their secretary, and a *Newton* their president." This new Society in Calcutta, he wishes, will eventually achieve similar sagacity and eminence.[4]

Jones's inaugural "Discourse" highlights two aspects of eighteenth-century empires and their material-discursive networks that I find particularly important for my argument in this book. He illustrates the first one when he speculates on the possible name for the Society and observes: "if it be necessary or convenient, that a short name or epithet be given to our society, in order to distinguish it in the world, that of *Asiatick* appears both classical and proper, whether we consider the place or the object of the institution, and preferable to *Oriental*, which is in truth a word merely relative, and, though commonly used in *Europe*, conveys no very distinct idea" (3: 5). Coming from one of the leading orientalists of the Enlightenment era, this outright denunciation of the "Oriental" is no doubt surprising. But it is also apparent that this rejection is meant to be a ground-clearing exercise, an intellectual *Aufhebung* of sorts, to usher in a new regime of knowledge characterized by the shift from conventional "Orientalism" to clearly bounded territorial inquiry. Indeed, the way he marks this shift, and conjures Asiatic territories as the putative object of the Society's "investigations," one cannot but feel that he is perhaps describing one of the maps that will soon adorn the walls of the learned society – taking India as his vantage point, he presents a panoramic view of the continent that includes vast regions like China, Japan, Tibet, Persia,

Introduction: Formations of the Literary Sovereign

the Arabian Peninsula and so on (3: 3–4). As we shall see below, this cartographic underpinning of a new regime of knowledge will soon saturate the daily business of colonial governance, and its longevity will transform the modes of knowledge production across the colonial divide, bringing together diverse histories and disparate territories.[5]

Perhaps Jones was inspired by the cartographic revolution since the eighteenth century and was referring to the new thickness maps had achieved since then.[6] At the same time, his seamless mixing of territorial and cultural representations, mediated by colonial institutions and officials, also pointed toward a new idea of territorial opacity and a new regime of knowledge that was not reducible to any orientalist antecedent. Rather, this new logic of territoriality was based on the colonial government's insistence on turning the land under its possession into anthropological *fields* of investigation and research, leading to a specific form of territorial governmentality. Jones was familiar with many of these works authored by Company officials in India: apart from James Fraser's *The History of Nadir Shah* (1742), John Zephaniah Holwell's *Interesting Historical Events, Relative to the Provinces of Bengal, and the Empire of Indostan*, 3 Vols. (1765–71), and Alexander Dow's *The History of Hindostan*, 3 Vols. (1768–72) and *The Tales Translated from the Persian of Inatullah of Delhi* (1768), he also knew some recent works such as Nathaniel Brassey Halhed's translation of a digest of Hindu personal law as *A Code of Gentoo Laws, Or, Ordinations of the Pundits* (1776) and *A Grammar of the Bengal Language* (1778). In addition, he possibly had access to some more translations from Arabic and Sanskrit into Persian.

In other words, Jones's formulation presupposed these works and hence was indicative of the idea that the colonial state in British India, much like professional anthropology, treated its territories as some sort of *Gestalt* that needed to be interpreted with standardized methods and expert investigators. Moreover, the transformation of territories into knowledge objects had an additional consequence – as another colonial official and prolific writer, William Wilson Hunter, put it succinctly, this new model of governance made it obligatory for British civil servants to devote themselves, simultaneously, to both "public work" and "services to scholarship" in their efforts to uphold "British suzerainty."[7] In sum, Jones's address defined one of the most crucial features of modern colonialism – that colonial governance was progressively a combination of political and nomological decrees, being simultaneously the site and source of new knowledge. Colonial governments became not only the preeminent authority but also the sole proprietor of this new knowledge about whatever lay under their possession.

However, this emphasis on local governance is by no means a sign of discursive insularity. Jones quickly introduces the second critical component of imperial networks by arguing that this bounded territory under the watch of its colonial masters is not as provincial as his description may suggest. Hence, almost in anticipation of what Raymond Schwab calls the "Oriental Renaissance" that will soon traverse the boundaries of Asia and Europe in the final years of the eighteenth century, and in which Jones himself will play a crucial role, he offers this additional rider: "since *Egypt* had unquestionably an old connection with this country [i.e. Hindustan or India], if not with *China*, since the language and literature of the *Abyssinians* bear a manifest affinity to those of *Asia*, since the *Arabian* arms prevailed along the *African* coast of the *Mediterranean*, and even erected a powerful dynasty on the continent of Europe, you may not be displeased occasionally to follow the streams of *Asiatick* learning a little beyond its natural boundary" (3: 4–5). Jones shortly discovered through his own work on comparative philology and law that these links between Asia and Europe were more than "occasional," and it was indeed difficult, if not downright impracticable, to disengage the contiguous lines of knowledge production across continents.

This idea of conjoined and comparative histories found its climactic expression two years later in his well-known "Third Anniversary Discourse" (1786) at the Asiatic Society, when he proposed a rudimentary structure of what later became the "Indo-European hypothesis" (3: 24–46). His suggestion of a linguistic family comprising Sanskrit, Greek, Latin, Old Persian, and other languages became so popular that it permeated almost every branch of human sciences around the turn of the century.[8] Goethe, who appreciated and imitated both Hāfiz and Kālidāsa via Jones's translations, observed that "[w]hoever knows others as well as himself must also recognize that East and West are now inseparable."[9] And, by 1808, Friedrich Schlegel had not only endorsed Jones's speculation on linguistic families, but even made a programmatic announcement: "The dwellers in Asia and the people of Europe ought to be treated in popular works as members of one vast family, and their history will never be separated by any student, anxious fully to comprehend the bearing of the whole."[10] Jones's inaugural "Discourse" thus characterized the newness of the colonial project on its own terms: the new knowledge about India, or any other colony for that matter, would henceforth be poised on this double register – its internal transformation through philological and anthropological governance, and its embeddedness within broader geopolitical networks. It would be challenging to accomplish one

Introduction: Formations of the Literary Sovereign

without the other, and it would be even more difficult to think of knowledge in its local isolation.

I begin with this meeting of the Asiatic Society, and especially with Jones's "Discourse," for a number of reasons, but most importantly for the way it captures the connected and supranational – or one could say, global – context of this book. As my brief overview of Jones's lecture shows, the imperial structures necessarily crossed spatial boundaries and produced a wide range of cross-cultural institutions, governmental practices, laws, texts, and subjects that marked the newness of the regime. Within this transition, and as part of the trans-continental connections, proliferated new ideas and discourses that carried the traces of this cultural encounter and became noticeably mobile across territories. It is this material condition that functions as the bedrock for this book. What Jones describes as the two nodal points of modern imperialism – colonial governmentality and conjoined yet comparative histories of empires – constituted the field within which I trace the genealogy of the idea of the "literary," its transformation from being what Johnson's *A Dictionary of the English Language* defined as "Learning; skill in letters" in 1755 to its almost exclusive reliance on the tropological dimension of language by the end of the century.[11]

My wager in this book is that the modern idea of the literary as a *sovereign order of textuality* since the late eighteenth century – autonomous, autotelic, and singular – was coproduced with an extraordinary model of colonial sovereignty at a place where Jones lived and worked during the final decade of his life, namely the far-flung colony of British India. The new colonial regime, as Jones points out, was poised on its ability to turn the territory into a readable space – with its cartographic and textual signs overlaid on each other – and on the ambition of constituting a totalizing schema of representation. At the same time, as his other point reminds us, such a fundamental transformation of the colony could not have been possible either in its territorial seclusion or within any single domain deemed to be properly governmental. Hence, drawing on disparate resources including local legal canons, "oriental" scribal cultures, Indian "manners and customs," English common law, European aesthetics, and the changing character of colonial occupation across continents, the new regime gave birth to what I call the *literary sovereign*. Within this new idea, the colonial administration sought to bring together political sovereignty and literary singularity, with the further aim of constituting a thoroughly textualized sovereign power modeled on what the colonial translators identified as a self-governing literary language evident in a host of Sanskrit, Persian, and Arabic texts. No doubt, this resolution was designed as a response to a number of crises the Company faced at the time, but its other outcome was decisive – it defined literary language within an autonomous, non-mimetic, and performative mode of textuality and constituted the modern field of "literature." The literary sovereign, in other words, set out two templates at the same time – one for colonial governance that would be repeated in different parts of Asia and Africa in subsequent centuries; and the other for the new idea of literature that would soon transform cultures across the colonial divide.[12]

I track the proliferation of this model of the literary sovereign then through the conceptual grid of *Weltliteratur* or world literature and show how this colonial history made its mark across literary cultures in Europe.[13] From the eighteenth century onward, this colonial history shaped and reshaped literary cultures at a global scale, and laid the foundations of what can be defined as the modern culture of letters.

Historians have argued that the specificities of colonial rule in the eighteenth century were determined by what is often called the "ideology" of early colonialism in the Indian subcontinent. During this period, and before settling for an unbreachable colonial "difference" in the nineteenth century, the colonial administration often overlapped with or appropriated what were seen as typically Indian practices and values.[14] This was evident in the construction of the literary sovereign as well. The model of state-based sovereignty popular in Europe since the Westphalian peace in 1648, and described by Hegel in the *Elements of the Philosophy of Right* (1821) as the effect of the "ideality" of a perfect "*Rechtsstaat*," faced serious challenges in the colonies during the eighteenth century.[15] In India, unlike in previous British colonies in Ireland, North America, and the Caribbean, the crisis was much more acute since a public joint-stock company with monopoly rights assumed a quasi-state status and performed some of the activities – from collecting revenues to waging wars – that were associated exclusively with the state in European political imagination.

This unusual status of the Company led Edmund Burke, one of its fiercest critics, to allege that the Company was in possession of "[t]hose high and almost incommunicable prerogatives of sovereignty, which were hardly ever known before to be parted with to any subjects, and which in several states were not wholly intrusted to the prince or head of the commonwealth himself." As a consequence, he famously declared, the "East India Company in Asia is a state in the disguise of a merchant. Its whole service is a system of public offices in the disguise of a counting-house."[16] In a similar vein, Adam Smith noted in *An Inquiry into the Nature and Causes of the Wealth of Nations* (1776) the "strange absurdity" of the

Company that treated the "character of the sovereign as but an appendix to that of the merchant."[17] This scandalous model of what historians have variously called the "dual sovereignty" or diarchy, the "company-state," a "distant sovereignty," or simply "anarchy," therefore, needed an equally unusual resolution.[18] It was also evident that this resolution could not have come either from normative legal–juridical discourses in Europe or from political institutions like the parliament and monarchy.

In my opinion, the key to understanding the colonial resolution to this rather elusive problem is the Company's investment in large-scale translations of local legal canons such as the Shari'a and the Dharmaśāstra (representing Islamic and Hindu laws, respectively) and its subsequent attempt to link these laws to what the administrators often called the "manners and customs" (the eighteenth-century name for *culture*) of indigenous populations. In 1772, while facing multiple crises at home and in the colony, Warren Hastings, the first Governor General of Bengal, sought to anchor the new regime within local legal traditions and proposed his "Regulations" to follow indigenous manners, understandings, usages, and institutions.[19] Hastings even claimed to have unearthed the "Ancient Constitution of the Country" and proposed to overhaul the administration of the new colony on the basis of this doctrine.[20] It was further held that the foreignness of Hindu and Islamic laws could be tamed only if one knew enough about the equally foreign cultural matrix within which they operated and, consequently, the colonial claim to sovereign power could be secured only if its new legal regime could be shown as originating from these ancient but continuous cultural roots. The cultural universe of India, according to Hastings's plan, had to function both as an internal framework for the new colonial regime and also as the eventual horizon of its political ambition. Any claim to sovereign power for the Company had to navigate this essential duality of culture.

What Jones describes as the transformation of colonial governance through philology and anthropology in his "Discourse" became especially useful in this context, and soon the colonial administrators not only translated native legal, religious, and cosmological texts but also wrote copious grammars and dictionaries of local languages with the belief that such philological tools were necessary techniques of governance. Through a remarkable assortment of legal and cultural registers, the Company established a Janus-faced regime – while the origins of its sovereign power could be traced back to India's ancient legal systems, its "rule of law" was modern enough to distinguish itself from various precolonial administrations. It was the strategic deployment of local culture as a justificatory narrative for its rule as also its final governmental telos that allowed the Company to secure such a unique form of sovereignty.

My name for this colonial resolution – the *literary sovereign* – is designed to map this new concept of power across the abstraction of law and an anthropological description of culture. While working on local "manners and customs," many of the colonial administrators identified a distinctly "Oriental" or "eastern" mode of writing, especially in poetry, that collapsed the ontic and the phenomenal aspects of a language in the very act of its performance. In stark contrast to the neoclassical aesthetic ideals of contemporary Europe, this mode of writing did not follow the principle of mimetic representation and certainly did not adhere to any classical model of order and decorum. Instead, what one encountered in such texts was a form of allegory that did not have any secondary referent, or a metaphor that made no distinction between the vehicle and the tenor, or perhaps even a mode of language that produced meaning only within its own limits. Unlike the classical or biblical allegories that these officials knew well, the uniqueness of this kind of "oriental" writing emerged from its suspension of reference to an extratextual world, or from its manifestly autonomous and autotelic being.

Colonial officials insisted that this was not simply a generic quality, but a broader mode of being – of language and its attendant culture – that separated "oriental" writing from its European counterpart. If one were to make sense of this "singular species" of writing, one not only had to place its *performative* language (as opposed to the *veridical*) within a self-sufficient textual world, but also had to assume a cultural consensus that would lend credence to such hermetic textuality. Way before any European precedence, colonial administrators identified this sovereign order of textuality in the "orient," across texts and territories, and proposed it as the proper domain of the literary. What I call the literary sovereign in this book is precisely the overlap between this form of "oriental" writing and the new colonial sovereignty as both espoused an autonomous textual order within a specific cultural milieu and both embodied a form of truth that could have been established only across this text–culture continuum. I do not mean that one imitated the other, but I do submit that *political sovereignty* and *literary singularity* were coproduced in this case, and they reinforced each other in their respective careers.

The literary sovereign, in other words, marked a form of textuality that was radically different from contemporary standards of Europe – especially of mimetic imitation or representation – in its self-enclosed performativity, and specific to the "orient" in its cultural details. It was, however, the potent combination of political expediency and textual autonomy in the new idea that marked its uniqueness in imperial history. Once language was dissociated from its role of mimetic representation, and once it was reimagined as a political instrument within a bounded space like the colony, it was possible for the colonial government to deploy this form of textuality to ever-expansive fields and purposes. Indeed, by the turn of the century the literary sovereign inaugurated translation and textualization as essential mechanisms of governance almost everywhere. This was of course facilitated by the Company's growing reliance on writing and print to define the distinctiveness of its rule, but this close association with governmental institutions shaped the other characteristic feature of the literary sovereign – that it became irrevocably inflected by the spirit of anthropology.[21]

In a sense, the very structure of the new textuality – and especially its proximity to political power – consigned it to such a fate, but the whole process was accelerated by the emergence of the master narrative of the time, namely the *nation*, that subsumed every other anthropological classification under its utterly seductive sway. What was a literary model of sovereignty found its final enframing in the momentous idea of the nation, and the ensuing decades witnessed the intense nationalization of an act of pure linguistic performance. Without taking into account this contiguity between the literary and the anthropological – as also their mutual imbrication in colonial governance – it would be impossible to explain why, by the middle of the nineteenth century, literatures and nations confirmed and almost implied each other. I shall even argue that the literary sovereign made available the central template for nationalist imagination and shaped the political landscape of modernity.

This book thus reopens the crucial question of the historicity of literature, but does so amidst a broader arena of multicultural and multilingual locations and within the *longue durée* of colonial histories. In standard literary history, the story of the modern idea of the literary is traced back either to the Jena Romantics and the fragments published in the *Athenaeum* (1798–1800) or to Germaine de Staël's *De la littérature dans ses rapports avec les institutions sociales*, 2 Vols. (1799), and it is often staged with an exclusively European dramatis personae.[22] What emerged in the final decades of the eighteenth century, and subsequently became the dominant critical idea in most scribal cultures over the next couple of centuries, we are told, is the universalization of a fragment of European history. Literature was thus soon transmuted into world literature, and its mode of being or its typical value assumed a normative standard, dictating the fate of other and very dissimilar practices of writing, circulation, and reception. Any discussion under the rubrics of national or world literatures was, by definition, meant to pay homage to this global domination of an idea, and any critical engagement with writings from diverse regions had to be guided by this initial article of faith. It was left to literary history as a new discipline in the nineteenth century to confirm the universality of the idea of the literary, across languages as diverse as Persian, Arabic, Sanskrit, Chinese, and so on, and it became a common practice to see replications of Europe almost everywhere, producing a "world republic of letters."

As with many other universalist fictions, this story is interesting more for what it conceals than for what it tells us about the modern culture of letters. It does not tell us, for instance, how and why a provincial history of European origin found its home across continents. It does not reveal the modalities through which its defining feature of anti-historicist intransitivity was almost immediately trapped in the teleological narration of the nation and its performative energies were rechanneled as unmistakable signs of a national *Geist*. And it certainly does not disclose the way literature straddled its dual life across academic institutions and a broader world of print and publics to become one of the most powerful cultural expressions of modernity. But, most importantly, this fiction does not shed light on the contradictory prerogatives and paradoxical desires of the literary: it is born out of a sectarian history, but with universal ambition; it is part of a series of modern political assemblages (nations, empires, etc.), and offers lines of flight out of them; it promises democratic equality in its very construction, yet lends itself to be part of regressive politics; it resists historicization, but shapes literary historiography in decisive ways.

My point in this book, thus, is that in order to step aside from this Eurocentric narrative, and to decolonize the very idea of literature, one needs to go beyond Europe and before Romanticism and place the genealogy of this new cultural idiom within the histories of modern colonialism. It seems to me that, like so many other critical concepts that dominate the global intellectual discussions today, the literary as a distinct mode of being of language does not belong to any one culture or history. Instead, it telescopes a range of ideas and practices from different cultural worlds and fashions its own being through histories of violent colonial encounters in the eighteenth century. Traces of this multicultural, multilingual, and intermedial history – generated through colonial governmentality and imperial networks, as Jones suggested – are still visible in the life and career of the new concept, and I wish to capture these traces and small histories through the theoretical grid of the literary sovereign. Once the myth of

Romanticism as the origin point is set aside, however, one is perforce led to the bewildering profusion of manuscripts, languages, scribal traditions, translation and untranslatability, appropriation, plain forgery, philological claims and counter-claims, archival records, and disciplinary rivalry, all put together like an enormous jigsaw puzzle by imperial histories. This book is an invitation to step into this world of entangled texts and territories, of philological inquiries and political powers, of the literary and the sovereign.

Politics of Indigeneity

In 1600, the English East India Company was formed through a royal charter from Queen Elizabeth I, and was declared "one body corporate and politick." Its status as a corporation in early modern England made the Company part of a network of similar bodies that controlled a range of activities, from ecclesiastical governance to overseas trade and territorial occupation. As Philip Stern points out, the idea of a corporation – "corpus politicum et corporatum" or "communitas perpetua" – was derived from Roman laws and it formed the very foundation of associational life in contemporary England. "Legally and conceptually speaking," he goes on to argue, "the early modern national state and even the monarch herself were forms of corporation." This was evident in the formation of such corporations, their rules and laws, and also in their common purpose "to bind a multitude of people together into a legal singularity, an artificial person that could maintain common rights, police community standards and behavior, and administer over and on behalf of the collectivity."[23] The Company was like various other similarly formed bodies and yet held a status that was quite unique, making it an eminently modern entity.

The Company enjoyed this governmental power from the beginning as it held complete authority over all English subjects who were part of its administration or were members of its overseas voyages. Over the course of the next few decades, the Company received further rights and powers: in 1609, its monopoly was made "perpetual," and in 1623 it was entrusted with the right to "rule of law" over every English individual residing east of the Cape of Good Hope and in the Southern Atlantic.[24] As the English Company joined the Portuguese *Estado da Índia* (1505), the Dutch *Vereenigde Oost-Indische Compagnie* (1602), and later its French counterpart, the *Compagnie française pour le commerce des Indes orientales* (1664), to exploit growing trade relations between Europe and Asia in the seventeenth century, its status as a "company-state" became more and more prominent. Stern suggests that the founding charters of the Company, its manifold claims based on its monopoly trade rights with the East Indies, and its increasing use of war and diplomacy to consolidate its power over individual subjects demonstrated the various aspects of this company-state. By the end of the seventeenth century, such developments further highlighted the fact that the Company was now "possessed of political institutions and underscored by coherent principles about the nature of obligations of subjects and rulers, good government, political economy, jurisdiction, authority, and sovereignty."[25]

A dramatic turn in the fortunes of the Company took place around the middle of the eighteenth century as it won two consecutive battles at Plassey (1757) and Buxar (1764) against Sirāj-ud-Daulāh – the *Nawāb* of Bengal – and his allies in India. As a consequence, the Company was recognized in 1765 by the Mughal emperor Shah Alam II as the *diwān* of Bengal, Bihar, and Orissa in eastern India, with the power of collecting revenues and administering local justice.[26] This was the beginning of the Company's imperial mission in many ways, as the emperor's *farmān* or charter formed the foundation for its claim to political authority, and certainly of its territorial governance that was to grow in the following decades.

These events, however, presented a new set of problems that Adam Smith identified as arising from a central paradox – namely the rival claims of monopolistic trade and sovereignty.[27] Smith sees it as a sign of "mercantile habits" that the Company prefers the "little and transitory profit of the monopolist" over the "great and permanent revenue of the sovereign," and suggests that the consequences of this paradox characterize the nature of the Company's functioning in India. The "council of merchants" lacks sovereign power, and, as a consequence, can "command obedience only by the military force with which they are accompanied, and their government is therefore necessarily military and despotical."[28] The reluctance of the merchants to act as sovereigns, even when they have de facto assumed that role, he maintains, will result in a disaster: "Such exclusive companies are nuisances in every respect; always more or less inconvenient to the countries in which they are established, and destructive to those which have the misfortune to fall under their government."[29]

By the time Smith made these damning observations in 1776 as part of his general attack on mercantilism, the idea of "Oriental despotism" as the prevailing political system in India (and across Asia, from Turkey to Persia and China) was well entrenched in European imagination, and his submission that the Company in practice resembled these much-maligned "despots" was nothing short of a scandal.[30] He was in fact following a well-established body of scholarship on "Oriental despotism" that included Montesquieu's *De l'esprit des loix* (1748) and Nicolas Antoine Boulanger's *Recherches sur l'origine du despotisme oriental* (1761), though his immediate source was perhaps the colonial official Alexander Dow, who, in the third volume of his *The History of Hindostan* (1772), implied similarities between the new colonial regime and its Indian predecessors.

Dow was one of the major voices of his time who shaped the public perception of India in Europe – buttressing his claims with his personal experience of serving as a lieutenant-colonel with the Company's army – and influenced a series of intellectual stalwarts including David Hume, Voltaire, Immanuel Kant, Johann Gottfried Herder, Georg Wilhelm Friedrich Hegel, and Friedrich von Schlegel.[31] In his opening chapter "A Dissertation Concerning the Origin and Nature of Despotism in Hindostan," he describes despotism as the inevitable outcome of the natural and cultural conditions of India – the abundance of nature, the fertility of land, the tropical climate, and the inherent indolence of the inhabitants all led to the inescapable slavery of the populace under despotic kings and princes. To this rather Montesquieuan list that connects climate to politics he adds Islam – described as "peculiarly calculated for despotism" – as the religion that not only encourages despotic rule but also gives it a moral hue.[32] This is evident, according to Dow, in the "manners and customs" of India that accept despotism as the preordained fate for its political institutions. For him, the Mughals represent a milder but archetypal version of oriental despotism.[33]

In a supplementary piece entitled "An Inquiry into the State of Bengal," he indicts the Company by suggesting that the colonial administration, despite its claims to the contrary, is almost an extension of this natural despotism of India. Like Smith after him, Dow also holds the monopolistic rights of the Company largely responsible for the mismanagement of the colony, but in his historical account he introduces an additional feature. He argues that Indian despots such as the Mughals, in spite of their enormous and mostly unaccountable power, did not rule according to their "caprice" or "whim." The sovereignty of such states was derived from a combination of despotic power and a clearly defined "code" of Islamic laws, and the success of such regimes depended on how effectively these codes could rein in the despot. Referring to the Mughals, he even contends that the "despotic form of government is not […] so terrible in its nature as men born in free countries are apt to imagine. Though no civil regulation can bind the prince, there is one great law, the ideas of mankind with regard to right and wrong, by which he is bound." The Company inherits the despotic core of these previous regimes but not the codes – hence, in the absence of any restraints over its rapacious officials, its government mostly depends on "preposterous policy" and the "abrupt expedient of barbarous conquerors." In effect, he notes, the Company's governance replaces one form of despotism with another, and the crucial question of sovereignty remains entangled in the messy business of everyday administration, without a legal framework or even a clear political vision.[34]

It is possible to see both Smith and Dow as part of the Enlightenment-era critique of imperialism, a position shared by a diverse group of philosophers including Denis Diderot, Kant, Herder, and Burke, among others.[35] Both of them, for instance, extended the rhetorical device of criticizing the monopoly company as a way of scrutinizing the functions of state sovereignty, made popular by Diderot's contributions to Abbé Raynal's *Histoire philosophique et politique des établissements et du commerce des Européens dans les deux Indes* (1770). For my purpose here, however, the most important feature of their critique, and of the Enlightenment anti-imperialism more broadly, is the rise of an anthropological notion of indigenous culture as the counterpoint to colonial occupation. For the first time, Europe witnessed the gradual consolidation of anthropology not only as a discipline but also as a field that could rival philosophy in its ambition to conjure an alternate episteme. This was partly indebted to Kant's well-known declaration that the crucial question of "What is man?" could not be answered fully by transcendental philosophy and needed to be posed as part of pragmatic anthropology, but it had other contributors – from George-Louis Leclerc, Comte de Buffon to Herder – and a broader set of concerns.[36]

I shall return to this moment of Kantian anthropology and its relationship with the new idea of literature in Chapter 4 with greater details, but let me focus here on the way this new disciplinary formation permitted contemporary anti-imperial critique to formulate its own tenets. As I shall demonstrate at different points in this book, this critique gradually crystalized around the notion of a precolonial indigenous cultural world with diverse elements like religion, language, race, and law as an autonomous domain that successfully retained its essence over the centuries. Even when a region was subjugated by external forces, this immutable cultural world was seen as continuing largely untouched, with its sway over the local populace more or less unaffected. One of the recurring themes in Enlightenment-era critique of imperialism thus portrayed the "manners and customs" or religion and law of an indigenous population as a self-governing site of freedom, at once in possession of its own history and unmediated volition, and also as a domain of social life that needed to be protected from colonial interventions. Dow also suggested that it was this distinctive cultural essence of India that survived past conquerors from Afghanistan or central Asia, and, in all probability, would outlive the present ones from Europe; and hence, any attempt at strengthening the colonial governance in the subcontinent would have to be mindful of its substance as well as nuances.

What began as a critique of monopoly trade rights, and especially of the Company as its foremost manifestation, thus, soon transformed itself into an endorsement of indigenous cultural practices and institutions. This phase of the Enlightenment critique coincided with the transition from Ernst Platner's medico-philosophical anthropology to Kant and Herder's efforts in delimiting the new discipline's borders within more empirical domains such as physiognomy, language, religion, race, and so on.[37] These two approaches were not mutually exclusive of course, and their combined effect gave birth to a vocabulary that was visible both in academic debates and in governmental decisions. This evolving connection between local culture and political sovereignty was not lost on the administrators of the Company either, and Hastings took special care to make it part of his calculations for the governance of Bengal. He was aware of this general intellectual drift of his time, and he received a copy of Dow's book almost immediately after its publication in London. Though he felt Dow misrepresented many issues relating to "Revenue, Forms of Office and Justice," he was nonetheless ready to admit that "some things which he asserts [about the Company] are true."[38]

Even before coming across Dow's criticism, however, Hastings expressed his fear of a parliamentary takeover, and lamented the fact that it would be a gross injustice to Indian subjects if they were to be ruled by the "English gentlemen of Cumberland and Argyleshire," who had little access to the colony's everyday realities and knew it only through the revenue amount it sent to England. He often claimed in his personal correspondences that the prevailing legal and juridical systems in Bengal resembled "a confused heap of materials" and that the only way out of this mess was the "vital influence which flows through the channels of a regular constitution," but he vehemently opposed the imposition of an alien system like English law to resolve the crisis.[39] Instead, the "reform" he envisaged had to emerge from Indian traditions – or the *cultural core* of the Enlightenment critique – and, like Dow, he thought a centralized administration for both fiscal and judicial governance during the Mughal era was a legitimate point to start from. He even suggested that the new regime should follow "the original constitution of the Mogul Government" and that though "[m]any other correspondent Regulations will be necessary, but not one perhaps which the original constitution of the Mogul Government hath not before established or adopted, & thereby rendered familiar to the People."[40]

As historians of colonial law have shown, however, this professed adherence to the so-called "Mughal constitution" was not as straightforward as Hastings made it out to be. While Company officials often expressed their admiration for the Mughals during their glorious days in the sixteenth and seventeenth centuries, they despised the remnants of the same empire in their immediate vicinity in the eighteenth. In popular opinion, the chief malaise affecting the contemporary state of affairs was the "juridical venality" of Mughal laws. In addition to this corruption – or, rather, as a consequence – they argued that the present system was designed to encourage "judicial discretion" or treating different subjects according to their rank, religion, caste, and so on, and this was fundamentally inimical to any standardized version of the "rule of law."[41] In order to overcome these legal residues of despotism, the Company officials made plans to introduce what was taken to be the underlying principle of English legal traditions – the "rule of law, and not by men" – but sought to anchor it within an existing cultural milieu of India. It was widely held that the robust structure of textualization and precedence that had held English common law in good stead over the centuries would function as a viable model for India as well. And before long, a number of officials started arguing that India indeed had such a tradition and one simply needed to resurrect it for the present cause of colonial governance.

Hastings, for instance, writes in a letter to Lord Mansfield, the Lord Chief Justice, that, contrary to popular opinion, the "Hindoos, or original inhabitants of Hindostan [...] have been in possession of laws, which have continued unchanged, from the remotest antiquity." Such laws exist in the esoteric language of Sanskrit and are expounded by the "professors of these laws" or the Brahmins all across the subcontinent. Even the "introduction of the Mahomedan government" in later centuries did not change the setup much, and if the present Christian rulers deviated from such settled practices, it would be a blatant abuse of power. In a rare gesture of generosity, he even adds that the "Mahometan law, which is the guide at least of one fourth of the natives of this province [...] is as comprehensive, and as well defined, as that of most states in Europe." On the basis of such insights into the legal history of India, he makes the following extraordinary plea to Lord Mansfield: "It would be a grievance to deprive the people of the protection of their own laws, but it would be a wanton tyranny to require their obedience to others of which they are wholly ignorant, and of which they have no possible means of acquiring a knowledge."[42] Such an appeal signaled many things: first, the Enlightenment idea of an autonomous cultural universe had become part of the colonial common sense; second, the Company was no longer satisfied with being a mere corporate tributary to the Mughals, but harbored serious political ambitions; and, finally, the notion of colonial sovereignty was taking root among the Company officials, beyond and besides the British model.

Lie of the Land

At this point, Hastings and his colleagues had to confront the critical question of "authenticity" of law and culture in all its complexities, and had to find ways of joining it with their political mission. They had to reinstate, in other words, the canons of Hindu and Islamic laws in all their pristine purity, and yet had to find a version of the same laws that would serve the practical purpose of everyday governance. The Enlightenment assumption of a precolonial cultural core was no longer a theoretical idea but a practical necessity, and the administrators soon realized that local languages and scribal cultures were their best bets to capture the essence of Indian legal systems.

Some preliminary accounts of Indian manners and customs, religion, cosmology, history, and poetry were made available by James Fraser in the appendix "A Catalogue of about Two Hundred Manuscripts in the *Persic* and Other *Oriental* Languages, Collected in the East" added to his *The History of Nadir Shah* (1742).[43] John Zephaniah Holwell, another Company official of some notoriety, took this idea further and suggested in 1765 that any European author wishing to describe the alien cultural world of India must be "skilled in the language of the people he describes, sufficiently to trace the etymology of their words and phrases, and capable of diving into the mysteries of their theology."[44] Though he never learnt Sanskrit himself, that did not deter Holwell from pleading the primacy of language or even from quoting random Sanskrit phrases to support his claims on a range of subjects, from political history to theological doctrines.

Once again, it was left to Dow to draw up a distinction between two different styles of writing – "oriental" and "European" – in the "Preface" to his *Tales Translated from the Persian of Inatulla of Delhi* (1768): while the first is described as "too florid and diffused" or full of "pompous diction peculiar to the East," the latter is characterized in terms of its "succinct and nervous manner of the ancients, and that concise elegance, which distinguishes many writers of modern Europe." Despite this dissimilarity, and the underlying values attached to these two styles, he nonetheless submits that the text of Inatulla was unique since the "species of wit contained" in those tales "depends very much upon the idiom of the Persian."[45] For him, this interdependence of cultural meaning and language – or the embedded cultural world within the space of the text – is a typically oriental phenomenon, and its remit is soon extended beyond poetry or fiction and into the domain of other genres of writing as well.

In the first volume of *History of Hindostan* (1768), hence, Dow repeats the proposition that oriental poetry is "too turgid and florid, and the diction of their historians too diffuse and verbose," but this time he points out the unusual ability of these texts to contain a cultural world almost without any external referent. He illustrates his case with the example of the Persian text he translates as the history of Hindustan – Muḥammad Qāsim Firishtā's seventeenth-century history *Tā'rikh-i-Firishtā* – that offers both the "history of a great empire" and its "literary treasures" concealed in the "obscurity of the Persian." As a translator, he feels it necessary not only to relate the "minute and authentic history of a great empire" as communicated by Firishtā, but also to explicate "a nervousness of expression, and a manliness of sentiment" that characterize the language of the original text.[46] This overlaying of different idioms, notwithstanding the charges of turgidity, came to signify the emblematic oriental style, and a number of colonial officials subsequently claimed that this feature was shared by a diverse set of texts in Persian, Sanskrit, and Arabic.

Many of these early leads found their coherent expression in the first text commissioned by Hastings – Nathaniel Brassey Halhed's translation of a digest of Hindu personal law as *A Code of Gentoo Laws, Or, Ordinations of the Pundits, from a Persian Translation, Made from the Original, Written in the Shanscrit Language* (1776). As the title itself suggests, this was a translation that traversed three different languages – Sanskrit, Persian, and English – and yet it claimed to access a version of India that was not available beyond the text or beyond its ability to embody cultural truth. As Halhed puts it: "[*A Code of Gentoo Laws*] must be taken as the only Work of the Kind, wherein the genuine Principles of the Gentoo Jurisprudence are made public, with the Sanction of their most respectable Pundits (or Lawyers) and which offers a complete Confutation of the Belief too common in Europe, that the Hindoos have no written Laws whatever, but such as relate to the ceremonious Peculiarities of their Superstition."[47] By segregating a body of law from the labyrinthine world of rituals and superstitions, he hopes to reinstate the "genuine Principles of the Gentoo Jurisprudence" for a public that hitherto had no access to such a doctrine.

His argument here relies heavily on the power of the original Sanskrit, although twice removed in translation, to represent authentic Hindu law, both as a refutation of widespread European misconception about India and also as a possible ground for colonial jurisprudence. Such an argument requires him to emphasize the authenticity and integrity of the original, turning the textual autonomy both of the original and of its translation as governmental resources. In fact, he sees an unbroken chain of succession between three different languages, and claims that the integrity of the first (Sanskrit) has been retained in the last (English) without any alteration, accretion, or abridgement. Textual autonomy and its straightforward connection with political power – the two most vital components of the literary sovereign – are clearly visible in his keenness to defend his translation.

As a result, Halhed seems especially eager to establish the integrity of the text, and insists that only the "English Dialect in which it is here offered to the Public, and that only, is not the Performance of a Gentoo." He renders his own role as the translator almost invisible, foregrounding instead other qualities such as the impeccable reputation of the Brahmin *pandits* who collated the original digest titled *Vivādārṇavasetu*, or the fidelity of the Persian translation to the original Sanskrit. Even when he comes to comment on the principles of translation for a text like this digest, this is what he records: "Less studious of Elegance than of Accuracy, the Translator thought it more excusable to tire the Reader with the Flatness of a literal Interpretation, than to mislead him by a vague and dubious Paraphrase; so that the entire Order of the Book, the several Divisions of its Contents, and the whole Turn of the Phrase, is in every Part the immediate Product of the Bramins."[48] This self-effacing humility is indeed astonishing, especially from a man who harbored considerable literary ambition and who collaborated with prominent figures of his time, such as Richard Sheridan. Such sentiments make sense only when placed against Halhed's overriding desire to impress upon his readers that what they hold in their hands is an uncontaminated text and that the act of translation is a mere device to bear that textual autonomy across linguistic borders.

Quite naturally, this quest for authenticity finds its final refuge in Sanskrit, both in its ability to exemplify what is quintessentially Hindu and in its status as an archive of civilizational values. I shall discuss Halhed's note on Sanskrit as a cultural artifact at length in Chapter 1, but let me briefly highlight here three points that made significant contributions to the literary sovereign. First, like Holwell and Dow before him, Halhed accords an exceptional status to Sanskrit among all Indian languages, both in terms of its antiquity and because of its complex grammar. He notes its "copious and nervous" nature, and observes that its "grammatical Rules also are numerous and difficult, though there are not many Anomalies," that "Shanscrit Poetry comprehends a very great Variety of different Meters," and so on.[49] He quotes several passages from ancient sources like the *Vedas* to establish the antiquity of the language, and inaugurates a kind of inquiry into Indian cultures that would later be christened Indology.[50] Second, he makes Sanskrit the exclusive repository of pre-Islamic Indian civilization by proposing a direct correlation between the land and the language. He elaborates on this idea further two years later in his *A Grammar of the Bengal Language* (1778) in the following words: "The grand Source of Indian Literature, the Parent of almost every dialect from the Persian Gulph to the China Seas, is the Shanscrit; a language of the most venerable and unfathomable antiquity; which although at present shut up in the libraries of Bramins, and appropriated solely to the record of their Religion, appears to have been current over most of the Oriental World."[51]

And third, he places Sanskrit within a comparative frame with other languages such as Arabic, Persian, Greek, and Latin. He tells his readers, for instance, that Sanskrit "far exceeds the Greek and Arabick in the Regularity of its Etymology, and like them has a prodigious Number of Derivatives from each primary Root."[52] And again in his *Grammar*, he notes the following: "I have been astonished to find the similitude of Shanscrit with those of Persian and Arabic, and even of Latin and Greek: and these not in technical and metaphorical terms, which the mutation of refined arts and improved manners might have occasionally introduced; but in the main ground-work of language, in monosyllables, in the names of numbers, and the appellations of such things as would be first discriminated on the immediate dawn of civilization."[53] This comparative framework is the first step toward what will later become the "Indo-European" hypothesis via Jones and others.

A second line of investment into the literary sovereign began with William Jones, especially with his *Poems, Consisting Chiefly of Translations from the Asiatick Languages* (1772). In this collection, and especially in the two essays he adds to explain the specific character of these "Asiatick" poems, he virtually declares mutiny against the aesthetic ideals of eighteenth-century neoclassicism. According to Jones, *pace* the vulgar Aristotelianism of the day, the true mechanism of poetry (or literature, more broadly) is not mimesis or imitation – which he discards as mere "*likeness of a likeness*" – but the "*rich and creative invention*" of imagination. He suggests that the spirit of the poetry of these Asiatic nations exemplifies this principle, and that the source of this aesthetic ideal has to be traced back not to some classical ideal of unity or decorum but to the abundance of their everyday lives, to the anthropological profusion of their cultures, that nurtures this unique faculty of imagination. He argues that the "manners" of the "four principal nations" of Asia – Arabs, Persians, Indians, and Turks – when combined with their characteristic climate, topography, and religion, give birth to this unusually different ideal of poetry. Indeed, the central achievement of this collection is this new formulation of poetry, evident in Asian poets and ancient Greek geniuses like Homer, but altogether missing in modern European authors.[54]

Along with this theory, Jones makes two other points which are central to my concern in this book. First, for Jones, this autotelic poetry is not a standalone idea. In each case, he portrays the major poetic traditions as expressions of their respective national spirit and character. For him, Arabic poetry is a result of the Arabs "being perpetually conversant with the most beautiful objects, spending a calm, and agreeable life in a fine climate, [...] and having the advantage of a language singularly adapted to poetry," whereas Persian poetry expresses the "general character of the nation [which is] *softness*, and *love for pleasure*, that *indolence*, and *effeminacy*."[55] Even when he uses a racial stereotype, he takes special care to expand it into national characteristics, and, consequently, to attach to it a rudimentary idea of national literature. The second point is the comparative framework – the new idea of literature can only be thought comparatively, only with reference to multiple literary cultures. Being a polyglot himself, Jones frequently uses comparisons between Arabic and Persian poetry on the one hand and ancient Greek and Latin poetry on the other, and maintains that the new idea of literature – both its singularity and its national character – has to be established with reference to numerous sources and civilizations. The new idea of literature, in other words, can only consolidate itself within a field that will soon be called *world literature*.

A Rule of Philology

Hastings's judicial "Regulations" of 1772, one of the early steps toward the literary sovereign, needs to be placed against this backdrop of colonial scholarship. For my argument, the important document here is a letter from the Governor and Council in Fort William, Calcutta to the Court of Directors of the Company in London, dated November 3, 1772. In this letter, Hastings proposed to "adapt [the Company's] Regulations to the Manners and Understandings of the People [of India], and the Exigencies of the Country, adhering, as closely as we are able, to their ancient Usages and Institutions."[56] This letter was more of a preamble to two other documents, a letter from the Committee of Circuits (August 15, 1772) and extracts from the proceedings of the Committee of Circuits (November 3, 1772) – both proposing a slew of reforms for the explicit purpose of better "Administration of Justice." It is important to note here that these new proposals were not voluntary acts of benevolence; rather, they were designed to address growing concerns about the "East India" affairs back in England that prompted the parliament to form a committee to look into the various scandals associated with the Company.

Ranajit Guha's classic study *A Rule of Property for Bengal* details the intellectual debates of the time and shows how a number of events between 1769 and 1772 created a pall of suspicion over the activities of the Company – and how this, in turn, forced the officials to take policy decisions with far-reaching consequences like the Regulations of 1772 and the Permanent Settlement Act of 1793.[57] The British parliament also responded to the gravity of the colonial question through successive acts like the Regulating Act of 1773 and Pitt's India Act of 1784. Even the Committee of Circuits admitted in its note of 1772 that some elements of "despotic Governments" had crept into the daily businesses of Company administration and new policies were required to protect people against "venal and arbitrary Innovations" as well as "general and allowed Abuse of Authority."[58] Against this backdrop of political exigencies, Hastings thought it fit to anchor his new policies in indigenous legal systems of India, and argued that such a move was dictated by the "plain Principles of Experience and common Observation."[59]

Hastings's rather practical suggestions had serious implications. At the very least, his plan required an enormous amount of translations from Persian, Arabic, and Sanskrit into English, and also some familiarity with local customs and religions. However, Hastings was not proposing these changes in some void – as I have mentioned above, there had been some previous attempts by Company officials including Fraser, Holwell, Dow, and others to master Indian languages and texts. What was perhaps of more serious consequence for Hastings was the publication of two other volumes in 1771, a year before his Regulations – Abraham-Hyacinthe Anquetil-Duperron's French translation *Zend-Āvestā, ouvrage de Zoroastre* and Jones's *A Grammar of the Persian Language* with a large number of translations from Persian literary sources. Moreover, Jones's *Grammar* was explicitly meant for the use of Company administrators in India. Hastings thus exploited a growing trend of translations from and philological inquiries into various Asian languages, and, at the same time, used this new knowledge to claim a different kind of authority, of a vague and hoary antiquity of the Indic civilization. This was evident in his prefatory note, framed as a letter to the Court of Directors of the Company, to the first outcome of his project, Halhed's *A Code of Gentoo Laws* – while defending some passages which presumably ran contrary to the current standards of European taste and propriety, he explained that "possibly these may be considered as essential Parts of the Work, since they mark the Principles on which many of the Laws were formed, and bear the Stamp of a very remote Antiquity, in which the Refinements of Society were less known, and the Manners more influenced by the natural Impulse of the Passions."[60]

An image of Indian antiquity was indeed necessary for the kind of authority Hastings wanted to muster for his project. But it also introduced an additional problem – how to read and interpret texts which were from different cultural contexts and embodied principles and ideals completely alien to European sensibilities. Hastings seems aware of this difficulty, and, in his prefatory note to Charles Wilkins's translation *The Bhăgvăt-Gēētā, or Dialogues of Krĕĕshnă and Ărjŏŏn* (1785), he offers a rather radical proposal:

> Might I, an unlettered man, venture to prescribe bounds to the latitude of criticism, I should exclude, in estimating the merit of such a production, all rules drawn from the ancient or modern literature of Europe, all references to such sentiments or manners as are become the standards of propriety for opinion and action in our own modes of life, and equally all appeals to our revealed tenets of religion, and moral duty. I should exclude them, as by no means applicable to the language, sentiments, manners, or morality appertaining to a system of society with which we have been for ages unconnected, and of an antiquity preceding even the first efforts of civilization in our own quarter of the globe, which, in respect to the general diffusion and common participation of arts and sciences, may be now considered as one community.[61]

Of course, cultural difference is the central point of this passage. What stands out more prominently, however, is Hastings's eagerness not so much to paper over this difference but to underscore it, and then to help the average European reader develop a critical framework to attenuate the text's foreignness. In his proposed extension of the "bounds to the latitude of criticism," thus, he not only calls for abandoning the literary-critical frameworks of Europe but also suggests the beginning of a new one involving the alien "language, sentiments, manners, or morality" of India – in short, an anthropological framework. Whether a legal digest or a literary tract, for Hastings, alien texts call for different aesthetic ideals, and he is quite categorical that the newness of this new aesthetics has to be fashioned with anthropological details of a foreign culture.

Hastings's ambitious plan, especially after Jones joined him in 1783, took a turn toward what I call a rule of philology as a form of governance that would function by *reading* cultural difference. By translating anthropological details of indigeneity into recognizable textual signs, this philological governance would extend the new "latitude of criticism," over time, into governmental habits. In a letter to Burke, Jones gave voice to the central belief that animated this new regime: "A system of *liberty*, forced upon a people invincibly attached to opposite *habits*, would in truth be a system of cruel *tyranny*." The remedy for Jones, following Hastings, was a return to native legal systems: any "system of *judicature* affecting the natives in *Bengal*, and not having for its basis the old *Mogul* constitution, would be dangerous and impracticable."[62] As Bernard Cohn has indicated, this obsession with native law led the early colonial officials to believe that India possessed in some uncertain antiquity "a fixed body of laws [and] codes," derived from the "law givers" and contained in an "Ur-text"; and though subsequent "accretions, interpretations, and commentaries" had corrupted this "Ur-text," it was still possible to reconstruct it from available manuscripts and by consulting native authorities.[63] Hastings, and later Jones and others, thought philology was the method through which these ancient legal tracts could be reassembled and made available to the District Courts and British judges for their daily use.

As part of this search, however, Sanskrit gradually but surely displaced Persian as the most representative language of the Indic civilization and its cultural values. Jones soon offered a canon of "*Hindu* Literature" with the following list: "*Véda, Upavéda, Védánga, Puránu, Dherma,* and *Derśana* are the *Six* great *Sástras*, in which all knowledge, divine and human, is supposed to be comprehended." Alongside this, he also enumerated a corpus of "*profane literature*, comprized in a multitude of popular books, which correspond with the several *Sástra's*, and abound with beauties of every kind," and mentioned texts on "*Rájníti, Nítisástra, Cávya Sástra, Alancára, Upác'hyána, Nátaca*" (4: 110–12). With these two lists, he was able to give shape to both a textual canon and a territorial nation that owned the canon, implying a natural correspondence between the two. This was not an accidental formulation – rather, it was closely related to the way Sanskrit was territorialized within the subcontinent since Halhed, and also the way the language was made a precondition for cultural authenticity.

The primacy of philological methods offered the possibility of interpreting an alien cultural world as a whole, with a sense of totality that only language could withstand and a will that required the enormity of the colonial state to realize. As such, and on a theoretical plane, however, there was little scope to distinguish between different usages of language as long as philological principles could underwrite the colonial structure. As is evident from Jones's two lists, for instance, poetry, law, philosophy, and rhetoric could, and in fact did, occupy their respective places in this expansive canon, and he had little means to distinguish their individual deployment of language. However, since this canon was also supposed to capture a national spirit, Jones quickly turned toward his other theory of anthropological peculiarities from the 1770s, and explained the typical literary works in Sanskrit as distinct from other forms or usages of the same language.

In his essay "On the Mystical Poetry of the Persians and Hindus," meant as a prefatory note for his prose translation *Gítagóvinda: Or, The Songs of Jayadéva* (1792), Jones identifies what he calls "a singular species of poetry, which consists almost wholly of a mystical religious allegory, though it seems on a transient view to contain only the sentiments of a wild and voluptuous libertinism" (4: 212). Evidently, the allegorical mode of writing in itself is not a problem for a polymath like him. What intrigues him more is the structure of this poetry of the "*Súfis* and *Yógis*" of Persia and India that admits an allegory without a literal reference, or, rather, a language folding upon itself and creating a double that remains stubbornly intransitive. Oriental poets like Háfiz and Jayadeva represent for him the idea that "the sublimity of the *mystical allegory*, which, like metaphors and comparisons, should be *general* only, not minutely exact, is diminished, if not destroyed, by an attempt at *particular* and *distinct resemblance*" (4: 223; emphasis original). At one level, Jones attempts to explain such writings with reference to theological schools such as Vedánta and Sufism; at another, however, he simply registers his perplexity at such statements: "they profess eager desire, but with no carnal affection, and circulate the cup, but no material goblet; since all things are spiritual in their sect, all is mystery within mystery" (4: 230). Coupled with his earlier belief in the anthropological specificities of literature, this recognition of the literary language within the bounds of national characteristics produces more convincing credentials for its sovereignty.

With the rise of Sanskrit and this typically oriental form of writing as the centerpiece of philological governance, we can now see the outlines of the literary sovereign with greater clarity. In his 1803 essay "On the Sanscrit and Prácrit Languages," for instance, Jones's colleague and one of the Company Sanskritists H. T. Colebrooke presents a summary of the inquiries made in the preceding decades and makes the contours of the new sovereignty virtually unmistakable. He accepts the suggestion that Sanskrit is the most ancient language of the subcontinent, but argues that its true characteristics can be ascertained only once it is placed in comparison with subsequent vernaculars. In this formulation, the antiquity of Sanskrit is kept intact, but its territorial reach is made to coincide with the possible extent of the empire, and the mutual constitution of language, culture, and governance is highlighted as the promising outcome.[64] Sanskrit grammar becomes an especially important focal point for such an argument, and Colebrook insists that its complexity must not be taken to mean that Sanskrit was not a language of everyday use in ancient times. In fact, he argues the opposite – he submits that all these grammatical refinements took place only when Sanskrit, like Latin in Europe, ceased to be a spoken language, and functioned more as a repository of knowledge. The complexity of a well-known text like Pāṇini's *Aṣṭādhyāyī* (c. fourth century BCE), for instance, does not suggest practical advice on Sanskrit grammar for Colebrook; rather he sees in such texts the gradual codification of the language.

To decipher the mystery of Sanskrit, and also to use it as the foundational point for governance, therefore, the colonial administrators had to access it in its more practicable form. Consequently, a series of Sanskrit grammars by Europeans appeared around the same time: Paulinus a Sancto Bartholomaeo's *Sidharubam seu Grammatica Samscrdamica* (1790), the first ever Sanskrit grammar in any European language, was followed by Colebrooke's *A Grammar of the Sanscrit Language* (1805), William Carey's *A Grammar of the Sungskrit Language* (1806), Wilkins's *A Grammar of the Sanskrita Language* (1808), and H. P. Forster's *An Essay on the Principles of Sanskrit Grammar* (1810). In Colebrooke and his contemporary administrators, one could witness the gradual emergence of a parallel between the codification of Sanskrit grammar and the collation of Hindu laws, with the additional belief that, if philology could decipher the arcane grammatical rules of the language, it would also be able to translate the recondite legal system into practicable laws. Grammar and law, in other words, came together as mutually dependent hermeneutic systems, and the Company officials assumed that the success of colonial governance depended on the efficacious interpretation of one with the other.[65]

Singularity as Sovereignty

In recent years, this early history of British India has been narrated within a Schmitt–Benjamin frame of *exception* – or suspension of law – that sees the Company and its political maneuverings as constituting a kind of sovereignty that stepped aside from a formal legal structure. In this narrative, the Company could claim sovereign power not because it was an extension of the British state – which, as a listed joint-stock company, it was not – but because it successfully portrayed its power as emanating from the so-called "right of conquest"; and it could further enforce this idea of exception by simply marking itself out from the rest of the political powers active in India, both local and European.[66]

It is difficult to explain, however, why, at a time when the administrators were desperately trying to defend the Company through the language of law, the idea of suspending the same law would have appealed to them as a political resolution. In my reckoning, apart from this empirical difficulty, the real problem with a theory of colonial exception is that it cannot account for the serious incommensurability between a modern rule of law and an anachronistic idea of sovereignty – a characteristic feature of early colonialism in India – and it cannot even begin to address the relationship between law and the contingency of colonial history. As Giorgio Agamben points out, the "state of exception," especially in Carl Schmitt's *Politische Theologie* (1922), eventually presents a paradox – it suggests a legal form for something that in reality cannot have a legal form.[67] Suspension is not absence of law for sure, but its very invocation implies a typical poverty of legal language which cannot be fully compensated from within the purview of law alone. The idea of exception, in other words, is a political idea at its core, but it always presents itself as a legal–juridical provision; and this essential ambiguity renders the notion of a "state of exception" fully accessible neither to politics nor to law and jurisprudence. When one invokes this same theory to explain the volatile history of early colonialism in the Indian subcontinent, one is practically caught between these two different registers of politics and law, and one is perforce drawn to frame colonial history either in terms of haphazard contingencies or as arbitrarily assembled juridical power. In each case, what one misses is the possibility to think of early colonialism as the beginning of a political form or even as a historical event.

The literary sovereign, in contrast, allows one to think political sovereignty in terms of textual singularity, and vice versa. It is not a coincidence that the same set of officials who "codified" native legal systems also translated literary texts and wrote grammars and dictionaries. Within the eighteenth-century colonial world, these officials saw little disagreement between the two enterprises, and often argued that one was a vital requirement for the other. The precolonial cultural world of the land, the much-celebrated ground for Enlightenment anti-imperialism, came back here as an ally of colonial governance and had a new lease of life as part of the ensuing legal regime. In the popular parlance of the time, it was held, to quote Jones from *Institutes of Hindu Law: Or, The Ordinances of Menu* (1794), that "[l]aws are of no avail without manners," or that even the "best intended legislative provisions would have no beneficial effect [...] unless they were congenial to the disposition and habits, to the religious prejudices, and approved immemorial usages, of the people, for whom they were enacted." This was even more pertinent in India, where the inhabitants were seen as so deeply religious that they "universally and sincerely believed, that all their ancient usages and established rules of conduct had the sanction of an actual revelation from heaven."[68] Translations like Wilkins's *The Bhăgvăt-Gēētā* or *The Hĕĕtōpādēs* and Jones's *Sacontalá* or *Gítagóvinda*, among many others, were meant to capture this cultural core of India – the manners, habits, prejudices, and customs of its inhabitants – that animated legal texts but remained somewhat buried beneath the surface. What attracted the officials to these texts was the secluded interiority or a sort of closed textual system that perpetuated itself without any external aid or any obligatory referentiality, and yet offered a reliable access to a foreign world of alien habits. The verbal arrangements of these texts neither imitated a world outside nor performed a preordained script; instead, for the officials at least, they suggested a veritable semantic web that offered both an enclosed verbal architecture and an "authentic" cultural world.

To put it differently, it was the literary singularity that offered the most potent model for colonial sovereignty. Unlike the "state of exception," singularity is not defined by absence or suspension – of law, language, politics – and its physiognomy is not distributed across different registers. Rather, what constitutes literary singularity is the marshalling of the resources of a culture, and, paradoxically enough, crossing the threshold of that same culture in the very actualization of the singular experience. Literary singularity is an open structure, responsive to the uniqueness of verbal configuration and always susceptible to the foreignness of the other. Formulated in this way, singularity is not a property or feature of literature; it is rather an event embedded in the verbal organization of a text but not necessarily reducible to its constitutive elements alone. It is the excess of crossing cultural limits, or the reorganization of cultural resources with hitherto unavailable form and meaning, that establishes the singular experience of literature.[69]

Such a definition of literary singularity matches well with the colonial encounter with "oriental" texts that I have discussed so far, and the way Wilkins or Jones recorded their perplexity at defining the newness of these texts provides material to build a case for the idea of crossing a cultural threshold and entering the realm of the other. However, a theory of such magnitude – of joining singularity with sovereignty – can be sustained only if one also agrees to treat culture as an autonomous domain and texts as specific engagements with that cultural world. The Enlightenment critique prepared the ground for the first, as I have noted above, but the important contribution made by colonialism was the status and scope accorded to literary texts. In important ways, such texts were taken to stand in for a totality of cultural tradition – in this specific case, a rarefied Indic culture – and, as a consequence, texts were invested with a sense of sovereignty that was commensurate with the enormity of what they supposedly embodied. By sovereignty I do not mean the usual sense of literary autonomy or uniqueness; what I have in mind is the authority or power that is seen as tautologically valid, or self-sufficiently evident. A textual unit was sovereign for these officials and translators because of this notion of power that emerged through its status of being representative of a culture and the way such power came to be articulated in its verbal particularity.

This idea of sovereignty was precipitated further by two related concepts from colonial archives – difference and translation. All the texts seen as representing the sovereign cultural world of India were first defined in terms of their difference from European texts. Though Jones occasionally referred to Greek antiquity as a possible parallel to the Indian past, the bulk of his argument relied on the cardinal point of cultural difference that he thought distinguished the verbal organization of these oriental texts. What confirmed this sense of distinction was the anthropological details that placed difference within a recognizable scheme of things, but this also made anthropology an essential part of the literary sovereign. This is of course a counter-intuitive argument, since anthropology is seen as capturing what the literary cannot, and as such marking its epistemic alterity; but the colonial context made it absolutely clear that these two were related projects insofar as governance was concerned. This was partly due to the way early anthropology relied on an eclectic mix of different discursive resources, including literary texts such as novels and travelogues, but its real origin lay in the colonial insistence on detecting the essential "manners and customs" of India within literary texts.

This was confirmed further by colonial translators through their repeated use of the untranslatables from the original. Although translation was the key motor behind Hastings's plan to indigenize colonial rule, at least in its legal systems, in practice what secured the authority of such texts was what remained essentially untranslatable, as tenacious remainders of local culture. Jean-Luc Nancy suggests in a different context that, in translational practices, "[w]hat is sovereign is the idiom that declares itself to be untranslatable."[70] In a somewhat similar spirit, as I shall show in Chapter 2, it was this untranslatable anthropological detail that clinched the authenticity – and eventually sovereignty – of these texts of law and literature, and this literary sovereign was reinforced through a range of paratextual devices such as commentary, notes, glossary, and so on. In the colonial scheme of things, translation was meant to temper the cultural difference of Sanskrit or Persian texts, and many of the officials, such as Halhed, suggested that it was indeed the invisible hand of governance, so to speak. But what came out of the mission that Hastings set in motion was a repertoire of strategies – textual, translational, critical – that converted untranslatable foreignness into the very ground for literary sovereignty.

This is the precise point when the colonial administration discovered the specific quality of these texts that it could deploy to confirm its sovereign power. Hastings gives it a precise shape in his defense of Wilkins's *The Bhăgvăt-Gēētā*:

> Nor is the cultivation of language and science [...] useful only in forming the moral character and habits of the service. Every accumulation of knowledge, and especially such as is obtained by social communication with a people over whom we exercise a dominion founded on the right of conquest, is useful to the state: [...] it attracts and conciliates distant affections; it lessens the weight of the chain by which the natives are held in subjection; and it imprints on the hearts of our own countrymen the sense and obligation of benevolence.[71]

And it was also the point when this sense of sovereignty was extended to literary texts as well. In the same note, Hastings describes *Bhagavadgītā* as "a very curious specimen of the Literature, the Mythology, and Morality of the ancient Hindoos," and cautions his readers that,

> Many passages [from this text] will be found obscure, many will seem redundant; others will be found cloathed with ornaments of fancy unsuited to our taste, and some elevated to a track of sublimity into which our habits of judgment will find it difficult to pursue them; [...] Something too must be allowed to the subject itself, which is highly metaphysical, to the extreme difficulty of rendering abstract terms by others exactly corresponding with them in another language.[72]

This sense of cultural otherness, coupled with some of its untranslatable components, confers sovereignty on the literary text. What is otherwise a personal experience of literary singularity is generalized in Hastings's account as a common reading experience for the community of his European readers. He acknowledges the gap between European aesthetic taste and a text like *Bhagavadgītā*, but his point is not to turn this gap into a taboo but to mobilize it to imagine the alterity of the text within the vocabulary of sovereignty. What remains "obscure" or "cloathed with ornaments of fancy" is not simply bad writing or repugnant morality but a sovereign world with its own mythology and metaphysics, organized according to its own cultural norms. Translation – and untranslatability – only reconfirms the conjoined sovereignty of the text and the world.

What emerged out of the colonial mission was this new idea of the literary as a sovereign form of textuality that hosted within itself a set of rules and values and produced meaning strictly according to these rules. This is not to suggest, I hasten to add, that the new idea of the literary was dissociated from similarly constituted texts or from a cultural universe of which it was a part. In fact, the rules and values that characterized a literary text were seen by the colonial officials as exclusively belonging to a specific culture, and they frequently recommended intertextual inquiry to unpack a given text. This is perhaps best captured by the most popular text coming out of this period – Jones's translation of Kālidāsa's classic *Abhijñānaśākuntalam* as *Sacontalá; Or, The Fatal Ring* (1789). In his "Preface," Jones describes the work as the expression of the "full vigour" of the "Indian empire" from the remote past, and informs his readers that the "machinery of the drama [...] is taken from the system of mythology, which prevails to this day, and which it would require a large volume to explain" (9: 370–1). Alongside this, he mentions three other projects he is simultaneously engaged in as translator: "the Law Tract of Menu, and the new Digest of Indian and Arabian Laws" (9: 373). These projects, directly related to his passion as a jurist and also to colonial administration, soon appeared in succession: his translation of *Mānavadharmaśāstra* as *Institutes of Hindu Law: Or, The Ordinances of Menu* (1796), *A Digest of Hindu Law on Contracts and Successions* (1798; completed and published by Colebrooke after Jones's untimely death), and *Al Sirájiyyah: Or, The Mohammedan Law of Inheritance* (1792). Clearly, Jones sees these projects as one and wants his readers to read *Sacontalá* not in isolation, but as part of the larger project of explicating the Hindu cultural world, as captured in *Institutes of Hindu Law* and *A Digest of Hindu Law*. The "system of mythology" he is so reluctant to include in his "Preface" can be addressed, at least partially, by these broader reflections on law, religion, and cosmology.

This effect of Jones's translation was not lost on his European readership. As Schwab notes, "*Shakuntala* was the first link with the authentic India and the basis on which Herder constructed an Indic fatherland for the human race in its infancy. From this sagacious work with its time-honored traditional refinement, a blasé Europe, thirsty for a golden age, could fabricate the notion of a primitive India, a concept that would prove long-lived and would obstinately seek to push back the date of Vedic poetry." With remarkably rich details Schwab shows how *Sacontalá* fundamentally transformed European cultures, especially in England, France, and German-speaking regions, and categorically states that the appearance of Jones's translation "was one of the literary events that formed the texture of the nineteenth century, not just by its direct influence but by introducing unexpected competition into world literature." Following Jones's lead, a number of prominent literary figures from Schlegel to Chateaubriand suggested parallels between Kālidāsa on the one hand and Homer, Theocritus, Tasso, or Ossian on the other, giving further life to the comparative frame that was so central to the development of the literary sovereign.[73]

The cardinal point of Europe's reception of *Sacontalá* was the sense that in its textual unity Kālidāsa's play presented an "authentic" picture of ancient and uncorrupt India with its characteristic manners, customs, political institutions, religious beliefs and so on. When read with Jones's other translations, or those produced by Wilkins, Halhed, or Anquetil, the play offered a glimpse into an alien culture, but did so through its sovereign singularity, or through a form of literary language for which there was little precedent in Europe. As the historian William Robertson argued in his immensely popular *Historical Disquisition Concerning the Knowledge Which the Ancients Had of India* (1791), for a play like this, one must not apply "rules of criticism drawn from the literature and taste of nations with which its author was altogether unacquainted"; instead, one needed to make "allowance" for "local customs, and singular manners, arising from a state of domestic society, an order of civil policy, and a system of religious opinions, very different from those established in Europe."[74] The literary sovereign paradigm I have been tracing through colonial archives so far surfaced in such pleas across Europe, and it was evident that the colonial history behind it was all set to make its mark beyond its culture of origin.

A Passage to Europe

One of the ways Europe made sense of the literary sovereign was the conceptual grid of *Weltliteratur* or world literature. As Goethe's discussions with his disciple Johann Peter Eckermann from 1827 onward indicate, the term was meant to bring together an anthropological description of the world and a new aesthetic idea of literature, and its primary aim was to domesticate the foreignness associated with what Europe saw as its essential other, both historically and textually.[75] This was part of what Gayatri Spivak has shown as the crisis of European thought in the era of expanding imperialism;[76] and, in this period of tenuous philosophical tenets and dubious claims of universality, the literary sovereign offered a unique way to make sense of a history that was larger than anything that Europe had ever had to grapple with. When Goethe suggested the idea of world literature to Eckermann, he was aware of the countless translations and retranslations of the texts that came out of the colonial world, creating what Schwab calls Europe's second or "oriental" renaissance.[77] He also knew, at least partially, the great amount of research material circulating in Europe through *Asiatick Researches*, the journal published by the Asiatic Society of Bengal. As a consequence, when he set out to formulate his version of world literature, he did so through an unusual combination of aesthetic and anthropological registers.

The immediate provocation for his reflections, as Eckermann notes, is Goethe's reading of a Chinese novel that he describes as "very remarkable." However, the discussion that follows, on January 31, 1827, sees Goethe develop two different aesthetic ideals – one represented by unnamed Chinese authors and their works and the other by a host of European authors including Pierre-Jean de Béranger, Friedrich von Matthisson, Alessandro Manzoni, Sophocles, William Shakespeare, Aeschylus, Euripides, and Goethe himself. His initial contention that the "Chinamen think, act, and feel almost exactly like us" quickly gives way to his more robust commitment to anthropological grounding of aesthetic traditions – he tells Eckermann that "with them all is orderly, citizen-like, without great passion or poetic flight"; "they likewise differ from us, inasmuch as with them external nature is always associated with the human figures"; that Chinese novels are replete with their legends, all "turning upon what is moral and proper"; and finally, "it is by this severe moderation in everything that the Chinese Empire has sustained itself for thousands of years, and will endure hereafter." It is difficult not to see traces of Hastings or Jones in this lumping together of Chinese texts into one single anthropological frame of propriety and moderation, and it is even more difficult to miss their influence on Goethe's further attempt to join this anthropological foundation to a national attribute and eventually to political sovereignty of the Chinese empire. This anthropological frame becomes even more prominent as Goethe sets it against individual authors from Europe – while Chinese texts collectively represent one single tradition, Béranger or Shakespeare revel in the bright light of their individuality.[78]

At this point, Goethe offers his well-known observations on world literature:

> But, really, we Germans are very likely to fall too easily into this pedantic conceit [of national pride], when we do not look beyond the narrow circle which surrounds us. I therefore like to look about me in foreign nations, and advise every one to do the same. National literature is now rather an unmeaning term; the epoch of World literature is at hand, and every one must strive to hasten its approach.[79]

The most striking feature of this passage is of course this idea of world literature superseding national literatures, within a frame of futurity that requires human efforts to materialize; but one needs to pay equal attention to the transition narrative that informs his contemplation at this point. What were the conditions of possibility that Goethe thought would be sufficient enough to hasten this move from the nation to the world? What were the signs of contemporary history that he read as suggesting the central idea of this passage – that the "epoch of World literature is at hand"? And, at a time of growing German nationalism after the Napoleonic invasion, why did he feel the obligation to pronounce the death of national literature? I think this is the moment where Goethe's reliance on Kant became critical, and he believed that the foreignness of colonial histories could be contained within the latter's proposal for a new concept of aesthetics.

Of course, it is possible to see his proposition of world literature as a parallel to Kantian cosmopolitanism.[80] But that is not the whole story. At stake in this formulation is the fundamental question of how to make sense of culturally different texts and how to rearrange aesthetic resources to account for this difference. Kant's argument across two texts suggests a model of what I call *impure aesthetics* (see Chapter 4 for details) – in the *Critique of the Power of Judgment* (1790) he registers his inability to identify a pure or practical domain with a priori norms for the operation of aesthetic judgment or taste, and subsequently in *Anthropology from a Pragmatic Point of View* (1798) he invokes a popular supplementary register which is thoroughly anthropological in nature. He argues that the judgment of taste or aesthetics (as defined by Alexander Baumgarten) is a subjective statement with universal pretension – in practice, such statements are validated only within a community, and that too comparatively. The impurity of this paradigm resides in the fact that aesthetic judgment is always beyond itself or that its being necessarily refers to an external anthropological logic, and this very impurity sets Kant apart from most of the works on aesthetics in the eighteenth century.

For Goethe, this impurity suggests a sovereign community that is anthropologically defined but internally delimited, and in the early decades of the nineteenth century such a community can only mean the nation. In his conversation with Eckermann, thus, he defines Chinese and German literatures in explicitly national terms; even when he suggests that "poetry is the universal possession of mankind," this *mankind* is effectively an assembly of nations. Such a frame made eminent sense, given what he already knew of the colonial enterprise in British India, especially of the literary sovereign paradigm. And conversely, Goethe's endorsement reconfirmed the new status of the literary – or its sovereign textuality – beyond the colony, and within the larger world. It is here, however, that Goethe also made the transition from the nation to the world, by converting the latter into an aggregate of discrete nations and national cultures. His world was not the globe or the planet – it was a site of difference, or a space held together by endless distinctions between nations. Every literary text that entered this arena was thus an agent of a nation, and every entry was an announcement of competition.[81]

This sense of the competitive world is further consolidated in his remarks immediately after the passage I have quoted above: "But, while we thus value what is foreign, we must not bind ourselves to anything in particular, and regard it as a model. We must not give this value to the Chinese, or the Servian, or Calderon, or the Nibelungen; but if we really want a pattern, we must always return to the ancient Greeks, in whose works the beauty of mankind is constantly represented. All the rest we must look at only historically, appropriating to ourselves what is good, so far as it goes."[82] Almost paraphrasing Jones, he imagines different aesthetic logics for different traditions as internally sovereign, and then poses them against each other. His fascination with Greek antiquity is perfectly consonant with the residues of eighteenth-century neoclassicism, but his conscious effort to restrict its legacies to western Europe – and to exclude, apart from the Chinese, "the Servian, or Calderon, or the Nibelungen" – indicates his eagerness to assert proprietorial rights over it. This is a precondition, across much of Goethe's contemporary Europe, to claim both literary and national sovereignty, and he feels little hesitation in extending it to cover a range of authors encompassing Shakespeare and Manzoni and their individual genius.

Goethe's world of world literature, therefore, was invested with two logics of seriality: national culture and aesthetic tradition. Within the two traditions of oriental and European aesthetics, he placed individual national literatures; and the European nations were further subdivided into individual authors. However, through these two serialities he reinvented the substantial claims of the literary sovereign at a global scale, and made the new idea of the literary a precondition for world literature. In fact, one of the qualifications for entering this world of world literature, from this point onward, would be to adhere to this new textuality of the literary sovereign, as an autonomous and autotelic realm unto itself.

This new textuality of the literary sovereign made its most distinct mark in what Jacques Rancière has identified as the "democratic petrification" of the literary language, or a form of writing that collapsed earlier hierarchies – formal and otherwise – within a democratic condition of readability. Taking its cue from contemporary developments such as Georges Cuvier's research in zoology and paleontology, Rancière contends, this new ideal of "literature as literature" embraced the maxim of "everything speaks." The historicity of literature, and also the autonomy of its own being, became thinkable only when it was "conceived neither as the art of writing in general nor as a specific state of the language, but as a historical mode of visibility of writing, a specific link between a system of meaning of words and a system of visibility of things."[83] It was in the democratic petrification both of language and of the world of things, and in the relationship between the two, that literature as an autonomous being materialized.

Rancière often cites the opening sequence of Honoré de Balzac's novel *La Peau de chagrin* (1831) as announcing this new idea of literature and its emblematic mode of doing politics. In this sequence Raphaël, the protagonist of the novel, enters a Parisian antique shop and encounters a range of objects from different ages and different parts of the world, put together on a gallery. This rather random juxtaposition not only made "all objects and images equal," but also indicated a new representational order in which "their random gathering made a huge poem, each verse of which carried the infinite virtuality of new stories, unfolding those signs in new contexts."[84] Balzac's novel is important for Rancière because it signaled the death of earlier aesthetic conventions that presumed representational hierarchy between forms and genres; and also because it signposted the arrival of a new mode of visibility for literary writing that relied on the principle of democratic petrification.

The near simultaneity of Goethe's formulation of world literature and Balzac's novel is important for my argument, but, for the time being, I want to place both on a longer chronology and within older traditions of translation and textualization. Both "world literature" and "democratic petrification" had a complex relationship with two traditions of translation. The first one, beginning with the Sanskrit original, the *Pañcatantra* (third century CE), entered Pahlavi or Middle Persian around the sixth century, and by the nineteenth it was available in almost every major literary culture across the world. In Europe, starting from the twelfth century, these stories circulated under the name of Bidpāi or Pilpay and influenced a large number of authors, including Boccaccio and La Fontaine.[85] The second one began with the "translation" of the Arabic story cycle popularly known as the *Arabian Nights*, and appeared in French and English from the early eighteenth century through successive translators including Antoine Galland, Edward William Lane, and Richard Francis Burton. Loosely assembled as a combination of translation, imitation, and forgery, and held together by the frame narrative of King Shahriyār and his wife Shahrazād, this collection of stories had a remarkable journey in different languages and inspired countless imitations across the continent.[86]

Srinivas Aravamudan has shown how these two translations, and their imitations, flooded eighteenth-century print cultures of western Europe, and had extraordinary afterlives across genres and texts as pseudoethnographies, travelogues, fantasy, and erotic tales, eventually crafting what he calls the "enlightenment orientalism."[87] While such translations created an orient for popular consumption, their intrinsic claims to be either "authentic" or "literary" were strongly contested by colonial officials in British India. Many of the new translations that came out of Hastings's mission in fact made it a point to denounce these earlier translations by suggesting that they were not grounded in the "original" language and, hence, they perpetuated a culture of counterfeit (see Chapter 2 for details). Jones even declared that all translations from Sanskrit into any European language prior to Wilkins's *The Bhăgvăt-Gēētā* in 1785 were invalid on similar grounds.

It became clear by the early nineteenth century, thanks to the transnational success of the literary sovereign, that long histories were not enough to qualify these translations as literature proper. Within the intellectual climate of world literature, they either had to access a different kind of autonomy or simply had to function as historical curiosities. Some of the retranslations of these texts – for example Wilkins's translation of the *Pañcatantra* as *The Hĕĕtōpādēs of Vĕĕshnŏŏ-Sărmă* (1787) and Edward Lane's version of the *Arabian Nights* (1838–40) – were attempts to reintroduce these texts according to the new standards of the era, and thereby to highlight their literary quality, but such attempts were rather few and far between. What survived of this tradition, however, was the set of techniques to convert the orient into a readable text, to create an everyday reality of distant lands through the sheer power of language. In an age that transformed its penchant for anthropological details into markers of authenticity, these earlier conventions of writing naturally found a warm reception.

As I shall demonstrate in Chapter 5, the textual mechanism of novels like Balzac's *La Peau de chagrin* deployed a complex mix of narrative techniques derived from the *Arabian Nights* and colonial documents like *Description de l'Égypte*, 23 Vols. (1809–29) or translations by leading orientalists Anquetil and Silvestre de Sacy; and they appropriated a different logic of readability that emerged through the spectacle of the "orient" in contemporary exhibitions like tableau *générale*, *tableau historique*, *Exposition Universelle*, and so on. The literary quality of these novels was intimately tied to the combined effect of these different forms of textual organization, to their ability to manipulate the anthropological and the fictional as interdependent narrative configurations. Within a multiplicity of languages, histories, and cultures, such novels developed their fictionality as participating in a worldwide reality of literature. Rancière's democratic petrification was indebted more to such narrative techniques of colonial provenance than to Cuvier, and the success of the nineteenth-century novel as a global genre ensured the survival of these techniques beyond their culture of origin.

Another entry point in this global trajectory of the literary sovereign can be found in Michel Foucault's work, especially in his account of the birth of literature in *The Order of Things* (1966). Foucault pegs the idea of the literary on its "radical intransitivity" and explains its emergence as determined by two different imaginations of language since the late eighteenth century – one through the newly minted discipline of philology and the other through literature as a reconstituted field of linguistic performativity. His central thesis in fact rests on the development of philology, first in the colony with the translations of Anquetil, Wilkins, and Jones, and then carried out in Europe by a group of philologists including Friedrich Schlegel, Franz Bopp, Jacob Grimm, and Rasmus Rask. In his reckoning, the fundamental achievement of philology was the historicization of language – or making history an internal property of language – that resulted in two vital developments: first, it ended the neoclassical tradition of treating language as a "thing" in nature; and second, it turned language into its own archive, making it a proper "object" of study. The result was that languages were now seen as akin to organic beings with inner teleologies, and were susceptible to familial groups like the Indo-European or the Semitic and so on. As opposed to this shift toward historicism, the literary language gradually became an act of performance. "From the Romantic revolt against a discourse frozen in its own ritual pomp, to the Mallarméan discovery of the word in its impotent power," Foucault argues, literature "folded back upon the enigma of its own origin and exist[ed] wholly in reference to the pure act of writing."[88] From this point onward, the literary language would remain beyond the reach of historicism, would function through the suggestiveness of analogy, and, as such, would occupy a zone of exception in the development of the modern episteme.

The problem with Foucault's theory is that his neat distinction between the historicized and the performative is not supported either by colonial archives (where he places its origin) or by the texts of comparative philology he cites as evidence. As I shall show in Chapter 3 with some details, the central feature of Jones's engagement with non-European languages such as Persian, Arabic, and Sanskrit was his insistence on the conjoined development of philology and literary conventions, making them interdependent and coterminous. He often advocated the view that the limitations of philology could be overcome only with the addition of literary texts that represented the precise "manners and customs" of the people who spoke specific languages. Even the early texts of comparative philology that Foucault cites extensively — for example Friedrich Schlegel's *Über die Sprache und Weisheit der Indier* (1808) and Franz Bopp's *Über das Conjugationssystem der Sanskritsprache in Vergleichung mit jenem der griechischen, lateinischen, persischen und germanischen Sprache* (1816) — continued with this tradition and were replete with references to classical literature as a way of establishing Sanskrit's philological specificities. Bopp in fact went even further — as part of his attempt to prove his theory of a linguistic family that stretched across the borders of Asia and Europe, he not only included extended citations from the *Vedās*, the *Rāmāyana*, and the *Mahābhārata*, but even produced a series of translations from Sanskrit literature such as *Nalus, carmen sanscritum e Mahàbhàrato* (1819) and *Indralokâgama, Ardschuna's Reise zu Indra's Himmel* (1824) as well as glossaries like *Glossarium Sanscritum* (1828–30), uniting the literary and the philological on the same analytical ground. This conflation was possible because much of Bopp's work on Sanskrit relied on the grammars and translations authored by Wilkins, Jones, and Colebrooke, and he extended the widely shared colonial view that "a nation, possessing a language so polished in so early a period [...], must be able to boast of a very ancient literature."[89]

What I am trying to get at is one of the central doctrines of the literary sovereign that Foucault misses completely — that is, a culture could most effectively be delimited through its languages *and* literary texts. In their eagerness to know India thoroughly, the colonial administrators, in addition to translating Indian literary texts, plunged headlong into local languages and scribal cultures, producing a flurry of grammars, dictionaries, comparative vocabularies, and so on. By 1798 the Company issued official decrees to make proficiency in local languages a mandatory condition for employment in its services.[90] In 1800, a college at Calcutta's Fort William was established under the stewardship of John Borthwick Gilchrist, a surgeon turned orientalist, to train both Company officials and the "writers" or clerks in local languages with the help of Indian *pandits* and *maulvis*. Over the next few decades, Fort William became one of the major centers to publish a series of translations, primers, grammars, and dictionaries both of classical languages such as Sanskrit and Persian and of popular Indian vernaculars.[91] Between the introduction of local laws in the governance of the colony in 1772 by the first Governor General, Warren Hasting, and the establishment of the college in 1800 by the sixth Governor General, Marquess Wellesley, the Company made an enormous investment in philological projects and literary translations to produce a manageable version of the cultural universe it sought to intervene into. Within this world, and within the emerging structure of the literary sovereign, the distinction that Foucault proposes was collapsed, and a definite image of Indian culture and civilization was created along the adjoined vectors of performative and veridical languages. In an important sense, it was this duality of languages such as Sanskrit that produced a culturally recognizable idea of India with unique form and content.

The text that captured this moment of the literary sovereign with great perspicuity, ironically enough, is the one Foucault cites in support of his argument – Schlegel's *Über die Sprache und Weisheit der Indier* (*On the Language and Wisdom of the Indians*). In his general scheme for the book, Schlegel considers language, literature, and philosophy as forming a continuous mode of representation of India and chooses Sanskrit as the archetypal language for this task. Throughout the text, in fact, he frequently deploys "Sanskrit" and "Indian" as interchangeable terms. The point of this exercise is to put comparative philology in the service of what will soon be recognized as the new discipline of literary history, and to recalibrate the insights derived from colonial missions to produce an account of India over the ages, through interconnected cultures and histories. Schlegel's theoretical armature, for instance, borrows heavily from Halhed and Jones's suggestion of the Indo-European family of languages, and he extends it further to imagine a global antiquity shaped by migration, settlement, and colonization. Within this expansive world, Sanskrit becomes his chief navigational tool – its grammatical refinement suggests an advanced civilization and its literary texts confirm this speculation. At the same time, Sanskrit puts into motion a series of comparative analyses – especially in Book 1 – and functions as the yardstick against which other languages are measured and classified. While some of these comparative arguments can be seen as logical extensions of colonial philology – and Schlegel himself admits to that – his efforts to rethink human history in the last two books, especially through literature and philosophy, mark the beginning of a new mode of thought.

Schlegel's seamless transition from comparative philology to comparative literary history – or the very discipline of literary history itself – belies Foucault's claim of literature being non-historicist or that it simply restricts itself to the "pure act of writing." In contrast, Schlegel argues that the "ancient forms of speech [...] constitute a record, far more valuable and instructive than all those monuments of stone [...] at Persepolis, Ellora, or in Egyptian Thebes." Access to such "ancient forms of speech" is provided by the "copious richness of Indian literature," and determined further by a combination of "philosophy, ancient history, and philology."[92] From such preliminary groundwork, he proceeds to define a series of ideas historically, about the orient and Europe, and eventually to unite them within one theoretical frame.

Thus, for instance, he echoes the idea that the "chief peculiarities of Oriental literature are supposed to consist in a bold and lavish pomp of imagery, and in the tendency to allegory usually combined with those qualities," but instead of tracing its origin to tropical climate or topography, as Dow and Jones do, he rather emphasizes "their highly intellectual religion" as the "operative cause." In the presence of such complex religious traditions, Schlegel submits, "poetry and the poetical temperament [...] will find scope for its richness and luxuriance in bold poetical imagery." In support of his claim, he cites both Persian and Arabic poetry on the one hand and the strikingly "Oriental character" of many medieval poets from Spain, Italy, and Germany on the other. If one wishes to push this idea further back in history, one can possibly see parallels even between the "soul-felt intensity of emotion" in Indian poetry and the "simple and severe" Greek writings. "Choruses" in Aeschylus or the "lyric boldness of the similes and allusions of Pindar" can be described as "highly Oriental, although clothed in an Hellenic form," confirming his claims of conjoined histories from ancient times. Such parallels inspire him to imagine a deeper structural affinity: "The deep-thinking philosophers of Europe have almost always shown a decided preference for ancient Oriental literature. Many great poets among the Greeks are distinguished by the same peculiar feeling; and Dante, among the moderns, approximates, though in a manner less universally recognised, to Oriental grandeur of style and diction."[93]

All these individual instances of comparative reading eventually lead Schlegel to a grand scheme of literary history:

> As in popular history, the Europeans and Asiatics form only one great family, and Asia and Europe one indivisible body, we ought to contemplate the literature of all civilized people as the *progressive development of one entire system, or as a single perfect structure*. All prejudiced and narrow ideas will thus unconsciously disappear, many points will first become intelligible in their general connexion, and every feature thus viewed will appear in a new light.[94]

He does not use the phrase "world literature" here, but his proposal for the study of the "literature of all civilized people as the progressive development of one entire system, or as a single perfect structure" is perhaps the first statement in that direction. Here Schlegel anticipates Goethe's formulation in 1827 or Marx and Engels's in 1848 in a number of ways, not the least in suggesting a conjoined yet comparative field; but the real breakthrough comes in the form of a history that transforms the basic model of Indo-European philology into a global itinerary of the literary. The crucial point of this single but global system is achieved not by treating the literary language as a universal exception, or as a linguistic performance that remained inaccessible to history, but by regarding it as the general unifier of a number of disparate and historical elements that would have stayed scattered and unconnected otherwise. For Schlegel, the literary is a privileged site because it can achieve a cohesion of its own where notions of culture, civilization, and race find their place, as supplementary domains, and such cohesiveness can be demonstrated historically. The Indo-European family of languages harbors this possibility of linking cultures across the continents, but it is left to literature to bring out the full import of such connected histories, to reconstitute the "great family" of Europe and Asia.

In England, and in direct conversation with the developments in the colony, this story of literary history unfolded along two different yet related tracks. The first one emerged through the question of a national canon that wavered for some time between the rather idiosyncratic attempts of Samuel Johnson's *Lives of the Most Eminent English Poets* (1779–81) and the more systematized account of Thomas Warton's *The History of English Poetry* (1774–81), before eventually culminating into the Romantic passion for assembling a vernacular canon that would have suited the school curricula.[95] By the time William Wordsworth penned his famous "Preface" for the 1798 edition of the *Lyrical Ballads*, and claimed to have represented the everyday – or even the "rustic" – language of ordinary people in his poetry, it was clear that along with the canon, or perhaps as a supplement to it, he also wished to identify an anthropologically inflected national-popular as the locus for the new literature. Any discussion on the canon, and any investment in the new training for a public that would be its ideal readers in future, therefore, needed an internal delimitation of culture. However, this rhetoric of a new canon had a parallel in the colony. From the early decades of the nineteenth century, and especially in the wake of what is known as the Orientalist–Anglicist debate in British India, English Literature was made a taught subject in Indian higher education.[96] Such an administrative decision needed a literary canon to teach in the first place, and soon the debates on a national canon in England and in the colony overlapped. The idea of the literary sovereign that was first developed to understand Indian literatures was transposed to this new set of debates, and national canons were repurposed as quintessential expressions of national *Zeitgeist*.

What distinguished this phase was the deliberate inculcation of race within the canon, forcing a corpus of texts to stand in for racial superiority. This invocation of literature–race–culture as a composite concept received its most prominent articulation in Matthew Arnold's *Culture and Anarchy* (1869) that borrowed some of its key ideas from the racialized philology of Ernest Renan.[97] But the very introduction of race within the politically charged space of the literary sovereign made the latter an inseparable ally of imperialism. Canons and literary histories were no longer simple expressions of literary singularity or cultural autonomy; in important ways, such cultural artifacts were thoroughly historicized using contemporary "race sciences" and consequently mobilized to signal imperial orders. Race assumed a polyvocal status within the imperial discourses and also in the literary sovereign – it turned difference into hierarchies, and generated typologies of cultural value out of literary texts. It was possible, in the second half of the nineteenth century, to see race forming intricate networks of physical and psychic domination – even violence – within the many-layered palimpsest that the literary sovereign had become by then. It is hardly a wonder that literary texts turned out to be one of the major sites to produce what Maurice Olender calls racialized "erudition."[98]

The Plan of the Book

Now we can see the full range of the literary sovereign across continents – from Jones's "singular species" of poetry and Hastings's "latitude of criticism" to Goethe's "world literature" and Schlegel's "literary history," that eventually reached its climax in Arnold's invocation of "culture" on a global key. Let me clarify here that what I track in this book under the general rubric of the literary sovereign is not a new mode of writing or a formal innovation. Rather it refers to a critical paradigm that first became visible through colonial governance in British India, and subsequently through Europe's encounter with alien textual traditions in Sanskrit, Persian, and Arabic. That it was a critical paradigm and not a recommendation for writing was obvious from the fact that the literary sovereign was developed with references to texts prior to its time – often ancient ones – in these languages, and it was never announced as an agenda or a manifesto for writing. Even when Jones recommended the idea of the literary as a possible model for European authors, he did not claim to have invented it, but referred to existing customs of the "Eastern nations." What it included, rather, was a set of contingent rules that gradually allowed a culture, through interconnected, contiguous, and comparative histories of modern empires, to recognize a particular form of writing as "literary" and to attach a certain value to that writing, with the hope that this set of rules and values together would be adequate to the novelty of the new idea. These rules no doubt constituted the literary sovereign, but the paradigm itself was not reducible to these rules alone or even to a regime that made these rules worthwhile, but was established in connection with other histories and events. As I shall show in the following chapters, the new paradigm responded to and shaped a range of histories – of colonial governance, legal innovations, crises of philosophical thought in the wake of imperial expansion, aesthetic values, the development of anthropology as a discipline but also as a governmental technique in the colonies, and so on.

To put it differently, a paradigm is neither a metonymic example nor a metaphorical archetype. Rather, it represents a set of rules and conventions that delineate a material-discursive field, with the power to engineer further rules and generalizations. The literary sovereign as a paradigm, likewise, is shaped by five broad sets of rules: it is a form of lettered sovereignty that becomes an epistemic habit of colonial governance; it embodies a set of aesthetic conventions that constitute the distinct field called literature; it thrives in the interim zone between aesthetics and anthropology and draws on both; it finds its political efficacy by oscillating between the nation and the world, as two dominant framings; and yet, it continues to function as an autonomous and autotelic performance of language. All five of these, often in combinations, allow one to see the specific arrangements on the surface of the new paradigm, to investigate how events and individuals or texts and territories are organized, or how their relationships are defined and distributed. When gathered together, at a deeper level, they even reveal the points at which the new paradigm broke off and separated itself from previous ones. It was the context of the colonial rule in the Indian subcontinent that made this transition to a new paradigm possible, and it was the strategic alliance with the emerging form of colonial sovereignty that made it distinguishable.

At the heart of this new paradigm lies a new thickness of language that would have been inconceivable even during the first half of the eighteenth century. What I have in mind is not only the historicist thickness advocated by philology, as Foucault notes, but a kind of thickness that evolved over time, borrowed its resources from diverse genres and disciplines such as travelogue, anthropology, cartography, *belles-lettres*, and so on, and eventually attained its form and content by aligning itself with political sovereignty. This was partly to do with Europe's historical association with India, going back to the military campaign of Alexander the Great in the fourth century BCE and renewed periodically by medieval travelers such as the Venetian Marco Polo; but it was more directly connected to early modern contacts through trade, diplomacy, missionary activities, and military interactions. Since the discovery of the Cape Route and Vasco da Gama's arrival in Calicut in 1498, maritime interactions between the two regions grew manifold. Scholars have chronicled these contacts between Europe and India over the centuries in great detail, and have shown how the representational patterns changed as Europe made the transition from being a trading outlier to being the political ruler between the fifteenth and the eighteenth centuries.[99] The kind of thickness that shaped the literary sovereign had its roots in this centuries-old tradition of representing India, through increasing traffic of people, texts, artifacts, images, trading goods, and ideas, and the new paradigm made use of some of these narratological conventions such as tropes or metaphors to fashion its own being. However, in an era of colonial dominance, with the task of governance at hand, the colonial officials found these earlier resources necessary but not adequate enough. At least from the 1770s, the new administration under Hastings sought to build on these earlier European engagements with India, but did so within a conscious frame of newness, of surpassing the discursive frames which were put in place over the last few centuries.

Part I of this book offers a detailed exploration of colonial archives to trace the evolution of this new thickness of language, as also of its gradual migration toward political institutions and practices. Any form of philological governance needs a stable "text" and a set of critical apparatuses to ensure that the authenticity of that text can be ensured with a fair amount of certainty. In a pre-print scribal culture, where texts survived in multiple manuscripts and in varying degrees of "corruption," this idea of an authentic text proved particularly challenging for colonial administrators. In Chapter 1, I explore in detail – through official and personal papers, published translations, letters exchanged between colonial officials, prefaces and commentaries, and so on – how the Company officials, in close collaboration with their local *pandits* and *munshis*, produced a tradition of what I call *ethnographic recension* that anchored an ethnographic world within the very space of a legal or literary text. Coming between the Renaissance humanists like Politian, Desiderius Erasmus, and Joseph Scaliger on the one hand and nineteenth-century textual scholars like Karl Lachmann on the other, these colonial administrators introduced a new model of textual authority by combining philology and ethnology that was the first move to mark the newness of colonial knowledge. This ethnographic world was seen as a guarantor of textual authenticity, but its very inclusion set off the dual career of the literary sovereign – its role in defining what is literary, and its participation in political sovereignty.

Within the colonial world, the textual density of the literary sovereign was calibrated through translation. However, as I show in Chapter 2, the idea of textual autonomy and singularity was secured not so much by the transparency of translation as by the opacity of what was essentially untranslatable. These untranslatables might include anything from ethnographic details of local cultures to "exotic" religious or literary practices, but the central point remained that their impermeability was a necessary guarantor of textual integrity and authenticity. Across literary and legal translations such as Charles Wilkins's *The Bhăgvăt-Gēētā* (1785) and *The Hēĕtōpādēs of Vĕĕshnŏŏ-Sărmā* (1787), Charles Hamilton's *The Hedàya, or Guide* (1791), and William Jones's *Al Shirájiyyah* (1792), I argue, the untranslatable emerged as a political category, as an essential ingredient of the literary sovereign. This political character of the untranslatable was eventually ratified in the sensational impeachment trial of Hastings. Analyzing the speeches and other documents from the trial, I demonstrate how the untranslatable Indian culture became the central point of contention, and how it was the autonomy of this cultural core that determined the course of colonial governance.

While ethnographic recension and colonial untranslatables defined a distinct mode of textual organization, the full potential of the literary sovereign was revealed within a frame of comparatism. Chapter 3 explores colonial archives to unearth two models of comparatism – one diachronic or chronological and the other synchronic or territorial. The first model emerged from Jones's works, both his translations and his speculative essays in *Asiatick Researches*, covering a broad range of subjects including Indian chronology, astronomy, literary history, and so on. Along with this, and in explicit opposition, the second model was developed by colonial officials like Brian Houghton Hodgson and William Wilson Hunter through their copious comparative vocabularies: Hodgson's numerous essays published in the *Journal of the Asiatic Society* since 1847 and Hunter's *A Comparative Dictionary of the Languages of India and High Asia, with a Dissertation* (1868). The potential of these two phases was realized fully in the ambitious Linguistic Survey of India (1894–1928) under the supervision of George Abraham Grierson. My claim in this chapter is that with Grierson's attempt to enumerate and describe modern Indian vernaculars, and with his seamless mixing of colonial structures and linguistic knowledge in the survey, we encounter the full range of the comparative method for the first time. Many of the critical tools used in comparative literary studies today have their origins in these colonial projects.

However, owing to the transnational and multilingual context of modern empires, the literary sovereign soon traveled across the seas to reach Europe and its cultures of polite letters, saturating its salons, literary circles, critical treatises, and almost every possible space that took up literature for serious discussions. Part II of this book explores this European career of the new paradigm through three different contexts – German philosophy, French novels, and English literary history. In Chapter 4, I concentrate on the evolution of the idea of *Weltliteratur* and argue that it was one of the most successful tools through which Europe negotiated with and made sense of the colonial history of the literary sovereign. Though it is mostly associated with Goethe, its clearest outlines were available through a combination of Kant's *Critique of the Power of Judgment* (1790) and *Anthropology from a Pragmatic Point of View* (1798). *Weltliteratur*, I argue, is the culmination of a set of ideas that Kant introduced to account for the peculiar nature of the power of judgement or taste – that such judgments cannot have any a priori or universal principles and yet claim universality in their application. Whether framed as the beautiful or the sublime, he suggested, such claims remained contingent, and relied on a communal consensus that could have been established only according to anthropological principles. Kantian aesthetics, thus, is an "impure" one as it always and already relies on something external to it, something that cannot be made sense of within the borders set by aesthetic judgment itself. Similarly, *Weltliteratur* was a combination of aesthetic and anthropological principles, advocating a form of comparative judgment that replicated the Kantian model.

Goethe's proposal renewed the core of Kant's formulation, and inaugurated the typically modern aesthetic regime.

In Chapter 5, I follow this lead further and demonstrate that one of the most prominent sites where this new aesthetic regime and its colonial history was articulated most forcefully was the nineteenth-century French novel. Discussing Jacques Rancière's influential work on novels by Balzac and Flaubert and his suggestion of the new idea of literature emerging through the "democratic petrification" of writing, this chapter shows how the context of such a development in France was historically much wider than developments within its national borders. Instead of thinking the historicity of literature only through Europe, this chapter shows how the literary sovereign shaped the central ideas of textualization and readability through colonial documents, translations, textual representation of the orient, and so on. This textual history is then embedded within larger registers of visuality in contemporary French cultures that extended the colonial paradigm further. The argument I make is the exact opposite of the usual novel theory that proposes the nation as the exclusive domain of the novel – rather, I argue that French novels in the nineteenth century presuppose a logic of world literature that is necessarily multilingual and multicultural. Such a trajectory of the form was made possible by the dynamic idea of the literary sovereign.

The final triumph of the paradigm, however, came in the form of literary history. Chapter 6 explores the gradual development of English literary history to trace how the autonomous and performative being of the literary came to be enframed within the nation, and how literary texts were seen as unmistakable expressions of national spirit. Some of these ideas were first expressed as part of the literary sovereign paradigm, and were reinforced through the successive stages of its travel across geographies. After the initial impetus from the colonial administrators, the idea of the literary and the nation as conjoined entities in history received a further elaboration in two publications from 1808 – Friedrich Schlegel's *On the Language and Wisdom of the Indians* and Johann Gottlieb Fichte's *Addresses to the German Nation*. Both Schlegel and Fichte identified an unbroken literary tradition as the most organic expression of a nation, and both advocated for a "literature" in vernaculars as the most legitimate ground for a national history. However, the bulk of this chapter traces the new discipline of literary history in England, from Thomas Warton's *The History of English Poetry* (1774–81) to Matthew Arnold's *On the Study of Celtic Literature* (1867) and beyond, and shows how such an idea emerged from colonial histories and contemporary "race sciences," and eventually became an important ally both of the nation and of the empire, making its anthropological underpinning more explicit than ever. In fact, the literary sovereign was progressively appropriated by different political formations, and by the middle of the nineteenth century it was made part of a number of different tasks that were not included in its initial remit.

To decolonize literature and literary studies, it is important to explore the organizational logic of both, to revisit the early years of their institutionalization. If the present moment of decolonization has to go beyond the canon wars of the 1980s and 1990s or beyond the token inclusion of postcolonial or black academics and texts while keeping the larger structure more or less intact, one needs to start by exploring the paradoxical character of the literary itself. The modernity of literature is precisely the expression of this paradoxicality – that literature is marked, simultaneously, by its autonomy and its submission to history, its sovereign order of signification and its subordination to political regimes, its supreme aestheticization of language and its deeply democratic commitments. Such a paradoxical existence marks the modernity of literature for sure, but it also signposts the colonial history that shaped its contours, leading us to newer archives and texts to account for its trajectory over the last couple of centuries of so. It is this paradoxical modernity of the literary sovereign that ensured its dual existence – its involvement in colonialism and its role in anti-colonial resistance. The decolonization of literature, in other words, must start from literature itself, from its constitutive protocols and its genealogy, from its diverse commitments and its multifarious responsibilities in modernity.

PART I
Epistemic Habits

CHAPTER I

Ethnographic Recension

A regime that wished to constitute a form of lettered sovereignty – and eventually the literary sovereign – needed a stable and repeatable idea of textuality in the first place. Such a textuality had to be supple enough to respond to the demands of colonial governance and, at the same time, had to exude a sense of cultural authenticity strong enough to distinguish the colonial engagement with India from any previous missions. It was this second point about the authenticity or purity of a culture that the colonial officials eventually settled on as the ground to claim sovereign power, and for this they needed an equally pure tradition of textual authority. This was especially important since translations of legal texts both from Hindu and from Islamic traditions into English, they felt, required this stamp of purity in order to make them effective. A form of sovereignty could be operationalized only if it conformed with established "customs and manners" of local populations; and, to secure such a legal regime, the officials had to first establish the details of the indigenous cultural world.

In the context of the eighteenth century, this search for authentic texts had a number of implications. In Europe, for instance, this was the time when hermeneutic and exegetical practices – or textual criticism, more broadly – were being extended for the first time to non-scriptural texts. A case in point is the proliferation of edited volumes of William Shakespeare's plays in England that appeared with detailed discussions on the authentic version, editorial notes on what was spurious in previous editions, and critical commentaries to help the reader understand a culture that was remote in time and yet important enough to draw attention to itself. This was the culmination of practices introduced by the Renaissance humanists who deployed similar techniques to ascertain the correct version of the New Testament. When transported to non-theological or non-liturgical contexts, these editorial practices were seen as one of the chief protectors of the authenticity of a culture and its texts. Soon, interpretation and textual criticism formed the core of a culture that took progressive steps to establish its pure origin.

Many of the colonial officials who landed in India in the eighteenth or early nineteenth century had some exposure to this new scholarship in Europe and the new trend of utilizing textual criticism to determine cultural purity. They also had some formal training in interpretative practices before they set sail for the new colony. But what they encountered in India was something vastly different from Europe – a scribal culture and a virtual cornucopia of manuscripts and languages with uncertain origin, authorship, or even date. These officials found it extremely difficult to instill any sense of order in this bewilderingly capacious textual world and its attendant culture with their knowledge of textual criticism in Europe. Horace Hayman Wilson, a translator and orientalist stationed in Calcutta, gave voice to the working conditions of early officials when he related to his readers the following: "The brevity and obscurity however of the technical definitions, the inconceivable inaccuracy of the Manuscripts, and the little knowledge of the subject which the Pundits generally possess, have rendered the taste of interpreting them, laborious and painful, to an extent, of which readers accustomed to typographic facilities can form no adequate conception."[1] Many of the officials and translators soon realized that they had to devise some new strategy to sift through this vast textual world of India and also to settle the thorny issue of authenticity.

My name for this new strategy is *ethnographic recension* or ethnographic worlding of texts. It marked a clear departure from contemporary textual criticism in Europe as the translators identified and highlighted ethnographic signs within the text and eventually calibrated those signs to claim a national culture. In fact, it was the presence of these ethnographic signs of a nation that was held to be the guarantor of authenticity of texts. Whether in a legal text or a literary one, therefore, the translators repeatedly searched for an identifiable national tradition and argued that such a tradition was capable of overcoming the usual corruption of manuscripts and other related technical details. As a result, when European scholarship was concentrating more and more on internal evidence of corruption, scribal mistake, interpolations in a manuscript, and so on, the colonial officials were busy establishing a recension of Indian manuscripts that would have displayed an unmistakable sign of a national culture.

This difference was not a mere technical one, but had larger philosophical consequences. In the colonial context, the texts were not seen in their isolation, or even in light of the complex history of individual manuscripts. Rather, texts and manuscripts were taken as representative of an organic national culture that had continued unbroken over centuries and that could still be recovered through correct philological practices. Learning languages such as Arabic, Persian, or Sanskrit was the first step in that direction; but the scholarship soon went beyond this initial stage as the officials started treating languages – and, by extension, texts – as some sort of archive of the nation. It was a reworking of the paradigm of historicism, but this time the history they searched for was not confined to the space of the text alone – it had to be corroborated continuously against the organic wholeness of a national culture, amidst its everyday ethnographic signs.

In this chapter, I set out the history of this ethnographic recension, and I explore the strategies different colonial officials/translators employed to achieve this new scholarship on textual criticism. One of my central interlocutors is the prolific colonial administrator and polymath William Jones, but I also take into account a host of other officials who made vital contributions to this story. After the "Regulations" of 1772, introduced by Warren Hastings, this engagement with local texts received official support, but the process has a longer and complex history. I argue in the following pages that it is by attending to this long history, and also by engaging with different attempts to arrive at a reliable version of the ethnographic recension, that we can see the genealogies of the literary sovereign. Some of these attempts were successfully incorporated into colonial governance, others were discarded in the long run; but, when taken together, they offer us a steady insight into the early formations of the new paradigm.

Colonialism and Textual Criticism

In recent scholarship Jones's work has been identified as possibly the most influential articulation of the encounter between European scholars/colonial administrators and the textual universe of the colony.[2] However, what seems missing in such discussions is a fuller appreciation of the fact that Jones (and other colonial administrators) assumed an ambiguous persona for these texts – a combination of author, editor, grammarian, philologist, and translator – in clear defiance of the available literary conventions of eighteenth-century Europe. This had several implications for the rise of the literary sovereign, as well as for what I have described as the progressive anthropologization of literature as an object worthy of serious scholarly attention. One of the central points of this shift from what Michel Foucault would have called an explicitly "authorial function" to a nebulous managerial one was the conscious attempt by Jones and others to align themselves with the mission of colonial governance, and to participate in the foundation of what would eventually become, in Nicholas Dirks's words, the "ethnographic state" in British India.[3] I suggest that the ambiguous persona Jones and his colleagues assumed for these texts was a precursor not only to the professional ethnographer, making their interventions an integral part of colonial governance, but even for the governmental process of turning literary texts into techniques of rule.

Jones's emphasis on this combined persona was consistent with his approach to languages or even literary texts. In his extremely successful *A Grammar of the Persian Language* (1771), which went through several editions during his lifetime and after, he first argues that the mere translation of a culturally different text is not sufficient ground either to attract attention to the text or to understand it satisfactorily. The result of men spending their entire scholarly lives on the minutiae of Persian grammars and dictionaries and ignoring the "manners and sentiments" is, in his opinion, very similar to that of "men who discover a precious mine, but instead of searching for the rich ore, or for gems, amuse themselves with collecting smooth pebbles and pieces of crystal." Or, better still, such scholarly labor of the grammarians, while laudatory, remains busy "adoring only [...] porticos and avenues" while it could have been better utilized "to beautify and enlighten the vast temple of learning."[4]

This is indeed a curious claim to make in the preface to a book ostensibly designed to teach Persian grammar. It is even more so since the text is primarily meant for the practical use of the colonial administrators of the British East India Company stationed in India who need the language to further both their administrative functions and their commercial interests. He is aware of this practical appeal of his book, and in fact pleads unsuccessfully with the Company to secure some advances for the book by citing its future usefulness for colonial administrators.[5] And yet, Jones seems convinced that mere grammatical rules, or even grammatically correct translations, cannot be trusted for the full appreciation of a language.

This belief is reinforced by the colonial experience of India, where, he notes, "[b]y one of those revolutions, which no human prudence could have foreseen, the Persian language found its way," and where knowledge of the language has become of paramount interest.[6] What is needed for a colonial official to successfully administer "important affairs [...] in peace and war between nations equally jealous of each other" is not only a technical knowledge of the language, but also an awareness of all the manners and sentiments associated with it, and even the cultural context within which it operates.[7] Hence, initially he plans to "prefix to the grammar a history of the Persian language from the time of Xenophon to our days, and to have added a copious praxis of tales and poems extracted from the classical writers of Persia."[8] The *Grammar*, however, is published without this paratextual material; but he soon fulfills his promise by publishing a great deal of such material with his *Life of Nader Shah* (1773), and in later editions insists that his grammar be read along with these other texts. Once Jones has linked the knowledge of a language with the explicit interests of the empire, he feels confident enough in saying that, now that the utilitarian muster has been passed, "the manners and sentiments of the Eastern nations will be perfectly known; and the limits of our knowledge will be no less expanded than the bounds of our empire."[9]

The point I am trying to highlight is of course the way Jones deviates from the established rules of General Grammar of the eighteenth century; but I am much more interested in the unique way he aligns this shift explicitly with colonial governance. This is made possible, among other things, by his willing acceptance of a managerial role, a combination of author–editor–philologist, that can do full justice to these culturally different texts. For instance, he cites three contemporary grammars of English – James Harris's *Hermes: Or, A Philosophical Inquiry Concerning Language and Universal Grammar* (1751), Robert Lowth's *A Short Introduction to English Grammar: With Critical Notes* (1763), and Samuel Johnson's "An English Grammar" prefixed to his *A Dictionary of the English Language* (1755) – and argues that he has "refrained from making any inquiries into general grammar" as established by these authorities and instead focusses on Persian grammar as part of a larger cultural milieu.[10] His new approach soon finds supportive echoes across the empire and its functionaries. Nathaniel Brassey Halhed's *A Grammar of the Bengal Language* (1778), one of the early outcomes of Hastings's project in colonial governance, to take just one example, reverentially mentions the "accurate and elegant grammar composed by Mr. Jones" that does "equal honour to the cause of learning, and services to his countrymen in Asia."[11]

This dual service to disciplinary knowledge and imperial interest, I suggest in this chapter, led to the typical ethnographic underpinning of the new idea of the literary sovereign, and made textual criticism a mandatory framework to elaborate on this immanent concept. What Jones and his colleagues in Calcutta were able to devise was not simply a new methodology, but a new way of looking at language and a new vocabulary to discuss its literary expression with far-reaching consequences. Within the colonial world this new approach to language found its legitimation through its extensive use by the colonial state, and within the larger world it gained popularity because of its close proximity with imperial circuits of circulation.

Jones's deliberate emphasis on a managerial/ethnographic function, especially when it was adopted as the working principle by the colonial officials, however, faced a serious challenge – that of producing the "authoritative" version of native texts. While it was crucial for the colonial authorities to arrive at a reliable version of the text they were championing, it was no less important for them to distinguish their efforts from what Srinivas Aravamudan has described as the texts of "enlightened orientalism" of the eighteenth century – "[o]riental tales, pseudoethnographies, sexual fantasies, and political utopias" – that inundated European markets after the astounding success of the French translation of *A Thousand and One Nights* in 1704.[12] They even had the additional task of distinguishing their work from earlier accounts of the East, mostly by travel-writers and amateur orientalists, and needed to stake their claims on a new idea of authenticity. As Jones's accounts suggested, this initial claim was often made through language learning, and through their claim that they had unmediated access not only to Indian texts but also to the immediate milieu of manners and customs that were required to interpret such texts. Indeed, this new generation of orientalists often calibrated this linguistic claim to distinguish themselves from their predecessors and dismissed the earlier generation's rather amateurish reliance on secondary sources as scandalous.[13]

And yet, this strategy had limited success. It was clear to these colonial administrators that, to prove their claims and to preserve the edifices of new learning, they needed something else, something more appealing, and something like a framework in tune with contemporary knowledge paradigms. Mere language learning, they realized soon, was not enough to claim authenticity in an age of rapid communication and a shrinking globe. At one end of these new practices was a set of rules which were gathered during the eighteenth century under the general heading of the *ars critica* or the art of textual criticism. These rules were established through progressive refinements on the principles introduced by the renaissance humanists like Politian, Desiderius Erasmus, and Joseph Scaliger, and were meant to perform the vital task of reconstructing the "lost original document, the "authoritative text."[14] Many of the colonial officials were familiar with these developments in Europe.

However, on the other hand, they also had to face the daunting task of mediating the momentous transformation of a largely scribal culture to its modern typographical standardization, which made most of the European rules rather redundant. As a result, while they adopted some of the critical insights offered by European editors, they also, owing to their peculiar location and the contingencies of colonial governance, introduced a number of consequential changes that later found their most coherent articulation in

Karl Lachmann's methods of *stemmatics* in the first half of the nineteenth century.[15] The central point for this colonial–philological engagement with Indian texts, and also for the contemporary European obsession with the New Testament, was to determine the most reliable version of a text, especially given their obscure histories, multiple manuscripts, and the constant fear of corruption. In the latter Lachmannian version, this would be termed the central problem of *recensio* and *emendatio*, with the former being the fundamental mechanism for determining the authoritative version.[16] The editorial strategy of *recensio* in the eighteenth century was primarily concerned with identifying the most dependable versions of a given text and separating them from other and allegedly spurious contenders. From these reliable versions, and through utmost care against possible scribal corruptions, the editors hoped to produce the emended or corrected account.[17]

When Jones made his early forays into textual scholarship in the 1770s, the European tradition was beset by what Sebastiano Timpanaro has described as the frequent search for a "systematic *recensio*." Several attempts were made by a host of classicists and philologists including Richard Bentley, Johann Jacob Wettstein, and Johann Albrecht Bengel to propose a systematized *recensio* against the other two prominent claimants – *vulgate* (transmitted text, primarily through print) and *textus receptus* (a succession of Greek texts, forming the foundation for the New Testament). While all three methods claimed to approximate the uncorrupted original texts (*constitutio textus*) of both theological importance (the New Testament in particular) and philological curiosity (classical texts from the Greco-Roman civilizations), it was the votaries of the systematic *recensio* who could most successfully tap into the overpowering idea of the era – that is, historicism – and, as a consequence, could secure a superior standing for their method.

Hence, Johann Jacob Reiske declared in 1770 that *recensio* "is the only way to demonstrate the historical truth of any text, be it sacred or profane, on the basis of the consensus of many ancient manuscripts of approved reliability."[18] Extending the organismic metaphor behind the *recensio* method, the philologist Friedrich August Wolf argued in the prefatory note to his *Prolegomena ad Homerum* (1795) that,

> A true, continuous, and systematic recension differs greatly from this frivolous and desultory method. [...] But a true recension, attended by the full complement of useful instruments, seeks out the author's true handiwork at every point. [...] Not uncommonly, then, when the witnesses require it, a true recension replaces attractive readings with less attractive ones. It takes off bandages and lays bare the sores. Finally, it cures not only manifest ills, as bad doctors do, but hidden ones too.[19]

Within the prevailing intellectual climate of Europe, such an argument made eminent sense, and appealed across a range of disciplinary formations that critically relied on historicism as an indispensable guarantor of truth. As we shall see later in this chapter and also in Chapter 3, this historicist idea and the organismic metaphor through which it circulated would come back again and again to shape the finer details of the new concept of literature and its eventual institutionalization.

Colonial *recensio*

The fact that Jones was familiar with at least some of these debates from his contemporary Europe is evident from his short French pamphlet on Abraham-Hyacinthe Anquetil-Duperron's French translation of *Zend-Āvestā* (1771). Entitled *Lettre à Monsieur A*** du P**** (1771), it is a blistering attack on the French orientalist for his alleged misrepresentation of the Zoroastrian faith and its central text. Jones's primary charge against Anquetil is the latter's purportedly sketchy knowledge of the original text and its language, but there are several passages suggesting that the Frenchman could have avoided embarrassing gaffes had he been familiar with contemporary editorial practices.[20] It is quite evident that Jones largely accepts the argument about a systematic *recensio*, and points out more than once that the surest way of avoiding forgery in textual scholarship is to be attentive to the histories of individual manuscripts. In his view, this is a necessary safeguard in an intellectual world flooded with forged texts and manuscripts from the orient, and in urgent need of expert intervention to adjudicate on specious claims of every possible kind. When combined with his claim of both language learning and cultural translation in his *Grammar*, this emphasis on meticulous editorial practices allows glimpses into an emerging conceptualization of literature, with its vicissitudes and vocations.

This break in Jones's theory happens a year later, with his *Poems, Consisting Chiefly of Translations from the Asiatick Languages* (1772). It is in this slim volume that he first clearly makes literary cultures dependent on territorial peculiarities, and recommends an ethnographic mode of knowing as the most reliable framework for literary criticism. The central clue is provided not only in the poems included in the volume, but also in the two essays Jones adds to it in order to explain the mission of the volume as well as the crux of his craft. The idea is developed in response to two of his immediate challenges – first, he has to defend a set of poems most of which, despite the title, are not exact translations from any extant

"Asiatick" sources and hence are open to the charge of forgery; and second, as a corollary, he has to devise a new aesthetic theory to uphold these poems against the neoclassical fashions of eighteenth-century Europe.

To put it differently, he is not engaged in unraveling the authorial intent (or what later became known in textual criticism as the "final intentions"[21]) of these poems through his editorial interventions since, strictly speaking, most of these poems did not have any clearly assigned author in the first place. This lack of an author figure also exposes Jones's collection to be clubbed with what Aravamudan describes as pseudoethnographic texts that "speculated about a largely imaginary East" and also "titillated European readers with armchair voyagings and vicarious imaginings."[22] The point needs to be stressed since Jones was not only familiar with this tradition, but even borrowed ideas in the past for some of his other poems from pseudoethnographic texts such as William Collins's *Persian Eclogues* (1742).[23] In the preface to his *Poems*, he makes a clear reference to this other tradition when he opens on this cautionary note:

> The reader will probably expect, that, before I present him with the following miscellany, I should give some account of the pieces contained in it; and should prove the authenticity of those *Eastern* originals, from which I profess to have translated them: indeed, so many productions, invented in *France*, have been offered to the publick as genuine translations from the languages of *Asia*, that I should have wished, for my own sake, to clear my publication from the slightest suspicion of imposture.[24]

He in fact makes no bones about his distaste for such spurious texts, especially ones of French origin.

One would have expected him, as a consequence, to make a strong case for the systematic *recensio* of his translations, since it is the authenticity of his text, against the corpus of forgery and fraudulence, that he wishes to establish. Instead, and quite surprisingly, Jones makes a completely different claim, and shifts the idea of authenticity from individual manuscripts or authors to literary traditions of a given land. "The first poem in the collection, called *Solima*," he tells his readers, "is not a regular translation from the *Arabick* language; but most of the figures, sentiments, and descriptions in it, were really taken from the poets of *Arabia*" (*Poems*, viii). Similarly, it turns out, all the other poems from the "Asiatick" sources, with the exception of the "Turkish Ode," are not "regular translations" at all. Rather, their authenticity is derived from a peculiar mode of ethnographic belonging to a given tradition and territory.

Take the poem "The Palace of Fortune" as a case in point. He informs his readers that the "hint" of this poem "was taken from an *Indian* tale, translated a few years ago from the *Persian* by a very ingenious gentleman in the service of the *India-company*." However, what the reader is confronted with is somewhat different since, he admits, "I have added several descriptions, and episodes from other *Eastern* writers, have given a different moral to the whole piece, and have made some other alterations in it, which may be seen by any one, who will take the pains to compare it with the story of *Roshana*, in the second volume of the tales of *Inatulla*" (*Poems*, x). In this case, the *recensio* thus is not concerned with the poem (or its manuscript) included in the collection, but with a preexisting literary tradition and a prior text by a colonial official, namely Alexander Dow's *Tales Translated from the Persian of Inatulla of Delhi* (2 Vols., 1768). He makes it a point to highlight the difference between spurious oriental tales and Dow's text by virtue of the fact that the latter is produced through the intricate mechanisms of colonial administration, including language learning, and hence through more authentic access to the cultural world of the text.

Endorsements by colonial officials, however attractive, are still external confirmations. Jones quickly recognizes that such claims cannot be repeated *ad infinitum* without spelling out the underlying "tradition" or without detailing the aesthetic components that will secure a more authentic status for his volume. At the outset, and especially in the second essay entitled "On the Arts, commonly called Imitative," however, his aesthetic theory seems very distant from any ethnographic consideration. If anything, it is a combative argument against the neoclassical dogma of mimetic art. In an oft-quoted passage he argues:

> If the arguments, used in this essay, have any weight, it will appear, that the finest parts of poetry, musick, and painting, are expressive of the *passions*, and operate on our minds by *sympathy*; that the inferior parts of them are *descriptive* of natural *objects*, and affect us chiefly by *substitution*; that the expressions of *love, pity, desire* and the *tender* passions, as well as the *descriptions* of objects that delight the senses, produce in the arts what we call the *beautiful*; but that *hate, anger, fear*, and the *terrible* passions, as well as objects, which are *unpleasing* to the senses, are productive of the *sublime*, when they are aptly expressed, or described. (*Poems*, 207–8)

This is an important intervention in a number of ways. As M. H. Abrams has noted in his magisterial account of the Romantic theories of poetry, this is perhaps the first instance in English of bringing together various threads like "ideas drawn from Longinus, the old doctrine of poetic inspiration, recent theories of the emotional and imaginative origin of poetry, and a major emphasis on the lyric form and on the supposedly primitive and spontaneous poetry of Oriental nations." What Jones achieves additionally, Abrams suggests, is "an explicit and orderly reformulation of the nature and criteria of poetry and of the poetic genres."[25]

While this initial step is not explicitly grounded in ethnographic conventions, his subsequent move of rejecting the Aristotelian maxim of mimetic or imitative art, and his valorization of oriental poetry as a counterpoint to European art, clearly lead to that direction. He argues that if one extends the scope of one's inquiry beyond the boundaries of Europe and into the heart of the Orient – in the spirit and manner of anthropology, so to speak – one would find irrefutable evidence in support of his theory. He cites the allegedly universal appeal of lyric poetry which has found a home in "some *Mahometan* nations; where *sculpture* and *painting* are forbidden by the laws, where *dramatick poetry* of every sort is wholly unknown, yet, where the pleasing arts, *of expressing the passions in verse, and of enforcing that expression by melody*, are cultivated to a degree of enthusiasm" (*Poems*, 192; emphasis original). If this non-mimetic tradition is so prevalent and universal, he insists, it has to be the original wellspring of all creative arts.

Jones's new theory of poetry, despite its buoyant claim of accessing a truer source for the genre, is premised on unstable grounds. As he notes passion and sympathy, or even taste, are notoriously individualistic: "As the passions are differently modified in different men, and as even the various objects in nature affect our minds in various degrees, it is obvious, that there must be a great diversity in the pleasure, which we receive from the fine arts, whether that pleasure arises from sympathy, or substitution; and that it were a wild notion in artists to think of pleasing every reader, hearer, or beholder" (*Poems*, 207). How can one argue for a theory based on such subjective responses to art, or how can one even hope for any degree of certainty, if the very ground of appreciation is so unpredictable and uncertain between individuals and their preference for pleasure or sympathy? To counter this subjective nature of passion and sympathy, Jones fleetingly mentions the "opinion of many able writers" who believe that "there is one uniform standard of taste" (*Poems*, 207) – but this is more a sign of desperation than a mark of reassuring authority.

He rather pins his hopes on the possibility that a theory of this kind will find support across cultures in their formative days, in the evidence provided by the early poetry of "the Hebrews, the Greeks and Romans, the Arabs and Persians" (*Poems*, 201). Abrams notes that such an argument implies that "Jones employs the lyric not only as the original poetic form, but as the prototype for poetry as a whole, and thereby expands what had occasionally been proposed as the differentia of one poetic species into the defining attribute of the genus."[26] At the same time, Jones is aware that such a generic expansion cannot be argued on the evidence of European literature alone, not even through the haloed sedimentation of Greco-Roman antiquity across the cultural landscape of Europe, but has to be shown as emerging from a larger milieu, larger than the literary corpus familiar to his readers. Consequently, he turns toward his other material he has long been mastering, especially Arabic and Persian, to advocate that a very different idea of literature indeed exists in these texts.

Jones's new theory is most notably evident in the first essay of this collection – "On the Poetry of the Eastern Nations." This essay, like the collection itself, is based on a curious assertion – he maintains that, even though he is recommending this new "species of literature" to a learned audience on the very basis of its novelty and richness, he does not want to take away anything from the supreme achievements of the Greco-Roman cultures. As he says in the preface, "It must not be supposed, from my zeal for the literature of *Asia*, that I mean to place it in competition with the beautiful productions of the *Greeks* and *Romans*; for I am convinced, that, whatever changes we make in our opinions, we always return to the writings of the ancients, as to the standard of true taste" (*Poems*, xiii–xiv). And again, in this essay, he repeats the point: "I must once more request, that, in bestowing these praises on the writings of *Asia*, I may not be thought to derogate from the merit of the *Greek* and *Latin* poems, which have justly been admired in every age" (*Poems*, 189).

Goethe repeated this strategy almost verbatim in his formulation of *Weltliteratur* nearly five decades later, as we shall see in Chapter 4; but here I want to draw attention to a very different implication of this claim as far as Jones is concerned. These repeated comparisons with "Greek and Latin" poems testify, I suggest, that he wants to contrast two different aesthetic logics which are based on larger territorial configurations. His touchstone or standard is the Europe that begins with Greece and Rome and then engulfs the whole continent within the singularity of its aesthetic ideal. This idea of Europe as a unified territory is more prominently manifest in the sphere of the literary than in anything else, and it is premised on the notion of a European core with clear frontiers that gradually moves from the Mediterranean to the northern shores. In order to suggest a different aesthetic tradition, and to find support for his own theory, Jones therefore has to imagine a similar form of cultural contiguity and comparable territorial logic for this new body of literature.[27]

His essay "On the Poetry of the Eastern Nations" does precisely this – it imagines a poetic ethos that travels across the geography of Asia, from the Arabian Peninsula to Persia and eventually to Central Asia and India. Its veracity is maintained through the peculiar sensibilities of the inhabitants of these lands as also through the spiritual integrity of Islam. The territorial, and eventually ethnographic, logic of this other tradition depends on the way the aesthetic production is shaped by the physical geography and its climate. As Jones states his case: "Now it is certain that the genius of every nation is not a little affected by their climate; for, whether it be that the immoderate heat disposes the *Eastern* people to a life of indolence, which gives them full leisure to cultivate their talents, or whether the sun has a real influence on the imagination, (as one would suppose that the ancients believed, by their making *Apollo* the god of poetry) whatever be the cause, it has always been remarked, that the *Asiaticks* excel the inhabitants of our colder regions in the liveliness of their fancy, and the richness of their invention" (*Poems*, 170–1).

He first establishes his case through the unique example of "Arabia [...] because no nation at this day can vie with the Arabians in the delightfulness of their climate, and the simplicity of their manners" (*Poems*, 163). He goes on to argue that "We may also observe in this place that *Yemen* itself takes its name from a word, which signifies *verdure*, and *felicity*; for in those sultry climates, the freshness of the shade, and the coolness of water, are ideas almost inseparable from that of happiness; and this may be a reason why most of the *Oriental* nations agree in a tradition concerning a delightful spot, where the first inhabitants of the earth were placed before their fall" (*Poems*, 165). This peculiarity of the Arabian topography and climate, he indicates, is the chief source of the poetry they produce, and it is the close connection with nature that secures its characteristic beauty. Jones points out that "an allegory is only a string of metaphors, a metaphor is only a short simile, and the finest similes are drawn from natural objects" (*Poems*, 167). It is only logical, then, that this peculiarity of nature will be part of their poetry, both *beautiful* and *sublime*:

> We must conclude that the Arabians, being perpetually conversant with the most beautiful objects, spending a calm, and agreeable life in a fine climate, being extremely addicted to the softer passions, and having the advantage of a language figuratively adapted to poetry, must be naturally excellent poets, provided that their *manners*, and *customs*, be favorable to the cultivation of that art; and that they are highly so, it will not be difficult to prove. (*Poems*, 182–3)

Of course, the point of such an argument is to link the text with the territory, but the very structure of this and similar other passages also makes it clear that Jones is pleading a different idea of the *recensio*, as also a different notion of authenticity.

As a parallel to this territorial logic, Jones also suggests an internal cohesion through Islam. The crucial connection, again, is supplied by the topography and climate: "*Mahomed* was so well acquainted with the maxim of his countrymen, that he described the pleasures of heaven to them, under the allegory of *cool fountains, green bowers, and black-eyed girls*, as the word *Houri* literally signifies in *Arabick*; and in the chapter of the *Morning*, towards the end of his *Alcoran*, he mentions a garden, called *Irem*, which is no less celebrated by the *Asiatick* poets than that of the *Hesperides* by the *Greeks*" (*Poems*, 180). This internal cohesion makes the poetic ethos both mobile and capable of appealing across territories, and it eventually finds local habitations in Persia, Turkish-speaking Central Asia, and India. As would be evident from this narrative strategy, Jones is eager to establish a territorial logic through the peculiarities of the land; but his second argument about the enclosed and itinerant nature of the poetic culture also makes this territorial logic somewhat detached from the land to which it originally belonged, and transforms the aesthetic coherence into a unit that is sustained through self-reference and intertextuality, without any external support.

His description of the Persian epics *Ferdusi* and *Shahnâma* (especially the section called "*the delivery of Persia by Cyrus*"), and his explicit comparison with the *Iliad*, leads to the conclusion that there is a wide chasm separating these oriental poets from their European counterparts, especially in the period after Homer. Hence, he argues, these eastern poets "possessed, in an eminent degree, *that rich and creative invention, which is the very soul of poetry*" (*Poems*, 186; emphasis original). Though there are occasional comparisons between the two groups – as, for instance, between a poem by Hāfiz and a sonnet by Shakespeare – the distinction is largely intact in Jones's mind, and he eventually uses it to condemn "European poetry," which he believes "has subsisted too long on the perpetual repetition of the same images, and incessant allusions to the same fables" (*Poems*, 189).

In fact, this distinction is at the heart of his reconfigured *recensio*, since through it he is able to refute the tradition of pseudoethnographies, including popular texts such as Montesquieu's *Lettres persanes* (1721) or Oliver Goldsmith's *Citizen of the World* (1761). In this reformulation, he distributes the *recensio* across the tradition and its anthropological underpinning, and, instead of a single text or manuscript as the original text (or source for "final intentions"), he deliberately privileges a textual culture. The authenticity he claims for his poems, thus, derives not from their status of being accurate translations of identifiable individual originals, but from their membership within a tradition of ethnographic textuality.

What Jones presents here is the beginning of a distinct tradition based on ethnographic *recensio*, a tradition different from the pseudoethnographies masquerading as "authentic" oriental tales or, more to the point, from the purported "translations" of oriental originals. The distinction can be ratified only through the singularity of the textual organization, and any reference to a generalized exoticism, though important, must stand as secondary confirmation. What he refers to as clear fabrications, especially in France, was a popular tradition running from Madame de Lafayette's *Princesse de Clèves* (1678) and Pétis de la Croix's *Les mille et un jours* (1710–12) to Thomas Gueullette and his series of tales from Persia, Central Asia, India, China, and even Peru (published between 1712 and 1755). Aravamudan shows that such Oriental tales were often placed within recognizable narrative genres such as the *petite histoire* or the *speculum principis*, and their regularization thus ran parallel to what would soon become the standardized "national realism" of modern novels.[28] I shall return to this question in Chapter 5 with reference to Balzac's novels, and argue that the neat separation Aravamudan poses between enlightened orientalism and the novel is not that neat after all.

Here, however, I want to suggest that, as opposed to these existing and emerging genres, Jones wants to draw attention to the newness of his little volume – and, by implication, of the whole of "Asiatick" poetry – on the ground that its *recensio* is accessible only through the textual organization the reader is about to encounter, through its "rich and creative invention" as opposed to the tired rhetoric of established European traditions. And, for this, the orient one encounters in these poems is an ethnographic textuality that, for its readers, opens onto the land and not the other way around. It is true that this argument is necessary for Jones, since the collection he is trying to defend is premised on this very idea; but it is equally true that through this defense he shifts some of the more accepted terms of textual criticism of the eighteenth century and reinvents them in the textual matrices of ethnographic details. In fact, Jones invokes a double register for his ethnographic *recensio* across these two essays – while its core has to be ascertained through the singularity of a tradition, this core is always and already distributed across ethnographic codes and values. In order to set his text as the exact opposite of eighteenth-century pseudo-ethnographies, he has to stress both these registers, often at the same time, and has to offer his translations as structurally dependent on them.

Sanskrit and Colonial Governance

This early formulation of ethnographic *recensio*, however, went through further changes after Jones reached India in 1783 and after he encountered what Mufti describes as a "sort of *philological sublime*, a structure of encounter with a linguistic and cultural complexity of infinitesimal and dynamic differentiations and of seemingly infinite proportions."[29] Though Jones harbored the ambition of knowing "*India* better than any other European ever knew it," he soon discovered that the colonial officials in Calcutta had already been set upon a similar task under the stewardship of Governor General Hastings, and he indeed entered the stage, as it were, *in medias res*.[30]

He also discovered that this new phase of knowing India was structured around a linguistic shift, from Persian–Hindustani to Sanskrit. Company officials stationed in India had made various unsuccessful attempts to master Sanskrit since the middle of the eighteenth century, but the project received a new lease of life after Hastings's 1772 plan of aligning the governance of the colony with local customs and sentiments.[31] As Bernard Cohn points out, the early colonial officials thought that "there was historically in India a fixed body of laws, codes, which had been set down or established by 'law givers,'" and, in order to revive that ancient tradition, "[a]n Ur-text had to be found or reconstituted, which at one and the same time would establish *the* Hindu and Muslim law as well as free the English from dependency for interpretations and knowledge on fallible and seemingly overly susceptible pandits and maulavis."[32] As a consequence, Sanskrit, just like Persian before it, became part of governmental apparatuses, and its harnessing was seen as crucial to the standardization of Hindu civil law (more on this in Chapters 2 and 3).

Alongside this, Sanskrit also represented the possibility of retrieving ancient learning unknown to Europe. In a letter written in 1787, Jones made the point in the following words: "*Sanscrit* literature is, indeed, a new world [...]. In *Sanscrit* are written half a million of Stanzas on sacred history & literature, Epick and Lyrick poems innumerable, and (what is wonderful) Tragedies and Comedies not to be counted, above 2000 years old, besides works on Law (my great object), on Medicine, on Theology, on Arithmetick, on Ethicks, and so on to infinity."[33] He even went as far as suggesting a parallel between this ancient treasure-trove of India and the classical civilization of Greece, "substituting Sanscrit for Greek, the *Brahmans*, for the priests of *Jupiter*, and *Valmic, Vyasa, Calidasa*, for Homer, Plato, Pindar."[34]

This duality of Sanskrit as a governmental apparatus and as a repository of ancient learning and literature is crucial for my purpose here. At the cusp of these two, the colonial officials had to find a credible *recensio* and a workable *emendatio*. Hastings makes the point with unusual clarity when he discards European "rules" of criticism to engage with Sanskrit texts and calls for a "latitude of criticism" to explore the "language, sentiments, manners, or morality" of India in his prefatory note to Charles Wilkins's English translation *The Bhăgvăt-Gēētā, or Dialogues of Krĕĕshnă and Ărjōōn* (1785).[35] Hastings first recommends *Gītā* as a valuable text on its own right: "I hesitate not to pronounce the *Gēētā* a performance of great originality; of a sublimity of conception, reasoning, and diction, almost unequalled." And then places it within a comparative framework: "I should not fear to place, in opposition to the best French versions of the most admired passages of the Iliad or Odyssey, or of the 1st and the 6th Books of our own Milton, highly as I venerate the latter, the English translation of Măhăbhărăt."[36]

Both these points, however, are not self-evident to a universe made exclusively of European ideals of judgement and morality. The reason that someone like Hastings can testify to the text's intrinsic greatness, the note implies, is his additional access to the ethnographic realities of India, to its everyday life with all its variedness and eccentricities. He illustrates the point by comparing a passage from *Gītā* on the extreme "separation of the mind from the notices of the senses" with his experience of witnessing "a man employed in this species of devotion, at the principal temple of Banaris."[37] While it would be difficult for "even the most studious men of our hemisphere" to achieve such a separation, he assures his readers, the Indian spiritual tradition has produced generations of such men, and for them the otherwise abstruse metaphysics of *Gītā* is but all too apparent.[38]

Towards the end of the note Hastings includes a special plea to the Company officials in London to encourage projects involving Sanskrit, and also outlines the basic structure of his plans that reinforce this ethnographic point even more forcefully. In an extraordinarily sympathetic passage, he informs the officials that "[e]very instance which brings their [Indians] real character home to observation will impress us with a more generous sense of feeling for their natural rights, and teach us to estimate them by the measure of our own." What is equally striking is his immediate qualification that "such instances can only be obtained in their *writings*: and these will survive when the British dominion in India shall have long ceased to exist, and when the sources which it once yielded of wealth and power are lost to remembrance."[39] Being a pragmatic man of business,

Hastings also appeals to a governmental sensibility: "Every accumulation of knowledge, and especially such as is obtained by social communication with people over whom we exercise a dominion founded on the right of conquest, is *useful to the state*: it is the gain of humanity: [...] it attracts and conciliates distant affections; it lessens the weight of the chain by which the natives are held in subjection; and it imprints on the hearts of our own countrymen the sense and obligation of benevolence."[40] For him, the comparative framework is a way of reinforcing his point that Sanskrit texts have innate worth of their own, and in India they function the way Greek classics do in Europe.

However, the inherent value of Indian texts for him cannot be a standalone argument; rather, comparatism is required as a way of putting an official stamp of approval on the *recensio* of texts like Wilkins's *Gītā*, and also as a means of introducing its significance to the company bureaucracy, who may not be enthusiastic about projects that do not "contribute to the immediate and substantial advantages of the state." In other words, Hastings gestures to his plan of establishing a system of governance on native textual traditions, and refers to Wilkins's translation as a positive step in the right direction; but he also enlists the idea of colonial comparatism and insights from textual criticism to strengthen his case. The rhetorical strategy of this note bolsters the ethnographic point, where he is seen as, to quote Cohn, "translating for a British audience theories and practices from one culture to another";[41] but the textual tradition he thus invokes is very different from what I have charted through Jones's works on Persian and Arabic texts above.

Returning to Hastings and his plan, we can now see why he commissioned several law digests to be compiled by Hindu pandits and translated by colonial officials. The first major outcome of this project was Nathaniel Brassey Halhed's *A Code of Gentoo Laws, Or, Ordinations of the Pundits* (1776).[42] Unlike many later volumes, especially Jones's *Institutes of Hindu Law: Or, The Ordinances of Menu* (1794) and Henry Thomas Colebrooke's *A Digest of Hindu Law, on Contracts and Successions* (1796–8), however, Halhed's *Code* was not translated directly from Sanskrit. A group of eleven Brahmin pandits were commissioned to compile a digest of Hindu civil laws between 1773 and 1775 under the title *Vivādarṇavasetu*. Zayn al-Dīn 'Ali Rasā'ī, a munshi (scribe or clerk) employed by the company, prepared a Persian translation of the Sankrit digest, and Halhed used this version for his English translation.[43] Despite this limitation, and the obvious conflict with the new orientalism of language learning, the *Code* was initially designed to be the "Ur-text" of Hindu laws Cohn mentions, and

Halhed buttresses the idea by comparing his compendium with Roman laws, to which "much of the Success of the Romans may be attributed, who not only allowed to their foreign Subjects the free Exercise of their own Religion, and the Administration of their own civil Jurisdiction, but sometimes by a Policy still more flattering, even naturalized such Parts of the Mythology of the Conquered, as were in any respect compatible with their own System."[44] He hopes that his *Code* will be a modern version of Roman laws for the colony.

Such a grandiose claim can be sustained only through a demonstrable mastery over his material. Hence, he offers a detailed account of how the correct *recensio* was produced through extreme care and rigor:

> The Professors of the Ordinances here collected still speak the original Language in which they were composed, and which is entirely unknown to the Bulk of the People [...]. A Set of the most experienced of these Lawyers was selected from every Part of Bengal for the Purpose of compiling the present Work, which they picked out Sentence by Sentence from various Originals in the Shanscrit Language, neither adding to nor diminishing any Part of the ancient Text. The Articles thus collected were next translated literally into Persian, under the Inspection of one of their own Body; and from that Translation were rendered into English with an equal Attention to the Closeness and Fidelity of the Version. Less studious of Elegance than of Accuracy, the Translator thought it more excusable to tire the Reader with the Flatness of a literal Interpretation, than to mislead him by a vague and devious Paraphrase; so that the entire Order of the Book, the several Divisions of its Contents, and the whole Turn of the Phrase, is in every Part the immediate Product of the Bramins.[45]

His eagerness to establish the authenticity of his *Codes* is all too apparent in such passages.

However, in the age of new orientalism, Halhed cannot sidestep the issue of language altogether and hence is forced to include a separate section on Sanskrit itself, including its alphabets, orthography, some grammatical rules, and a longish note on literary styles. His observations on Sanskrit are based on the idea that, while it is imperative for the colonial government to anchor its legislation in these texts, there are very few resources to distinguish between legal texts and others, since they are often mixed with each other and written in a manner that demands close reading. Halhed also complains frequently that very few of the Brahmins he met could claim any degree of authority, given the obscurity of these texts and the language they are written in. He presents the case of the four *Vedas* as an eminent example: "From the many obsolete Terms used in the Beids

[Vedas], from the Conciseness and Obscurity of their Dialect, and from the Particularity of the Modulation in which they must be recited, they are now hardly intelligible; Very few of the most learned Pundits, and those only who have employed many Years of painful Study upon this one Task, pretend to have the smallest Knowledge of the Originals."[46]

Faced with such obscurity of the original texts, and equally bewildering traditions of commentary, Halhed employs two devices which would soon become the cornerstone of comparative philology – grammar and prosody. He first suggests that such texts can be read properly and used for the purpose of governance only if the grammatical rules are clearly set. From the "abstruse" and "prolix" grammar books, he indeed extracts a few rules which, according to him, are intelligible and useful. Halhed also observes that grammatical rules are of limited value in his case, since many of these source texts are composed not in prose but in verse; hence, a clear account of the Sanskrit prosody is equally warranted. He offers a rough sketch of Sanskrit prosody as well, including its various "chhund" or meters, and then, armed with the twin techniques of grammar and prosody, he sets out to decipher a few texts in the preface.[47]

Halhed's engagement with Sanskrit continued and his confidence grew, so much so that in his next major publication, *A Grammar of the Bengal Language* (1778), he could chastise the Jesuit missionary Dupont on his faulty knowledge of the language. The point of disagreement is vital for us, since in its elaboration Halhed sets out some of the central tenets of comparative philology, a discipline that would flourish further in the next decade under the influence of Jones, and also of the governmental principles behind translations. The central point of contention is Dupont's alleged misrecognition of verb roots for "the *caput mortuum* of the language; as not being words of themselves, but certain sounds bearing a relation to certain ideas."[48] For Halhed, the distinction between the two is critical since it is on these finer points of grammar that Sanskrit can be compared with other classical languages such as Greek. Indeed, almost a decade before Jones's "Third Anniversary Discourse" (1786) proposing the rudiments of comparative philology, Halhed observes the "similitudes" between Sanskrit, Greek, Latin, Persian, and so on. From these similitudes, he further deduces the territorial reach of Sanskrit as covering the area stretching from the "Persian Gulph to the China Seas." In support of his thesis, he cites a range of items of archaeological evidence such as coins and seals with Sanskrit inscriptions recovered from different parts of the Indian subcontinent, and even argues that, on the evidence of a text in the possession of the "Raja of Kishenagur," one can surmise ancient links between India and Egypt.[49] In effect, he establishes Jones's territorial principle for oriental literature on the solid grounding of a classical language, suggesting that it is through the antiquity of Sanskrit that a theory of such magnitude can be sustained. What is equally important for my purpose is the suggestion that the evidence for such a theory comes from within the language, through its grammatical rules and literary conventions.

This is the point at which Jones enters the scene, and, although he is critical of Halhed's *Code* for being too derivative and erroneous, he almost immediately picks up a number of Halhed's other arguments. In his "Third Anniversary Discourse," for instance, he accepts two of Halhed's central points – the boundaries of India as a linguistic territory and the antiquity of Sanskrit. In fact, he makes these two interdependent: "By *India* [...] I mean that whole extent of country, in which the primitive religion and languages of the *Hindus* prevail at this day with more or less of their ancient purity, and in which the *Nágari* letters are still used with more or less deviation from their original form."[50] What is only a speculative suggestion in Halhed thus becomes a theoretical commonsense for Jones, that the core of the Indic civilization is essentially Hindu and the evidence of this Hinduness is available in the languages – most conspicuously in the way Sanskrit and its offspring define the limits of this civilization. In his methodology, as a result, he makes it clear that "in all these inquiries concerning the history of *India*, I shall confine my researches downwards to the *Mohammedan* conquests at the beginning of the *eleventh* century, but extend them upwards, as high as possible, to the earliest authentic records of the human species."[51] In a subtle move, he replaces his earlier formulation through Islam with Hinduism, and reworks his territorial argument about oriental cultures by using the antiquity of Sanskrit. For him, the next logical step in this argument is to show a continuous line of literary descent through the ages and to argue that, despite regional differences, it is the core of Sanskritic culture that provides any sense of cohesion to the political idea of India.

He elaborates on this textual tradition in "On the Literature of the Hindus, from the Sanscrit," published in the very first volume of the *Asiatick Researches*. It is essentially his translation (with commentary) of a Sanskrit tract called "*Vidyádersa*, or a *View of Learning*," "communicated by" an Indian *pandit*. In his commentary, Jones proposes that the core of Hindu India has always existed within a dense intertextuality of the *Shastras* or scriptures. However, given the secretive nature of the Brahmins, the custodians of these *shastric* texts, one is forced to employ close and philological readings to unlock their reservoir of learning. The central texts in this tradition are the four *Vedas* as well as the tract of *Gītā*, but the everyday reality of Hindu cultures needs to be explained through a number of other texts like the "*Upavéda, Védánga, Purána, Dherma,* and *Derśana.*" This list is supposed to exhaust the history of Indic civilization by establishing a connection between its antiquarian past and its historical present, and yet it proposes an ahistoric status for these *Shastras* since they have always been part of the core Hinduness without change. In order to argue his case, and also to convince his readers, he quickly enumerates a vast number of texts, disciplines, and schools of learning, suggesting that this bewildering profusion of *shastric* knowledge is almost as extensive as the land.[52]

Jones, however, also notes that the caste system of the Hindus makes many of these *Shastras* inaccessible to the "*Súdra's*, or *fourth* class of *Hindus*"; instead they (and especially "the *Vaidya's*, or those, who are born Physicians") have access to a body of "*profane literature*":

> Instead of the *Véda's* they study the *Rájaníti*, or *Instruction of Princes*, and instead of *Law*, the *Nítisástra*, or general system of *Ethicks*: their *Sahitia*, or *Cávya Sástra*, consists of innumerable poems, written chiefly by the *Medical* tribe, and supplying the place of *Purána's*, since they contain all the stories of the *Rámáyana, Bhárata,* and *Bhágawata*: they have access to many treatises of *Alancára*, or Rhetorick, with a variety of works in modulated prose; to *Upác'hyána*, or Civil History, called also *Rájatarangini*; to the *Nátaca*, which answers to the *Gándharvavéda*, consisting of regular *Dramatick* pieces in *Sanscrit* and *Prácrit*: besides which they commonly get by heart some entire Dictionary and Grammar.[53]

Through these two traditions of textuality – one *shastric* and the other *profane* – Jones produces a unique map of India, and claims that any point of contention in the present has to be resolved with reference to this dense textuality of the land.

By the 1780s and through successive hands including Hastings, Wilkins, Halhed, and eventually Jones, this technique of textualization became commonsensical, so much so that any discussion on India was perforce premised on this central assumption. It was further held, as a logical corollary, that the habits, manners, sentiments, and characters of the Indians were somewhat immutable, and hence the best guide to such unassailable qualities could have been these ancient texts. However, this new order of knowability had another implication for the colonial engagement with Sanskrit. Jones notes in his essay that "[s]ince *Europeans* are indebted to the *Dutch* for almost all they know of *Arabick*, and to the *French* for all they know of *Chinese*, let them now receive from our nation the first accurate knowledge of *Sanscrit*."⁵⁴ In each case, he imagines these non-European languages as primarily functional, serving larger goals of governance and commerce. Sanskrit as a language thus gradually made its claim against Persian as the sole representative of India, and also as the chief governmental instrument. He even sets a precise date for this new engagement with India and its linguistic universe – anything before the publication of Wilkins's translation of *Gītā*, he announces emphatically, should henceforth be treated as inauthentic and unreliable.

Texts, Territories, Nations

All these ethnographic detailing of texts and all the methods to ascertain authenticity eventually needed a frame. As I shall argue in Chapter 6, this framing for the literary sovereign emerged in the form of the nation and, in important ways, this was the final culmination of the ethnographic underpinning of the new paradigm. This was evident in Jones's celebrated translations of Kālidāsa's *Abhijñānaśākuntalam* (popularly known as *Śakuntalā*) as *Sacontalá; Or, The Fatal Ring* (1789) and of *Manusmṛiti* or the *Mānavadharmaśāstra* as the *Institutes of Hindu Law: Or, The Ordinances of Menu* (1794). These two texts had profound influence in their respective fields, and impacted the story I tell in this book in decisive ways. Jones's translation of Kālidāsa led to what Raymond Schwab has described as "A Shakuntala Era" in Europe. A range of prominent figures in the turn-of-the-century Europe, including Herder, Goethe, the Jena Romantics such as the Schlegel brothers, Chateaubriand, and many others, came under the spell of Jones's translation, and responded to its novelty in their own and often competitive terms – Alphonse de Lamartine went as far as detecting in it "the threefold genius of Homer, Theocritus, and Tasso combined in a single poem."⁵⁵ In many ways, Jones's translation was significant for the kind of debates it generated about the idea of literature, and the way it led to radical rethinking across Europe.

On the other hand, the *Institutes* was the outcome of a long-held dream of the colonial government to produce a digest of Hindu laws from the original Sanskrit sources, which would, unlike Halhed's *Code*, reflect accurately the nuances of their cosmology as well as their legal system. In his preface, Jones elaborates on this goal, and, while doing so, proposes the central tenet of what I call the ethnographic worlding of a text – he argues that a collection of legal codes like this one does not have any chance of success if it is not "congenial to the disposition and habits, to the religious prejudices, and approved immemorial usages, of the people, for whom they were enacted."⁵⁶ Referring to the maxim "Laws are of no avail without manners," he indicates further that this intertwining of the textual and the ethnographic indeed has been the policy of the Company, and also his guiding principle; he even wishes that "all future provisions, for the administration of justice and government in India, will be conformable, as far as the natives are affected by them, to the manners and opinions of the natives themselves; an object, which cannot possibly be attained, until those manners and opinions can be fully and accurately known."⁵⁷ Thus legal codes, and their textual inscriptions, are distributed over a host of ethnographic details encompassing manners and religious duties, and, in one stroke, made intertextual as well as mutually conditional.

Jones's strategy here departs from his earlier practices in significant ways – in his translation of the poem-cycle *Mu'allaqāt* (1782) just a decade earlier, he was quite willing to accept that the "Discourses and Notes" he added to explain similar points of cultural obscurity, were, after all, "ornamental only, not essential to the work." They were added as supplementary or even paratextual devices to aid the reader.⁵⁸ But here, in the *Institutes*, these glosses and commentaries on ethnographic details are an integral part of his translation, even its principal *raison d'être*, allowing little distinction between the text and its discursive elaboration.

In an important sense, Jones also suggests a departure from the European standards of textual criticism, since in the editorial practices of his contemporaries anything external to the text is treated as a sure sign of corruption. In contrast, Jones regards the ethnographic markers as necessarily prior to the text, as its essential precondition, and hence legitimate inhabitants of the textual space. Jones emphasizes this ethnographic principle for two related reasons. First, as he points out in his descriptive essay on "Hindu literature," one of the central challenges for him and other colonial officials was to ascertain the correct or standard *recensio* of these texts – obscure histories of manuscripts and the secretive cult around *shastric* texts made it almost impossible to arrive at any sense of authenticity. As a counter, he believes that importing the ethnographic details within the text, and relating the text to the present inhabitants of India, will allow him to ascertain the standardized version. The governing idea behind this strategy is of course the *unchanging orient*, where present generations can and do conform to their ancient rituals and belief-systems. Within the text, however, this integration of the ethnographic and the textual means that the textual organization is not an independent phenomenon; rather, its *recensio* is possible only because of a preexisting set of rules, forming its necessary condition of possibility. Even when the ethnographic details are made part of the text itself, as in *Sacontalá* or the *Institutes*, neither their origin nor their function is erased, and, if anything, they are clearly signposted as a mark of authenticity.

His second reason to emphasize the ethnographic details is to arrive at another level of authenticity, of finding a national tradition in *Sacontalá* or the *Institutes*. In a marked departure from contemporary practice, he spends very little time in establishing the authenticity of the manuscript, and, like Halhed before him, simply asserts its status through the authority of native pandits such as his Indian teacher "Rámalóchan."[59] Instead, he feels more confident in citing a series of ethnographic details about the manners and customs of the Hindus, suggesting the immutable "national vigour" that runs through an unbroken tradition, and manifests itself in texts like these. Once he has established a seamless and unbroken ethnographic tradition both inside and outside the text, he is able to suggest that the text is representative of a continuous national essence. Ethnographic density is where this national disposition makes its appearance most noticeably, and, as a result, he can suggest a different usefulness for the eventual *recensio*.

Alongside this, Jones also proposes a close connection between this ethnographic detailing and the intertextuality argument, and recommends a larger textual web within which a text like *Sacontalá* needs to be situated. "Dramatick poetry must have been immemorially ancient in the Indian empire," he tells his readers, and adds that "all the Pandits assert that their plays are innumerable; and, on my first inquiries I had notice of more than thirty." He records the following works by Kālidāsa (whom he also describes as the "Shakespeare of India"): "a second play, in five acts, entitled Urvasí; an heroick poem, or rather a series of poems in one book, on the Children of the Sun; another, with perfect unity of action, on the Birth of Cumára, god of war; two or three love tales in verse; and an excellent little work on Sanscrit Metre, precisely in the manner of Terentianus." Apart from these iconic texts, he mentions another group of plays that includes "the Malignant Child, the Rape of Ushá, the Taming of Durvásas, the Seizure of the Lock, Máláti and Mádhava, with five or six dramas on the adventures of their incarnate gods."[60]

Taken together, these two lists form a kind of textuality that not only privileges Sanskrit over any other Indian language (including the different versions of the *Śakuntalā* story in other languages), as historian Romila Thapar points out,[61] but also takes the reader back to his earlier argument about the core of Indic civilization existing within an intricate web of textuality. The point becomes clear when he tells his readers that he took special care to get rid of the "stiffness of a foreign idiom" and yet "prepared the faithful translation of the Indian drama" – such mediated fidelity to the text is possible only because of the larger textual network with its ethnographic markers, and of course because of the translator's ability to draw on and, in turn, verify against this textual world.[62] Sanskrit and intertextuality remain the quintessential markers of a national culture.

My point about the ethnographic details leading to a national culture can be seen in the next two major colonial engagements with Kālidāsa – Horace Hayman Wilson's *Select Specimens of the Theatre of the Hindus, Translated from the Original Sanscrit*, 3 Vols. (1827), and Monier Williams's publication of the Devnāgarī recension of the play (1853) and the subsequent translation *Śakoontalá; Or, The Lost Ring; an Indian Drama* (1856). All these texts share a number of theoretical positions Jones articulates, and often repeat verbatim his insights into Sanskrit literature. For Wilson, the idea suggested by Jones becomes a literary ground-rule, that "Hindus had a national drama" and that "Hindu theatre" requires serious attention. He then extends this idea by arguing that it is Hindu theatre above anything else that embodies the core Hindu nation. This extension, again following Jones, is made through a comparative framework – all modern European nations, he submits, have their distinct theatrical traditions, but, at the same time, they owe their origin to Greek antiquity: despite their widely different "mysteries and moralities [...] from the plays of *Æschylus* or *Aristophanes*," eventually the "compositions of Shakespeare, Lope de Vega and Racine [remain indebted to] the Songs of Bacchus and the Monologues of Thespis."[63] In contrast, Hindu national theatre is completely autochthonous, without any influence from any other nation.

In Wilson's opinion Europe never had any influence on Hindu theatre since the "nations of Europe possessed no Dramatic literature before the 14th or 15th century, at which point the Hindu Drama had passed into its decline." On the other hand, the "Musselman conquerors of India" came from a culture that prohibited theatrical performance, and hence they "could not have communicated what they never possessed [i.e. theatre]."[64] Therefore, he deduces that, while other branches of learning in India may have had some external influence, "Hindu Drama" is representative of a quintessential Hindu nation because it presents "characteristic varieties of conduct and construction, which strongly evidence both original design and national development."[65] While Jones hints at a national cultural tradition in individual texts like *Śakuntalā* by showing how these texts internalize ethnographic detailing, Wilson stretches the idea further by establishing national culture at the heart of the genre, by making it an absolute precondition for the form itself. From such a position, Kālidāsa, or any other playwright from the hallowed tradition of Hindu drama, becomes a purveyor of this essential core of a Hindu/Indian nation.

Williams, on the other hand, explicitly links this national tradition with the goals of colonial governance: "The need felt by the British public for some such translation as I have here offered can scarcely be questioned. A great people, who, through their empire in India, command the destinies of the Eastern world, ought surely to be conversant with the most popular of Indian dramas, in which the customs of the Hindus, their opinions, prejudices, and fables, their religious rites, daily occupations and amusements, are reflected as in a mirror."[66] Since "Hindu drama" represents the quintessential core of India, as Jones and Wilson argue, Williams feels it is important to make available the best specimen of it for a robust colonial government. Equally important is the way he deliberately invokes ethnographic categories to flesh out this core Hinduness and also to support his argument of colonial utility.

In a post-Lachmannian period, however, this ambitious project needs further corroboration through textual criticism and editorial conventions, and a clear defense of the *recensio* needs to be established. In his Devnāgarī recension of 1853, he takes great care to ascertain his version of the text, claiming, quite predictably, that it meets all the current standards of textual criticism. One of the central points for Williams is the distinction between the "Bengálí recension" used by Jones (and later by Antoine-Léonard de Chézy in 1830) and the "Devnāgarí recension" that forms the foundation for his text. He tells his readers that the manuscripts in Devnāgarī are "older and purer" and that they retain the "bold and nervous phraseology" of Kālidāsa. In contrast, the Bengali manuscripts are considerably corrupt because of frequent interpolations by later authors. One good example, he points out, is the beginning of the "third Act of the Bengálí recension, where the love-scene between the King and *Śakuntalá* has been expanded to five times the length it occupies in the MSS. of the Devnāgarí recension, and the additions are just what an indelicate imagination might be expected to supply."[67] In support of his case he cites six manuscripts (both in Bengali and in Devnāgarī characters, collected from different parts of British India by various colonial officials) and commentaries on the play by three "Indian Scholastics."[68] Similarly, he defends his version against Otto von Böhtlingk's German edition of 1842 (which also uses a Devnāgarī recension) by pointing out a series of inconsistencies and alleged errors in the latter. Writing in the 1850s, Williams thus brings various threads together – national core, textual criticism, correct recension, necessary emendation, and the authority of colonial administration – which were dispersed across the pages of Jones, Wilson, and other colonial administrators and which I have been charting in this chapter as belonging to the new idea of textuality that the paradigm of the literary sovereign required.

However, even in this updated *recensio* of Kālidāsa's magnum opus, the central problem remains – that is, how to interpret this culturally different text and how to develop a framework beyond what Hastings calls the "latitude" of European criticism. This problem crops up repeatedly in Jones, Wilson, and Williams, especially during their engagement with distinct traditions of commentaries that clearly presume a local critical convention. Wilson thus suggests that, just as there exists a national theatrical tradition in India, so does a critical tradition of interpretation and criticism that is peculiar to Hindu sensibilities. He adds a long note with the title "On the Dramatic System of the Hindus" to the first volume of his translation of Sanskrit plays to provide this other tradition, and quotes copiously from a number of "authorities" to argue his case. This note is subdivided into different sections like "Different kinds of Dramatic Entertainments," "Dramatic Arrangements," "Conduct of the Plot," or "Diction" that are designed to furnish an old but lively tradition of critical reflections on theatrical performance. At the beginning of this note, Wilson takes his readers through a long list of "Treatises on Dramatic Literature" like *Dasa Rūpaka* and *Saraswatī Kanthābharana*, works on "Rhetorical Composition in general" like *Kāvya Prakāśa* and *Sāhitya Darpana*, and other "works which treat generally de Arte Poetica" like *Kāvyadarśa, Dasa Kumāra, Chandrāloka, Rasa Gangādhara*, and many more.[69] Somewhat like Jones before him, Wilson also indicates a dense textual world as the context for his claim of an authentic Hindu tradition of critical thinking.

It is this textual density that Wilson claims to be the sure sign of the national culture around theatre, both creative and critical. While he celebrates the plays themselves as comparable to Grecian plays of antiquity, however, he is dismissive of the critical tradition itself. "Indian Criticism," he observes, "has been always in its infancy. It never learned to contemplate causes and effects: it never looked to the influence exercised by imagination or passion in poetry: it never, in short, became either poetical or philosophical." In Wilson's opinion, this absence of poetical or philosophical criticism, and the almost exclusive attention to mere "technicalities," is what defines Indian critical tradition. In a striking passage, he sums up the effort of all the critics he has consulted by declaring that the "critics of the Hindu school set themselves to classify Plays, persons and passions, until they wove a complicated web out of very spider like material."[70] It is quite evident from his account that he aligns the poverty of critical tradition with a general drift of civilizational decline, suggesting that, while the zenith of the national culture produced excellent plays, its gradual degeneration over time resulted in the tiresome inanities of its critical thinking. Both Hindu theatre and Hindu criticism, in other words, demonstrate the national cultural tradition, but from two very different moments in its life and with very different consequences.

What I have called the ethnographic recension was the new conceptualization of textuality produced by the colonial encounter with the Indian subcontinent. The reason that it became the ground for the new paradigm of the literary sovereign was this assumption of national cultural tradition behind this form of textuality. For the colonial officials, text after text, whether legal, juridical, literary, or otherwise, confirmed the existence of this national identity. They were not only eager to retain this quality in their translations, but also wanted to associate it with colonial governance. At this stage, the question of translation became crucial, since it was through translation that they hoped to capture the essence of India, and hence we now need to turn to the translational practices they deployed.

CHAPTER 2

Colonial Untranslatables

My suggestion of ethnographic recension was critically dependent on translation as both a governmental apparatus and a pedagogic practice, especially because of the colonial belief that by converting the native legal universe into English the incipient government would find a better grip on an essentially Indian version of sovereignty. At the same time, the new notion of the literary as a sovereign order of textuality took shape within this world of colonial translations, as an active ingredient in the textualization of sovereign power. Almost all the translations commissioned by the English East India Company in the final decades of the eighteenth century – whether legal, literary, or otherwise – shared this literary model of accessing the sovereign and singular truth about native cultural worlds, and believed that the textual mechanisms required to define a work of literature would equally distinguish other realms of governmental intervention.

The literary, in other words, was both an autonomous order and an administrative technique, and this duality became especially useful for the colonial officials in investigating what was seen as unbroken and self-governing traditions of local habits, manners, religions, and customs over centuries if not millennia. Translation, as a consequence, was no longer a governmental or ideological necessity alone; it soon became the chief instrument to build a new ideal of textual sovereignty based on native authorities, and it was equally central to the Company's design to resist a Parliamentary takeover of the new colony. In fact, translation and textual sovereignty were so enmeshed in the early colonial imagination that they almost implied each other, and their joint career was believed to pave the way for a new colonial "rule of law" as opposed to previous instances of "oriental despotism," especially of the Mughals.[1]

For some time now, this connection between translation and early colonial rule in South Asia has been studied by historians, anthropologists, and literary scholars.[2] However, I argue in this chapter that, notwithstanding this faith in translation, what settled the central question of translational authority and authenticity for the colonial regime was, ironically enough, the exact opposite of translation – what I call, following Barbara Cassin and Emily Apter, *colonial untranslatables*. The "untranslatable," as Apter defines it, is "a term that is left untranslated as it is transferred from language to language [...], or that is typically subject to mistranslation and retranslation."[3] At one level, this was a practical consequence of the choices the colonial translators made – their obsession with ethnographic signs representing an authentic India led to a host of terms, concepts, and practices in different languages for which they did not have adequate lexical equivalents in English. Even though these ethnographic signs were often labeled as "superfluous" remnants of a different cultural universe, and hence alien to European taste, they were duly highlighted and commented upon.

At another level, however, these untranslatables were mobilized to claim a deeper, and deeply philosophical, idea of authenticity. Instead of considering them as mere cultural detritus that somehow managed to cling to the text, these untranslatables were invested with a different temporality, turning them into cultural agents and, as such, internal guarantors of the culture they represent. Like the land or the people they stood in for, these untranslatables were retained as essentially immutable signs, and, once they were dissociated from the constraints of simple lexical correspondence or referential fidelity, it was possible for the translators to treat them as cultural sedimentation capable of surviving what Lawrence Venuti calls the "violence' of translation.[4] Through mistranslation and retranslation, through copious notes and commentaries, and of course through non-translation, these untraslatables came to signify the *original* textual organization. Colonial untranslatables, in short, were supposed to reveal a deeper textual logic that a straightforward translation was unable to do – they were expected to unveil the original and singular truth of the indigenous culture.

This colonial formulation was not fashioned in some textual void. As I argue in this chapter and elsewhere in this book, this was a necessary safeguard against older traditions of what can be called pure translation, especially of an Indian story cycle that had circulated across languages since the sixth century CE under the signature of Bidpāi or Pilpay. By the eighteenth century, when colonial translation projects were undertaken in British India, these fables had been translated into almost every major language of Asia Europe, and Northern Africa. The situation was further exacerbated after the stunning success of Antoine Galland's *Les mille et une nuits, contes arabes traduits en français* (1704–17) that inspired countless imitations, pseudoethnographies, purported translations from various Asian languages, and a plethora of spurious texts representing an exotic "Orient."[5]

The complex network of translation and untranslatability that ran across the texts of new colonial projects, I argue, was designed to distinguish the new translations from those older ones. It was suggested that this combination invoked a sense of the sovereign local that was impossible to capture either in the seamless transparency of the Bidpāi fables or through the specious authority of texts that appeared in Europe after Galland. Across genres and historical periods, and traversing diverse languages such as Sanskrit, Arabic, and Persian, this sovereignty found its definitive expression in the dual idea of textual *autonomy* and *singularity*. Translation did not only offer access to an alien cultural world – when combined with the critical element of untranslatability, it also produced a governmental version of truth about the native culture.

Paradoxically enough, this textual sovereignty – born through a heady fusion of governmental exigencies and philological erudition – was ratified in an impeachment trial that was designed to condemn the Company's rule in India, and especially its first Governor General, Warren Hastings. Between 1788 and 1795, the English public was engrossed with the spectacular trial of Hastings by Edmund Burke, Richard Brinsley Sheridan, Charles James Fox, and others at the House of Lords on charges of both personal "misdemeanor" and "high treason" during his tenure in India. Burke took the lead and attacked Hastings on the ground that the latter exercised a form of arbitrary or despotic power that did not have approval either in British law or in India's ancient legal systems – whether Hindu or Islamic – and thus committed a crime against both the British imperial mission and local history.

Burke's biographer P. J. Marshall suggests that at the beginning of the trial "Burke almost certainly knew more about India than any other man in public life who had not actually been there," and that his knowledge allowed him to substantiate his allegations against Hastings with greater clarity.[6] On closer scrutiny, however, it becomes apparent that the source of Burke's exceptional "knowledge" was in fact the translation projects initiated by the man he sought to impeach. Burke not only quoted liberally from texts that Hastings had commissioned and supervised as the Governor General of Bengal, but readily agreed with the general colonial principle that it was through these texts, and through the complex cultural world they represented, that a sovereign rule of law had to be established. Notwithstanding their personal acrimony, both men enthusiastically supported something that was being implemented for the first time anywhere in the modern world – the production of legal codes from local texts through translation – as a necessary precondition for colonial governance. In this chapter, I track this complex history of colonial untranslatables across texts and territories.

The Tradition of Pure Translation

In 1570, Sir Thomas North, the well-known Elizabethan justice of the peace, published a small quarto of translations entitled *The Morall Philosophie of Doni: Drawne out of the ancient writers*. North is usually remembered for his English translation of Plutarch's *Lives* (from Jacques Amyot's French), which served as the primary source for William Shakespeare's Roman plays,[7] but this small translation of only 116 leaves with about 40 animal tales of Indian origin was equally noteworthy since it marked the first entry of a popular fable cycle into English. His immediate source was the Italian author Anton Francesco Doni's *La Moral filosofia del Doni, tratta dagli antichi scrittori* (1552), but, as Joseph Jacobs, the nineteenth-century editor of North's text, notes, it was in fact the "English version of an Italian adaptation of a Spanish translation of a Latin version of a Hebrew translation of an Arabic adaptation of the Pehlevi version of the Indian original."[8] North acknowledged both the Indian origin and multilingual translations in his extended subtitle – *A worke first compiled in the Indian tongue, and afterwardes reduced into divers other languages* – but the real diversity of its bibliographical history was perhaps beyond his wildest imagination.

According to Jacobs's calculation, these "tales have been translated into thirty-eight languages, in 112 different versions, which have passed into about 180 editions" between the sixth and the nineteenth centuries CE.[9] Indeed the story cycle, derived through a combination of the Sanskrit original, the *Pañcatantra* (dating from the third century CE) and even older Jātaka fables from the Buddhist tradition (primarily in Pāli), reached almost every major literary culture in Asia, Europe, and Northern Africa and "probably had more readers than any other [text] except the Bible."[10] Designed as a "Mirror for Princes" or *speculum principis*, these stories were known either by the name of their alleged author (variously called Bidpāi or Pilpay, presumably corruptions of the Sanskrit for Bidyāpati or Bidyāpriya) or by the names of the two jackals from the frame narrative, Kalilā and Dimnā (again, presumably corruptions of the Sanskrit for Karataka and Damanaka).

The tales of Bidpāi or Pilpay, and their success across the ages, present an unparalleled history of transculturation.[11] The translational history roughly followed what Janet Abu-Lughod calls the "world systems" that existed before the beginning of the "European hegemony" in the sixteenth century. Her description of the "long distance trade system that stretched through the Mediterranean into the Red Sea and Persian Gulf and on into the Indian Ocean and through the Strait of Malacca to reach China" comprising "numerous preexistent world economies" matches well with the circuitous routes these fables took between the sixth and the thirteenth centuries. As Europe – "an upstart peripheral to an ongoing operation" – joined these systems in the twelfth and the thirteenth centuries, these fables gradually started showing up in various European languages.[12] Even then, almost all the translations acknowledged the Indian origin of these tales, and, at the same time, included brief accounts of the translational history that immediately preceded their respective versions. North, in his "Prologue," for instance, mentions Persian, Arabic, Hebrew, Latin, Spanish, and Italian translations as his precursors.[13] *Les Fables de Pilpay, philosophe indien ou la Conduite des rois*, a late seventeenth-century popular French translation by an unknown author (possibly by David Sahid d'Ispahan), to take another example, likewise proffers a list of its predecessors in its "Avertissement": Pehlevi, Arabic, Hebrew, Greek, Latin, and so on.[14]

This recorded history and somewhat secular trajectory of these fables made them particularly attractive to nineteenth-century Orientalists and Indologists. Friedrich Max Müller, for instance, argues that it is this inbuilt historical record of migration that distinguishes these fables from earlier and pre-historic diffusion of "Indo-European myths" across Asia and Europe, and further makes them available for examination under the aegis of the *literary-cultural*.[15] He illustrates his case with the example of the seventeenth-century French author La Fontaine's fable "La Laitière et le Pot au Lait" which was included in the second edition of his well-known *Fables* (1678). Several of his fables, including this story of Perrette the milkmaid, as La Fontaine himself admitted in the preface, were taken from "Pilpay the Indian sage." And this admission allows Müller to explore various translational routes – historical and interconnected – that the fables might have taken from India to reach France.[16] Müller's central point about history relies on a notion of pure translatability of these tales, an itinerary that could be traced and attested with textual evidence, and invokes something akin to Walter Benjamin's idea of the "afterlife" of translation.[17] In his imagination, however, this afterlife becomes so powerful that it overshadows the "original" and releases translation as a form within a spectral frame of history – a form that kept transmuting between languages without necessarily repeating the "original."

This historicity of translation appealed to a host of Indologists including Theodor Benfey, I. G. N. Keith-Falconer, Thomas William Rhys-Davids, Johannes Hertel, and others as they produced scholarly editions of different translations. After Benfey's classic study *Pantschatantra: Fünf Bücher indischer Fabeln, Märchen und Erzählungen* (1859) drew attention to parallels between European texts and the many translations of the *Pañcatantra*, these fables also became one of the central reference points for the new discipline of Comparative Literature. La Fontaine was of course a well-known case, but other authors were also probed for possible influences, and Jacobs went as far as saying that the "idea of stringing a number of stories together by putting them in a frame as in Boccaccio's *Decamerone*, Chaucer's *Canterbury Tales*, Basile's *Pentamerone*, and so on down to Mr. Pickwick and Mr. Stevenson, is one that is distinctly to be traced to the East in the Fables of Bidpai, the book of Sindibad, and the *Arabian Nights*."[18]

Srinivas Aravamudan has explored another dimension of this spectral or pure translation and has shown how the transcultural character of these fables had a profound impact on what he calls the "Enlightenment Orientalism" of the eighteenth century, especially in Britain and France, in its search to go beyond "national realism and identity politics." Referring to eighteenth-century classics such as Jonathan Swift's *Gulliver's Travels* (1726) and Voltaire's *Zadig* (1747) and *Micromégas* (1752), he argues that the tales of Bidpāi or Pilpay and the *Arabian Nights* offered possibilities of generic plurality for radical political imagination – from theriophily and *conte philosophique* to pseudoethnography and early novels. In an age that is otherwise overshadowed by the rise-of-the-novel narrative and that is generally viewed through the prism of nascent realism as an emerging bourgeois sociolect, the spectral presence of these animal fables kept the literary horizon open, even infused it with possibilities that remained more indebted to transculturation than to national parochialism.[19]

By the eighteenth century, when the earlier world systems that Abu-Lughod charts were under firm European hegemony, these beast fables operated within the fissures of this new dominance, representing its antecedent as well as alternative potentials. In fact, the translational history of these fables would eminently qualify them as "world literature," especially the way David Damrosch has defined the term in recent years: "I take world literature to encompass all literary works that circulate beyond their culture of origin, either in translation or in their original language. [...] a work only has an *effective* life as world literature whenever, and wherever, it is actively present within a literary system beyond that of its original culture."[20] In translation, Bidpāi fables reached almost every major literary culture around the world, and their "effective life" – or afterlife – was readily visible in the way they functioned as both model and source for generations of writers across languages.

Colonial Departure

And yet, toward the end of the eighteenth century and in the distant colonial outpost of Calcutta, a group of British officials challenged this history on the very ground of its pure translatability – where translation as a form merely passes through languages – and put forward their claim of unearthing the singular text in Sanskrit in its pristine purity. For these colonial officials, translation did not simply mean transaction or transference of meanings across languages – rather, they considered it as the primary technique to fix the singularity of a text. This shift was visible in the way the Bidpāi or Pilpay stories were recorded in colonial archives. In the first instance, James Fraser, a Scotsman and Company servant who worked in India in the 1730s and 1740s and collected and annotated a large number of manuscripts in different languages, simply records the various translations of the *Pañcatantra* story-cycle into Persian and Arabic in his *A Catalogue of Manuscripts in the Persic, Arabic, and Sanskerrit Languages* (1742). In his gloss, Fraser offers a brief account of the first translation of the Sanskrit "*Kurtuk Dumnik*" – described as a "Treatise" compiled by the "ancient *Brahmins* of *India*" with the "choicest Treasures of Wisdom, and the perfect Rules for governing a People" – into Pehlevi, and then records the subsequent translations as "*Anuar Sohéli, Kulila Dumna,* [and] *Ayar Danish.*"[21] In a second iteration, Alexander Dow, another Scottish servant of the Company, published a somewhat similar story-cycle in 1768 with the title "The Baar Danesh; or, Garden of Knowledge" that combined motifs from the *Pañcatantra* and the *Arabian Nights.*[22]

Fraser or Dow's innocence, however, is lost by the time we encounter the next major account of the story-cycle in William Jones's "Third Anniversary Discourse" (1786) at the Asiatic Society of Bengal:

> We are told by the *Grecian* writers that the *Indians* were the wisest of nations; and in moral wisdom, they were certainly eminent: their *Níti Sástra*, or *System of Ethicks*, is yet preserved, and the Fables of VISHNUSERMAN, whom we ridiculously call *Pilpay*, are the most beautiful, if not the most ancient, collection of apologues in the world.[23]

Jones carefully marks the distance between the "ridiculously" derivative "*Pilpay*" and the authentic "VISHNUSERMAN" and, unlike Fraser or Dow, uses these two proper names to discredit the long history of translation I discuss above. He of course realizes that the familiarity of his audience with the fables will probably run against his radical views. To counter this, he turns the very multilingual translation of the text against itself, and argues that it is this long history, without any access to the Sanskrit original, that is responsible for the corrupt "Pilpay" and much other cultural distortion. History of translation or the Benjaminian notion of an "afterlife" is thus held against the singularity of the original: "they [i.e. the apologues of Vishnusherman] were first translated from the *Sanscrit*, in the *sixth* century, by the order of BUZERCHUMIHR, or *Bright as the Sun*, the chief physician and afterwards *Vézír* of the great ANÚSHIREVÁN, and are extant under various names in more than twenty languages; but their original title is *Hitópadésa*, or *Amicable Instruction*."[24]

This is an unusual move given that in this very discourse Jones also proposes the rudimentary structure of the "Indo-European hypothesis" and suggests a deep history of intertwining cultures across Asia and Europe. While he recognizes the plausibility of shared linguistic origins across cultures, manifest in grammatical details such as roots and inflections, he denies the same shared past to translation. Jones rather marshals his philological expertise to establish the singularity of the original text – hence, the decisive tone of "but their original title is *Hitópadésa*" – and to liquidate the translations "extant under various names in more than twenty languages." He indeed translated *Hitopadeśa*, but never published it during his lifetime.[25]

Instead, his ideas found their fuller elaboration in the first colonial translation of the fables, Charles Wilkins's *The Hĕĕtōpādĕs of Vĕĕshnŏŏ-Sărmă* (1787). Wilkins's "Preface" begins with the exact quote from Jones's "Discourse" I have reproduced above, and follows it up with longer passages from Fraser and other unnamed sources. Against this history of multilingual translations, and as a potential remedy, he submits his own theory:

> In executing this work I have scrupulously adhered to the text; and I have preferred drawing a picture of which it may be said – *I can suppose it a strong likeness, although I am unacquainted with the original*, to a flattering portrait, where characteristic features, because not altogether consonant to European taste, must have been sacrificed to the harmony of composition.[26]

The hint of visual mimesis in this passage – especially in the portrait image – is somewhat misleading, since it was this kind of repetition in translation that the colonial regime resisted. Hence, almost immediately, Wilkins qualifies his theory with two other claims: first, he states that he has been mindful of the literary "form" of the original and has preserved "what was originally in verse distinct, by indenting every line but the first of each distich"; and second, more importantly, he claims to retain certain proper names untranslated with the belief that "they would appear always awkward, and often ridiculous, in an English dress," and instead decides to offer a phonetic "uniform plan" to guide his readers to pronounce these foreign names correctly (*H*, xv). When put together, these scattered statements point not only to a new theory of translation, but also to an order of textual autonomy that can be ascertained only within the limits of the text, as its immanent quality, and cannot be fully represented in any other language.

However, the precise import of Wilkins's point about translational autonomy can be grasped only when one frames these observations through the full title of his translation: *The Hĕĕtōpādĕs of Vĕĕshnŏŏ-Sărmă, in a Series of Connected Fables, Interspersed with Moral, Prudential, and Political Maxims; Translated from an Ancient Manuscript in the Sanskreet Language with Explanatory Notes*. As would be evident, he follows Jones's lead in ticking all the appropriate boxes – the original title *"Hĕĕtōpādĕs,"* the name of the author, namely *"Vĕĕshnŏŏ-Sărmă"* (and not Bidpāi or Pilpay), the nature of the content, and so on. But what most explicitly distinguishes his translation from numerous earlier attempts is his emphasis on the last part, that his text is *"Translated from an Ancient Manuscript in the Sanskreet Language with Explanatory Notes."* Apart from authenticity, this implies that in his effort to retain the singularity of the text – always immanent but identifiable – he remains so faithful to the original Sanskrit that he does not alter anything significantly in the text beyond what would have been permitted by the original author himself.

Hence, though he is forced to append a large number of explanatory notes as subsidiary tools for his readers, in order to remain loyal to the original, or to its textual autonomy, he is willing to allow the untranslatable right in the middle of his translation. Any attempt to avoid such untranslatables, or to integrate them as transparently legible signs, would have disturbed the original organization of Viṣṇuśarmā and would have even falsified his authorial intention. These explanatory notes, as a result, cease to be simple external interpretations of cultural foreignness – they are, in an important sense, designed to mark out the untranslatables as markers of textual integrity. In other words, Wilkins's insistence on the ancient Sanskrit manuscript and the paratextual commentary – or what Jacques Derrida would have called the "outwork" or *hors livre/hors d'œuvre*)[27] – when put together as the central mechanism of translation, conjure a distinct sense of textual autonomy that transmits itself across languages largely through what remains in essence untranslatable. Untranslatability in this formulation, contrary to expectations, is not a threat to the text's singularity or its literary qualities; instead, Wilkins suggests that the untranslatables can assure the literary text's autonomy and yet can make it available to new readers who would experience it by proxy, as it were.

Colonial Departure 91

In contrast, and by implication, then, all previous translations of *Pañcatantra* or *Hitopadeśa* were liable to violate this textual singularity by their twin folly – reliance on secondary languages and interpretation/translation of local details or untranslatables within the main text.[28] Wilkins makes the point even more prominent by comparing his own text with two immediately preceding translations of the same corpus in French and English. He records that "in the year 1709, the *Kulila Dumna*, the Persian version of *Abul Mala Nasser Allah Mustofi* made in the 515th year of the *Hegira*, was translated into French with the title of *Les Conseils et les Maximes de Pilpay Philosophe Indien sur les divers Etats de la vie*. This edition resembles the *Heetōpadēs* more than any other I have seen, and is evidently the immediate original of the English *Instructive and Entertaining Fables of Pilpay, an Ancient Indian Philosopher*, which in 1775 had gone through five editions" (*H*, xiii). He strategically mentions successive translations through various languages except Sanskrit – namely Arabic, Persian, French, and English – and reinforces the idea of derivativeness of his recent predecessors by repeating their titles twice with the misattribution of Pilpay. Against this tradition of triteness, he cements his claim further by elaborating on the very title of the text, presumably to explain its real solemnity, through etymological details: "*Heetopades*, (or *Heetopadesa*, with the addition of the final short vowel *a*, which is often omitted in repeating *Sanskreet* names of persons and places) is a compound of *Heeta*, health, welfare, *oopa*, a preposition implying *proximity*, and *dēsa* signifying a *shewing* or *pointing*. The common acceptation of the word is *useful*, or *beneficial, instruction*." (*H*, 293–4.)

Within the text this distinction is stressed with greater care. Let us look at the opening passage of the fable "The Lion and the Rabbit," a popular narrative in the story-cycle and available in all three versions, to get a better sense of Wilkins's formulation:

First, from *Les Conseils*:

> Aux environs de Raydet il y avoit une fort agréable prairie que plusieurs bêtes sauvages avoient choisi pour demeure à cause de la beauté du lieu. Parmi tous ces animaux il y avoit un Lion furieux qui troubloit le repos des autres par des meurtres continuels.[29]

Then from *Instructive and Entertaining Fables*, which more or less faithfully translates the French version:

> In the neighbourhood Mianstol there was a very delightful meadow, where several wild beasts had taken up their habitations, by reason of the pleasantness of the place. Among those creatures was a furious lion, who disturbed the peace of all the rest with his continual murders.[30]

Wilkins, however, begins the episode with a little instructive verse or "distich": "He who hath sense hath strength. Where hath he strength who wanteth judgment? See how a Lion, when intoxicated with anger, was overcome by a rabbit" (*H*, 139). And then he introduces the fable:

> Upon the mountain Măndără, there lived a lion, whose name was Dŏŏrgāntă, who was perpetually complying with the ordinance for animal immolation. (*H*, 139–40)

He not only gets his Sanskrit names right against the incongruous "Raydet" and "Mianstol" of his predecessors, but even explains in his notes that "Măndără" refers to a "fabulous mountain" and that the lion's name means "Hard-to-go-near." In his gloss on "animal immolation," again, he points out that the "Hindoos still offer kids and young buffaloes in their sacrifices" (*H*, 314), in an apparent effort both to highlight the untranslatable nature of the original and to render it more transparent to his readers. With the distich and the cultural references in Sanskrit, Wilkins is able to invoke the untranslatable as the marker of literary sovereignty in his translation, as a sign of its integrity, and position his version as superior to all previous attempts.

Wilkins's notes are full of similarly copious glosses on a wide range of subjects: Hindu religion, mythology, Sanskrit grammar and prosody, South Asian landscape, names of Hindu deities, popular customs and rituals, local flora and fauna, and so on. What arrests our attention, however, is his eagerness to qualify these notes as necessary but external tools – or *obligatory outwork* – to the untranslatable cultural references in the main text. Consider, for instance, the following note:

> This verse is written in a kind of measure which they call *eendra-vajra*, (the lightning of the God of the heavens). The curious may not dislike to see it in its original form; from which, and the verbal translation, he may judge of Sanskreet composition in general, and find an excuse for the quaintness of the translation in some parts:
>
> > swa-karma-santâna-veechêshteetânee
> > *own-work-offspring-seekings*
> > kâlâ-'ntarâ-'vreetta-soobhà-'soobhânee
> > *time-within-shut-good-not-good*
> > eehî-'va dreeshtânee mayî-va tânee
> > *here even seen by me even those*
> > janmâ-'ntarânêê-'va dasâ-'phalânee
> > *birth-within as it were stage of life fruits.*
>
> The first and second lines contain but one compound word each; for there is no sign of either case, gender, or number, till you get to the end, where there is the termination of the plural number in the neuter. This manner of

writing, which is very common, is called *samāsa*, (throwing or placing together) and is a most happy mode for the Brahmans, who are the interpreters of the law. (*H*, 307)

And now let us read the actual translation of the verse in the text:

By me have been experienced, even here, as the fruits of the state of existence, in some certain birth, the good and evil shut up in time, which are the seekings of the offsprings of our own works. (*H*, 86)

Wilkins clearly wants his readers to read these two together, but not as supplementary texts designed to illuminate what is obscurely hinted at in the translated verse.

The point of this exercise rather is to highlight the awkward syntactic structure of the translated text and the theological maxim that lies hidden under it as unmistakable signs of the text's original literary organization. In the notes, he offers an interlinear and "verbal" translation of the original Sanskrit, with further comments on how grammatical devices like "*samāsa*," popular with the Brahmin authors of these verses, force certain prosodic patterns like the "*eendra-vajra*" on literary compositions, with the hope of uniting the obscure reference within the text with the cultural world it represents. In his view, these ethnographic details of rituals and customs, with corresponding representation in the verbal architecture of the text, produce both the sovereign organization of the literary text and its singular experience. Any effective translation that respects the singularity of the original, therefore, needs to go beyond the preliminary task of finding analogous syntactic arrangement in the new language. It must also highlight the peculiarly untranslatable components – both *anthropological* and *textual* – that do not yet have adequate equivalents in the new order of words or sentences and yet hold the key to the original's sovereign singularity.

Wilkins, however, first proposed these ideas in his "Translator's Preface" to *The Bhăgvăt-Gēētā, or Dialogues of Krĕĕshnă and Ărjŏŏn* (1785):

The reader will have the liberality to excuse the obscurity of many passages, and the confusion of sentiments which runs through the whole, in its present form. It was the Translator's business to remove as much of this obscurity and confusion as his knowledge and abilities would permit. This he hath attempted in his Notes; but as he is conscious they are still insufficient to remove the veil of mystery, he begs leave to remark, in his own justification, that the text is but imperfectly understood by the most learned *Brāhmăns* of the present time; and that, small as the work may appear, it has had more comments than the Revelations. These have not been totally disregarded; but, as they were frequently found more obscure than the original they were intended to elucidate, it was thought better to leave many of the most difficult passages for the exercise of the reader's own judgment, than to mislead him by such wild opinions as no one syllable of the text could authorize.[31]

Even in this early, and somewhat tentative, formulation, he emphasizes his points about the singular textual organization and its untranslatability, adding another layer by suggesting that he is in fact emulating an extant Indian practice. Just as the Brahmins produce copious commentaries for their readers without disturbing the original text or its obscure passages, so does he, with the further burden of making the text accessible to an audience who are culturally far more removed. His translation, thus, is both the text and its commentary, both the representation of the singular original and the acknowledgment that its full import is practically untranslatable.

For Wilkins, and within the world of colonial translation more broadly, thus, the ethnographic soon became a guarantor of the literary, of both its singular universality and its textual autonomy. Significantly enough, it was translations like Wilkins's *The Bhăgvăt-Gēētā* and *The Hēētōpădēs* that explored this intimate suturing of the ethnographic and the literary, bringing together two very different yet significant concerns of colonial governance in British India. Wilkins carefully assembled these diverse forces through the powerful mix of translation/untranslatability, and, in the process, laid the foundations for the literary sovereignty that colonial governance was to introduce. The distance between North's *The Morall Philosophie of Doni* and Wilkins's *The Hēētōpădēs* was no longer that of simple chronology but rather that of a distinct method that characterized the new idea of the literary.

Cultures of "Superfluity"

With Jones and other colonial officials after Wilkins, this method received further elaboration and refinement, and became the central translational mechanism for governance. This was most prominently visible in translations of Hindu and Islamic personal law as a necessary premise for the "rule of law," and the close intertwining of the anthropological and the textual through the intricate network of translation and untranslatables shaped the outcome in decisive ways. This project was usually narrated using two histories, one of colonial contingencies and the other of a hermetic chronology internal to respective legal traditions. Both histories converged around the idea of translation as a transformative practice with the power to standardize texts as also to fix the discursive borders within which such texts were supposed to operate.

In his "Preliminary Discourse by the Translator" to *The Hedàya, or Guide: A Commentary on the Mussulman Laws* (1791), Charles Hamilton, an army lieutenant with the Company, offers a fairly standard account of both histories. The first part of the "Discourse" begins by acknowledging the exceptional status of the British colony in India, and offers a brief account of the events that led to this unusual arrangement. Hamilton describes the British entry into the subcontinent in the seventeenth century as determined by previous histories since Indian territories were already under the control of a mighty empire of the Mughals and most Indians lived under the jurisdiction of the "MUSSULMAN CODE" as well as their "courts of justice." Unlike the New World, the British believed, India had an entrenched medieval state and its own institutions of justice that followed the "general maxims of government" and "a rigid and undeviating adherence to their own LAW." Though Hamilton registers his unease at the alleged unfair treatment often meted out to the Hindus under Muslim rulers and their Islamic law, he nevertheless maintains that "these abuses did not alter the spirit of law, which continued unvaried in its ostensible operation."[32] In fact, he believes that this differential practice of applying personal laws to litigants according to their religion and criminal laws only according to the Islamic "codes" served India well through the centuries.

When the Company took over the administration of Bengal after 1765, it decided to "introduce as few innovations in those particulars [of administration of justice] as were consistent with prudence." The reason behind this decision, according to Hamilton, is a maxim: "The permanency of any foreign dominion (and, indeed, the justification of holding such a dominion) requires that a strict attention be paid to the ease and advantage, not only of the *governors*, but of the *governed*." In more practical terms, this implies "preserving to the latter their ancient established practices, civil and religious, and protecting them in the exercise of their own institutes." Even if the British were to introduce a uniform system of law and administration, he contends, they had to be mindful of "an infinite number of usages, essential to the ease and happiness of a people differing from us as widely in customs, manners, and habits of thinking, as in climate, complexion, or language."[33] Therefore, unlike North America, the Caribbean, or even Ireland, the Indian subcontinent was not subsumed under the legal and administrative institutions of Britain. Instead, through successive acts such as the Regulating Act of 1773 and Pitt's India Act of 1784, a system of dual sovereignty was put in place – while the

Company was free to administer the territories under its control according to native laws and with quasi-state characteristics such as collecting revenues or waging wars, the British Parliament retained the power to oversee, review, and pass regulations to check the efficiency of the colonial government.

Hamilton's account follows some of the earlier discussions on the same set of issues by other colonial administrators, and reproduces a broad colonial commonsense of his time. To sustain such a position on governance, however, the colonial administration needed a second history proclaiming the internal cohesion and legitimacy of these native legal traditions – which were largely *untranslatable* – through what Hamilton calls "ancient established practices" and "institutions." He in fact devotes the bulk of his "Discourse" to demonstrate precisely this, that is, Islamic law as a closed but fully functional system from the days of Muhammad and the Qur'ān to his contemporary times. This other history is diverse and fractured, with details on individuals, institutions, exegetical traditions, and competing claims of authority. Hamilton rearranges this complex history through three broad narratives: the first one follows a somewhat schematic history of early Islam and recommends it as the groundwork for Islamic law; the second one offers details on different legal schools ("the *Haneefites*, the *Màlekites*, the *Shafëites*, and the *Hanbalites*") and various methods of exposition in Islamic law ("*Osool*, *Sonnàn*, and *Fatàvee*"); and the third one presents a brief history of the text under translation, "*AL HEDAYA* [by] Sheikh BURHAN-AD-DEEN ALEE."[34]

In his gloss on the text, Hamilton informs his readers that the "HEDAYA is an extract from a number of the most approved works of the early writers on jurisprudence, digested into something like the form of a regular treatise" with the "singular advantage of combining, with the authorities, the different opinions and explications of the principal commentors on all disputed points."[35] A digest of this nature calls for a detailed textual history, and Hamilton likewise offers a meticulous list and brief biographical sketches of the "persons whose opinions are chiefly quoted" in the text, then follows it up with a further list of legal treatises mentioned and/or quoted in the compendium, and finally invokes the general principles of Hanafi jurisprudence within which this text needs to be situated and read.[36] In effect, he creates a textual world that was put together through religious conventions and internal rules, and submits it as the exclusive frame within which a text like *The Hedàya* makes sense. The power of the Hanafi compendium originates in the authority of the text for sure (which is the reason for its translation), but Hamilton also suggests that it is the wider cultural world alluded to within the text that historically bestows such treatises with the requisite influence and exclusivity.

At this juncture, Hamilton confides to his readers that as a translator he feels it is his obligation to explain this alien world lurking behind the text, and to "notice certain peculiarities which will occur in the perusal of [the text], and an explanation of which is requisite to the elucidation of what might otherwise appear unintelligible and obscure." Following Wilkins, and almost echoing a professional ethnographer, he tells his readers that these "peculiarities" – often so quaint as to appear "unnatural or improbable" or simply "frivolous and absurd" to a European audience – constitute a large part of the digest since they are perfectly consonant with the general laws of Islamic jurisprudence and are seen as unexceptional by Muslims all over the world.[37] The explanation, however, is not far to seek – such oddities simply need to be traced back to the "peculiar manners, customs, and language, of the people among whom they have originated" and the "state of the society in *Arabia* at the time when MOHAMMED and his companions began to introduce something like a system of jurisprudence among the followers and subjects of *Islâm*." In a spectacular display of orientalist stereotypes, Hamilton describes the sixth-century Arabs as essentially violent, immoral, and bereft of any civilizational virtues.[38]

If the world of Islamic law represents an interconnected network of texts and authorities with its own hermeneutic autonomy, he argues, its characteristic features – or "peculiarities" – are to be ascertained with reference to this history and to distinctly ethnographic categories such as customs and manners or even classifiable racial dispositions. The parallel between his description of these "superfluous" and "peculiar" traces in the Arabic text and Wilkins's account of the "obscurity and confusion" in Sanskrit texts suggests itself. As a result, just like Wilkins, Hamilton argues that, since it is an autonomous world doubly removed from his immediate audiences – first through its textual density and then through "superfluous" ethnographic "peculiarities" – he as the translator must take up the daunting task of shepherding his readers through this gulf of cultural unfamiliarity.

The task of the translator in a colonial project like this is in fact manifold. At the heart of the translation is the rather practical idea of joining the two histories recounted above – of the Company's political ascendancy in the subcontinent and of Islamic law – and subsequently making available to the magistrates a body of laws for everyday use. Hamilton, however, places this rather practical enterprise within a larger narrative of the empire's contribution in the "diffusion of useful knowledge, and the eradication of prejudice" through its effort to "open and to clear the road to science; to provide for its reception in whatever form it may appear, in whatever language it may be conveyed."[39] In both cases, these untranslatable and "superfluous" cultural elements present the central hurdle for him. As a resolution, and to continue the pursuit of legal sciences to arrive at a practicable version of Islamic law, he employs two different layers of translation – from Arabic into Persian, and then from Persian into English.

This unusual model is defended on two grounds: first with reference to the rather "close and obscure" style of the Arabic original that needs something more than a literal translation and then with reference to the time-honored tradition in India of producing "*Fattàwees*" or expositions on Islamic law in Persian. Instead of being inadequate or unreliable, therefore, this method of double translation involving a group of Company *maulavis* and Hamilton himself is seen as an advantage over a direct rendering of the Arabic into English; its result is projected as some sort of translational gain since it not only offers a copious gloss from competent Islamic scholars on what remains somewhat abstruse and "superfluous" in the original, but even makes it possible to arrive at a textual version of these laws that will unite "the dictum and the principles" and eventually serve as both "an exemplar and an instructor."[40] In effect, thus, this twofold labor allows the translators to elucidate on particular points in the Arabic text, and also to gloss on what is considered "superfluous" or "ingenious sophistry," much like Wilkins's untranslatables; as the final arbiter, Hamilton of course has the power to select and edit – and, in an important sense, *fix* – the version of Islamic law to be adopted by the courts of the Company. The definitive English version, hence, is a curious mix of exegetical authority and colonial expediency – although the translation establishes the text of *The Hedàya* in the name of the Arabic original and its revered author, its editorial practices remain more beholden to contemporary governmental concerns than to any purported textual authenticity.

What we encounter in Hamilton's "Discourse," however, is not his personal eccentricity, but one of the central tenets of the colonial search for a "rule of law": the creation of an essentially textual universe that would establish and regulate the meaning of native law within its own limits. The point was made repeatedly by almost every translator of legal texts during the early years of the Company's rule. Jones, for instance, in his "Preface" to *Al Shirájiyyah: Or, The Mohammedan Law of Inheritance* (1792) recasts the idea in a comparative frame. He first introduces two of the foundational texts of English common law – Thomas de Littleton's *Treatise on Tenures* (1481) and Edward Coke's *Institutes of the Lawes of England* (1628–44) – and then juxtaposes them with two influential texts from the Hanafi school of Islamic jurisprudence – Sirāj al-Dīn Muḥammad's treatise on inheritance *al-Sirājīyyah* and Sayyid Sharīf's commentary on it entitled *al-Sharīfiyyah* (both from the twelfth–thirteenth centuries). While the common law in Littleton or Coke for him is "always too clear to need a gloss," the "extreme brevity" coupled with "a needless anxiety to remove every little cloud" about the largely customary law of *al-Sirājīyyah* warrants clear commentary and editorial intervention.[41]

Jones's editorial policy is important for my argument here, and needs to be quoted in full:

> [I]t would have been a far easier task to have dictated and written a verbal translation of the two comments on my text, than to have made a careful selection of all that is important in them; for which purpose I perused each of them three times with the utmost attention, and have condensed in little more than fifty short pages the substance of them both, without any superfluous passage, that I should wish to be retrenched, and with as much perspicuity as I was able to give, in so short a compass, to a system in some parts rather abstruse: lest men of business, for whom the book is intended, should be alarmed at first sight by the magnitude of it, I have omitted all the minute criticism, various readings, and curious *Arabian* literature; most of the anecdotes concerning old lawyers, and all their subtil controversies with the arguments on both sides; together with the demonstrations of arithmetical rules and the very long processes, after the prolix method of the *Arabs*, in words instead of figures.[42]

He makes a critical distinction between what is substantial in the two Arabic texts and what survives in them as mere cultural detritus of an alien world – as "superfluous" – with its peculiar practices. This distinction forms a subset within a larger division between common law and what he poses in contradistinction as customary law – one substantial, the other riddled with difficult cultural codes. Hence, the obvious clarity of Littleton and Coke and the alleged obscurity of both *al-Sirājīyyah* and *al-Sharīfiyyah*. In his mind, English common law's primary dependence on precedence makes it internally coherent and practical. On the other hand, customary law's reliance on traditional practices and secondary sources – which can be bundled together under the general name of *anthropological* or *cultural* – makes it difficult to follow, especially for an outsider.

From this preliminary distinction, he also infers that common law operates within a domain that can be delimited as universally legal while customary law imposes the further condition of cultural familiarity. The superfluity in the Arabic texts, as a result, is directly connected to the cultural world that law refers to and draws its authority from; and yet, in

Jones's practical schema, this cannot be represented within the body of the law. In fact, he castigates a previous translator, Muhammed Kasim, who translated *al-Sirājīyyah* into Persian following Hastings's commission, for his blending of "the text and comments" in such a manner that "it is often impossible to separate what is fixed law from what is merely his own opinion."[43] The point about "fixed law" is so central to Jones's mind that he even offers a mathematical table and a "synthetical method" to get rid of the cultural addenda, though he admits at the same time that such methods are not often "very consistent with the dignity of science."[44] To be clear, Jones does not dismiss the cultural context of law altogether, but prefers to move such additional material from the main text to the "commentary," keeping intact what he considers the essential characteristics of law – abstract, universal, and yet fixed. The additional materials – or notes, like those of Wilkins – form a necessary "outwork" within which finer legal points have to be ascertained or contested, but the very "substance" he wishes to capture in those "little more than fifty short pages" has to have a different ideal of law altogether.

It becomes apparent toward the end of the "Preface," however, that his eagerness to distil a structure of fixed Islamic law of inheritance and succession through translation has a specific goal – to challenge a prevalent conception regarding the source and nature of Mughal sovereignty: "*whether, by the* Mogul *constitution, the sovereign be not the sole proprietor of all the land in his empire, which he or his predecessors have not granted to a subject and his heirs.*"[45] Though he confesses that the "Arabian phraseology both in law and arithmetick" of his source does not translate well into English, and that in some cases he can convey the sense only through "circumlocution," he nonetheless feels confident enough to declare such a view about Mughal sovereignty both spurious and uncorroborated by Islamic law.[46] His chosen method to prove this "fixed law" is instructive: on the one hand, with a characteristic rhetorical flourish, he assembles the verdicts of the "*Korán* and the *dicta* of MUHAMMED," and various established legal authorities such as Ābu Hānifā – all of them supporting his view; and, on the other, he places some unnamed "foreign physician and philosopher" who "too hastily believed [lower law officers], and ascribed to such a system all the desolation, of which he had been a witness."[47] The outcome of such a comparison between textual authority and mere hearsay is obvious.

What is even more, once he takes the Mughal emperor out of the equation and replaces the body of the "oriental despot" with an equally powerful body of texts, he feels emboldened enough to argue that in effect even

Islamic law supports the non-despotic idea of sovereignty. The purpose of this translation of *al-Sirājīyyah* – and many others by his colleagues – is thus not to impose an alien legal system on Indian subjects, but to reveal to the people the true nature of their own law and transform it into reliable codes. A few years earlier, in his first "Charge to the Grand Jury" in Calcutta on December 4, 1783, he made a similar distinction between "power in the hands of men" and "prescribed rules" – the first was bound to be abused, whereas the second held the promise of justice. He even argued that the latter would let "the natives of these important provinces be indulged in their own prejudices, civil and religious, and suffered to enjoy their own customs unmolested." The larger point about law for Jones was its abstract and impartial nature, a quality achievable only through textual standardization and not through individual caprice: "The use of law, as a science, is to prevent mere discretionary power under the colour of equity; and it is the duty of a judge to pronounce his decisions, not simply according to his own opinion of justice and right, but according to prescribed rules."[48]

Fixed law or "prescribed rules" founded on verifiable textual authority, akin to the English legal system, for Jones, is not an external goal to be achieved but an immanent feature of Islamic law that needs to be reinstated through translation. In fact, Jones submits that it is only through such methods of translation and interpretation of local laws that the Company will be able to assure its subjects that "their laws of property, which they literally hold *sacred*, shall in practice be secured to them," and that this will, in turn, "secure the permanence of [British] dominion."[49]

Jones's argument assumes here not only that English common law must triumph over other (and primarily customary) legal systems, but also that it must function as the template for legal reforms, and this was undergirded by the hypothesis that it was the precise textuality of English law that gave it an edge over others. In the eighteenth century, and in an era of expanding imperialism, this idea was fast becoming one of the central precepts of British legal philosophy and was defining the metropolitan center with increasing sharpness. It also became a crucial part of the concept of sovereignty in Britain and its colonies, as a differential system that distinguished between different forms of power and accordingly separated despotic rules from proper rule of law.

The supposed universality of common law, in other words, became the yardstick against which every other legal system had to be judged. Such a sentiment was given a precise expression by Jones's friend Burke across different fora. In his influential treatise *Reflections on the Revolution in France*

(1790), for instance, Burke portrays English common law as an almost organic or quasi-natural expression of Englishness. Promoting the English legal system over the French, Burke describes the combination of common and statute laws of the former as "emanating from the common agreement and original compact of the state, *communi sponsione reipublicæ*, and as such are equally binding on king, and people too, as long as the terms are observed, and they continue the same body politic."[50] In his mind, the tradition behind English common law – through its long history and rich archive of antecedents – is the source of sovereign power, and also a necessary safeguard against what he sees as the excesses of Jacobinism in France.

Jacobinism, however, is not the only frame against which Burke counterposes the consensual sovereignty and common law of England; he is equally eager to refute the evolving imperial ideology as it passes from North America to Asia (or India, more specifically), producing what he terms "Indianism" under the Company as a despotic political force as dangerous as Jacobinism. As Sunil Agnani points out, what Burke represented in political philosophy, and what his position meant for the empire, have to be measured against this shifting backdrop, and his trenchant critique of the Company or Hastings has to be assessed in the context of this multifaceted imperial history of the late eighteenth century.[51] It is possible to argue that his spirited defense of the English legal system in *Reflections on the Revolution in France* is his way both to navigate through the shifting imperial terrain and also to find a historical anchor against which to judge the emerging political realities in England and its colonies.

Thus, even if English common law demonstrates the central liberal maxim that the "society is indeed a contract" – a claim about which Burke remains ambivalent here and elsewhere – he nonetheless maintains that such a view can be held only with the additional proviso that this "partnership" with the state is unlike any other business contract since it is premised on a much longer history and a grand intergenerational vision: "It is a partnership in all science; a partnership in all art; a partnership in every virtue, and in all perfection. As the ends of such a partnership cannot be obtained in many generations, it becomes a partnership not only between those who are living, but between those who are living, those who are dead, and those who are to be born."[52] Significantly enough, the exact opposite to this solemn contract in Burke's imagination is contracts drawn out in trades of pepper, coffee, calico, and tobacco – all associated with the colonies in the two Indies.[53] In an effort to make the case even stronger, he announces the grandness of the former through the calculated invocation of Justinian law – "*communi sponsione reipublicæ*" or the consent of the commonwealth – as a historical model against both a revolutionary France and a chaotic India. Such an appeal to Roman legal codes makes it possible for him to gather together the abstract notions of citizenship, civil society, and the state on a pan-European platform, and then to argue that the English arrangement is the most natural outcome of that history. Roman legal regimes stand as the frame of reference as well as the *raison d'être* for English common law partly because of their antiquity and partly because of their civilizational claims that European empires progressively borrowed in the eighteenth century.

Against this legal–philosophical backdrop, then, we are faced with two different models of legal translation here. For Hamilton, the "superfluous" features connect legal codes to a national culture, a quality that Burke proposes as a necessary condition for any legal regime claiming sovereign power. Jones, on the other hand, emphasizes the other half of Burke's formulation – that is, fixed and unambiguous law – and considers the "superfluous" elements distractions. However, in the absence of a tradition of common law, an organic legal system for both of them could only find its resources in texts or, more specifically, in what I have described in Chapter 1 as the *ethnographic recension* of law and customs, and could use the English model as a blueprint. This is where the idea of superfluity becomes crucial as it directly impacts not only the everyday efficacy of the new legal regime (after all, these legal tracts were intended for use in Company courts) but also the new imagination of sovereignty that is text-based and hermeneutic in nature.

Hamilton addresses this idea through a model of excess translation – involving Arabic, Persian, and English – and suggests that it is in the textual surplus that the "superfluous" can be tamed and made sense of. What remains "unnatural or improbable" in the Arabic original becomes accessible, and somewhat naturalized, once it is made part of the governmental world of textuality through successive stages of translation. For Hamilton, translation is both a governmental technique and a device to make two different cultures transparent to each other. Jones, however, chooses a different path and proposes an intellectual division of labor between the substantive "fixed law" and its commentary, with the suggestion that whatever is superfluous in the original text, and whatever lingered as remainders of an alien culture, could form a lateral second order of textuality. At its basic conceptualization, Jones also remains committed to the idea that the cultural world of laws – as "customs and manners" – must be included in a translation, but he favors a more governmental logic of separating substantive laws from commentaries in the name of everyday practicality. Being a trained jurist himself, Jones perhaps fancies himself to be a modern-day Justinian entrusted with the job of codifying and textualizing Indian law, but he also sees translation as the central governmental instrument in his mission.

In each case, however, the issue of superfluity, like Wilkins's untranslatables in *The Hĕĕtōpādēs* and *The Bhăgvăt-Gēētā*, surfaces at the moment of translation since neither Hamilton nor Jones contests the organization of the original Arabic texts with these details or doubts their worth in the cultural milieu they are supposed to operate in. Superfluity becomes a concern only when the text is taken out of its immediate culture of production, or when translation literally displaces the original. To put it differently, textual superfluity becomes a concern for colonial government at the moment when disparate texts are pressed into service to produce a perfect "rule of law" or "partnership" (in Burke's words), and when such a textual–legal regime is claimed to be the foundation for sovereignty. As such, my suggestion is that the "superfluous" occupies the same ontological status as the untranslatable, being a form of cultural sedimentation that cannot be represented in its entirety and yet is needed to define the text with its unique autonomy. As I show in this chapter and elsewhere in the book, such ideas of cultural vestiges or textual excesses are typically expressed in ethnographic terms – custom, manner, religion, and so on – and are often held as external to the core textual organization that a translator seeks to capture in a different language.

But, as we have seen in the successive cases of Wilkins, Hamilton, and Jones, this is often a futile exercise. Even the translators acknowledge so, and devise different models to conjoin the two. What is more interesting for me, however, is how this ambivalent status of the untranslatable superfluity – both external and integral to the text, at the same time – is repeatedly harnessed to claim textual autonomy, and how such a move is proposed as the very ground for colonial power. The new model of colonial sovereignty is designed to be a translational one, but its legitimacy is sought within a set of ethnographic superfluities that defy translation and yet function as a guarantor of the text in translation. This double bill for the untranslatable cultures or superfluity, ironically enough, brings the colonial legal regime closer to the vision Burke sets out in *Reflections on the Revolution in France* – that is, it marks out a fixed body of universal law while it also ensures a national consensus behind it.

Burke's intervention offered another context for these translations. By the time Hamilton and Jones published their respective translations, debates on "rule of law" or its reliance on cultural superfluity were not restricted to India and instead had become an intrinsic part of what Nicholas Dirks calls the "scandal" of the empire.[54] Burke himself advocates this connection when he remarks in *Reflections on the Revolution in France* that the continuity of the English constitutional rule or even the power of the House of Commons will remain intact as long as the latter "can keep the breakers of law in India from becoming the makers of law for England."[55] It would have been impossible for colonial officials like Hamilton and Jones to be oblivious of these larger debates and political bickering when they considered the idea of a possible legal regime in India.

Consider, for instance, the paradox of Hamilton's translation. Hamilton dedicates his translation to Hastings, and waxes eloquent on the "wisdom and benevolence" of the latter in initiating the project during his tenure as the Governor General. He even hopes that such translations would facilitate the "administration of Justice throughout our Asiatic territories, and [unite] us still more closely with our *Mussulman* Subjects." While identifying Hastings as the executive source of many such translations, Hamilton wishes further that his "humble" efforts would bolster the project of colonial governance in India and as such would add "some additional lustre" to his employer's considerable reputation as an administrator.[56]

However, Hamilton's dedication in 1791 must have struck an ironic note for most of his readers, since the subject of his eulogy was then embroiled in one of the most sensational impeachment proceedings in British history. The irony of the situation became ever more prominent because Burke sought to discredit Hastings for flouting the very thing that Hamilton describes as his supreme achievement in India – the "rule of Law." In 1786, barely a year after Hastings's return to England from India, Burke identified him as the chief culprit among the "breakers of law in India" and urged the House of Commons to impeach him with twenty-two "Articles of Charge of High Crimes and Misdemeanors" ranging from corruption and private profiteering to more serious charges of instigating native princes against the Company.[57]

In fact, this was Burke's second attempt at restraining Hastings, following an unsuccessful one in 1783 to introduce a regulatory structure for the Company through the Whig leader Charles James Fox's East India Bill in the parliament. But, four years later, in 1787, he was able to convince the House of Commons to pass the resolution that Hastings would be prosecuted before the Lords under seven out of the twenty-two charges (now called "Articles of Impeachment"). In 1788 the trial began with an almost national sensation, and presented over an extended period a political spectacle commensurate with the contemporary penchant for melodramatic performances on the English stage.[58]

106   Colonial Untranslatables

Sovereignty on Trial

As historians have noted, the sensational impeachment was not restricted to Hastings and his alleged "misdemeanor" in India, but encompassed other and larger issues relating to the empire, the idea of the rule of law, and eventually the critical issue of sovereignty.[59] My point here is that the impeachment was also about translation as both a governmental and a pedagogic apparatus – as seen in Hamilton and Jones, for instance – and, as a corollary, that colonial translational projects were instrumental in deciding the trial's final outcome. Burke condemned Hastings for violating the local legal codes by resorting to despotism, and indeed cited many of the translations the latter commissioned in support of his own argument. For him, the "high crime" of despotism became visible only when the Company's misrule was set against these legal texts and the unfortunate victims – both anthropologically defined – and when translations were able to make available an indigenous legal tradition to the rest of the world.

To argue his case, he had to make a distinction between an earlier phase of orientalism that grappled with the unknowable and untranslatable cultural other in India and a later phase that I have discussed above, where those untranslatables in fact became the primary means of knowledge. Hastings, on the other hand, defended himself by invoking a precolonial and pre-translational legal regime that he allegedly inherited from a decrepit Mughal empire and was forced to work with. He presented his translations as offering legal salvation for India, delivering the people not only from the tyranny of despots but also from the confusing and conflicting legal systems extant across the land. That Hastings was exonerated of all charges at the end of the trial, and that his plans of translational sovereignty won categorical approval in the House of Lords, was perhaps a testimony to the public faith in the Company's claim that the new translations restored India's ancient laws – both Hindu and Islamic – and thus saved the subcontinent from reverting back to its precolonial misery. It was also a sign that the translational sovereignty Hastings championed was to become a dominant feature of British imperialism from this point in history.

Burke himself makes the nature of the trial abundantly clear in a series of statements at the beginning of his "Speech in Opening the Impeachment," on February 15, 1788: "the business of this day is not the business of this man [Hastings], it is not solely whether the prisoner at the bar be found innocent or guilty, but whether millions of mankind shall be made miserable or happy"; "It is not only the interest of India, now the most considerable part of the British empire, which is concerned, but the credit and honor of the British nation itself will be decided by this decision"; and finally, "there is another consideration [...] something that [...] comes more home to the hearts and feelings of every Englishman: I mean, the interests of our Constitution itself, which is deeply involved in the event of this cause."[60] Against such grave charges, the figure of Hastings indeed dwindles to that of a petty renegade – too tiny to be burdened with the enormity of these accusations.

Yet, for Burke, Hastings is not inconsequential to the broader scheme of colonial things, no "poor, puny, trembling delinquent," but the "first man of India [...] the chief of the tribe, the head of the whole body of Eastern offenders, a captain-general of iniquity, under whom all the fraud, all the peculation, all the tyranny in India are embodied, disciplined, arrayed, and paid" (9: 338–9). At the same time, Burke places both sets of concerns – the larger issues of law, constitution, and sovereignty as well as Hastings's individual culpability – at the center of the imperial project, as a litmus test for the British empire and its legal sustainability. He frequently urges the Lords to consider the possibility that it is through the outcome of this impeachment that the laws of the ancient constitution of Britain will be tested, and it is through the moral deliberations on the rights of a culturally alien population – "different in language, in manners, and in rites" (9: 340) – that the future of the British empire will be decided.

At the heart of Burke's speech is the issue of sovereignty and law. His initial distinction between the larger imperial project and Hastings as an aberration is a strategic one. At no point in the speech does he question the legality of the empire itself, or seriously interrogate the origins of empires anchored in the so-called "right of conquest." If anything, he is too eager to suppress these early histories of the empire as a morally reprehensible yet necessary condition for its continuity and legitimacy: "There is a secret veil to be drawn over the beginnings of all governments. Ours in India had an origin like those which time has sanctified by obscurity. Time, in the origin of most governments, has thrown this mysterious veil over them; prudence and discretion make it necessary to throw something of the same drapery over more recent foundations, in which otherwise the fortune, the genius, the talent and military virtue of this nation never shone so conspicuously" (9: 401–2). In order to strengthen his point about legitimacy, he adds further "[t]he first step to empire is revolution, by which power is conferred; the next is good laws, good order, good institutions, to give that power stability" (9: 402). It would follow that, even though Hastings has been put on trial for his misdemeanors in India, in Burke's opinion this fact in itself does not delegitimize either the empire or its claim to sovereignty.

To mount an attack like this one, Burke needs a clear account of what he means by sovereignty in this specific case. Indeed, it is possible to argue that his position during the impeachment, in addition to clarifying his own ideas, signals a clear shift in the broader understanding of imperial sovereignty, from the territoriality of the American colonies to what I call the *hermeneutic imperium* of the Indian case. Dirks has suggested that the crux of the American experience for Burke and many of his contemporaries was the untenable nature of territoriality as the foundation for sovereignty. In an age imbued with growing nationalist spirit, they realized, it was impossible to maintain territory as the sole basis for sovereignty at the cost of the "far more significant contradictions of race, language, religion, and history" across the empire.[61] From a territorially expansionist model that underpinned the American case, thus, the idea of sovereignty gradually shifted to a set of issues that crystalized around the principle of colonial difference and became reflected in textual-hermeneutic codification of law. What is equally important to note is that British discussions on sovereignty and nationhood from an earlier period – as represented by Hobbes and Locke, for instance – underwent broad transformations thanks to the imperial experience, first in America and then in India; and Burke perhaps was the first political philosopher who addressed the issue of sovereignty within the imperial frame.

His engagement with the Indian colony had been in the making for quite some time, and it revolved around the question of difference and the more philosophically inflected idea of knowing the colonial other. In a speech in response to Fox's East India Bill in December 1783, as Sara Suleri points out, Burke directly addresses the inchoate political discussions around the "Indian question" and recasts the issue of colonial difference within a conceptual structure similar to that of the "sublime" he outlined earlier in his *A Philosophical Enquiry into the Origin of Our Ideas of the Sublime and Beautiful* (1757) – that is, beyond reason or causality, unreadable, and always in proximity with the terrible.[62] As Burke himself puts it:

> All this vast mass, composed of so many orders and classes of men, is again infinitely diversified by manners, by religion, by hereditary employment, through all their possible combinations. This renders the handling of India a matter in an high degree critical and delicate. But, oh, it has been handled rudely indeed! [...] It is an empire of this extent, of this complicated nature, of this dignity and importance that I have compared it to Germany and the German government – not for an exact resemblance, but as a sort of middle term, by which India might be approximated to our understandings, and, if possible, to our feelings, in order to awaken something of sympathy for the unfortunate natives, of which I am afraid we are not perfectly susceptible, whilst we look at this very remote object through a very false and cloudy medium.[63]

Sovereignty on Trial

Building on the principle of difference, he proposes India as unknowable or unpresentable in its entirety, much like the sublime, and approachable only through a "middle term" that falls between cognition and sympathy.[64] Even though the rule of the Company clearly sets a moral question for him, and he repeatedly castigates the officials for their failings, he is nonetheless willing to harbor the possibility of the colonial other being shrouded in some sort of mysterious veil or being beyond the reach of European knowledge practices.

This was to change soon, however. During the impeachment speech of 1788, and notwithstanding the charge that he often aestheticizes what is essentially a historical question, as Hayden White has alleged most forcefully,[65] Burke indeed submits a political resolution to this unpresentable colonial sublime – of translating and textualizing cultural difference into ethnographic codes of legibility. Within the conventions of ethnography, he detects a force that is not only commensurate with the unnamable colonial sublime, but also capable of summoning the much-required emotion of sympathy across cultural barriers. His faith in the cognitive powers of ethnography is on full display in his opening speech – he requests the Lords for certain "latitude" to introduce the people of India with their "characters, lives, opinions, prejudices, and manners" as a way of making the victims of Hastings's carnages as vivid as possible (9: 376).

What arrests one's attention in Burke's speech is indeed his almost exclusive reliance on distinctly ethnographic categories such as religion and the caste system to describe the uniqueness of the "Gentoos" or Hindus for his audience. At the outset, he informs the Lords that "these Gentoo people are the original people of Hindostan," and by far "the most numerous." The essential defining feature of this original population is their reliance on the caste system, derived from their ancient religious beliefs, as both originary and immutable: "The Gentoo people, from the oldest time, have been distributed into various orders, all of them hereditary: these family orders are called castes; these castes are the fundamental part of the constitution of the Gentoo commonwealth, both in their church and in their state." He spends some time explaining to his audience various aspects of the caste system – that the Hindus are "divided into four castes, – the Brahmins, the Chittery [kṣatriya], the Bice [baiśya], and the Soodur [śūdra], with many subdivisions in each. An eternal barrier is placed between them. The higher cannot pass into the lower; the lower cannot rise into the higher." He carefully notes that this division is not only social but religious: "They have all their appropriated rank, place, and situation, and their appropriated religion too, which is essentially different in its rites and ceremonies, sometimes in its object, in each of those castes" (9: 379–80). In Burke's opinion, this immutability of the caste system gave the Hindu religion and its institutions their most distinctive features – "great force and stability" and "excellent moral and civil effects" – that remained largely unaffected "before it was distorted and put out of frame by the barbarism of foreign conquests," first by Muslim invaders and eventually by the Company rule under Clive and Hastings (9: 382–5).

Using this ethnographic foundation, Burke then offers a sketch of Indian history with a somewhat schematized design, and divides it into six separate eras to suit his principal objective of condemning Hastings as the apostle of destruction and mismanagement. Relying primarily on John Zephaniah Holwell's *Interesting Historical Events, Relative to the Provinces of Bengal, and the Empire of Indostan*, 3 Vols. (1765–71) and possibly on Alexander Dow's *The History of Hindostan*, 2 Vols. (1768), he offers a teleological narrative that begins with an almost idyllic Hindu past, followed by various periods of Islamic invasion, and eventually culminating in the political ascendency of the Company.[66] In its bare structure, Burke's narrative sets the tone for subsequent colonial historiography of India, including James Mill's highly influential textbook for Company officials – *The History of British India*, 3 Vols. (1817).[67]

But, unlike Mill, Burke is much more eager to establish an unbroken tradition of Hindu "customs and manners" that, through its inherent inertia, not only persisted through the ages but defied the upheavals of successive military invasions. He again turns to Holwell's description of the Burdwan province in Bengal to illustrate the "beauty, purity, piety, regularity, equity, and strictness of the ancient Hindostan government" that survived through millennia, bearing testimony to the "wisdom and benevolence" of the "original people" of the land (9: 384–6). It is this ethnographic foundation of his historical narrative that allows Burke to declare one of his central postulates during the impeachment debate:

> If we undertake to govern the inhabitants of such a country, we must govern them upon their own principles and maxims, and not upon ours. We must not think to force them into the narrow circle of our ideas; we must extend ours to take in their system of opinions and rites, and the necessities which result from both: all change on their part is absolutely impracticable. (9: 378–9)

Such a plea surely does not refer back to what Suleri calls the mysterious "colonial sublime," but displays its confidence in unlocking the same mystery with an ethnographic key.

For my purpose here, this ethnographic–historical description of India – as opposed to the sublime colony – is important since it is against these rather unchanging "customs and manners" leading to the static society that he poses the Company era as an anomaly. Referring to the Company's history from the early seventeenth century to the period of Restoration, he argues that the Company's gradual appropriation of power, especially its capacity to declare war and peace in India, marked something unprecedented in world history: a joint-stock company grabbed "[t]hose high and almost incommunicable prerogatives of sovereignty, which were hardly ever known before to be parted with to any subjects, and which in several states were not wholly intrusted to the prince or head of the commonwealth himself." In effect, the "East India Company was no longer merely a mercantile company, formed for the extension of the British commerce: it more nearly resembled a delegation of the whole power and sovereignty of this kingdom sent into the East" (9: 348–9).

Burke fleshes out his point about the extraordinary situation "not dreamt of in the theories of speculative politicians" through the trope of reversal, or a complete reorganization of normative principles as its necessary condition. The central act of reversal lies in the fact that whereas in every other instance "a political body that acts as a commonwealth was first settled, and trade followed as a consequence of the protection obtained by political power," here the reverse was true – "[t]he constitution of the Company began in commerce and ended in empire." If this original reversal was unprecedented in imperial history, both ancient and modern, its outcome was nothing less than scandalous – the "East India Company in Asia is a state in the disguise of a merchant. Its whole service is a system of public offices in the disguise of a counting-house" (9: 349–50).[68] Burke enumerates several other cases of reversal that flow from this initial one and include the bureaucracy, the administrative organization of the Company, its institutions, and so on (9: 355–6, 402, 454).

This curious arrangement poses the central challenge to normative sovereignty: "They [the Company] are a nation of placemen; they are a commonwealth without a people; they are a state made up wholly of magistrates. There is nothing to be in propriety called people, to watch, to inspect, to balance against the power of office" (9: 353–4). For someone extremely critical of the French revolution, this lamentation for the absence of a people as a necessary balancing factor for the "power of office" is indeed ironic. For Burke, however, the situation in India under the Company is different from France since the absence of a people in the former undermines the very precondition of sovereignty, and, as a natural consequence, aids and abets unbridled despotism. In the English constitutional system that Burke uses as his template, the only source of power is the "power of office," and this singular source gives both its sovereignty and its legal system a united and cohesive purpose. In a significant extension of the Leviathan metaphor of Hobbes, Burke lauds the "*esprit du* [sic] *corps*" of the English system for its ability to enforce the same "spirit of the body" over "all its parts," and argues that it is the people who offer the justification for this singularity of power and provide its necessary checks and balances (9: 354–5). In short, without the people, there is no substantive sovereign power.

As a consequence, and as a countervailing argument against the Company rule, he decides to concentrate on the ethnographic description of the people of India both as the legitimate candidate to claim sovereignty and as an element in the larger discursive structure to support a claim of this magnitude. The advantage of such a move is not readily visible. But, on closer scrutiny, it becomes apparent that he is in fact borrowing heavily from a plan devised by the man he puts on the dock, namely Hastings himself, and is recalibrating an ongoing colonial project with a different name. Burke admits as much when he says that the resources for an argument like his are actually "furnished" by the "gentleman" at the bar, that is, Hastings (9: 482). And again, in his "General Reply" of May 28, 1794, he acknowledges more specifically that "[o]ne of the books which I have quoted was written by Mr. Halhed" (11: 222). Apart from Holwell and Halhed's *A Code of Gentoo Laws, Or, Ordinations of the Pundits* (1776), he in fact borrows heavily from his friend Jones – both through their personal association over the years and from the latter's published works – to etch out the details of the unchanging customs and manners of the Hindus or the age-old resilience of their civil and religious laws. Burke's ideas about the colonial legal regime in India, including his fundamental proposition that it should be based on native legal texts and traditions, have strong resemblances with, if they are not actually derived from, Jones's short and programmatic pamphlet "The Best Practicable System of Judicature for India" that he sent to Burke from Calcutta in 1784.[69]

Hermeneutics of Law

Burke's strategy of invoking an ethnographic description of India has a further advantage – once he is able to establish his first point about victimhood, he can then mobilize the same people as providing the solution to the Company's misrule through their own legal systems. This becomes most patently visible as he draws on colonial translations of Hindu and Islamic

Hermeneutics of Law

laws to suggest that neither of them supports despotism, and that Hastings's argument about despotic sovereignty as the norm in India is a serious misrepresentation of native legal traditions (9: 463–82). Since India was primarily ruled under Islamic law for centuries before the Company arrived on the scene, he takes special care to underscore its rational and moral structure. "To name a Mahomedan government," he submits, "is to name a government by law. It is a law enforced by stronger sanctions than any law that can bind a Christian sovereign. Their law is believed to be given by God; and it has the double sanction of law and of religion, with which the prince is no more authorized to dispense than any one else." Apart from this characteristic moral foundation, Burke also cites a tradition of legal "interpreters" or "*men of the law*" throughout the Islamic world from Turkey to India, who are responsible for the correct interpretation of law and who are protected from the wrath of the sovereign so that they can discharge their duties without fear or prejudice. The result of such restrictions is quite astounding: "Even their kings are not always vested with a real supreme power, but the government is in some degree republican" (9: 463–4).

Again in 1794, as part of his "General Reply" on May 30, he goes as far as saying that Islamic law is "binding upon all, from the crowned head to the meanest subject – a law interwoven with the wisest, the most learned, and most enlightened jurisprudence that perhaps ever existed in the world" (11: 232). Parallel to this, he charts out a somewhat similar structure for Hindu law: "[t]hese people in many points are governed by their own ancient written law, called the *Shaster*," and observes that, as with the Islamic "men of the law," the Hindu legal tradition is also aided by "interpreters and judges" called the "*Pundits*." He even adds that from the extant texts it becomes obvious that Hindu laws are "comprehensive, extending to all the concerns of life, affording principles and maxims and legal theories applicable to all cases, drawn from the sources of natural equity, modified by their institutions, full of refinement and subtlety of distinction equal to that of any other law" (9: 482).

This particular point becomes critical for Burke and other "Managers" of the impeachment, since Hastings contests the charges by arguing that the central legal problem in India is the confusing profusion of laws, which makes arbitrary power inevitable as well as effective. In his opinion, the Company had to face a wide array of "mischiefs, doubts, and inconveniences [...] arising from the *variety* of tenures, rights, and claims in all cases of landed property and feudal jurisdiction," and then had to intervene in the "unavoidable anarchy and confusion of different laws, religions, and prejudices, moral, civil and political, all jumbled together in

One unnatural and discordant mass." Hastings traces the origin of this confusion to "Mahomedan conquests," and asserts that the Hindus "were kept in order only by the strong hand of power."[70] From this he deduces the following: "The constant necessity of similar exertions [of arbitrary power] would increase at once their energy and extent. So that rebellion itself is the parent and promoter of despotism. Sovereignty in India implies nothing else. For I know not how we can form an estimate of its powers, but from its visible effects; and those are everywhere the same from Cabool to Assam. The whole history of Asia is nothing more than *precedents* to prove the invariable exercise of arbitrary power."[71]

Such a defense, Burke argues, is problematic on a number of counts, and not least because of its moral depravity. But he takes particular exception to the fact that Hastings practically "disenfranchised" all of Asia in a "single stroke": "Its inhabitants have no rights, no laws, no liberties; their state is mean and depraved; they may be fined for any purpose," and all this under the pretension that every act of arbitrary power was sanctioned by the "authority of this country" (11: 199–200). What is even more scandalous for Burke is the revelation that this particular section of Hastings's defense was composed by none other than Halhed in association with almost the entire "Indian Cabinet Council" (11: 202). Contemporary accounts of the impeachment also note that in "every charge except two, the answers were supplied [...] by various friends of Mr. Hastings." As it transpires from the list of "friends," most of them were employed by Hastings in India.[72] Quite naturally, Burke believes that the whole of the colonial machinery supports Hastings and as such becomes guilty by association.

What Burke describes as "detestable and abominable doctrines" (11: 202) of Hastings and Halhed, however, is very close to his own earlier position, his conceptualization of the colonial sublime, with a minor difference. In that earlier moment, the cultural untranslatables made India both unpresentable and terrifying, aligning it with the experience of the sublime. What Burke proposed then had its roots in the eighteenth-century obsession with the sublime, of course (more on this in Chapter 4), but it also hinted at a direct link between language and reason, with the further suggestion that what cannot be represented in language – or in translation – must remain outside the reach of rational intelligibility. Aravamudan has argued that, by the time Burke made his parliamentary speeches against Hastings in 1788, this idea of the terrifying sublime had migrated from India as an alien culture to the horrific consequences of the Company's rule, and especially to Hastings's alleged despotism.[73]

This second formulation of the sublime is not reliant on the absence of language and reason; rather, its contours become visible only when it is set against an abundance of language, made available through translation, and only when it is seen as an anachronistic embodiment of untranslatability. In both cases, the idea of the sublime implies an absence of translation, but in the first instance it is related to cultural difference while in the second it is related to governmental techniques. Burke's indignation at Halhed and Hastings is prompted by this duality of the sublime – while they make the language of native law available to colonial governance through translation, they nonetheless defend the Company's misrule on the grounds of cultural untranslatability. Burke reverses his idea of the sublime – from *culture* to *governance* – on the basis of colonial translations, and his proclamations on indigenous legal traditions of India constituted his attempt to overcome the earlier moment of the unreadable and the unpresentable.

Textual Imperium

At issue here in this impeachment trial or in the translation projects in the colony is the nature of the sovereignty the Company sought to implement. Despite their differences, or even enmity, there is a broad agreement between Hastings and Burke that India possessed a form of sovereign power in an earlier period that was perfectly compatible with the modern idea of rule of law. Both cite (often identical) texts from Hindu and Islamic legal traditions to substantiate their cases. And both agree on the point that it was the final phase of the Mughal era that destroyed this Indian form of sovereign power. During his defense, Hastings describes the kind of legal regime he inherited from the ruins of the Mughal empire in the following words: "this [Indian] sovereignty will be found a burthen instead of a benefit; a heavy clog rather than a precious gem to its present possessors [i.e. the Company] [...] unless the whole of our territory in that quarter shall be rounded, and made an uniform compact body, by One grand and systematic arrangement."[74] This idea of erecting "One grand and systematic arrangement" as part of colonial rule, he tells his audience, has been his mission during his years as the Governor General. All the translations he commissioned in India were designed to retrieve the original legal system and then to make that textual universe the ground for the new regime. In fact, way back in 1774, he assured the Court of Directors of the Company that this was indeed his plan, and defended his "Regulations" by saying that "[i]n this establishment no essential change was made in the ancient constitution of the province [of Bengal]. It was only brought back to its original principles, and the line prescribed for the jurisdiction of each Court, which the looseness of the Mogul government for some years past had suffered to encroach upon each other."[75]

Hastings, like Burke after him, also informs his employers in London that "Hindoos [...] have been in possession of laws, which have continued unchanged, from the remotest antiquity"; and that "Mahometan law [...] is as comprehensive, and as well defined, as that of most states in Europe."[76] Even if something appears as "most injudicious or most fanciful" from a European perspective (like the untranslatable or the "superfluous" in Wilkins, Hamilton, and Jones), he assures his readers that such customs are nonetheless "interwoven with their religion, and are therefore revered as of the highest authority." For him, then, the logical conclusion from such observations is the "legal accomplishment of a new system which shall found the authority of the British government in Bengal on its ancient laws, and serve to point out the way to rule this people with ease and moderation according to their own ideas, manners, and prejudices."[77] This shared awareness of Burke and Hastings also implies that they saw sovereignty in the colony as essentially encoded in native legal systems and believed that any access to it had to be textually mediated.

To put it differently, sovereignty in India for both Burke and Hastings was not so much the result of British principles or standards, however lofty they might have been, but the outcome of native legal texts and their interpretations – in short, of specific textual functions. The exceptional power of the Company in ruling over vast lands of India with what Burke calls "subordinate sovereign power" (9: 349) had to be justified, and the impeachment debates made it clear that there was a common agreement on this textualization of sovereignty across political divides. Hastings's critical-philological project of translating native legal tracts was premised on a similar assumption that, in order to ensure maximum compliance from the Indian people, they first had to be convinced that the new colonial dispensation was anchored in their own customs and manners, as enshrined in their ancient legal and religious tracts. In this model, Hindu or Islamic law operated within a closed textual world where texts referred to other texts and one authority on law to yet another, through an incessant chain of referentiality and within the limits set by legal as well as interpretative conventions. Sovereignty, as a result, mutated from the will of the despot to an internal function of a dense and distinctly bounded world of textuality, a world that sustained itself purely by investing its own verbal signs with absolute meaning.

CHAPTER 3

Comparatism in the Colony

After the ethnographic recension and the intricate web of translation/untranslatability, the colonial paradigm of the literary sovereign still needed a framework to realize its full potential and also to make the new idea of the literary visible. This final frame came in the form of comparatism, as a method that was capable of uniting many of the strands on textual scholarship developed as part of colonial governance. The origin of this comparative method can be traced in the germination of comparative philology as proposed by William Jones, and the importance of this history has been noted in no uncertain terms over the years: Ferdinand de Saussure, in his foundational text *Cours de linguistique générale* (1916), identifies the Orientalist "discovery" of the Indo-European language family with the help of Sanskrit as the beginning point for new or "comparative" philology;[1] Raymond Schwab's *La Renaissance Orientale* (1950) and David Kopf's *British Orientalism and the Bengal Renaissance* (1969), from different perspectives, narrate the centrality of both British India and its use of comparative philology to reorganize cultures in Europe and its colonies;[2] Michel Foucault's *Les Mots et les choses* (1966) proposes the comparative philology initiated by William Jones as one of the central characteristics of the modern episteme;[3] Edward Said's *Orientalism* (1978) recognizes the contribution of Jones and other colonial officials both to the secularization of cultural discourses and to the consolidation of modern humanistic disciplines;[4] and Bernard Cohn in his iconic essay "The Command of Language and the Language of Command" (1985) observes that the discovery of the "comparative method" was made possible by the British experience of encountering, "at a phenomenological level," the bewildering profusion of "hundreds of languages and dialects" in India and by their subsequent efforts to develop adequate theoretical resources to deal with this linguistic cornucopia.[5]

In recent scholarship, this history has been calibrated to recast the history of world literature as a paradigm. Aamir Mufti, for instance, has demonstrated the long genealogy of "world literatures" through the orientalist production of a unified cultural space called India, and Siraj Ahmed has suggested that Jones "could [...] justifiably replace Goethe at the beginnings of comparative literature."[6] In this chapter, I extend these early leads along and against the archive of the empire to propose that the fundamental paradigm of comparatism was fashioned through colonial governance in nineteenth-century British India as part of the literary sovereign and also as a disciplinary field distinct from the classical philology that Friedrich Nietzsche denounced with some vehemence in *The Birth of Tragedy* (1872) and "Notes for 'We Philologists'" (1875). What began with Jones as a suggestion of comparative philology and the "discovery" of the Indo-European language family, I suggest in the following pages, developed into an epistemic habit of the colonial state in the subsequent decades and saturated the daily business of running the empire. It all started in 1772 with Warren Hastings's plan to "adapt our Regulations to the Manners and Understandings of the People [of India], and the Exigencies of the Country, adhering, as closely as we are able, to their ancient Usages and Institutions"[7] and Jones's academic elaboration on the codifying and textualizing practices in his "Anniversary Discourses" (1785–92) delivered at the Asiatic Society of Bengal.[8]

Soon, however, the principle of temporal coevalness that underpinned Jones's comparative method migrated to other colonial documents and reinvented itself as territorial equivalence. As is evident in countless comparative vocabularies and grammars of Indian languages produced throughout the nineteenth century, often with active state patronage, comparatism as a governmental practice adopted this territorialization as a more secure method of classification and systemization of knowledge. My reading of this migration is structured around two prolific colonial officials – Brian Houghton Hodgson and William Wilson Hunter – and their consolidation of the comparative table as the most reliable method for articulating territorial comparatism.

The potential of these two phases was realized fully in the ambitious Linguistic Survey of India (1894–1928) under the supervision of George Abraham Grierson.[9] I argue in this chapter that with Grierson's attempt to enumerate and describe modern Indian vernaculars, and his seamless mixing of colonial structures and linguistic knowledge in the survey, we encounter the full range of the comparative method for the first time. With the survey, Grierson was able to resolve the central contradiction of British Indian archives – between the Orientalist desire to know India and the colonial mission to produce India as a governmental space – and also to regulate different energies within the neat tables of comparatism. Indeed, what remained scattered across a range of archival material – discourses, treatises, official dispatches, comparative tables, survey maps, census data, statistical reports, and so on – came together in this survey as concise and programmatic indices not only of the organicohistoric characteristics of modern Indian languages but also of India as a linguistic field that could be known only through comparative methods. Grierson's emphasis on the unity of the discipline of philology found a uniquely supportive echo in the territorial unity of the colony, and his voluminous survey was evidence of the successful suturing of colonial governance and comparatism in the service of the empire.

It is of course possible to see this survey as a pinnacle of what Cohn defines as the "investigative modalities" of British India that turned the vast social world of the colony into a mass of abstract "facts" through practices including historiography, museology, survey, census, and so on.[10] My claim in this chapter, however, is somewhat different: I propose that it is the *longue durée* of such modalities, with the survey as its culmination (and not Goethe/Marx or the exilic philology of Leo Spitzer and Erich Auerbach), that made available by the end of the nineteenth century a new disciplinary field called literature and a set of methodological devices under the generic name of comparatism. This was made possible by the new paradigm of the literary sovereign.

Archives as Lettered Governance

In other words, my account of the colonial government's investment in comparatism expands the terms of the very concept of literature in the late eighteenth century – what Foucault calls "literature as such" (*littérature comme telle*) as a supplementary ground for philology and what Philippe Lacoue-Labarthe and Jean-Luc Nancy identify with the contemporaries of Jones, especially the Jena Romantics.[11] Such a history, however, cannot be narrated through any one discipline or any one region. As I have showed in Chapters 1 and 2, the archive is full of mobile and circulating texts, ideas, and people that range across disciplinary boundaries and colonial geographies: voyages made by company officials like Jones and others; Jones's translation of Hāfez's "A Persian Song" (1771), the *Mu'allaqāt* (1782), and Kālidāsa's *Śakuntalā* (1789); circulation of Sanskrit manuscripts within Europe; availability of pirated copies of the journal *Asiatick Researches* across western Europe from 1796 onwards; and the formation of repositories of oriental manuscripts in London and Paris after the Napoleonic invasion of Egypt in 1798.

All these historical details suggest that a strictly disciplinary history is at best partial. Even within the colonial context, Jones hardly restricted his interests to philology. He was a puisne judge of the Supreme Court of Judicature of the East India Company, and he joined his legal and philological skills to serve Warren Hastings's plan of textualizing indigenous legal systems such as the Shari'a and the Dharmaśāstra.[12] This blurring of disciplinary boundaries is similarly evident in the research agenda he outlined for the Asiatic Society of Bengal. Roughly defining "MAN and NATURE" within the vast expanse of Asia as the "intended objects of [...] inquiries," he urges the members of the society to concentrate on three human faculties, "memory, reason, and imagination," which would lead to three "main branches of learning" in the form of "history, science, and art." Hence the list he produces includes "annals, and even traditions" under history; arithmetic, geometry, mechanics, mensuration, grammar, rhetoric, chirurgery, medicine, and similar subjects under science; and "musick, architecture, painting, and poetry" under "inferior arts." To this rather capacious list Jones also wants to add Sanskrit, Chinese, and other Asian languages, which he believes are indispensable in unlocking the "immense mine" of Asiatic knowledge.[13]

It is equally important to note that, as the colonial power consolidated itself during the nineteenth century, this early multidisciplinary energy was progressively appropriated by the colonial state. Indeed, during the course of the nineteenth century philologists became, to echo Nietzsche's wry judgment, "passionate slaves of the State."[14] Three important developments followed from this state interest in and eventual takeover of philology. First, the gap between a historicist conception of language and a contrarian definition of literature was reduced to make literature a historical being. The colonial state in India gradually aligned these different energies to codify and textualize colonized cultures, across its own institutions and practices, and enlisted literature as a necessary ally. Second, in a related move, the colonial state in India introduced literary studies to train its subjects, with the explicit acknowledgment that humanities education encouraged qualities important for the successful running of the state.[15] This also required institutionalizing English literature as the model national literature, a move that would train colonized minds and standardize the very category of literature across geographical difference. And third, through these two moves of codification and institutionalization, a model of comparativity was created as a template for institutional literary studies in the twentieth century.

Together, these three moves created a new way of organizing the field of literature as an object of knowledge, one that is very different from the notion of literature that Foucault identifies at the end of the eighteenth century. This model shaped comparative methods as the privileged way of conducting study. Grierson's voluminous survey epitomized these points and demonstrated how things had changed over a century thanks to active state patronage and interest in the field of literary studies. Indeed, Grierson's survey embodied the prototype of comparative literary studies – a colonial discipline that was institutionalized in a new way after the Second World War and reinvented as *Weltliteratur* after the end of the cold war.

Colonial Comparatism

But we are getting ahead of our story. To return to our plotline, we need to start with Jones and his brand of orientalism. Anthropologists, philologists, historians, and literary critics rightly identify Jones and his colleagues in Calcutta as the beginning of modern comparative philology and modern Indophilia.[16] However, restricting Jones within a rigorously evolutionary history of philology is misleading. Apart from his academic pursuits during Supreme Court recesses, he also supported Hastings's long-cherished dream to "found the authority of the British Government in Bengal on its ancient laws" and willingly joined Hastings's project.[17] The flurry of texts on Indian languages that followed from Hastings's plan, in which Jones played a pivotal role, resulted in, to use Cohn's words, "the establishment of [a] discursive formation [which] defined an epistemological space, created a discourse (Orientalism), and had the effect of converting Indian forms of knowledge into European objects." Jones's efforts thus need to be seen as part of this project that converted not only existing native epistemological fields but also native subjects into "instruments of colonial rule."[18]

Even Jones's work on philology, including the "Anniversary Discourses," needs to be seen as prompted by what Thomas Trautmann describes as "Mosaic ethnology" or "an ethnology whose frame is supplied by the story of the descent of Noah in the book of Genesis, attributed to Moses, in the Bible."[19] His annual lectures were not, strictly speaking, only philological. Instead, he planned to deliver these lectures on the major nations of Asia. Hence, his third to seventh discourses (1786–90) addressed, respectively, the Hindus, the Arabs, the Tartars, the Persians, and the Chinese. He added an eighth lecture on the "Borders, Mountaineers, and Islanders of Asia" (1791), and in the ninth he sought to arrange all of them under the title "On the Origins and Families of Nations" (1792). "It becomes clear in the ninth discourse," Trautmann observes, "that the entire project is one of forming a rational defense of the Bible out of the materials collected by

Orientalist scholarship, more specifically a defense of the Mosaic account of human history in its earliest times."[20] It also becomes clear that from the beginning these lectures employed "Mosaic ethnology" to outline a framework for comparative studies of different nations across Asia, with the implicit belief that comparatism as a method would reveal their typical characteristics better than individual studies of their peculiarities.

However, if Jones initiated this philological revolution and employed comparatism in the service of colonial governance, it was brought to its complete fruition almost a century later by Grierson and his *Linguistic Survey of India*. Producing a linguistic map of India with 179 languages and 544 dialects, the survey achieved something that, in Grierson's own words, "has been done for no other country in the world."[21] Grierson, as the superintendent and the author of the survey, recognizes that Jones was the transitional figure between "old philology" and "modern comparative philology" (*I*, 10), and he acknowledges the importance of the work done by new philologists such as Jones and Franz Bopp for his survey. But he also maintains that an entirely theoretical investigation of the orientalist variety will be inadequate to the purpose of making philology an arm of governance. Rather, he identifies as his predecessors the "Serampore missionaries" (*I*, 11) – William Carey, Joshua Marshman, and William Ward – who initiated the "first attempt at a systematic survey of the languages of India" in 1816 and thus brought the lofty discipline down to mundane needs of governance (*I*, 12). The central characteristic of this phase was the emphasis on modern vernaculars as opposed to the classical languages Jones and Bopp studied, and the phase thus inaugurated an engagement with India's historical present rather than the orientalist dream of accessing its glorious past.

Despite this early lead by Carey and others, no comprehensive survey of Indian languages was taken up in the following decades, and research was channeled through monographs on individual languages. Eventually the project received a decisive push in the Oriental Congress at Vienna in 1886, when a group of scholars including the well-known Indologists Friedrich Max Müller and Monier Monier-Williams "passed a resolution urging upon the Government of India to undertake 'a deliberate systematic survey of the languages of India'" (*I*, 17). After a brief hiatus, work began in 1894 under the supervision of Grierson, and with the help of various local governments an estimated 224 million Indian subjects were brought under the direct purview of the survey. Grierson notes at various stages that this ambitious project, stretching over thirty years, would not have been possible without the help of government officials and missionaries or

Colonial Comparatism

without an active overlapping between technical knowledge of the discipline and disciplinary techniques of governance.

It is clear from the beginning that the survey was modeled on the census of 1891, and there are striking parallels between Grierson's methodology and the administrative account of the census commissioner for India, J. A. Baines.[22] In many cases, the same set of colonial officials and their Indian interlocutors doubled as informants for the census and the survey. Thus the survey, like the census, imagined India as a unified site with the proviso that it was also "a site for integrating the different branches of linguistics as a modern European discipline (phonetics, historical linguistics, dialectology, etymology, and philology) into a unified working project."[23] The premises of such overlapping projects were established when Grierson contributed a chapter on Indian languages to the monumental *The Imperial Gazetteer of India* (1881) under Hunter's editorship and offered some of the preliminary ideas that later found fuller elaboration in the survey.[24]

However, I want to concentrate on the methodology of the survey. It is here that we can locate most succinctly the governmental foundation of the project and also a distinct shape of modern comparative literary studies. Let me quote Grierson on his methodology to underscore my point:

> After some discussion it was decided that it was primarily to be a collection of specimens, a standard passage was to be selected for purposes of comparison, and this was to be translated into every known dialect and sub-dialect spoken in the area covered by the operations. As this specimen would necessarily be in every case a translation and would, therefore, run the risk of being unidiomatic, a second specimen was also to be called for in each case, not a translation, but a piece of folklore or some other passage in narrative prose or verse, selected on the spot and taken down from the mouth of the speaker. Subsequently a third specimen was added to the scheme – a standard list of word and test sentences originally drawn up for the Bengal Asiatic Society in 1866 by Sir George Campbell and already widely used in India. [...] The foundation of the Survey is thus these three specimens, – the standard translation, the passage locally selected, and the list of words and sentences. It was then determined that the first specimen should be a version of the Parable of the Prodigal Son, with slight verbal alteration to avoid Indian prejudices, a passage which has been previously used and is admirably suited for such purposes. (*I*, 17–18)

It is this framework that sustained the survey over the years and across several volumes.

Now, if we place Jones and Grierson next to each other, despite the century that separates them, we may obtain an outline of the colonial genealogy both of comparative literature and of its methods. Grierson largely follows the census reports in subscribing to linguistic families suggested by Jones and works with classificatory groups such as "Indo-Aryan" or "Tibeto-Burman" (*I*, 115, 53), though he often refers to later research that corrected a number of mistakes Jones made in his anniversary discourses. The larger point of convergence lies in the methodology Grierson adopted for the survey and in the status he accorded English in its execution. Out of the three specimens, as seen in the extract above, the first was supposed to be a translation of the biblical parable in respective Indian languages. But it soon became apparent that in many cases translators did not know English, or their grasp of the language was wobbly at best, and, to help them, "a volume of all the known versions of the parable in Indian languages was compiled with the help of the British and Foreign Bible Society, of local missionaries, and of one or two Government officers" (*I*, 19).

To minimize the distortion of translation – which was multilingual by this stage and offered a proliferating field without fixed direction or location – a second specimen of a local folktale or narrative in verse or prose was recommended. However, even in this case translation remained central. As Grierson notes, "instructions were given that all specimens were to be written (a) in the vernacular character (if there was one) and (b) in the Roman character with a word for word interlinear translation. The second specimen was also to be furnished with a free translation into good English" (*I*, 20). English, in its original or translated form, was placed at the heart of this methodology, with the belief that it was the sole resource for knowing and classifying Indian languages. Even though the survey wished to enumerate and document existing Indian languages, English was seen as providing the structure to tame the otherwise bewildering abundance of data.

The point about English needs further elaboration, and I shall return to it toward the end of this chapter, but let us first consider the central problem of time or chronology that both Jones and Grierson had to deal with and that had considerable impact on comparatism as a method. Jones frequently records his uneasiness with the "chronology of the Hindus" or their "civil history" because all the Sanskrit texts he could lay his hands on suggested an absurd chronology for India's past – absurd because it defied both "*Mosaick* history" and natural laws.[25] Indians are so convinced of their own antiquity that even blatant incongruities do not bother them, but to any rational mind, he notes, these chronological lists call for investigation with "sound reasoning from indubitable evidence." The problem is further compounded by various myths perpetuated by Brahmin pundits, who for their vested interests give currency to doubtful chronology and thus secure an ahistorical ground for their authority.

Colonial Comparatism 125

A
CHRONOLOGICAL TABLE,
ACCORDING TO

One of the HYPOTHESES *intimated in the preceding Tract.*

CHRISTIAN and MUSELMAN.	HINDU.	Years from 1788 of our era.
ADAM,	MENU I. Age I.	5794
NOAH,	MENU II.	4737
Deluge,		4138
Nimrod,	Hiranyacaśipu. Age II.	4006
Bel,	Bali,	3892
RAMA,	RAMA. Age III.	3817
Noah's death,		3787
	Pradyóta,	2817
	BUDDHA. Age IV.	2815
	Nanda,	2487
	Balin,	1937
	Vicramáditya,	1844
	Dévapála,	1811
CHRIST,		1787
	Nárdyanpála,	1721
	Saca,	1709
Walīd,		1080
Mahmūd,		786
Chengiz,		548
Taimūr,		391
Babur,		276
Nádirṣháh,		49

Figure 3.1 Jones's table showing parallels between Christian, Islamic, and Hindu chronologies. William Jones, "On the Chronology of the Hindus," in *The Works of Sir William Jones*, 13 Vols. (London: John Stockdale and John Walker, 1807), 4: 47.

Jones devises an ingenious strategy to amend this faulty history. Initially he poses the problem in the form of a question: "whether [Indian chronology] is not in fact the same with our own [that is, Mosaic history], but embellished and obscured by the fancy of their poets and the riddles of their astronomers."[26] At the end of his long and often fanciful discussion of various textual traditions, he indeed establishes that these two chronologies run parallel and that they may even have been the same despite their different forms of recollection. Thus, in the final chronological table, characters from the Bible and Hindu mythology appear next to each other as contemporaries or possibly identical figures, with the hope that, by superimposing biblical chronology on Hindu myths he could get rid of the wild claims made by wily Brahmin pundits (Figure 3.1).[27]

This chronology, he insists, is obtained through internal textual evidence, albeit with a combination of reason and evidence. Such claims of authenticity are important because this chronological table is an integral part of his comparative method; any proposition regarding family resemblance between different languages, or even the language tree of comparative philology, had to pass this test of chronological simultaneity. Mosaic history and "Hindu chronology" had to agree with each other, and Adam and "Menu I" had to appear parallelly as preconditions for comparativity. Hence Jones had to repeatedly claim that his table was supported by reliable textual traditions. In a supplementary note, Jones thus produces further evidence from texts related to the "Astronomical Computations of the Hindus" (*Sūrya Siddhānta* and *Varāhīsanhitā*) in support of his chronology and states: "the *Mosaick* and *Indian* chronologies are perfectly consistent; [...] that a considerable emigration from *Chaldea* [Iran] into *Greece, Italy*, and *India*, happened about *twelve* centuries before the birth of our Saviour; that SĀCYA, or SĪSAK, about two hundred years after VYASA, either in person or by a colony from *Egypt*, imported into this country the mild heresy of the ancient *Bauddhas*; and that the dawn of true *Indian* history appears only three or four centuries before the *Christian* era."[28] The "indubitable evidence," however, comes not exclusively from Sanskrit texts but from comparative philology and etymology, and Jones claims that several words in Greek, Persian, and Sanskrit related to his calculation are of the same root and hence they bear out his larger hypothesis on history. Jones of course gestures toward his proposition of a language family, but here he also contends that, if languages could be part of historical dispersal, so could communities who spoke those languages. Philology and ethnology, in other words, should conform to a shared and universal chronology.

Jones's otherwise confident chronology, however, falters at literary texts. He notes in "On the Literature of the Hindus, from the Sanscrit" that legal texts such as *Manusmṛti* or more recent ones including "an excellent treatise on *Inheritance* by JĪMUTĀ VĀHANA, and a complete *Digest*, in *twenty-seven* volumes, compiled a few centuries ago by RAGHUNANDAN" easily lend themselves to close philological readings and are thus of great interest to the "*British Government*," but this cannot be repeated for literary texts in Sanskrit.[29] And again in "On the Mystical Poetry of the Persians and Hindus," he admits difficulty in explaining the Persian poet Hāfiz strikingly sensuous poems as either literal or figural, with the observation that "it must be admitted, that the sublimity of the *mystical allegory*, which, like metaphors and comparisons, should be *general* only, not minutely exact, is diminished, if not destroyed, by an attempt at *particular* and *distinct resemblances*."[30] He even acknowledges that this is a general problem for all Sufi poets, whose great Maulavi states that "they profess eager desire, but with no carnal affection, and circulate the cup, but no material goblet; since all things are spiritual in their sect, all is mystery within mystery."[31]

Surely, allegory in itself cannot have posed serious challenges to a polymath like Jones, who knows several literary traditions well and is familiar with allegorical texts in other languages. What confounds him is the literary practice that makes sense only within the bounds of language itself – an allegory, so to speak, without the literal referent. This is manifestly different from European literatures Jones knows. In "Essay on the Poetry of Eastern Nations," he makes a fundamental distinction between European and Eastern poetry: "European poetry has subsisted too long on the perpetual repetition of the same images, and incessant allusions to the same fables" and remains trapped in "the likeness of a likeness"; Eastern poetry avoids referentiality altogether by embodying "that rich and creative invention, which is the very soul of poetry."[32]

This multiplicity of the being of language did not find any final resolution in Jones's work, and, though Jones made comparative philology subservient to the state, he at least left the field open. Grierson, understandably, could not afford such an open-ended theory of language, because it was the finitude of language within history that he wanted to capture through his survey. To fix this finitude, he had to update the chronology established by Jones and others, and, to make his effort worthwhile, he also had to account for modern Indian vernaculars as part of this revised chronology. Grierson made two vital changes to Jones's schema: first, he dropped the Mosaic framework; and second, while Jones and early modern philologists treated grammar as the true means of knowledge and used it to support the history of a language, Grierson turned established and recognizable grammatical rules into preconditions for linguistic evolution. Every language, potentially at least, was regarded as both a vernacular and a dynamic speech act. Clear grammatical rules not only fixed its being in history but also removed it from the earthly realm of spoken words, leaving the space open for more vernaculars.

Grierson insists in his notes that this process occurred repeatedly in history, and thus it is reasonable enough to adopt it as a reliable methodology for his purpose (see *I*, 121–2). The earliest instance was the development of classical Sanskrit, which emerged from one of the vernacular dialects when its rules were fixed by successive generations of grammarians and Brahmins and when it was raised to a status similar to "that of the Latin of the Middle Ages" (*I*, 121). As opposed to this secondary language, for centuries "Aryan" vernaculars were known as Prakrits; the difference, and support for his theory, is evident even from their very names – "Prakrit, *prākṛita*, i.e., the natural, unartificial language, as opposed to Sanskrit, *saṃskṛita*, the polished, artificial, language" (*I*, 121). Grierson is on solid grounds here; as we have seen in Chapter 1, this distinction was accepted as early as Nathaniel Brassey Halhed's prefatory notes to his *A Code of Gentoo Laws, Or, Ordinations of the Pundits* (1776). Hence he claims that, from assorted sources (both textual and archaeological), it is possible to establish that the vernaculars from which Sanskrit was segregated as an artificial language should be named the "*Primary Prakrits*," followed in subsequent eras by "*Secondary*" and "*Tertiary Prakrits*" (*I*, 121).

Grierson's argument here faces an internal paradox. While he suggests that classical Sanskrit was recognizable through its regularized and somewhat artificial grammatical structure, he does not specify the rules through which the three different stages of Prakrit could have been recognized. He even remains largely silent up to this point on the emergence of modern "Indo-Aryan" vernaculars from the Tertiary Prakrit and works largely within the chronology established by Jones. However, at this stage he introduces two new concepts to resolve this paradox that redoubtably end Jones's legacy of chronological comparatism. First, he points out that all that is known about different stages of Prakrit is "founded on the literature in which they have survived, and in the grammars written to illustrate that literature" (*I*, 122–3). By his own rule of thumb, however, Grierson then has to argue that the moment they became recognizably distinct (primarily through literary language rather than through their grammatical structure) these Prakrits realized their own standardization, like Sanskrit before them, and were removed from everyday language practices. Unlike Jones, Grierson does not posit any opposition between grammar and literary language. On the contrary, he suggests that both standardized languages with fixed identities – grammatical rules restricted the dynamism of vernaculars, and literary conventions fundamentally misrepresented the nature of spoken dialects. Grammar and literature thus participated in equal measure in regulating the historicist being of languages.

In his second move, Grierson introduces the forceful concept of *apabhraṃśa* or "'corrupt speech' or 'decayed speech'" to explain the origins of modern "Indo-Aryan" vernaculars (*I*, 124).[33] *Apabhraṃśa* in his account ensures continuity of vernaculars even when, or particularly when, Prakrits were standardized through literary texts, and this account formed the foundation for contemporary languages (*I*, 123–5). With the notion of corruption, however, Grierson changes the very ground of modern philology, as it is no longer the strict grammatical rules but rather the deviations from them that define the new set of vernaculars. Even when a literary *apabhraṃśa* eventually emerged, unlike Prakrit, its local variations kept the possibility of further corruption open by borrowing *dēśya* or local words and also by affecting phonetic changes.

As should be evident, Grierson's formulation of corruption does not follow any historical trajectory; that is to say, in his imagination specific forms or even mechanisms of corruption do not change over time. It remains constant – or ahistorical – and updates vernaculars over time. This is why he can identify corresponding *apabhraṃśas* for all the "Indo-Aryan" vernaculars of his contemporary India and can confidently say that his method of identification relies not on languages with fixed identities like Sanskrit or Prakrit but on the very mechanism of corruption and evolution that avoids such fixity by being responsive to local forces and aspirations. While languages change under the pressure of corruption, his methodological tools (that is, the apparatus of such changes) remain active yet unaffected between roughly 1000 CE and his time. It is then possible for him to establish their vicissitudes with a fair degree of accuracy.

To prove his point further, on the one hand, Grierson replaces an earlier emphasis on grammar with vocabulary by insisting that there is little affinity between modern "Indo-Aryan" vernaculars of northern India and Sanskrit insofar as their grammatical structures are concerned; he argues that a more direct connection can be established through the persistence of shared vocabulary.[34] On the other hand, though, to sustain this rather territorial view of language, he relies heavily on the colonial state's ability to territorialize itself. By using the colonial state's lateral networks of governance as well as its territorial map, he was able to suggest geographical boundaries between languages and also to settle controversial distinctions between languages and dialects. "The first thing done in this Survey," he notes, "was to obtain lists of dialects from each of the local areas [...]. They were furnished by the officers in charge of these areas in 1896 and the following years. Each local official had at hand the language totals of his District or State according to the census of 1891. With the aid of his local knowledge, and as the result of local inquiries, he was able to state what dialects of each language were spoken in his charge, and how many speakers there were of each" (*I*, 25). What began with the notion of corruption – the territorialization of languages – thus found its final approval from the colonial state.

Comparative Tables and Territorial Imagination

Grierson, however, indicates a second genealogy for this territorialization of comparatism. In volume one, part two of his survey, he cites Hodgson's extensive lists of comparative vocabularies published since 1847 in the pages of the *Journal of the Asiatic Society* and Hunter's *Comparative Dictionary of the Languages of India and High Asia* (1868) as his models and sources for the ongoing project. Although both Hodgson and Hunter primarily dealt with "non-Aryan" languages, and to complete his survey Grierson had to collate additional lists for "all the languages of India and the neighbouring countries," their central achievement of standardizing linguistic knowledge of India through comparative tables remains undisputed in his estimation (see *I*, 13–14).[35] In his introductory volume, he even states that, through their extensive lists of "non-Aryan" languages on the fringe of the empire and with their unusual "clearness of arrangement, and accuracy of treatment," Hodgson and Hunter established the comparative table as the central paradigm of comparatism in the service of the colonial state and produced the fundamental model for the survey (*I*, 14). The unique economy of the comparative table, its ability to replicate territorial equivalence and interchangeable values within the adjacency of its precise columns, he seems to suggest, responded to the original aspiration of Carey and others and allowed him to consolidate his methods against the philological legacies of Jones.

The table, for Foucault, was the "centre of knowledge, in the seventeenth and eighteenth centuries," as it was seen to be the "ground of all possible orders, the matrix of all relations, the form in accordance with which all beings are distributed in their singular individuality" (*OT*, 82, 273). During the nineteenth century, as "history" displaced the classical notion of "order" from its preeminence, the table also ceased to be the ideal paradigm for knowledge and was seen as "no more than a thin surface film for knowledge" (*OT*, 273). In the colonial order of things, it seems, Hodgson had a very different notion of the table; he considered it a vital instrument for stabilizing languages and for strengthening governance. In the brief note added to one of his initial lists of comparative vocabulary in 1857, for instance, he argues that, although the "arrangement and nomenclature" of these languages on the tables "are not quite correct," they may still serve the "present end" of knowing the "'broken tribes'" bordering the empire.[36] Elsewhere he reiterates this belief in the useful nature of comparative tables and argues that comparative vocabularies and "grammatical analysis" of languages are essential means of determining "territorial limits" of languages and their speakers.[37] This foundational model of comparative tables, as Hunter puts it in his biography of Hodgson, led to subsequent and more comprehensive knowledge of "non-Aryan" races: "disdaining a word of introduction, [the comparative table] starts with the vocabularies which Hodgson had for the first time collected among the hill races. It then evolves, also for the first time, a grammar of their speech. Finally, it sets forth in a learned disquisition the origin, location, numbers, religion, customs, character, and condition of the tribes."[38]

Grierson's precise debt to Hodgson, and later to Hunter, was much larger than a single table and encompassed the very foundation of comparatism in the service of the state. He inherited Hodgson's central ambition to mobilize the comparative table as a counterpoint to Jones's chronological model and, as a consequence, to make it respond to the needs of colonial governance. Hunter describes this project as an attempt "to explore the ethnical affinities of the non-Aryan races in India, and to establish the common origin of many of these widely dispersed remnants of primeval man."[39] Hodgson is more explicit in engaging Jones; he suggests that, if it is possible to assume that "Hindús, Persians, Germans, English, Irish, Russians, are members of one family, viz., the Iranian," as Jones's thesis implies, it may equally be possible to demonstrate that "Tamúlians, Tibetans, Indo-Chinese, Chinese, Tangús, Mongols, and Túrks are so many branches of another single family, viz., the Turanián."[40]

Hodgson's point of departure was marked by his chosen method to prove this hypothesis; instead of drawing chronological trees, he employed the comparative table to track languages spoken by different "non-Aryan" races or "aborigines" across the subcontinent and offered to conceptualize the spread of the "Turánian" family of languages as lateral networks of communities.[41] He realized that the table was fundamentally incompatible with any notion of chronological succession, and Jones's table could be better utilized if it were employed to map the territorial spread of languages. As a result, he not only freed the table from any chronological burden but also offered to load it with copious lists of comparative vocabularies covering an astonishing range of "aborigines" and their territorial spread – northeastern frontier, eastern frontier, Indo-Chinese borders (subdivided into Arakan and Tenasserim), central India, Eastern Ghats, northern "Sircars," Nilgiris, southern India and Ceylon, and so on. As Grierson notes, "he gave comparative vocabularies of nearly all the Indo-Chinese languages spoken in India and the neighbouring countries, and of the Muṇḍā and of the Dravidian forms of speech" (*I*, 13) and, in the process, secured the centrality of the comparative table in colonial engagement with Indian languages.

This is a key moment in our story, as Hodgson embarked on demonstrating not only the "lingual affinities of all the Aborigines of India" and even their shared ethnic characteristics, but also the possibility of a philological framework that would supersede the kind of orientalism Jones initiated.[42] Let us look at a typical page from these lists to underscore my point (Figure 3.2). As we saw earlier, in its bare form the table reproduces the structure established by Jones. But the chronological table has been evacuated of its temporal content to minimize the suggestion of temporal affinity or even of the mythical common origin. Individual names (both mythological and historical) have been replaced by languages, and the chronological organicity of the former has been substituted by territorial proximity of the latter. The effect of this new organizational plan is that languages do not attain their historical being over time or through membership to a given family; rather they reveal their true being through comparison in the present, through juxtaposition designed to uncover mutual identity and difference. Individually they remain opaque, but the moment they are related to each other, the moment they enter the scheme of a comparative table, they become accessible.

While this somewhat protosynchronic view of language was developed into structural linguistics by Grierson's contemporary Saussure, Hodgson chose to align it with governmental projects. Indeed, the lateral organization of his tables is inspired by the scopic drive of survey maps, and the principle of territorial contiguity has been deployed in these tables to create the illusion of looking at a map as a reliable spatial guide. Such tables not only suggest bounded and contiguous territorial organization, but also use the reach of the colonial state as the very ground for comparison. With his grand plan of including all the "non-Aryan" races of the subcontinent within the organizational schema of comparative tables, Hodgson had the dream of producing a linguistic map of India that would rival Jones's hypothesis.

This governmental approach is much more frontally stated in Hunter. In his little "Dissertation" appended to his *Comparative Dictionary*, he offers two "political" or practical needs for such a project.[43] First, he refers to a "painful" episode in imperial history, the colonial state's troubled relationship with the "hill and forest peoples who surround the frontier and inhabit the interior table-lands and mountain ranges of India," which leads to the "perpetual probability that each cold season will have its highland rising or frontier war." He cites a series of such wars and concludes that the reason behind such a sorry state of colonial management is that "English administrators understand the Aryan, and are almost totally ignorant of the non-Aryan, population of India." Hunter's second reason is even more startling. The challenge before the colonial state, he argues, is no longer to find ways of taming these "non-Aryan" races, but to find opportunities to "utilize" them. As such, the task is twofold: "the first consists in supplying the place of the old sources of subsistence by new ones; the second, in

English.	Dardhi vel Dahi.	Dénwár.	Pahrí vel Pahi.	Chepáng.	Bhrámú.	Háyu, or Váyu.	Kuswár.
Air	Batás	Batás	Phú-sá	Má-rú	A-sí	Hujum	Batás
Ant	Cheunta / T-seu-n-ta	Cheu-ti / T-seu-ti	Mig-za	Túl-ti	A-nap	Chiki-bulla	Kimili
Arrow	Kánr	Kánr	Bá-rá	Lá	Pá-rá	Sár	Sár
Bird	Chárí	Chárái	Bú-khíncha / Bu-khin-cha	Wá. Mó-á	Jyá-ling	Chín-chí	Chárí
Blood	Rágat	Ráktái	Hí	Wé-í. W í	Chí-wí	Ví	Rakti
Boat	Dúngo. Dun-go	Dúnga. Dun-ga	Dón-ga	Dún-ga	Dun-ga	Dun-ga	Dun-ga
Bone	Had	Had	Ku-sá	Rhu-s	Wot	Rú	Hadh
Buffalo	Bhainsa	Bhainsi	Mé-sá	Mí-syá,	Bhai-sa	Caret	Bhainsa
Cat	Biralo	Mai-ni	Bhí	Biral	Manzyí	Dána	Bíralo
Cow	Gai	Gai	Mó-sá	Mó-syá	Syá	Caret	Gai
Crow	Káwá	Kowa	Kó-kó	Kág. Ká	Káng-kang	Gá-gín	Kág-lé
Day	Din	Di. ni	Nhí-ma-ko	Nyí. Ngí	Di-ná	Nu-ma	Di-ní
Dog	Kúkúr	Kú-kúr	Ku-ju. Ku	Kwí. Kú	A-kyá	Urí	Ku-kol
Ear	Kán	Kán	Nhua-puru	Né. Nó	Ká-ná	Nak-chú	Kán
Earth	Máti	Máto	Chá	Sá	Ná-sá	Kó	Mati
Egg	Anda	Dimba	Khén-ja	Wá-khím. Lu-m	Hom	Chalung	Dimba
Elephant	Hathi	Hatti	Ki-si	Há-thi	Caret	Caret	Hathi
Eye	Ánkhí	Ánkhá	Mí-gí	Mi. Mi-k	Mi-k	Mé-k	Ankhí
Father	Búbó	Bábá	Bá	Ba-bú	Ba-bai	U'-pá	Bábáik
Fire	A'-gé	Agí	Mí	Mé. Mí	Má-i	Mé	Aghi
Fish	Má-chha	Ma-chhe	Nyó-já	Nyá. Ngá	Na-ngá	Hó	Jhá-in
Flower	Phúl	Phúl	Só-nó	Dó. Ró	A-wai	Púm-mí	Phúl
Foot	Gód	God	Lí	La	Un-zik	Lé	Gor
Goat	Chág-ri / Cha-g-ri	Chá-gár / Cha-ga-r	Chá-lá	Mé-syá. Mí-chá	Mí-chha / Mí-ch-ya	Chí-lí	Chá-gari / Cha-ga-ri
Hair	Bár	Bár	Són	Mén	Syám	Sóng	Bár
Hand	Hát	Háth	Lá	Kút-t. Kút-pa	Bhi-t	Gót	Háth
Head	Múd	Mú-dek	Chhé	Tá-Tó-long	Ká-pá	Pú-chhi	Ká-pá
Hog	Sú-er	Sú-gúr	Phó	Pyá. Pyák	Pak-syá	Póg	Sú-ri

Figure 3.2 A list of comparative vocabulary. B. H. Hodgson, "Comparative Vocabulary of the Languages of the Broken Tribes of Nepál," *Journal of the Asiatic Society*, Vol. 26, No. 5 (1857), 320.

enabling the people themselves to augment the productiveness of such of the old means of subsistence as remain to them" (*CD*, 3, 8, 11).

However, the practical solution to both is to exploit the gulf that exists between different "races" within India: "in interest, in race, in religion, in habits of life, they [the "aboriginal tribes" of India] are cut off from the Hindus and Mussalmans by a gulf of whose breadth the people of Christian States can form no idea; and their ethnical repugnance is kept in a constant glow by the remembrance of ancient wars and recent wrongs." Given this chasm and deep-seated antipathy, Hunter suggests, it would be but natural for the colonial state to use the "aboriginal races" of India to establish a standing army and military police that would be in charge of overseeing the "Hindus and Mussalmans" and would thus share the administrative burden of white officials. As an aid to this objective, he offers his comparative grammar of these "aboriginal" races with the hope that it would "supply a more accurate basis upon which European philology may work; but these vocabularies, notwithstanding their defects, will henceforth enable every frontier administrator to hold direct communication with the races committed to his charge" (*CD*, 11–12, 6, 16).

In his text, Hunter offers a visual parallel to his political argument. His tables of comparative vocabularies realize Hodgson's dream of creating a linguistic map that would chart the spread and density of the "aboriginal" population across the subcontinent. Languages are thus grouped under definite territorial markers such as Southern India, Central India, Nepal, Chinese Frontier and Tibet, Eastern Frontier of Bengal, and so on. These territorial and governmental divisions are preceded by three philological categories: "Inflecting," "Compounding," and "Isolating" (Figure 3.3). With the intersection of these two groups, Hunter seeks to consolidate philology as an essential part of governance. Only after weaving philological insights into the territorial imagination of the state and arranging academic disciplines and disciplinary techniques within the economy of the comparative table is he able to imagine the full extent of colonial governance.

The significance of Hunter's argument is that he imagines linguistic knowledge as a field allied to colonial governance with its internal rules and argues for an independent means to consolidate and verify its components. Building on Hodgson's initial plans, he is now able to suggest that this new colonial world of knowledge needs to be fashioned by the colonial state alone and hence there is a need to revise available sources. This is evident in his complaint that the chief reason behind the "painful" episode is that colonial officials have not made any independent attempt to know these

82 NUL (NON)—NEIN—NO—NYET—NON. [CHAP. III.—ADVERB

	Types.	
Inflecting.	SANSKRIT,	*Na* (*nad*=not).
	ARABIC,	*La, lam, lan.*
Compounding.	BASK,	*Ez.*
	FINNIC,	*En, ej, ei,* etc. (neg. particle [-e]).
	MAGYAR,	*Sem.*
	TURKISH,	*Yok.*
	CIRCASSIAN,	*Sigeh.*
	GEORGIAN,	*Nu.*
	MONGOLIAN,	*Ugei.*
	MANTSHU,	*Ako.*
	JAVANESE, Ngoko,	*Ora.*
	JAVANESE, Krama,	*Boten*
	MALAY,	*Bukan.*
Isolating.	CHINESE, Nankin,	*Puh-shi.*
	CHINESE, Pekin,	*Pu-shih.*
	CHINESE, Canton,	*'M-hai.*
	CHINESE, Shanghai,	*Veh.*
	AMOY, Colloquial,	*Bô, -m-si.*
	JAPANESE,	*Nai, iye, iye.*
	Brahui,	*Ahd.*
Chinese Frontier & Tibet.	Gyámi,	*Pusitikyo.*
	Gyárung,	*Dimoh.*
	Tákpa,	*Men.*
	Mányak,	*Ma-zyi.*
	Thochú,	*Mángwó, mang.*
	Sokpa,	*Bi-si.*
	Horpa,	*Nyir.*
	Tibetan (written),	*Ma, mi.*
	Tibetan (spoken),	*Men.*
Nepal (east to west).	Serpa,	*Men.*
	Súnwár,	*Ma-mai.*
	Gúrung,	*A'ni.*
	Múrmi,	*A'nin.*
	Magar,	*Mali.*
	Thákṣya,	*Al.*
	Pákhya,	*A'sin.*
	Newár,	*Makhú, mai, ahang.*
	Limbu,	*Men, ná.*
Kiranti Group (East Nepal).	Kiránti,	*Mang.*
	Rodong,	*Ai-ma.*
	Rúngchhenbung,	*Ma-ang.*
	Chhingtángya,	*Mahd.*
	Náchhereng,	*Ma, nad-á.*
	Wáling,	*Main, mdang.*
	Yákha,	*Manna, imánna.*
	Chourásya,	*A'tti.*
	Kulungya,	*Ma.*
	Thulungya,	*Mi.*
	Báhingya,	*Mah'-á.*
	Lohorong,	*Caret.*
	Lambichhong,	*Mahd, mále.*
	Báláli,	*Ho-gnane.*
	Sáng-páng,	*Mand.*
	Dúmi,	*Mo-á.*
	Kháling,	*Ma-ao.*
	Dungmáli,	*Man, ji, mi.*
Broken Tribes of Nepal.	Dárhi,	*Hai-na.*
	Denwár,	*Boy-in.*
	Pahri,	*Makhi.*
	Chepáng,	*Caret.*
	Bhrámu,	*Mami, alek.*
	Váyu,	*Ma, ma-non.*
	Kuswar,	*Na.*
	Kusunda,	*A'yend.*
	Tháru,	*Nahi.*
	Lepcha (Sikkim),	*Ma ni.*
	Bhútáni v. Lhopa,	*Ma-tóp, men.*
N.-E. Bengal.	Bodo,	*Onga, agoi.*
	Dhimál,	*Ma, mánthá.*
	Kocch,	*Nah, nahin.*
	Garo,	*Akd.*
	Káchári,	*Caret.*
Eastern Frontier of Bengal.	Manipuri,	*Nate.*
	Mithán Nágá,	*Mantai.*
	Tablung Nágá,	*Mangcha.*
	Khári Nágá,	*Nonga.*
	Angámi Nágá,	*Mose.*
	Námsáng Nágá,	*Ma.*
	Nowgong Nágá,	*Mau, nenga.*
	Tengsa Nágá,	*Nonga.*
	Abor Miri,	*Mamd.*
	Sibságar Miri,	*Ma.*
	Deoria Chutia,	*Hhya.*
	Singpho,	*Gaiai.*
Arakan & Burmah.	Burman (written),	*Mahut.*
	Burman (spoken),	*Mahok, mohok bú.*
	Khyeng v. Shou,	*Hi-a.*
	Kámi,	*Na-u-ká.*
	Kúmi,	*Na-a.*
	Mrú v. Toung,	*Caret.*
	Sák,	*Caret.*
Siam & Tenasserim.	Talain v. Mon,	*Ha-sien.*
	Sgau-karen,	*T'mabah, tho-mi-bah.*
	Pwo-karen,	*Mawi-ai.*
	Toungh-thu,	*Ta-maróla.*
	Shán,	*Ma-ivuk.*
	Annamitic,	*Không.*
	Siamese,	*Mai-hsa, michi.*
	Ahom,	*Bubbrnro*
	Khámti,	*Ma-tsru.*
	Laos,	*Bo-tici.*
Central India.	Ho (Kol),	*Banno.*
	Kol (Singhbhum),	*Báno.*
	Santáli,	*Ah, bang, bdi, bánu,—*
	Bhúmij,	*Báno.*
	Urâon,	*Mala.*
	Mundala,	*Báno.*
	Rájmahali,	*Malla.*
	Goṇḍi,	*Halli, hilli.*
	Gayeti,	*Caret.*
	Rutluk,	*Caret.*
	Naikude,	*Caret.*
	Kolami,	*Caret.*
	Mádi,	*Caret.*
	Mádia,	*Caret.*
	Kuri,	*Caret.*
	Keikádi,	*Illa.*
	Khoṇḍ,	*Caret*
	Sávara,	*Yafan.*
	Gadaba,	*Vure.*
	Yerukala,	*Villa.*
	Chentsu,	*Nahi.*
Southern India.	Tamil, anc.,	*Caret.*
	Tamil, mod.,	*Illei, alla.*
	Malayálma, anc.,	*Caret.*
	Malayálma, mod.,	*Illa, alla.*
	Telugu,	*Ledu.*
	Karṇáṭaka, anc.,	*Caret.*
	Karṇáṭaka, mod.,	*Illa, alla.*
	Tuḷuvu,	*Idhi.*
	Kurgi,	*Alla.*
	Toduva,	*Caret.*
	Toda,	*A'.*
	Kóta,	*Illa.*
	Badaga,	*Illei.*
	Kurumba,	*Illa.*
	Iruḷa,	*Ille.*
	Malabar,	*Alla, illi.*
	Sinhalese,	*Na.*

Figure 3.3 Table from W. W. Hunter, *A Comparative Dictionary of the Languages of India and High Asia, with a Dissertation* (London: Trübner, 1868), 82.

"aborigines" of India; while their considerable efforts in knowing "Aryan" languages and related cultural practices have produced new scholarship, they have been happy so far to gather their information from the texts written by the victorious "Aryans." He notes that "the Brahminical religion has ever treated them as outcasts, hateful to gods and men; and this traditional and superstitious abhorrence is kept in a glow by the actual necessities of the superior race" (*CD*, 4). To avoid this prejudice, and also to make a fresh start for the colonial state, he offers his comparative tables as instances of independent research modeled on efforts made by officials like Hodgson.

Subject to National Literature

Grierson inherited the legacies both of Jones and of Hodgson–Hunter and their mutual tension. He still had to find a framework to resolve some of this tension and to fashion his model of comparatism. He answered with the powerful concept of national literature. He of course had the option of turning to a body of scholarship that extended Jones's insights and offered India as an integrated national field with a distinct literary tradition.[44] Instead, Grierson chose to propose national literature as a problem that had to be resolved within the linguistic protocols of a language and along the two axes of chronology (Jones) and territoriality (Hodgson–Hunter). Grierson begins with the thorny issue of distinguishing among languages, or between a language and its dialects, and cites the case of Assamese:

> This form of speech is now admitted to be an independent language, – yet if merely its grammatical form and its vocabulary are considered, it would not be denied that it is a dialect of Bengali [...]. Yet its claim to be considered as an independent language is incontestable. Not only is it the speech of an independent nation, with a history of its own, but it has a fine literature differing from that of Bengal both in its standard of speech, and in its nature and content. (*I*, 24)

This is the ground upon which he proposes to elaborate on national literature.

Grierson offers an analogy – though English peasants have little difficulty in their conversation with Dutch peasants, this cannot be taken to negate their separate English and Dutch identities. Similarly, Bengali and Assamese may not pass the test of mutual unintelligibility, but they are not to be grouped under one linguistic identity. In both cases "nationality and literature," or national literature, mark their separate beings (*I*, 24). For Grierson, or anyone working in India in the final decades of the nineteenth century, this identification between language, literature, and nationality was a settled question not so much because of any European precedence but because of the immediate experience of the colonial state's endorsement of English literary studies as the study of a national culture rather than of a mere collection of texts; and Grierson adopted this premise as the reconciliatory ground for various legacies he dealt with.

The latter is indeed the story of literary studies in India as it developed in the early decades of the nineteenth century and as it increasingly promoted a set of secular values held together by the national narrative. Gauri Viswanathan suggests that after the Charter Act of 1813, and especially in the 1820s, "when the classical curriculum still reigned supreme in England despite the strenuous efforts of some concerned critics to loosen its hold, English as the study of culture and not simply the study of language had already found a secure place in the British Indian curriculum" (*MC*, 3). English literature, she notes, stood for a host of values and ideas – often expressed in the critical shorthand of the "ideal Englishman" – that were deemed necessary training for colonial subjects (*MC*, 20). In this process, the notion of national literature was given an official stamp of approval.

One may not agree entirely with Viswanathan's thesis of the unidirectional intentionality of the colonizer, but the point remains that the national orientation and the core of literary studies could not have happened without the colonial context. It would be quite difficult, without the colonial question, to account for the vastly different curricula introduced in England and India around the same time. It would be even more difficult to explain the progressive secularization of Indian education under colonial rule without the volatile circumstances in the colony that warranted religious neutrality on the ruler's part. In such cases, and as a response to sundry other crises and contradictions within the colonial regime, national literature emerged as the preferred narrative – preferred because it showed extraordinary flexibility in addressing the concerns of warring groups and interests, and it offered a resilient model of cultural hegemony that suited the colonial state.

I wish to discuss two important threads from Viswanathan's larger argument to make my point on Grierson and the survey. First, she suggests that the initial transition from language teaching to teaching of culture happened when colonial rulers discovered that certain aesthetic qualities said to be inculcated by literature – for example, "industriousness, efficiency, trustworthiness, and compliance" – were also qualities that could be harnessed gainfully for the successful running of the government (*MC*, 93). It was important to think of a unified field that would demonstrate such qualities and that would train colonial subjects aesthetically rather than through explicitly religious texts. English literature representing national cultural and moral values was the answer, allowing the colonial regime to secure a curious aesthetic dimension for its political rule. Grierson extended this thesis further and suggested national literature as the ground upon which distinct identities could be established. Just as English literature represented national characters and proved beneficial to colonial rule, national literatures in different Indian languages had a similar effect and comparable political advantage. For instance, he discusses a number of languages overcoming the vagaries of dialects and pronunciation through the standardization of a literary version that could consolidate a political identity. The "ideal Englishman" thus found his local counterparts almost everywhere, and it was possible for Grierson to place them on neat tables of comparison.

More important for my purpose here is Viswanathan's account of the Orientalist–Anglicist debate, which allows one to track an alternative version of the secularization thesis (see *MC*, 77, 99). It would be misleading to see the debate purely as two distinct schools of thought staking claims on Indian education, since these two schools shared a number of common concerns. Chief among them were anxieties regarding the indigenous educated classes (mostly *maulvis* and *pundits*), who exerted enormous influence on native populations and the status of religion in their pedagogical practices. Viswanathan suggests that, behind these concerns, one can detect larger philosophical questions about the status of knowledge and methods of learning and the suitability of Indian texts as acceptable means of training. Through a set of strenuous arguments, the Anglicists tried to show that European literature in general and English more specifically shared a less direct relationship with religion, and consequently the status of the literary work was primarily marked by intellectual labor and not divine intervention. In contrast, Indian texts – especially classics such as the *Rāmāyana* and the *Mahābhārata* – were debilitatingly dependent on religion. As a result, the status of the literary in them remained stilted at best.

Such texts, aided by *maulvis* and *pundits*, perpetuated error and falsehood and could not aspire to have the same effect as their Western counterparts; as the missionary Alexander Duff observed in this context, Indian literature could not offer "a single volume on any one subject that is not studded with error, far less a series of volumes that would furnish anything bearing the most distant resemblance to a complete range of information in any conceivable department of useful knowledge" (quoted in *MC*, 109). Indian texts could not be trusted, both James Mill and Hegel asserted,

Subject to National Literature 139

even for historical instructions, because a combination of lack of historical records and excessive reliance on poetic imagination rendered these texts unsuitable for the purpose. As a remedy, Viswanathan notes, the "Protestant Reformation provided a historical model for the relocation of authority in the body of knowledge represented by English literary texts. The characterization of English literature as intellectual production implicated a different process of reading, requiring the exercise of reason rather than unquestioning faith" (*MC*, 109). If Orientalists attempted a gradual erosion of the authority of native learning without disturbing its religious underpinning too much, the Anglicists ironically used a religious model to block such efforts and hasten the death of Oriental learning.

The irony of the situation was not lost on everyone. Soon such debates concentrated on the central question of truth that might not need a religious frame in order for it to be articulated. This new concept thus had to find a new model to replace religion, not only Christianity but also Hinduism and Islam. History was seen as the ideal choice for this purpose. Viswanathan demonstrates how history pervaded the domain hitherto occupied by religion and how a narrow historicism came to define literary studies in India (see *MC*, 121–6). This new historicism made conscious efforts to justify both colonial occupation and the new educational model, as well as to explain the national character of the new literature. By the end of the century, when Grierson began working on his survey, he readily borrowed this historicist model of literature and used it as his foundation.

Let me make my point with an example from the survey. In volume five, part one of his survey, Grierson offers a detailed account of two of the major Eastern "Indo-Aryan" languages, Bengali and Assamese. For Bengali, as for all other languages, he cites a series of authorities to authenticate his conclusions about the language. Interestingly enough, he quotes the same sources for both the language and its literary tradition and makes little distinction between the two as historical phenomena. These authorities include a long description of European citations of the language, people from Bengal, or even texts in the language: João de Barros's *Décadas da Ásia* (vol. 1, 1552); David Wilkins's letter to LaCroze of Berlin (1714); Chamberlayne's *Sylloge* (1715); the first Bengali grammar in Portuguese (1743); Johann Fritz's *Orientalisch-und-occidentalischer Sprachmeister* (1748); Cassiano Beligatti's Latin pamphlet *Alphabetum brammhanicum seu indostanum Universitatis Kasi* (1771); and finally Halhed's Bengali grammar (1778).[45] This list, intended to establish historical antecedents, is then followed by further lists of texts under the following headings: "General" (twelve titles), "Grammars and Reading-Books" (thirty-four titles), "Dictionaries" (forty-six titles), and "Literature, etc." (seventeen titles). Only one heading – "Grammars and Reading Books" – includes a large number of texts written in Bengali, while the others mostly rely on texts written by British experts and a small number of texts written by Indians in English. There are a few overlaps; for instance, J. Beames's *Comparative Grammar* appears both under "Grammars and Reading-Books" and under "Literature, etc."[46]

The point I am trying to make is that the underlying assumption behind the layout for Bengali (or any other language for that matter) in the survey is both historicist and territorial. Grierson works here and elsewhere within a framework that requires him to establish the identity of a language for the survey. Accordingly, he includes a series of markers that are verifiable historically and thus attest to the essence and extent of a language. Classifying Bengali literature along with other categories such as the area in which it is spoken, the general character of the language, or the total number of speakers of Bengali introduces a way of seeing and conceptualizing languages that makes little distinction between descriptive categories as long as they are subjected to the key rubric of history. This law of equivalence is extended not only to larger categories through which a language's identity has to be established but also to its inner mechanisms. Thus the survey consciously avoids making any distinction between literary texts and grammar/lexicography on the grounds that both are closely tied to the language and in similar historical ways.

But this historicist notion can only be related territorially. Grierson has the census reports of 1891 in mind when he proposes this law of equivalence as both an external and an internal organizing principle for a language. Census reports in the colonies gave credibility to the method that suggested that discrete objects and facts could be placed next to each other without any inherent value claim just because they happened to be territorially simultaneous. The logic of this organization of land and language was necessary for the colonial state; it claimed to unearth newer, governmental relations between objects under survey through a juxtaposition that other forms of record keeping could not reveal. Grierson thus readjusts the vital lesson of English literary studies in India – that languages and literatures ought to be seen as historical beings programmed with an internal telos – and expresses it as part of a governmental technology that seeks to access knowledge of the governed through equivalence and comparison.

Nowhere is this more prominent than in the map from the fifth volume of the survey, where extents of different "Indo-Aryan" languages of eastern

Subject to National Literature

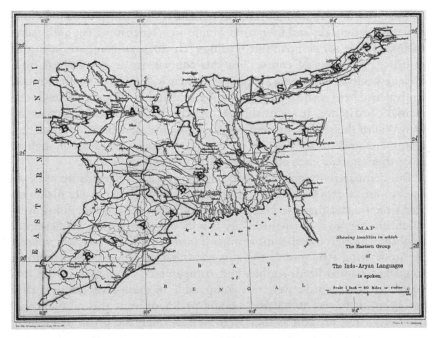

Figure 3.4 George Abraham Grierson, "Map Showing the Localities in Which the Eastern Group of the Indo-Aryan Languages Is Spoken," in *Linguistic Survey of India*, 11 Vols. (Calcutta: Government of India Central Publication Branch, 1903–28), vol. v, Part 1, frontispiece.

India are arranged carefully to correspond to the administrative map generated by the census reports of 1891 and 1901 (Figure 3.4). This map is the culmination of the two philological–governmental legacies I have charted in previous sections because here Grierson combines Jones and Hodgson–Hunter within the space of the map as supplementary philological techniques in the service of the colonial state. The map's two outlines duplicate each other, with the clear signal that the area demarcated is a legitimate object of appropriation. When the two merge in neat correspondence, when their symmetry and intertexuality are established without too many rough edges, the new method of organizing languages achieves its final approval. It can now claim, like the colonial state, that it has produced new knowledge of the land by calibrating its methods through the vital principle of historicity and territoriality.

Quite crucially, this map (and other similar maps scattered across the eleven volumes of the survey) represents the foundational model of comparative literary studies. It territorializes, with the help of colonial cartography, languages and literatures caught in a synchronic cut and makes them available for comparative readings. The logic of comparison in this case is equivalence, of course, but this equivalence is not derived from their respective evolutionary histories or their individual richness. Rather, equivalence here is surprisingly value-neutral and is achieved through territorial coexistence. It seems the fact that Bihari, Assamese, Bengali, and Oriya (with their speaking communities, literatures, dialects, dictionaries, grammars, and so on) exist in territorial contiguity is reason enough to place them next to each other and within a comparative frame.

But comparativity does not stop here. To get the full measure of it, we need to return to Grierson's methodology as quoted above. He makes no secret of the fact that the crucial transition from Jones's fanciful universal chronology to this synchronicity is achieved through the mediation of English. Through translations from and into English, he was able to erect the underlying structure of the survey, which rendered different Indian languages standardized, legible, and comparable. The languages he surveyed, in other words, were not comparable in themselves. Even if they had been, there was no reliable method to demonstrate this mutual comparability. But, as soon as they were seen through the prism of English, they became amenable to the cause of the survey. This method implies the violence of the colonial linguistic policy that prevented Grierson from comparing these languages amongst themselves despite his own historiography, which established their common descent and overlapping growth. Reading languages thus would have amounted to a return to the orientalist dream of family resemblance. On the other hand, English, whose historical being was already established (not least through literary studies), had the potential to mediate in the same way that colonial cartography did without going back to the orientalist narrative. It could unburden languages of their histories, and it could place them side by side without disturbing their synchronic beings. The map indeed highlighted graphically this underlying principle of comparatism; if one replaced Bengali, Assamese, and others with their European counterparts, one would get the template for our modern programs of comparative literary studies.

Archiving Newness

Such a project of comparative literary studies was no mere speculation for Grierson. Indeed, in 1888, long before the survey, he published a lengthy comparative study of vernacular literatures of northern India in a special issue of the *Journal of the Asiatic Society of Bengal*. The issue was published as a separate volume the following year as *The Modern Vernacular Literature of Hindustan*. As if in anticipation of the survey and its methodology, Grierson in this study employs both chronological simultaneity and territorial contiguity to offer a comparative study of three literary languages – "Mār'wārī, Hindī, and Bihārī" – and of their various "dialects."[47] For the chronological claim he states that the "muse of History, so silent in Sanskrit literature, has been assiduously cultivated by these authors [of vernacular literature], and we have still extant historical works founded on materials which were written so far back as the ninth century" (*MVL*, x–xi). And on the territorial point, he adds that "by Hindūstān I mean Rǎj'putānā and the valleys of the Jamunā and of the Ganges as far east as the river Kōsī, and that I do not include under that term either the Pañjāb or Lower Bangāl" (*MVL*, viii).

The point of this dual exercise is of course to set limits to the scope of the study and to produce a manageable field within which comparatism as a principle could produce the desired results. But Grierson uses such limits to vigorously identify the Indian modern with the Indian vernacular as coproduced phenomena in history and hence coterminous. In his scheme of things, these two qualities together constitute an independent field of vernacular literature that supersedes earlier methods of understanding literary work and makes comparatism not only possible but even the exclusive means. When he criticizes earlier attempts such as Garcin de Tassy's *Histoire de la littérature hindoui et hindoustani* (1839) – which Grierson cites as somewhat limited in ambition and scope – he does so with the conviction that comparatism remains weak in such studies because de Tassy and others miss the central point of vernaculars being essentially modern and vice versa.[48]

In a striking passage Grierson elaborates:

> When they [vernacular authors of India] wrote, the language spoken was practically the same as that spoken now in the rural parts of India, and they must have felt the same hesitation which Spenser and Milton felt in writing in their vernacular. Spenser chose the wrong method and cast his *Faërie Queene* into an antique mould, but Milton, though he once thought of writing his *Paradise Lost* in Latin, dared to be right, and thenceforward the English language was made. So was it in India, – the first vernacular authors dared greatly, and succeeded. (*MVL*, xix)

He makes the important claim that vernacularization of literary traditions is at the root of both national literatures and comparative methods, with the rider that English literary history, once again, provides the theoretical framework. This is a point that will receive its fuller treatment in

Auerbach's *Mimesis* (though via Dante Alighieri and not Edmund Spenser or John Milton) as the great moment of vernacularization in European literature.[49]

But what Grierson proposes is, in effect, the very ground for comparative literature as a modern discipline. Away from Jones's project of universal comparatism that stretches across time and territory, Grierson offers the possibility of exploring a unified field with strictly demarcated borders and internal rules. The distinction he makes between "an antique mould" and vernacularization, for instance, is a markedly modern one. For my purpose, however, what is more immediate is Grierson's suggestion that through this distinction, and through the constrictions posed by the very notion of the vernacular, one can approach literature as a delimited field – a field founded on the colonial territory and explored through its ethnographic modalities. Within this limited field, within its contours, comparatism unfolds as a methodological paradigm.

Grierson's text makes conscious attempts to replicate this idea through myriad sources divided into two major groups. The first consists of "innumerable texts bought in the bazārs" and other "native sources." He lists eighteen such sources, published between 1550 and 1887 (from *Bhakt Mālā* by Nabhājī Dās to *Bichitrōpadēs* by Nak'chhēdī Tiwārī), and suggests that he has been particularly reliant on a previous, and somewhat similar, text by an Indian authority – *Sib Siṅgh Sarōj* (1878) by Sib Siṅgh Sēgar (*MVL*, xiii–xiv). An Inspector of Police from Avadh in northern India, Sēgar or Semgar collated information about 1,000 poets and published detailed accounts of 836 of them in his anthology. As Stuart Blackburn and Vasudha Dalmia note, his primary aim was to "fill a gap in vernacular poetry, that is, historical information regarding the poets themselves," and this desire effectively suggested in the text "an unbroken, hermetically sealed lineage, encompassing the entire Hindi-speaking heartland of North India."[50] Grierson states that, although he frequently crosschecked information provided in this text, especially dates, he nonetheless used it as his primary guide.

The second set of sources for Grierson includes texts by European authorities: apart from Garcin de Tassy, he also lists H. H. Wilson's *Sketch on the Religious Sects of the Hindus* (1828–32, *Asiatic Researches*, Vols. XVI and XVII) and James Tod's *Annals and Antiquities of Rajasthan* (1829) (*MVL*, xiii).[51] Wilson was Assistant Surgeon of the East India Company and later Boden Professor of Sanskrit at Oxford, while Tod was colonel and Government Agent of the Company to various princely states in Rajasthan. Within this detailing of sources, Grierson performs a fundamental change – if the "idea that India is a unique national civilization in possession of a "classical" culture was first postulated on the terrain of literature," which emerged from the early orientalist working in Calcutta in the 1780s, as Mufti argues, Grierson now shows that the modernity of that literature lies in the vernacular traceable only through a network of native sources, colonial records, and intricate governmental networks.[52] Within this new territory, literature takes on new meanings, and departs from classical models in its quest to embody the vernacular spirit of northern India.

Grierson contends that his text, strictly speaking, is not "a formal History of Literature," though he hopes that "as a collection of *materials* [it] will form a foundation upon which others more fortunate than I am, and with more time at their disposal than a Bengal District Collector, may build" (*MVL*, ix). And yet, in his text he offers some important insights into the new idea of literature emerging from the colonial missions in the late nineteenth century. In his text, for instance, he provides entries on individual poets and their works (following de Tassy and Sēgar), with additional information including dates and place of birth and so on. In closely set columns, and through copious citation of his sources, these entries, however, replicate the comparative tables we have encountered in Hodgson and Hunter. Every page is arranged to give us a sense that we are indeed moving through comparative tables of literary figures and texts, and we are invited to place them next to each other. At the same time, his extraordinary emphasis on precise dates for each poet, and his desire to produce a chronological literary history of the territory under consideration, unmistakably evoke Jones's legacy across these individual entries.

My point is that this text in many ways anticipated the survey in its method, with the proviso that colonial governance could now justifiably rely on literature as a useful source. This connection with the survey is reinforced in the second feature of the text – in its introduction, Grierson effectively spells out the historical schema he was to later invoke for his survey, at least for North-Indian languages. He clearly conceives vernacular literary tradition as an organic one, passing through different phases of infancy, maturity, and so on, culminating in its "Augustan age" during the sixteenth and seventeenth centuries. It is a fascinating coincidence, he notes, that all the great authors of this age "were contemporaries with our masters of the reign of Elizabeth, and, to us English, it is interesting to note that when our country first came into contact by its ambassadors with the Mughal court, and when the East India Company was first founded, each of the nations, separated so widely by sea and land, was at its culminating point of literary glory" (*MLV*, xix). This coincidence also gave him a clue, it seems, encouraging him to narrate the Indian story along lines of the structures and periods of the English one. And this historical narrative, as I have shown above, also underscored the survey and its documentation of modern Indian vernaculars.

What is distinctly new in Grierson's account, however, is the closing of gaps between literature and ethnographic documentation of the colony. Indeed, it is possible to argue that for him the integrity of the colony was largely manifest in its literary production, since literature managed to overcome political rivalry resulting in territorial fragmentation. In his story, hence, the vernacular tradition lost its vitality with the decline of the mighty Mughals. As the subcontinent descended into a period of political instability and chaos in the final decades of the Mughal era, vernacular tradition also entered into its barren period. Things changed, however, with the entry of the British, as print technologies and sponsorship rejuvenated the sagging careers of vernacular literatures and resulted in nothing short of a "renascence" in the first half of the nineteenth century (*MVL*, xxii). With this newfound verve, aided by colonial institutions such as the Fort William College in Calcutta, according to Grierson, vernacular literature in India secured a stable being. This new literature, so to speak, in his texts and the survey appears through the intense and extensive network of colonial governance, with a clear ethnographic foundation, and displays its modernity through its ability to be part of the colonial territory. In its new avatar, literature chose the colony as its world, and remained beholden to governmental technologies for the affirmation of its being.

PART II
Aesthetic Conventions

CHAPTER 4

Impure Aesthetics

With the colonial paradigm of the literary sovereign, as I have defined it in the first part of this book, the modern culture of letters was all set to be transformed, not only in the colony but also across imperial borders and beyond. In a way, this was the natural outcome of the imperial culture with its connected geographies and channels of rapid communications; and the new scholarship on the literary originating in British India exploited these communication routes to the fullest to become the dominant paradigm across traditions and cultures. One of the ways Europe made sense of the new paradigm, I argue in this chapter, was the concept of *Weltliteratur* or world literature. This idea of world literature is usually traced back to Johann Wolfgang von Goethe.[1] Though he did not coin the term – it was already in circulation among some members of Weimar Classicism such as Christoph Martin Wieland[2] – Goethe nevertheless first articulated a consolidated vision and program for world literature, which was later appropriated by a range of enthusiasts, including the Romantics in the nineteenth century and the Anglo-American votaries of comparative literature as an academic discipline in the twentieth.

In his conversations with Johann Peter Eckermann, Goethe offered two important observations which have had different fates in subsequent discussions – while his projected opposition between "world literature" and "national literature" received enthusiastic support both as an ideal and subsequently as a virtual reality in globalization, his other point about the characteristic aesthetic experience (of ascribing certain "value" to "what is foreign") of this new corpus got somewhat lost.[3] It is important to note that for Goethe the invocation of the age of world literature was an essential gesture in prolepsis – yet to come and in need of deliberate labor. Within this temporal image, with what Mikhail Bakhtin identifies as Goethe's unusual ability to "*see time* [...] in everything,"[4] unfolded the distinct aesthetic experience he associated with world literature. Only as part of this unbound future did world literature as a manifestation of the literary sovereign with its unique aesthetic value and modes of circulation make sense to him.

In this chapter, I argue that Goethe's proleptic vision (of time, aesthetics, and circulation) was grounded not in any single concept of the Enlightenment era – say, Alexander Baumgarten's "aesthetics" or the more generalized notion of "disinterested" pleasure – but within a salient trajectory of late-Enlightenment aesthetic theory best captured by Immanuel Kant's anthropological lectures between 1772–3 and 1796 and finally by his *Anthropologie in pragmatischer Hinsicht* (*Anthropology from a Pragmatic Point of View*, 1798): that is, the confluence of *anthropology* and *sensibility*.[5] I propose to read Kant's *Anthropology* and *Kritik der Urteilskraft* (*Critique of the Power of Judgment*, 1790) together as constituting an aesthetic field that launched this futuristic encounter with foreignness, as a way of coming to terms with the new history and scholarship on the literary that was invading Europe since the eighteenth century.

Anthropology as a discipline, with its deep ties with imperialism, was indeed Europe's response to the experience of colonial otherness, as many scholars have noted; but, combined with the new notion of aesthetics (as distinct from, say, the earlier idea of *aisthetikos*), it offered a way of engaging with texts that came from different cultural milieus. It prepared a ground for evaluating the combination of beauty and morality in culturally different texts, of appraising what Kant often called the former's "feeling of life" (*Lebensgefühl*) and the latter's "feeling of spirit" (*Geistesgefühl*).[6] Both for the literary sovereign and for world literature, this combination of anthropology and aesthetic judgment, and its popularity after Kant and Goethe, was going to be a crucial development.

Partly, this argument rests on Goethe's appreciation of Kant's work – especially the *Critique of the Power of Judgment* and *Anthropology* – despite their radically opposing views on a number of other issues. Ernst Cassirer has claimed that "Kant's *Critique of Judgement* […] constructs, as it were, *a priori* the concept of Goethe's poetry, and […] what the latter presents as achievement and act is founded and demanded in the former by the pure necessity of philosophical thought."[7] Both Cassirer and Géza von Molnár argue that Kant's aesthetic theory had a profound influence on Goethe after 1790 at the latest and deeply influenced some of his major works, including *Wilhelm Meisters Lehrjahre* (*Wilhelm Meister's Apprenticeship*, 1795–6) and *Faust* (1808).[8] This is evident in Goethe's own assessment of Kant's work as well – during a conversation with Eckermann on April 11, 1827, for instance, Goethe suggested, invoking Kant as the most important proponent of the "new philosophy," that Kant's "doctrines […] have penetrated most deeply into our German civilization." Even if Eckermann was not familiar with Kant's work firsthand, he was nonetheless influenced by those doctrines. Goethe maintained that Kant's influence on "German civilization" was so profound that it could be taken as forming a sort of philosophical common sense that entered ideas and conversations without conscious effort or direct citation. Of all these "doctrines," he singled out the third *Critique* and told Eckermann that if he wished to read Kant he should start with the "'Critique on the Power of Judgment,' in which he has written admirably upon rhetoric, tolerably upon poetry, but unsatisfactorily on plastic art."[9]

Equally important for my purpose is Goethe's interest and investment in anthropology from the 1770s, which began almost immediately after he joined the administration of Saxony-Weimar, and his progressive reliance on the works of Kant, Blumenbach, Herder, and others for both literary and scientific writing.[10] This conjoining of aesthetics and anthropology in Goethe was no doubt quickened by his exposure to a range of texts coming out of the colonial world (including Wilkins's and Jones's translations, which I have discussed in Chapters 1–3), and this had a profound influence on his musings on world literature. What distinguished this phase in both Kant and Goethe, I propose, is the emergence of an *impure aesthetics* that was designed specifically for the newness of the era.[11] This impurity was the product of a constitutive dilemma in Kantian aesthetics – between the universalist claims of aesthetic judgment and its limited empirical application – and the subsequent quest for a reconciliatory ground. He figured out that, in the absence of any a priori principle for a "critique of taste," he would have to find this reconciliation elsewhere, and likewise he suggested that anthropology offered that empirical ground.

In a significant departure from contemporary discussions by Baumgarten and Hume, Kant took aesthetics away from cognition and rearticulated it (following Rousseau) within anthropological categories such as that of "human nature" or "character." Such a move was mediated by his interest in race and racial difference, and he found it appropriate to enlist the insights of the so-called "race sciences" in fashioning his concept. Racial difference and hierarchy in this case worked as a template and a parallel, and allowed him to explain the contingencies of aesthetic judgment. Goethe used this Kantian formulation to define the "world" of world literature, and then deployed this anthropologically inflected formula to build the new aesthetic regime. As I demonstrate below, it was through Kant's idea of bringing anthropology and aesthetics together that Goethe could imagine the coming epoch of world literature.

Kant and the Modern Aesthetic Regime

Kant has been placed at the beginning of the modern aesthetic regime or even modernity in a number of philosophical accounts over the years. Here I want to briefly discuss three of them that I find particularly important for my argument. In the first instance, Philippe Lacoue-Labarthe and Jean-Luc Nancy maintain that the modern conceptualization of literature arose with the Jena Romantics and the journal *Athenaeum* (1798–1800), and that this theory was a response to Kant's critical projects. While events like the French Revolution or widespread economic depression occasioned major upheavals in late eighteenth-century Europe, it was the crisis of philosophical thought, prompted by Kantian critiques, they argue, that the early German Romantics addressed most directly. At the heart of this crisis was Kant's proposition in the first two *Critiques* that the Idea of the subject, the fulcrum of his project, is unpresentable to itself by way of reason alone. In the transcendental schema of Kant, as presented in the *Critique of Pure Reason* (1781), the most radical suggestion is not the partition between the sensible and the intelligible or even between understanding and reason, but the point that there is no adequate correspondence between the Idea and its presentation. Even in Kant's transcendental aesthetics in the *Power of the Critique of Judgment*, Lacoue-Labarthe and Nancy suggest, this problem recurs as the text repeatedly points out that whether "situated as *arche* or as *telos*," the Idea of the subject can never present itself to itself as a substantial unity. As a result, they declare, the "Kantian 'cogito' is empty."[12]

At stake in this Kantian schema is the question of *Darstellung* (variously translated into English as presentation, exhibition, figuration, description, or staging), which was introduced in the very first *Critique*. Irrespective of whether one conceives the subject "by means of the Beautiful in works of art" or through the "sublime, taken as the presentation of the unpresentable," Lacoue-Labarthe and Nancy insist, *Darstellung* remains an analogical approximation in Kant's oeuvre and especially in the third *Critique*. To put it differently, in the absence of a subject "whose self-presence is guaranteed by originary intuition," as would have been required by transcendental aesthetics, the Kantian critical project remains unresolved.[13] Consequently, across the three *Critiques*, one witnesses a chasm that can neither be sublated nor wished away, forcing him to admit that the crucial question of "What is man?" cannot be effectively answered by philosophy.

The Romantic breakthrough came in the form of what Lacoue-Labarthe and Nancy call "eidaesthetics" (combining both *eidos* and *aisthetikos*), which "gathers, concentrates, and brings to a climax the metaphysics of the *Idea*, of the Idea's self-knowledge in its auto-manifestation."[14] Eidaesthetics for them marks a "double determination," where the form or Idea is not complete in itself, but "must be seen for itself" through a process of "auto-illumination." The Jena Romantics captured this point by reconstituting the problem of *Darstellung* within the realm of aesthetics – within, more specifically, the metagenre of *literature* – as a space available for both production and reflection, by placing "criticism simultaneously in the space of the 'auto-illumination' of the beautiful work and in the space, in every work, of the absence of the Work."[15]

This formulation is precisely what allows them to say finally that Romanticism, in a crucial sense, completes the Kantian project:

> If the Kantian *schema* was the never *truly* explained union of concept and intuition, the romantic *character* is its explication and the figure provided for its truth. It fulfills the most proper power of the proper; that of engendering itself in its proper form, and of grasping its unity and beauty in a single trait. It restores the *idiom* of judgment, that idiom which appears in the "mother tongue" whose fate "On the Essence of Criticism" links to that of "romantic poetry." Characteristics – as might have been suspected – is an idiomatics; and as an idiomatics, romanticism seeks to perfect eidaesthetics, according to the sole eidaesthetic motif to which it cares to respond. The literary genre is the idiomatics of the Idea.[16]

If Kant's subject-system remained empty because of its lack of unity between the Idea and its *Darstellung*, or stayed divided between *arche* and *telos*, in Lacoue-Labarthe and Nancy's opinion Romanticism addressed it with the concept of eidaesthetic literature that illuminates its own being through self-presentation.

I shall return to this argument and its implication in a moment, but let me register here two problematic areas of Lacoue-Labarthe and Nancy's argument. While they note Kant's position that the crucial question of "What is man?" cannot be satisfactorily resolved by philosophy, they remain surprisingly silent about the other half of this statement – Kant also suggested at the same time that this question can be answered only by anthropology.[17] Throughout the text, this point gets elided, and they deploy various maneuverings to gloss over the final phase of Kant's life that combined anthropology and critical geography from what he called "*pragmatische Hinsicht*" or a "pragmatic point of view" as a counterpoint to philosophy.[18] This suppression of anthropology occasions the second difficulty in *The Literary Absolute* – their methodology does not allow one to see the specificities of eidaesthetics, especially why and how it crossed

European borders in the nineteenth century and reached different cultures and textual traditions across the globe.

However, Kant again makes an appearance in Jacques Rancière's work as the beginning point for modern aesthetics. Almost echoing the first *Critique*, Rancière suggests that aesthetics is "the system of *a priori* forms determining what presents itself to sense experience."[19] In this formulation the problem of *Darstellung* is addressed obliquely, by making aesthetics the very constitution of the "distribution of the sensible in any politics."[20] If Kant's project of describing the cognition of the sensible world by a reasonable subject remains inconclusive, as Lacoue-Labarthe and Nancy argue, Rancière proposes an innovative solution – he anchors this impasse within politics, with the suggestion that this problematic in Kant can be adequately addressed only if one situates it within the history of the modern political subject. Aesthetics is not simply added to the Kantian schema, as Romanticism allegedly sought to do, but is made a condition of possibility for the subject of modern democratic politics, and as such it is seen as the very mechanism of the subject's auto-presentation. Rancière in fact states that, in Kant's third *Critique*, the beautiful is "a promise of equality" that "seeks the anticipation of the perceptible equality to come, of the *humanity* that will be the joint surpassing of the culture of the dominant and the culture of Rousseauist nature."[21] For him, this Kantian utopia was partially realized in Friedrich Schiller's grand proposal for the aesthetic education of humankind.

What makes this reformulation of Kant particularly important for us is the way Rancière narrates the emergence of the modern idea of literature within this aesthetic regime, and, additionally, the way he links this event not only to philosophy or philology but also to other knowledge paradigms of the early nineteenth century. The historicity of literature, and also the autonomy of its own being, cannot be separated from this distribution of the sensible – Rancière points out that "literature as literature" becomes thinkable only when it is "conceived neither as the art of writing in general nor as a specific state of the language, but as a historical mode of visibility of writing, a specific link between a system of meaning of words and a system of visibility of things."[22] It is in the democratic petrification both of language and of the world of things, and in the relationship between the two, that literature as an autonomous being materialized.

What was only a utopian promise of equality in Kantian aesthetics found its final destination in the works of such authors as Gustave Flaubert and Honoré de Balzac, in their ability to establish a new and democratic connection between the order of words and the order of things. Rancière often cites the opening sequence of Balzac's novel *La Peau de chagrin* (1831) as announcing this new idea of literature and its mode of doing politics. In this sequence Raphaël, the protagonist of the novel, enters a Parisian antique shop and encounters a range of objects from different ages and different parts of the world, put together on a gallery. This rather random juxtaposition not only made "all objects and images equal," Rancière submits, but also indicated a new representational order in which "their random gathering made a huge poem, each verse of which carried the infinite virtuality of new stories, unfolding those signs in new contexts."[23] Balzac's novel is important for him because it signaled two things at once: first, the death of earlier aesthetic conventions that presumed representational hierarchy between forms and genres; and then the arrival of a new mode of visibility for literary writing that relied on the principle of democratic petrification. I shall take up Rancière's proposition below and in Chapter 5 for detailed discussion.

In the final instance, Michel Foucault locates Kant at the threshold of modernity but within an ambiguous space – Kant is simultaneously lauded for awakening philosophy from its "dogmatic" slumber and censured for lulling it into the "anthropological sleep." Referring to Kant's *Logic*, Foucault argues that it is the final question of "*Was ist der Mensch?* [What is man?]" – which Kant added to his three questions enumerated in *Critique of Pure Reason* in 1781 ("What can I know? What ought I to do? What may I hope?"[24]) – that prepares the ground for the anthropologization of philosophy and introduces the crucial uncertainty between the empirical and the transcendental.[25] Kant does not stop at adding yet another question to the existing list but goes on even to say: "*Metaphysics* answers the first question, *morals* the second, *religion* the third, and *anthropology* the fourth. Fundamentally, however, we could reckon all of this as anthropology, because the first three questions relate to the last one."[26]

Kant's reduction of earlier questions from his critical period to the singular notion of anthropology prompts Foucault to suggest that anthropology as an "analytic of man" in this formulation constitutes man within an irreducible duality – human being is the empirical object of knowing while the same human being is also the transcendental ground for this knowledge to take place. "In this Fold," he writes, "the transcendental function is doubled over so that it covers with its dominating network the inert, grey space of empiricity; inversely, empirical contents are given life, gradually pull themselves upright, and are immediately subsumed in a discourse which carries their transcendental presumption into the distance."[27] From this point and during the nineteenth century, anthropology defined the limit or "finitude" not only of the human being but also of any form of philosophical thinking by tying such thought to the human being in the transcendental–empirical duality. Anthropology, in other words, performed a fundamental restructuring of knowledge in modernity by instating the human being at both ends of knowing and by making the human being both its alibi and its final destination.

In his *Introduction to Kant's Anthropology*, however, Foucault offers a larger framework within which Kant's anthropology needs to be located, and I want to borrow this frame as a historical parallel to the project of *Weltliteratur*. Foucault locates at the heart of Kant's *Anthropology from a Pragmatic Point of View* the overpowering drive to connect with physical geography under the conceptual paradigm of *Weltkenntnis* or knowledge/cognition of the world.[28] Within Kant's anthropological vision, Foucault suggests, the human being is always a *citizen of the world* and hence, in order to develop anthropology as a disciplinary ground of inquiry, it becomes necessary for him not only to define this *world* but also to distinguish between a cosmological view of the *universe* "that would organize geography and anthropology in advance and by rights" and "a cosmopolitical perspective with a programmatic value, in which the *world* is envisaged more as a republic to be built than a cosmos given in advance."[29]

The resultant "world" of the cosmopolitical perspective is not an inert natural unit reaching the purported "man" of anthropology as a finished product that can hardly be changed or acted upon; rather it is an earth (*Erde*) that is built around habitation and labor. Kant further highlights the contrast by making a distinction between "to *know* the world [*die Welt kennen*]" and "to *have* the world [*die Welt haben*]" – the first is analogous to watching a play, whereas the latter is more like performing in it. Kant's anthropology is pragmatic and not physiological precisely because it does not stop at investigating "what *he* as a free-acting being makes of himself, or can and should make of himself."[30] The cosmopolitical world underwrites the space inhabited by this free-acting being, and it is produced, Kant insists, through knowledge ("schooling" in his words) and not through intuition. Knowledge of the world becomes pragmatic anthropology not only when it includes "*things* in the world" but when it "contains knowledge of the human being as a *citizen of the world*" (A, 4; emphasis original).

Foucault's gloss on the "world" in Kant's anthropology is of some importance for my purpose here. He argues that Kant's question "What is man?" is hardly answered in the text of *Anthropology* alone, though ostensibly it is this very question that prompted Kant to compose the text out of his lecture notes towards the end of his life. Rather, one needs to take both the *Logic* and the *Opus Postumum* to complete the philosophical query Kant sets to answer and the eventual resolution he comes up with. The central insight offered by these three texts together, Foucault notes, is that knowledge of the human being already implies knowledge of the world, but not in a naturalist way. Kant is not repeating the naturalist position that the human being as an animal is but an extension of nature, and hence knowledge of one would automatically lead to that of the other. Far from it. His primary concern in *Anthropology* is the human being as a moral agent who masters the art of self-fashioning according to given universal laws and practices. In order to follow Kant's formulation, it is perhaps more productive to start with the trio Kant often repeats in the fragments of his *Opus Postumum* – "God, the world, and man as a person"[31] – and one can also argue that the totality of the first two elements is properly revealed in the third one.

In response to his fourth question, Kant seems to pose the human being as the "universal synthesis" in which the "personality of God and the objectivity of the world are rejoined" (*IKA*, 78). The difficulty of taking this as Kant's final statement is that, since he has already argued the human being to be primarily a citizen of the world (both *Weltbürger* and *Weltbewohner*), he cannot restrict this universal synthesis to the fragile boundaries of the human being and has to have a corresponding notion of the world within which the human being will face himself/herself as if in a depthless mirror. He has to have, in sum, a new notion of the world which is different from the naturalist view of the universe and at the same time in possession of its own internal operations in a way that would make it intelligible enough to the anthropological human being. Foucault suggests a number of ways to think of this world as part of Kant's transcendental philosophy: "It is in the implications of 'I am' that the world is discovered"; "the world of the *Opus Postumum* is the concomitant of the determination of the self as the objective content of experience in general"; and finally, "[i]t is no longer the correlative of a *Zeitbestimmung*, but the presupposition of a *Sinnenbestimmung* of the self" (*IKA*, 79–80).

From these preliminary observations, Foucault derives three major characteristics of the cosmopolitical world to which the human being belongs as a citizen. First, unlike the physical universe, the "world is the root of existence, the *source*, which, *containing* existence, manages both to *retain* it and to *set it free*" (*IKA*, 79–80; emphasis original). This duality is captured in Kant's use of the word *Inbegriff* or embodiment which suggests that the world is not the sum of physical laws leading to *Physis* but both the condition of experience and the eventual goal of its totality. Second, again unlike the physical universe, which is by definition one, the worlds of anthropology can be many. The naturalist universe is the totality of all possible relations, and hence its unity can be achieved only in its singularity. On the other hand, the world is made of a subset of all possible relations – which Foucault calls "real" relations – and thus it leaves room enough to imagine different worlds with different relations (*IKA*, 79–80). These two points define the world in an essential opposition to the universe and suggest that Kant's anthropology imagines the world as a "synthesis" of present where culture as both practice and labor provides the essential fabric of real relations between individuals. Whether seen as experience or as relations, what the world inexorably leads to is cultural practices in their immediacy, and Foucault observes that anthropology, in making these relations explicit, indeed functions like texts in the German *Bildungsroman* tradition and shares a close resemblance with Goethe's iconic rendering of it in *Wilhelm Meisters Lehrjahre* (*IKA*, 54).

In the third characteristic, however, Foucault suggests a paradox between the *real* and the *possible* – while the feasibility of imagining more than one world is never in doubt, such imaginations are necessarily restricted by the real one within which one imagines, since all the other possibilities are implicitly organized by the real one as either its alternative or its extension. The real as "a given system of actuality" thus facilitates one's ability to inhabit the world, and also functions as the limit of this ability. These three different characteristics of the world allow one to see it as its own "source, domain, and limit" and hence as a cultural totality within which "man appears to himself" (*IKA*, 81). When Kant suggests that *Weltkenntnis* is an integral part of the knowledge of the human being or anthropology, he does not imply that the knowable world is just an extension of nature, but rather assumes that the world is made part of and hence experienced by the human being as his/her immediate cultural totality.

The "World" of World Literature

The parallel between this anthropological/cosmopolitical world and the world of *Weltliteratur* practically suggests itself, but not necessarily within the frame of influence. I have suggested that Goethe knew his Kant well and that there are tantalizing parallels between his novels and Kant's anthropology (as Foucault, Cassirer, and Molnár note), but it would be counterproductive to restrict the connection to a purely biographical level. At this stage of my argument, it is also necessary to think of a larger frame within which this connection can be located and the special place I have accorded anthropology can be accounted for.

I suggest that both Kant and Goethe were participating in a general crisis in European philosophy that set in during the final decades of the eighteenth century when its insularity and internal coherence were repeatedly challenged by the vastly expanding colonial experience and when demands for new concepts and formulations were felt more acutely than ever. Gayatri Spivak has argued that the "end of the 'German' eighteenth century [...] provides material for a narrative of crisis management: the 'scientific' fabrication of new representations of self and world that would provide alibis for the domination, exploitation, and epistemic violation entailed by the establishment of colony and empire."[32] It is in this context of colony and empire, I suggest, that anthropological comparatism replaced the Kantian critical phase, and allowed both Kant and Goethe to put forward the new notion of the world which used itself as source, domain, and limit for whatever followed it (knowledge, citizenship, or literature). Within this larger climate of crisis management, anthropology emerged as the preferred space where the comparative paradigm could flesh itself out.

Let us take a closer look at the shared world of anthropology and literature to underscore my point. It is well known that Goethe's initial observations on world literature were made in the context of his recent experience of reading a Chinese novel, and he prefaces his discussion with the following remarks to the astonishment of a near-scandalized Eckermann: "the Chinamen think, act, and feel almost exactly like us; and we soon find that we are perfectly like them, excepting that all they do is more clear, more pure, and decorous than with us."[33] To elucidate further, Goethe first suggests that there are "many similarities [*viele Ähnlichkeiten*]" between Chinese novels and his own *Hermann und Dorothea* (1797) or Richardson's English novels, and then tells Eckermann that the Chinese have "thousands of them [novels], and had already when our forefathers were still living in the woods."[34] These two observations form a curious aesthetic field for us – the resemblance is strong enough to rebut Eckermann's quip that a "Chinese novel [...] must look strange enough," but it bears no guarantee that their histories would be comparable. His parallel between Chinese and European novels, when seen at a purely literary level, hints at a possible comparative frame, but this is a form of comparatism that is not yet anchored in a larger frame.

Goethe's remarks rather seem to suggest that generic resemblance is a necessary but insufficient ground for comparison, and that to take comparatism further one must juxtapose the worlds which produce comparable texts. Though he initially proposes poetry as the "universal possession of mankind [*Gemeingut der Menschheit*]" and hence a possible candidate to sustain comparison, his later insistence on translation belies such confidence. I think the real turn in his argument comes when he tells Eckermann that, in order to overcome nationalist pride, one must "look beyond the narrow circle which surrounds us" and goes on to declare "I therefore like to *look about me* in foreign nations [*Ich sehe mich daher gern bei fremden Nationen*]."[35] These foreign nations, if we go by Goethe's biography, are rather limited; but if we turn to his reading practices, they stretch far beyond Europe and into different parts of the world. Immediately after this he offers the following much-quoted statement on world literature: "National literature is now rather an unmeaning term; the epoch of World literature is at hand, and every one must strive to hasten its approach [*Nationalliteratur will jetzt nicht viel sagen; die Epoche der Weltliteratur ist an der Zeit, und jeder muß jetzt dazu wirken, diese Epoche zu beschleunigen*]"[36]

My point is that the transition from looking about oneself in a foreign country to the approaching epoch of world literature is anchored in a world analogous to the anthropological world I have tracked in Foucault's gloss on Kant – a set of "real relations" producing its own source, domain, and limit to sustain itself. What could be the meaning of "I therefore like to look about me in foreign nations" other than the intimate and anthropological suturing of the human being and the world? What could be the vision resulting from this act of looking about oneself in foreign lands if not the anthropological one that establishes the order of knowability on boundless proliferation of the natural universe? Goethe's point is in fact twofold here – he suggests that, since the gaze is directed toward the self in the middle of foreignness, it signifies that the foreign condition offers insights on the self which are not otherwise available. It is a gaze that is inherently comparative as it brings together the self and whatever is foreign to it; and, as such, it is shaped by an anthropological world that is limited and different from the natural universe. But the fact that the gaze is enabled by "foreign nations" also suggests that this anthropological world is designed to tame the profusion of foreignness and to reorder it with a manageable mechanism of recognition. In both cases the invocation of foreignness – and the call to move beyond nationalism – is an invitation to think of many possible worlds, comparable and limited.

It is of course of additional interest for us that in Goethe this vision is generated primarily, if not exclusively, through literary texts, but that in itself does not take away the anthropological foundation. Rather, the anthropological point is reinforced further when Goethe cautions

Eckermann by saying that, while the foreign is valuable, one must not fall into the trap of elevating it to the status of a model, something "exemplary [*musterhaft*]"; it is historically useful, and one needs to appropriate from it whatever is "good" without any nationalist inhibition.[37] The *world* of world literature is thus at once the source of this historical usefulness, the domain within which the foreignness of texts can be approached, and also the limit that circumscribes one's ability to participate in the history that leads to this world.

To put it differently, it is the finitude of this world – including of human beings – that makes the very idea of world literature thinkable. Goethe's world literature does not refer to a seemingly endless canon of texts from different locations; rather, it offers a way of regulating this chaotic corpus through internal limits and a set of norms, by delimiting its aesthetic scope through anthropologically charged categories. Within this delimited world, *literature* attains its meaning. The search for finitude, however, is fraught with the danger of being restricted within finite boundaries, and hence the notion of finitude is often coupled with a comparatism that seeks to replicate finite worlds side by side to make sense of each. Kant recognizes this fundamental paradox of comparatism – especially vis-à-vis art – when he suggests that "ideal taste has a tendency toward the external advancement of morality" on the evidence that any form of pleasure or satisfaction (indicated by taste as a "formal sense") beyond subjective perception "must contain necessity" and hence "an *a priori* principle" (*A*, 141). Necessity and principle – or necessity as principle – constitute the shared world of taste, and, in given social circumstances, this often manifests itself in a "well-mannered" individual insofar as his/her necessity is commensurate with the universally valid law and hence with everyone else's necessity.

In expressive or "speaking" arts such as poetry, however, it works differently. In his effort to explain the creative process of imagination, Kant proposes the following formulation – "Spirit and taste: *spirit* to provide ideas, *taste* to limit them to the form that is appropriate to the laws of the productive power of imagination and so to *form* them (*fingendi*) in an original way (not imitatively)" (*A*, 144; emphasis original). While "spirit" or *Geist* is the "principle of the mind that animates by means of *ideas* [*Man nennt das durch Ideen belebende Prinzip des Gemüts Geist*]," taste is what makes this power of spirit sociable and conformist; while spirit embodies the "productive faculty of reason," taste is "a merely regulative faculty of judging form in the combination of the manifold in the power of imagination" (*A*, 143). Thus individual manners and fashion (reliant on taste alone) represent the subject's efforts to conform within a shared world of dominant taste, but poetry (combining taste with spirit) always exceeds this initial threshold by fixing its eyes on taste "in respect to form" (*A*, 145).

The comparative potential of finite worlds is revealed here in this tension between what Kant calls spirit and taste. Idea animated by spirit is the proper domain of poetry, since Kant believes the painter (whether with brush or pen) of nature is a mere imitator, whereas the painter of ideas can be called a proper artist; and this would imply a more universal domain for art. But the inescapable route of taste places conditions on this universal drive and ties it down to given cultural contexts or anthropological worlds. Kant is not discarding the possibility of innovation here, and indeed he concedes that great poetry is distinguished from rhetorical speeches precisely on the ground of originality. What he is concerned with, rather, is the logic of aesthetic representation and its internal limits or even the possibility of identifying the finitude of such representation within the realm of form. Taste, as he points out more than once, is what turns representation worldly, by making it harmonious with existing networks and norms of interpretation.

Even in his brief statement on the sublime in *Anthropology* – which he discusses in greater detail in *Critique of the Power of Judgment* – Kant maintains that, although the sublime is "not an object for taste," its "artistic representation" has to embrace the norms of taste in order to avoid being "wild, coarse, and repulsive" (*A*, 141). Thus the logic of representation is available at two levels – formal (spirit/idea) and social (taste/manner), and the former perforce circulates through the latter. In Kant's text, spirit is not an anthropological category but taste is; and since taste is part of the social, it belongs to the finite world I have tracked above. World literature is thus constituted through these finite worlds of taste and judgment, as anthropological worlds, and its totality can be approached only through comparative models not only of texts but also of taste. When Goethe invokes the foreignness of other worlds and insists that such worlds be set against one's national context, he has something similar in mind. Both for Kant and for Goethe, world literature makes itself available within competing worlds of taste with a "tendency toward the external advancement of morality."

Race and Impure Aesthetics

Kant's repeated insistence that aesthetic judgments are determined by anthropological communities, or that, through a comparative study of different communities, one can understand the larger world within which such judgments take place, leads us to the precipitous zone of race and physical anthropology. Most scholarship on Kantian aesthetics, however, mentions neither race nor anthropology. This is not surprising, given Kant's own reticence on race in his three *Critiques* and, more surprisingly, in *Anthropology*. And yet, it remains crucial that Kant first formulated his views on race as an advertisement for his course on physical geography at the University of Königsberg in 1775 and then published his essay "Of the Different Human Races" in 1777, precisely during the period he was writing the *Critique of Pure Reason* (1781). In the published version of *Anthropology* in 1798, his exceptionally brief statement on race, however, has an important reference. It comes as an endorsement of Christoph Girtanner's *Ueber das Kantische Prinzip für die Naturgeschichte* (1796), as offering "so beautifully and thoroughly in explanation and further development [on theories of race] [...] (in accordance with my principles)" (*A*, 223). Though *Anthropology* does not explicitly refer to Kant's earlier work on race, I think this reference to Girtanner's text as continuing his own views makes his investment in racial theory abundantly clear. It seems more productive, then, to assume, against the dominant trend in Kant scholarship, that Kant did not abandon his early theories of race or racial evolution in his mature days.[38]

My reason for invoking Kant's views on race is to point out a particular crisis point in his anthropology that has larger bearings on our discussion regarding both world literature and its underlying premise of comparatism. Before I discuss this theoretical problem, let us recall here that the central characteristic of Kant's views on race is his rejection of a polygenetic origin of the human species in favor of a monogenetic one. Drawing on Buffon's multivolume *Histoire naturelle, générale et particulière* (1749), he suggests that, since "animals that produce fertile young with one another belong to one and the same physical genus" and since people from different races are capable of reproducing across racial lines, they should be considered as belonging to the same species and sharing the same origin.[39] Race for Kant is not a difference of species, but is restricted to skin color and physiological features derived from given climactic conditions. He suggests that several "seeds" or "natural predispositions" are present in different races, and only certain natural conditions such as climate or dietary habits quicken a few of those dormant features and suppress others.[40] Furthermore, Kant's anthropology at this stage does not show any sign of his deeply racist remarks on Native Americans, Indians, and Africans.[41]

But, even in its benign version, Kant's account betrays a theoretical problem that he never manages to solve completely. It is the distinction between physiological and pragmatic anthropology – as I have suggested above, Kant's preference for the latter is informed by the fact that it is able to access the human being not as a purely natural or physiological being, but as a rational actor who makes his/her own self out of natural resources. But the way he defines race – skin color depending on natural forces such as climate – it would qualify as a physiological characteristic and not a pragmatic one, because race not only precedes human action but remains beyond human limit. Even the consideration of race under the heading of pragmatic anthropology would undermine the disciplinary protocols of the latter – this is partly the reason why Kant previously included race in his lectures on physical geography and not on anthropology. But, once race is included within the bounds of anthropological discipline, and once it is made part of natural history of mankind, he needs a different methodology to justify his choice.

Emmanuel Eze locates the origins of this new methodology in Kant's selective appropriation of Rousseau's writings on nature. Kant produces an unusual reading of Rousseau (especially of *On the Origin of Language, Discourse on the Origin of Inequality among Men*, the *Social Contract*, and *Émile*) when he argues that the latter's call for "back to nature" or even his invocation of nature need not be taken literally because Rousseau's *primitivity* is more of a "hypothetical" construction for launching moral critiques of his contemporary human condition than an empirical observation. One can look back at this idyllic nature from one's historic situation, and one may even form a comparative understanding of different periods in history, but going back to such natural innocence would be tantamount to denying the civilizational and moral progress attained so far. Kant, in Eze's reading, rejects the oppositional values of nature versus culture implicit in Rousseau's account and instead prefers to split the notion of nature into two – a baser version, which belongs to "natural nature," and a moral one, which is "human nature" proper. Eze further suggests that Kant reformulates Rousseau's suggestion of "human nature" once more in his *Anthropology* by calling the essentially "moral" human nature "character."[42]

Once he proposes this fundamental duality of human nature, *character* becomes the preferred domain for anthropological investigations, because it is character that answers to his quest for man as a "free-acting being" capable of self-fashioning. Eze argues that, in this transition from the baser nature to human nature, Kant also seeks to solve the methodological problem of a pragmatic anthropology faced with physiological characteristics; his accounts restrict *lesser* and darker races to the natural conditions of being, while the *superior* white races emerge as capable of achieving human nature or character proper. His racist remarks on the Africans or the Native Americans consistently maintain that these races are incapable of cultural refinement and that, compared with the superior white races of Europe, they show a spectacular lack of the predispositions necessary for them to qualify as moral agents of the world.

Eze and others have connected these racialized assumptions of Kant's anthropology to his metaphysics with varying degrees of success. In this chapter, my line of inquiry is much more restricted – I am concerned with how to connect this racial inflection in Kantian anthropology to the modern aesthetic regime and how to locate Goethe's vision of world literature within this new aesthetic idiom. My suggestion is that race functions in two different ways in Kant's aesthetic theory. First, Kant uses race as a counterpoint to the central paradigm of anthropology – which he identifies to be *empiricism* – and attempts to secure a more stable field for aesthetic judgment. Taste – as opposed to spirit – is an anthropological and empirical category for him, and, to make it the ground for a critique of the senses, he needs something that will regulate the vagaries of empiricism. Since anthropology or anthropologically defined community cannot provide such a secure ground, he uses the racialized idea of a superior nature as the final location for aesthetic judgment. Goethe borrows this idea in his comparison between Chinese and European novels and distributes racial predisposition across cultures. These novels are comparable with each other because of the racial predispositions that underscore them. His point is that it is this elevated racial predisposition of the Chinese people that puts their novels on a par with *Hermann und Dorothea* or *Clarissa*. The world as a limited space makes comparison possible, but its true extent is revealed only when this underlying framework of racialized dispositions is made explicit.

This investment in race has another implication in Kant's theory – race is also the template for the community within which the aesthetic judgment is validated. Let us look at a cardinal distinction Kant makes between the "agreeable," the "beautiful," and the "good" in the *Critique of the Power of Judgment* to illustrate my point.[43] Kant first proposes an opposition between the logical and the aesthetic – the logical is based on concept and reason, and hence leads to the universal (*universale*); the aesthetic is devoid of any concept and is based on feelings of pleasure and displeasure and hence can only claim the general (*generale*) and not the universal. He maintains that the "judgment of taste about the beautiful ventures or claims" the universal, but, like all empirical rules, must remain confined to the general (*CPJ*, 98). On the basis of this preliminary distinction, Kant groups the agreeable and the beautiful under the aesthetic and places only the good under the logical. The agreeable is a private feeling and is restricted to individual experience; but the beautiful, though devoid of any rational underpinning, is a public declaration of taste with the assumption that it pleases the senses of everyone else. Away from these two aesthetic judgments, the universal is reserved only for the good: "With regard to the good, to be sure, judgments also rightly lay claim to validity for everyone; but the good is represented as an object of a universal satisfaction only through a concept, which is not the case either with the agreeable or with the beautiful" (*CPJ*, 98).

Almost immediately, he qualifies this even further by arguing that it would be merely boastful of a person to claim something beautiful and then to restrict it to his/her own self because the judgment of taste necessarily exceeds individual contentment. What is important in this formulation is the additional suggestion that this belief in the seeming universality of beauty is not borne out by past experience (or not necessarily), that the subject does not assume acceptance of his/her judgment because he/she witnessed similar validation of his/her taste in past cases; but rather the assumption rests on a "demand" that the judgment on beauty must be endorsed by everyone with taste (*CPJ*, 98). In the absence of historical consensus – or even of history itself – judgment of taste relies on representation with the possibility of its shared acceptance.

But, if there is no necessary historical antecedence for the judgment of the beautiful, what would be the ground for its acceptance? What would be the condition on which the "demand" for acceptance could be made and its validity asked for? Kant specifies the conditions in the form of two types of taste – the "taste of senses" and the "taste of reflection" (*CPJ*, 99). It is the second form of judgment or "taste of reflection" which concerns us more directly, as it always and already exceeds individual or subjective satisfaction. Kant even mentions a peculiar character of it – the alleged universality or "common validity" of the taste of reflection is poised on the typical constitution of it which demands such judgment to be universally valid, but always with the rider that its individual validity is open to contestation. That is to say, while its constitution as a judgment with universal ambition is never contested, the applicability of such universality is always left open as a contingent one (*CPJ*, 99–100).

This seeming universality of reflection exposes another peculiarity of its constitution. Its very demand that it is not subjective and is valid across a range of subject positions also makes it a judgment without subject. Reflection is not grounded in any given subject but is structured on the assumption of multiple subjects and their assent, but, the moment reflection is made part of taste, it assumes a regulatory quality. Within the demand of reflective taste, it is assumed that this regulatory power will assign subject positions to those who agree and thus will further its territory of operation, and Kant proposes this regulatory power as a counterweight to history (or its absence) in the judgment of taste. In his gloss he says that, although the "taste of reflection [...] is often enough rejected in its claim to the universal validity of its judgment (about the beautiful), [it] can nevertheless find it possible (as it also actually does) to represent judgments that could demand such assent universally." Moreover, "those who make those judgments do not find themselves in conflict over the possibility of such a claim, but only find it impossible to agree on the correct application of this faculty in particular cases" (*CPJ*, 99). As proof for such claims, quite uncharacteristically, he is able to cite only experience. In the absence of history, experience offers the evidence that the senses of pleasure or displeasure are capable of defining a subject position, but only with reference to similar subjects, and, though a provisional subjectivity may eventually be arrived at, reflection offers no guarantee that it would be anything other than an analogy of the moral subject.

I want to suggest a parallel between the racialized higher nature we have encountered in Kant's deliberations on race and this superior "taste of reflection." In both cases, the individual subject is not a pre-given but constituted through either a predisposition or a practice like the act of judging. In fact, it is possible to argue that in their collectivity both race and the community of reflective judgment are devoid of any individual subject position and open to ascription of subjects by other means. However, since the higher nature is a precondition of racial superiority and is not a product of human labor, it is possible to think of a similar community of individuals who are already predisposed with the ability to reflect, as a collectivity of characters, so to speak.

From this point onward, this assumption of the anthropological and racial community structuring the judgment of taste becomes almost an unstated assumption for Kant – he uses a somewhat similar structure of argument in defining taste, sociability, common sense, and a number of other ideas related to the act of judgment. Let us look at another formulation that Kant offers in support of his aesthetic theory. In *Anthropology* he offers two distinct notions of taste – *rationalizing* and *empirical* – with the qualification that the "former is *gustus reflectens*, the latter *reflexus*" (*A*, 137). Rationalizing taste as an anthropological category corresponds to the "taste of reflection," since, in "aesthetic power of judgment, it is not the *sensation* directly (the material of the representation of the object), but rather how the free (productive) power of imagination joins it together through invention, that is, the *form*, which produces satisfaction in the object" (*A*, 137; emphasis original). Indeed, Kant struggles across these two texts to secure a reliable foundation for this aesthetic judgment which, in the absence of a concept, cannot be logically universal and yet demands universal validity. In the third *Critique* he proposes "cognition" based on "imagination" and "understanding" (in a form of "free play") as the ground (*CPJ*, 102–3); in *Anthropology*, he suggests that it is the form which secures universality for aesthetic judgment (*A*, 137).

Both these points are necessary to understand the impurity of aesthetic judgment, since in a dual movement Kant is trying to record the essentially empirical nature of aesthetic judgment which relates to empirical faculties such as pleasure or displeasure; and, simultaneously, he is suggesting that, within a given social condition, this empiricity can have universal communicability (*Mittheilbarkeit*) like form (*A*, 137–8; *CPJ*, 103). What is cardinal in pulling this argument through is the nature and status of this given *social condition* that allows the empirical judgment to pose as universally valid communication – based on cognition and/or form – and yet maintain its contingent nature. To this end, Kant defines taste as an interpersonal phenomenon arising out of the context of sociability. If this sociability is stretched enough, if it is forced to match a community who share enough cultural experience, the empirical taste can lay claims on some form of stability. It is not yet, or will never be, strictly universal, but will at least have *common validity*.

"Sociability with other human beings," Kant writes, "presupposes freedom," and freedom in this case only reiterates the higher nature or racialized character Eze tracks in Kant. I shall return to this final impurity in a moment, but first I want to retrieve a relatively unnoticed passage in the *Critique of the Power of Judgment* (§ 8, 5: 215), which clearly relates this anthropological common ground to comparatism, and significantly anticipates the project of *Weltliteratur* as Goethe envisions it. In this passage, Kant is yet again engaged with the central problematic of the relationship between the empirical and the universal, and almost as an afterthought adds a further qualification – the central difficulty of the empirical judgment is its singularity, but this singularity can be overcome "if the singular representation of the object of the judgment of taste in accordance with the conditions that determine the latter is transformed into a concept through comparison" (*CPJ*, 100).

If enough singular experiences can be gathered together and can be shown to agree with each other through comparison, he argues, this comparative collectivity can indeed form "a logically universal judgment." He explains this with the example of admiring roses – any personal declaration of the beauty of a single rose is a singular judgment, but, if enough such statements can be gathered together to establish that roses are generally beautiful, it would be "an aesthetically grounded logical judgment" (*CPJ*, 100). Comparison, in other words, can escape the conundrum of empirical–logical or singular–universal by its sheer pressure and volume, by yet another form of empiricity that surpasses its own limitations through strategic and repeated iteration. Within comparatism the taste of sensation (*Sinnenempfindung*) embodies a characteristic form of empiricism that cannot be recognized as such or that is couched within a logic which is neither absolute nor universal but nonetheless effective with common validity. This transition from empiricity to quasi-logical judgment is premised on numerous comparable instances, and behind each instance and behind the entire project of sociable comparatism one can detect a free individual who is capable of judgment. Without this community, the comparative project would not have worked.

Here, race makes its powerful appearance once again. As would be evident from my discussion so far, in whatever way one approaches it – whether through a linear progression from individual to collective taste or through a lateral route of comparatism – the aesthetic judgment is eventually based on the crucial component of a "social condition" or a sharing community. In the *Critique of the Power of Judgment*, Kant has a name for this condition – "common sense." For him, common sense is what unites the various elements of taste into one communicable unit, and it is also responsible for turning a subjective judgment into an objective one. It does not refer to any psychological operation or reasoning but is the "effect of the free play of our cognitive powers" (*CPJ*, 122).[44] Kant insists that this common sense is an absolutely essential condition for the judgment of taste for two reasons. First, he points out that, in order to have any semblance of objectivity for the universal assent, the judgment of taste must be grounded in a given or a priori faculty which, theoretically at least, belongs to everybody. This ground is the common "feeling," which does not impose its own authority but nonetheless "demands" consent (*CPJ*, 123).

And second, more to the point, this belief in shared common sense makes cognition communicable; and since cognition is a universal "disposition," its association with common sense must be taken as attestation of the latter's universality as well (*CPJ*, 122). It needs little effort indeed to push this argument on cognition as a *disposition* onto Kant's theory of race, which also depends on a pre-cultural notion of natural *predisposition*.

Such dispositions are restricted to the community capable of overcoming mere individual sensuality or mere "natural nature" that revels in the sensuous pleasure of objects. What such a community aspires to is the higher form of pleasure that is empirically immediate but nonetheless in search of attestation from similarly cultivated minds. In other words, this concerns a form of pleasure affirmed through the condition of sociability; its universality – whether as *possibility* or *promise* – is available within a restrictive community of individuals with higher moral character and corresponding dispositions.

Literatures of the World

Let me briefly recapitulate here the two major strands of argument I have proposed so far. First, I have traced a line in Kant's texts that connects anthropology, community, and race and transforms the aesthetic field into a limited territory hospitable only to qualified individuals possessing suitable moral character. Aesthetic judgement in the Kantian sense is thus not a universal capability but selective disposition. And second, I have also identified a number of moments in Kant's oeuvre where his belief in the validity of the first argument appears tendentious and where he hurriedly reaches out to a host of other parameters from outside the field of aesthetics to support his case. In this second move, he increasingly relies on comparatism, as against his earlier critical phase, to support his views on aesthetics.

These two movements reach their climax in Kant's musings on art in general and on literature as a specific subset within it. Art, Kant argues, is distinguished from nature, science, and handicraft on the principle that it is "beautiful art" or *schöne Kunst* and it is beautiful because it "pleases in the mere judging [*Beurtheilung*] (neither in sensation nor through a concept)" (*CPJ*, 185). Hence the beautiful in art (available at the mere act of judging and nowhere else) for him also signifies that it is never an individual judgment; he then qualifies this further by relating this non-subjective judgment to the non-purposiveness in art – that is, even if there is an intentional purposive end to a work of art, the true judgment of the beautiful takes place only when this purposiveness is concealed and not explicitly displayed. In the absence of any precise law governing this judgment or defining the beauty, Kant is forced to consider the role of the genius as providing certain rules for this beautiful art, but doing so unconsciously. That is to say, what makes art beautiful is hidden in the enigma of the genius and is not available for empirical inspection and, while one can appreciate a work of art, one cannot explain the laws which produce it. Any great work of art is thus "exemplary" in its own right. The point is explained through a comparison between Newton, whose natural philosophy is explicitly verifiable, and poets such as Homer or Wieland, whose genius is undecipherable because even they do not know or cannot profess how to produce "inspired poetry" (*CPJ*, 187). In Kant, this absolute unreason or nature functioning through the genius becomes the ground where art can be located and judged.

However, this is not an isolated phenomenon in the third *Critique*. What was implicit in the aesthetic judgment of the beautiful (as opposed to the strictly individual enjoyment of the agreeable), in the form of an absent individual capable of completing the judgment, thus leads to a larger problematic in Kantian aesthetics when related to art more specifically. Lacoue-Labarthe and Nancy propose that the *Critique of the Power of Judgment* is aware of this central problematic and indeed is structured to resolve it through two concepts – "reflection" and "presentation" (*Darstellung*). Kantian "reflection" is not speculation but "only a pure referral or reflecting back, obtained by a simple, optical pattern and presupposing, moreover, the mediation of an inert, dead body, of a blind tain." When Kant introduces the taste of reflection as part of the "free play of imagination," they suggest, he wants it to operate as a synthesizing power so that the "subject sees itself in the image (*Bild*) of something without either a concept or an end."[45]

This is, however, a process without guarantee. Hence Kant introduces the additional possibility of presenting (*Darstellung*) the subject "by means of the Beautiful in works of art (the formation of *Bilder* able to present liberty and morality analogically), by means of the 'formative power' (*bildende Kraft*) of nature and life within nature (the formation of the organism), and finally by means of the *Bildung* of humanity (what we retain under the concepts of history and culture)."[46] Reflection and presentation build on the central suggestion of the image, and extend it across diverse fields such as the beautiful as caught between nature and culture, between what is given and what is made out of it. In both cases, however, we are returned to the central problem of Kantian aesthetics – the absentee subject and its supplementary ground in anthropology. His repeated attempt to find a priori principles for the critique of taste or for the feelings of pleasure and displeasure brings him face to face with the empty cogito, and he is forced to turn to anthropology in its pragmatic and popular form for an answer. Art or poetry only exacerbates the situation, since poetry as the highest form of beautiful art offers merely an impression of resolution but not a real answer.[47]

My suggestion of impure aesthetics is the name for this central confusion in Kantian aesthetics between universality and empiricity, between the urge to propose an a priori principle and the resultant synthesis of the subject that judges and the repeated undoing of that subject in the act of judging. Kant admits the possibility of this impurity when in the section on poetry in *Anthropology* he largely repeats his earlier position on the same subject in the *Critique of the Power of Judgment*. In the 1798 text he seems ready even to invert the quest initiated in the third *Critique* – that of finding a synthesized subject of judgment in anthropological categories such as taste and common sense – and proposes that anthropology may instead be the starting point.

He suggests, for instance, that sources for anthropology may include novels and plays by authors such as Richardson and Molière because they are based on a high degree of empirical observation. Novels and plays are "not actually based on experience and truth," he concedes, because they exaggerate characters and situations "as if in a dream" and thus offer precious little "concerning knowledge of human beings." Even then, "in such characters as are sketched by a Richardson or a Molière, the main features must have been taken from the observation of the real actions of human beings: for while they are exaggerated in degree, they must nevertheless correspond to human nature in kind" (*A*, 5). What strikes one immediately is the distance between his notes on poetry in both texts and this hesitant admission here of the utility of novels and plays. In fact, what Kant is trying to secure here is closer to what he says about "travel books" (for which he had a special penchant), namely that they are "means of broadening the range of anthropology" (*A*, 4). The difference implies not only a generic distinction (between poetry on the one hand and novels and plays on the other), but also a methodological reshaping. And this new methodology starts from anthropology and all it implies for aesthetic judgment instead of positing anthropology as a supplementary ground.

Goethe's vision of world literature emerges from this paradox across the two texts of Kant, and as a resolution spreads itself across the new world of anthropology. Like human character, which is the result of human labor and not a natural given, literature also is part of this world under the condition of cosmopolitical belonging. This mode of belonging is called "pragmatic" in Kantian vocabulary because it is neither spiritual nor juridical in the strict sense, but is part of a human universe which is produced and not discovered. Foucault argues that cosmopolitical belonging in Kant in effect means belonging "to the realm of the concrete universal, in which the legal subject is determined by and submits to certain laws, but is at the same time a human being who, in his or her freedom, acts according to a universal moral code" (*IKA*, 42). These universals are not abstract ideas but as concrete and precise as "an ensemble of precise juridical rules, themselves as universal as moral law" (*IKA*, 42). The anthropological world in Kant and Goethe is thus a differentiated and hierarchized space which has its own set of norms resembling juridical rules (in their preciseness) and moral laws (in their supposed universality).

What emerged as the literary sovereign in the colonial world found its entry into Europe through this impure aesthetics, through the complex coupling of anthropology and aesthetic judgment. The anthropological component of the new paradigm was exploited further in new aesthetic theories starting with Kant, and it soon became the precondition for aesthetic judgment. Any entry into world literature, from now on, was determined by this duality of anthropology and aesthetics, by their precision as well as their universality. However, this was by no means a settled principle for either Kant or Goethe, and this is partly the reason why world literature was a proleptic category in early discussions. As we shall see in the next two chapters, this entry of the literary sovereign through the impure aesthetics of Kant went through further changes and modifications in the subsequent decades.

CHAPTER 5

Sanskrit on Shagreen

A major change in the discussion of literature took place during the first few decades of the nineteenth century. Different ideas associated with the literary sovereign constituted a specialized language and an epistemic field within which, from this point in history, "literature" had to be cited and analyzed, its properties disentangled and scrutinized, and its very being understood as forming a distinct mode of textual organization. Within the supranational and polyglot structures of nineteenth-century empires, this paradigm circulated with unprecedented rapidity and soon found its way into literary texts, critical discourses, philosophical treatises, political pamphlets, and just about every other document that took up literature for serious and sustained discussion. Within Europe, as I have discussed in Chapter 4, *Weltliteratur* or world literature as a conceptual grid captured the exclusivity of this "new" being of literature over other competing claims, and facilitated the literary sovereign's popularity across territorial and cultural borders as signaling the emergence of new aesthetic ideals. As Goethe noted in 1830, the new idea of world literature was a necessity "for all the nations [that have become] aware of having imbibed much that was foreign, and conscious of spiritual needs hitherto unknown," and was also an aesthetic framework to make sense of this foreignness.[1] This new aesthetic ideal, likewise, had to be broad enough to match the geographical reach of this foreignness and yet specific enough to clarify what was characteristically new. This chapter charts out the newness of this aesthetic ideal of the nineteenth century, marked both by the diversity of colonial histories and by the intellectual ambition of world literature.

In recent years, there have been several attempts to theorize an aesthetic regime of literature under the sign of modernity that would respond to the historical events of the early nineteenth century and would still be amenable to more contemporary realities of literature as a worldwide phenomenon. The most fascinating one, in my opinion, has been the works of the French philosopher Jacques Rancière, especially what he calls the "democratic petrification" of literature as a prerequisite for democratic politics.[2] At the heart of his reformulation of this aesthetics–politics combination is his conviction that aesthetics is "neither art theory in general nor a theory that would consign art to its effects on sensibility"; rather, for him, aesthetics "refers to a specific regime for identifying and reflecting on the arts: a mode of articulation between ways of doing and making, their corresponding forms of visibility, and possible ways of thinking about their relationships (which presupposes a certain idea of thought's effectivity)."[3] Within this larger constellation, literature occupies a special position, and Rancière has been relentless in his search for an adequate theoretical language to match the emergence of what he calls "literature as literature" in the early decades of the nineteenth century.[4]

To explore literature and its politics within this modern aesthetic regime, he suggests, the precise definitions of the two need to be established first – the former is "a definite practice of writing," whereas the latter implies a "definite way of doing." Politics is primarily a framing for sensory data, a way of regulating what can be seen or said in given discursive-material configurations, and hence is "a specific intertwining of ways of being, ways of doing and ways of speaking." When Rancière suggests a specific mode of politics for literature, he argues that "literature as literature is involved in this partition of the visible and the sayable, in this intertwining of being, doing and saying that frames a polemical common world."[5] In more concrete terms, literature becomes political in this sense when it discovers the democratic petrification of literariness, when it becomes conscious of the "mute speech" engraved in mundane objects of everyday life, and, following Georges Cuvier's new paradigm of geological investigations in the early nineteenth century, embraces the non-hierarchized democracy of the maxim "everything speaks."[6] This new paradigm of universal readability is often taken as the sign of the realism of the nineteenth-century novels, or what Erich Auerbach calls the final triumph of mimesis.[7] But, for Rancière, this is nothing short of a democratic revolution against older paradigms of literature, mimesis included, that relied, like priests or orators, on imposition of will and form. The modern regime of literature, in short, is the very condition of possibility for democracy.

In this chapter, I make two related points vis-à-vis Rancière's argument: first, I demonstrate that he insufficiently imagines the knowledge paradigms informing this allegedly democratic petrification of literature, and ignores vital shifts in history; and second, I argue that, because of this initial poverty of imagination, Rancière fails to address the most crucial impediment to the regime's "universal" reading strategy – that is, *colonial history* and *racial difference*. While the metropolitan culture yields its innermost secrets to the hermeneutic eye of democratic petrification, the colonial other, shrouded in racial alterity, remains mysterious, illegible, and even invisible. This is particularly so since Rancière misses the way colonial histories had made vital inroads into European texts by the end of the eighteenth century (as I suggest in Part I of this book), and how it was impossible to revisit the metropolitan culture without taking into account its critical reliance on this other history.[8]

As opposed to this model, I suggest in the following pages, if we go back to the intellectual context of the late-eighteenth- and early-nineteenth-century imperial culture, and to the constitution of the literary sovereign, we can locate a partition at the heart of this universal readability paradigm – between aesthetic reading and governmental reading. This was partly a result of the way modern empires functioned, with a displacement of their political enterprise onto the cultural domain of civilizational values, creating a justificatory framework where different aesthetic forms (including literature) were mobilized and enlisted. On the other hand, this was also the result of the enormous investment in race-management and actual governance of colonies from the eighteenth century. The consequence was that the question of race remained peripheral to aesthetics and presented itself as a pressing concern exclusively for governmental regulations, and subsequently found expression in a range of "scientific" disciplines including anthropology, criminology, criminal anthropology, eugenics, and so on. I have elsewhere described this other paradigm as "somapolitics," or a biohermeneutic paradigm of readability around race, and here I want to suggest that it is the other and darker side of Rancière's democratic petrification.[9]

In the following pages I address the central problem of reading as it figures in Rancière's argument, and I suggest that its contours were shaped by various disciplines and generalizations surrounding race from the eighteenth century, under the master narrative of what Edward Said calls "Orientalism" and what Maurice Olender describes as racialized "erudition."[10] With reference to Honoré de Balzac's novel *La Peau de chagrin* (1831), which also functions as the central text for Rancière's theory of democratic petrification of literature, I show that the conditions of reading everyday life, and hence the new literariness, could emerge only under the strict orders laid down through these new disciplines and, behind them, by the coercive structures of colonial governance. Democratic and universal legibility was neither accidental nor benign, and, far from being an outcome of European history, it telescoped the myriad ways Europe struggled to make sense of its colonial encounters. As a result, I suggest, this new literariness needs to be situated within the same trajectories of the literary sovereign or world literature – that is, as a code developed to make sense of the newness of history since the eighteenth century.

The Old Curiosity Shop

Rancière cites the opening sequence of Balzac's novel *La Peau de chagrin* (translated as *The Wild Ass' Skin*, part of his *La Comédie humaine*), where the protagonist Raphaël surveys the showrooms of a Parisian curiosity shop, and suggests that the sequence is the "best example [of] and commentary" on the new politics of literature, which is not external to it but characteristic of its modern being. This is how the sequence in Balzac begins:

> At a first glance the place presented a confused picture in which every achievement, human and divine, was mingled. Crocodiles, monkeys, and serpents stuffed with straw grinned at glass from church windows, seemed to wish to bite sculptured heads, to chase lacquered work, or to scramble up chandeliers. A Sèvres vase, bearing Napoleon's portrait by Mme. Jacotot, stood beside a sphinx dedicated to Sesostris. The beginnings of the world and the events of yesterday were mingled with grotesque cheerfulness. A kitchen jack leaned against a pyx, a republican sabre on a mediaeval hackbut. Mme. Du Barry, with a star above her head, naked, and surrounded by a cloud, seemed to look longingly out of Latour's pastel at an Indian *chibook*, while she tried to guess the purpose of the spiral curves that wound towards her. Instruments of death, poniards, curious pistols, and disguised weapons had been flung down pell-mell among the paraphernalia of daily life; porcelain tureens, Dresden plates, translucent cups from China, old salt-cellars, comfit-boxes belonging to feudal times. A carved ivory ship sped full sail on the back of a motionless tortoise.[11]

Such seeming randomness of discrete and unrelated objects extends over several pages and, in this encyclopedic arrangement of different lands and ages, the text suggests, unfolds for Raphaël "a poem without end" (*WAS*, 18).

Rancière argues that the fundamental principle animating this sequence in Balzac, and creating this "poem" for Raphaël, is that all these objects are democratically equal in the way they occupy a homogeneous space of literariness. Within this democratic space, each object becomes "a poetic element," "a fabric of signs," and wears "a history on their body." The way they embody different histories and civilizations within a horizontal space is such that they not only compose a new poeticity, but even, as individual verses, "carried the infinite virtuality of new stories, unfolding those signs in new contexts."[12] This arrangement of Balzac's novel reveals the typical doubling of the politics of literature – it "upsets" the hierarchy of the earlier representational regime by releasing this democratic equality; and it also initiates a range of substitutability between the "deciphering of the mute meaning written on the body of things" and the "democratic chattering of the letter."[13]

Rancière's reading of the sequence in Balzac is selective and hence built on a series of elisions. He notes that the text abbreviates distant lands and histories in these odd objects, but leaves unexamined the modality of this abbreviation. The organization of objects in Balzac's text reveals a pattern when studied closely – apart from local French history and its signs, they mostly invoke great "civilizations" such as Egypt, Rome, China, and India. This calculated randomness functions only when there is a homogeneity of space withstanding not only such an extended inventory of objects but also the diversity of readers, when such readers share a consensus about civilizational values or a certain understanding of history.[14] From this catalogue, Balzac's readers were supposed to pick up clues about history and the way it had been periodized and taxonomized in recent times, clues they would be able to unpack and relate to. His readers were supposed to share and confirm, for instance, what Raymond Schwab describes as the "Oriental renaissance" in Europe during the eighteenth century with the rediscovery of India, resulting in radically altered notions both of civilization and of history.[15] It was visible, for instance, in the intellectual euphoria in France and elsewhere surrounding Abraham-Hyacinthe Anquetil-Duperron's translation of *Zend-Āvestā* (1771) and the *Upanishads* (1786), or around William Jones's translation of literary texts such as the *Muʿallaqāt* (1782) and Kālidāsa's *Śakuntalā* (1789), and had a profound impact on a long list of prominent figures in Europe, from Voltaire to Hegel.

One of the central outcomes of this period was, to borrow again from Schwab, the realization that, alongside the "Greco-Latin heritage of the Renaissance" and apart from the Biblical civilizations, there existed "innumerable civilizations from ages past, [and] an infinity of literatures; moreover the few European provinces were not the only places to have left their mark in history."[16] Balzac's readers were also supposed to share the subsequent phase of this renaissance that was sustained through the newly initiated projects in British India to codify, taxonomize, and make useful native knowledge for effective use. From the 1770s, as I have demonstrated in Chapters 1–3, this group of colonial officials and orientalists expanded European knowledge paradigms at an unprecedented scale through their translation of a vast amount of texts, codification of local legal systems

The Old Curiosity Shop

such as the Shariʻa and the Dharmaśāstra, proposals for the foundation for what later became the Indo-European language family, publication of their extensive research on the pages of *Asiatick Researches* and in sundry monographs, and indeed through their plan to explore the entire breadth of Asiatic "history, science, and art."[17] European knowledge was thus transformed across a colonial vector; as Said puts it succinctly, "Calcutta provided, London distributed, Paris filtered and generalized."[18]

As a consequence, this period produced a distinct textuality of the Orient, turning the land away from its present realities into a series of textual representations. This triumph of textuality was confirmed in France, ironically enough, through the Napoleonic invasion of Egypt in 1798. Said has argued that Napoleon saw Egypt through a maze of textual precedence and citations, almost like a professional Orientalist, and even modeled his military invasion on the Comte de Volney's two-volume travelogue *Voyage en Égypte et en Syrie* (1787). This is evident in Napoleon's own account of his Egyptian campaign, contained in General Bertrand's *Campagnes d'Égypte et de Syrie, 1798–1799* (1847).

Said suggests that the real turn in this history of textualization, and its close collaboration with colonial governance, came with Napoleon's reliance on orientalist scholars during the invasion to know and govern Egypt and with their eventual scholarship contained in the enormously ambitious twenty-three volume *Description de l'Égypte* (1809–28). It marked a new phase in the history of Orientalism, as its central ambition was, Said notes,

> to formulate the Orient, to give it shape, identity, definition with full recognition of its place in memory, its importance to imperial strategy, and its "natural" role as an appendage to Europe; to dignify all the knowledge collected during colonial occupation with the title "contribution to modern learning" when the natives had neither been consulted nor treated as anything except as pretexts for a text whose usefulness was not to the natives; to feel oneself as a European in command, almost at will, of Oriental history, time, and geography; to institute new areas of specialization; to establish new disciplines; to divide, deploy, schematize, tabulate, index, and record everything in sight (and out of sight); to make out of every observable detail a generalization and out of every generalization an immutable law about the Oriental nature, temperament, mentality, custom, or type; and, above all, to transmute living reality into the stuff of texts, to possess (or think one possesses) actuality mainly because nothing in the Orient seems to resist one's powers.[19]

Egypt emerged through such enterprises as a text, and existed as such over a period of time – "from Chateaubriand's *Itinéraire* to Lamartine's *Voyage en Orient* to Flaubert's *Salammbô*, and in the same tradition, Lane's *Manners and Customs of the Modern Egyptians* and Richard Burton's *Personal Narrative of a Pilgrimage to al-Madinah and Meccah*";[20] but its textuality was an unmistakable manifestation of power, its details dependent on the exigencies of colonial governance.

My point is that the textuality of everyday life, on which Rancière places such a huge premium, had a different and colonial route. What Balzac's readers encountered in these passages was the opacity not of objects but of historical signs, a form of textuality created with explicit reference to the Orient and made available since the final decades of the eighteenth century. If these objects "wore a history on their body," as Rancière contends, that history referred less to the innocence of chronological events through the centuries and more to this recent rearrangement of epistemic fields in which history came to signify a new order of knowledge and went through radical textualization itself. Within the novel, Raphaël's initial confusion gradually disappears as he becomes conscious of the connection between these objects and various forms of the "life of nations," as he manages to use the dense textuality as an opening into the larger histories of lands and peoples, into a sort of world history. It is of no small significance that Raphaël's sudden ability to *read*, leading to the "enchanted palace of ecstasy," begins with Egypt (*WAS*, 16–18). What is equally important is that this new vision of history was shared by the text and its readers, and without this shared ground the very technique of readability would not have worked. Balzac was critically reliant on this new epistemic textuality as well as his readers' familiarity with it to produce the effect of this sequence.

What Balzac achieves here and elsewhere in his novels has been described by Jonathan Culler as the "Balzacian ethnology": "Balzac purveys ethnological information about Parisian habits and types, as if for readers who view them from a distance, but at the same time evokes a community of readers through the presupposition of shared knowledge."[21] The immediate context for this observation is Culler's discussion of Benedict Anderson and the latter's insistence in *Imagined Communities* (1983) that old-fashioned realist novels like Balzac's were instrumental in shaping the typical national imagination of modern times. I shall return to this point below, but here I want to follow a second line of argument implied in Culler's text. The Balzacian ethnology of Parisian life essentially reverses the rules of ethnological representation, because here the explanatory narrative about a community is directed toward the same community and not an external group of readers. It has the status of auto-ethnology, which, Culler seems to suggest, produces a paradoxical excess in the text – the reader of Balzac's novel gets to know what she or he is supposed to know already.

But that certainly is not the entire story. In order to sustain the novel, Balzac has to introduce information which is external to this little pact between the author and the reader, and he has to manipulate the ethnological subtext to support the novel's fictionality. It is this paradoxical ethnology that generates historical excess in the objects of the antique shop and produces the dizzying experience of traveling through different lands and civilizations, traversing time and space, all at once. Reading (or, rather, correct practices of reading) was designed to discipline this excess, and to contain history within the bounds of its signs. Far from being a democratic practice based on formal or universal equality, this regime of reading was a disciplinary practice that sought to replicate a template generated through orientalism. Indeed, one of the central implications of what Said calls "modern Orientalism," to which I have briefly alluded above, was that its new textuality demanded fairly standardized and disciplined reading practices.[22] If it turned the Orient into a form of text, it also insisted that access to that textuality – that is, reading – must be regulated.

Let me introduce here a second tradition of readability at work in Balzac's text, which, once again, predates Rancière's chronology and offers further clues about this historical excess and its containment through legibility. As Ruth Yeazell has shown, at least since the 1830s Balzac's novels have regularly been compared with Dutch or Flemish paintings from the late seventeenth century. In 1833, for instance, the *Revue des deux mondes* suggested parallels between Balzac's characters in *Le médecin de campagne* and the paintings of Gerrit Dou. In England, his *Eugénie Grandet* was described in 1836 as "a Dutch picture of an interior," and Balzac himself was seen as "a painter of the Flemish school" or even a "Dutch painter in prose." In fact, the parallel was so popular that, by 1875, Henry James could confidently state that "[w]here another writer makes an allusion, Balzac gives you a Dutch picture."[23]

Bernard Weinberg, on the other hand, suggests that this explicit parallel between Balzac's status as "a descriptive artist and as a 'painter'" on the one hand and "Flemish and Dutch masters" on the other allowed his supporters to extol the virtues of his "style as 'éblouissant' and 'prestigieux,' of his manner as 'éclatant, taillé à facettes, incorrect quelquefois, coloré toujours'"; it is the same connection that was mobilized to defend, Weinberg notes, "this phantasmagoric quality, this oriental luxuriance associated usually with *La Peau de chagrin*."[24] Such paintings had been in circulation in France since the eighteenth century, and were made popular through countless cheap prints as well as significant collections such as

Jean Baptiste Pierre Lebrun's three volumes of engravings, *Galerie des peintres flamands, hollandaise et allemands* (1792–6). Both Balzac and his critics, therefore, could assume a reader's familiarity with "Dutch painting" as both "a phenomenon and as a paradigm for criticism."[25] Hence, when his early critics made this connection between his novels and Dutch paintings, they meant to offer ways of responding to Balzac's extended attention to details, his painstaking depiction of everyday minutiae.[26]

This reference to Dutch and Flemish paintings, however, was not a simple technical tool to make sense of a complex novelistic device. The invocation of "Dutch paintings" in nineteenth-century discussions of novels often carried a moral charge and implied definite reading practices. Yeazell argues that this regulatory aspect was visible most prominently through two broad associations of such paintings (and, by analogy, of such novels) – undignified or morally distasteful life and feminine domesticity. In a conscious reference to this critical paradigm and current debates, the novel incorporates a gallery full of such paintings as part of the opening sequence in the curiosity shop: "one by one there passed before his wearied eyes several pictures by Poussin, a magnificent statue by Michael Angelo, enchanting landscapes by Claude Lorraine, a Gerard Dow (like a stray page from Sterne), Rembrandts, Murillos, and pictures by Velasquez, as dark and full of color as a poem of Byron's" (*WAS*, 20). A little later, we also come across a lengthy description of the renaissance painter "Raphael's portrait of Jesus Christ" (*WAS*, 26–7). Through this deliberate ensemble of different periods and styles of painting, the novel seems to respond to the pejorative association of low lives and domestic confines, and to counter it by displaying these "Dutch paintings" of Rembrandt or Gerrit Dou, for instance, along with other classics of Michelangelo and Raphael Sanzio in a public gallery. It acknowledges and defies in the same move the critical constraints imposed by the association with genre paintings and the moral charge made against such vivid description of everyday life.

It is especially striking since the move is located right in the middle of boisterous visual opulence – which Sainte-Beuve and others explicitly described as Balzac's "oriental style"[27] – that could have been the subject of a Rembrandt still life. The larger point made in this sequence, however, is about reading. If it demonstrates the readability of everyday life, and thus confirms the doctrine of "everything speaks," as Rancière maintains, it also refers unambiguously to the sources of this textuality as well as to the regulations imposed on readability. Indeed, my wager is that reading as an event or legibility as an attribute is neither external to the novel nor temporally subsequent to its textual organization. Rather, the novel anticipates certain forms of reading and makes every effort to control it, challenging the belief that it can be read in its supreme innocence and poeticity. Rancière seems unable or unwilling to engage with any of the passages in the sequence, or elsewhere in the novel, that critically reflect on readability as a paradigm for literature. Instead, he flattens the novel's different sources and diverse commitments within the single, and somewhat constraining, frame of democratic petrification.

Persia or Bengal

Let us now look at another set of elisions or non-readings in Rancière, this time his non-reading of Balzac's *La Peau de chagrin* itself. The history I have charted above – of modern orientalism and its investment in textuality and disciplined reading – is at the heart of the novel, indeed its very *raison d'être*, and yet Rancière seems completely unaware of it. A number of commentators have noted the close parallel between Balzac's text and the *Thousand and One Nights*, which was first translated into French in 1704.[28] The novel was dedicated to Jean-Julien-Marie Savary, brother of the well-known orientalist and translator of the Qu'rān Claude Étienne Savary. In his foreword to *La Comédie humaine*, appended to the 1842 edition of *Scènes de la vie privée*, Balzac described the novel as "a work of almost *Oriental fancy* [*d'une fantaisie presque orientale*]" (*WAS*, liv; emphasis added). The orient is present in virtually every episode of the novel and on every other page through artifacts, commodities, objects, images, and texts, ranging from Indian *chibook* and *hookah* to Chinese mantelpieces and the *Arabian Nights*, from oriental amulets to troops of oriental women.[29] In fact, the orient – or, to be more precise, India – assumes a "ghostlike" status in the novel as it is, simultaneously, the source of inheritance both for Raphaël and for Pauline, and also the mark of the impossibility, at least for Raphaël, of benefiting from that bequest.[30] One of Raphaël's friends jokingly responds to his sudden change of luck by saying that what he inherits is "An *incalcuttable* fortune," with an obvious pun on the name of the place the money comes from – Calcutta (*WAS*, 180). As the novel unfolds, however, these scattered references to the orient come together and, coupled with Balzac's "oriental style," the novel creates its own internal orient and its corresponding textuality. But nothing really prepares us for the novel's central thesis on reading and its implications, and to this I now turn.

The episode is part of the novel's first section, "The Talisman," and appears right at the end of the opening sequence in the curiosity shop that Rancière cites. After surveying different galleries and pavilions full of objects, paintings, household artifacts, and other oddities, Raphaël meets the old merchant of the shop, and is led to a "leathern skin" or "a piece of shagreen" hanging on the wall. Raphaël's careful eyes notice that the "Oriental leather" bears the "mark of a seal which they call in the East the Signet of Solomon" (*WAS*, 29–31). This encounter with the talisman has been arranged carefully in the text; it not only appears at the end of this confusing montage of visual registers and historical fragments, but also takes place, as the narrator points out, at a crucial juncture in Raphaël's life, when he is seriously contemplating the possibility of suicide after losing in gambling. Hence, the translucent skin, with its brilliance and enigmatic aura, literally introduces a ray of hope in his otherwise gloomy life, and the merchant makes the case more obvious by saying that, with its help, he can be "richer, more powerful, and of more consequence than a constitutional king" (*WAS*, 29).

This promise is no empty boast, no clever business strategy of the shrewd old man, and it is not contained in the shagreen's material value. Rather, as the merchant points out, this is announced in "some characters inlaid in the surface of the wonderful skin, as if they had grown on the animal to which it once belonged" (*WAS*, 30). Raphaël's familiarity with the details of the skin convinces the merchant that he is indeed an "Orientalist" and he should be able to read the mysterious characters. Confirming this, Raphaël, the "man of science," reads the following message, arranged in the shape of an inverted pyramid:

> POSSESSING ME THOU SHALT POSSESS ALL THINGS, BUT THY LIFE IS MINE, FOR GOD HAS SO WILLED IT. WISH, AND THY WISHES SHALL BE FULFILLED; BUT MEASURE THY DESIRES, ACCORDING TO THE LIFE THAT IS IN THEE. THIS IS THY LIFE, WITH EACH WISH I MUST SHRINK EVEN AS THY OWN DAYS. WILT THOU HAVE ME? TAKE ME. GOD WILL HEARKEN UNTO THEE. SO BE IT! (*WAS*, 31)

As he translates the enigmatic characters, the old man remarks, with an obvious note of satisfaction, "So you read Sanskrit fluently [...] You have been in Persia perhaps, or in Bengal?" (*WAS*, 32).

The episode appears in two different versions. In early editions of the novel, the original engraving is not part of the text, and we are left with Raphaël's translation. Only he and the merchant are allowed to "read" the inlaid characters of the "Oriental sentence [*sentence orientale*]" (*WAS*, 31). From the edition of 1838, however, the novel includes a facsimile of the message and invites its readers to read it alongside Raphaël (Figure 5.1). In

40   LA PEAU DE CHAGRIN.

لو ملكتـني ملكت آلكل
و لكن عمرك ملكى
و اراد الله هكذا
اطلب و ستننال مطالبك
و لكن قس مطالبك على عمرك
و هى هاهنا
فدكل مرامك ستنزل ايامك
أتريد فى
الله مجيبك
آمين

qui voulait dire en français :

SI TU ME POSSÈDES, TU POSSÉDERAS TOUT.
MAIS TA VIE M'APPARTIENDRA. DIEU L'A
VOULU AINSI. DÉSIRE, ET TES DÉSIRS
SERONT ACCOMPLIS. MAIS RÈGLE
TES SOUHAITS SUR TA VIE.
ELLE EST LA. A CHAQUE
VOULOIR JE DÉCROITRAI
COMME TES JOURS.
ME VEUX-TU?
PRENDS. DIEU
T'EXAUCERA.
SOIT !

Figure 5.1   Honoré de Balzac, *La Peau de chagrin* (Paris: Charpentier, 1839), 40.

both versions, the oriental origins of the skin and its message are emphasized without any ambiguity. In the second version, as the facsimile shows, however, the enigmatic message is not in Sanskrit but in Arabic! As if to anticipate Rancière's argument, the novel literalizes the metaphor of "mute speech" on the object itself, but does so within the essential ambiguity of two different languages.[31] Is it a case of sheer negligence, that Balzac inserted this text in Arabic and forgot to change the sentence that comes right after it, leading to this embarrassing gaffe?[32] Is it, in that case, another instance of what Said calls the "casual [...] confusion of Arabic with Sanskrit," which was so widespread in the early phase of modern orientalism?[33] Or should we interpret this episode as a complex gloss on the novel itself, on its organization and structure?[34] Whatever way we approach this paradoxical event with two "Oriental" languages, there is no getting away from the fact that the point of this episode is indeed about reading, a form of reading that is not anticipated in the novel's organization but staged right at its outset.

At any rate, the episode, across its two versions, implies a certain substitutability between Sanskrit and Arabic. In the first instance, the novel does not represent the Sanskrit message, and only confirms Raphaël's translation of it into French through the merchant's endorsement of his fluency in the tongue. In the second version, the novel asks the reader to take part in the translation, but, by reproducing an Arabic text, erases the Sanskrit one from its space and renders it absolutely invisible and unreadable. We are faced with the possibility of reading or translating a text that is invisible but not altogether absent, a kind of conundrum that challenges the central assumption of reading anchored in visuality. This invisibility is neither a dead end nor a cipher, since the novel uses it as its condition of possibility, as an alibi to invade the space of the mysterious oriental characters. Whatever the original message is, and however unreadable, the novel makes it a mission to decode it and then projects itself as an extended reading, as a prolonged commentary on its truth, so that various wishes of Raphaël and their realizations, leading to his misery and eventual death, allow the reader to read the inscription all over again. If the first attempt at reading was thwarted through invisibility, the second one is saturated with excessive visibility and formal garrulity, as if to compensate for the momentary interruption of the coordinates between visuality and reading.

As a result, the novel offers two different sequences of reading – Raphaël reading the Sanskrit text, and the reader reading the novel – and suggests that they are synchronized, if not identical, since the novel simply elaborates the cryptic codes on the magic skin. *La Peau de chagrin* is indeed a supplementary reading of an oriental text that is invisible but extant, and is available only through the authority of an orientalist (that is, Raphaël), though within the world of the novel there is no guarantee either of its real existence or of its putative meaning. We are simply invited to take the novel at its face value, and convince ourselves that what the novel performs in its extended unraveling is indeed the intended meaning of the invisible text. We are faced with the prospect, in other words, through a supreme act of displacement, that the novel is that enigmatic text; in its capaciousness Balzac's novel can, and indeed does, occupy the space on the wild ass's skin and reproduce the message contained in an oriental language. *La Peau de chagrin* is both a novel and a talisman, a French novel and an oriental enigma – no wonder, then, that, as the novel progresses toward its end, the magic skin shrinks, and as the novel draws to a close the skin disappears altogether.

Once the Arabic text is introduced, however, this ambition of the novel looks doubtful. The Arabic text is visible but unseen and unread. Neither Raphaël nor the merchant takes note of it, and the reader is left with its enigmatic presence not on the skin but on the page of the novel. But it allows the reader to compare this text with Raphaël's French translation, and two important discrepancies are readily visible – the Arabic version does not mention the skin's shrinking with every wish fulfilled, and it does not exhort its reader by saying "TAKE ME [*PRENDS-MOI*]."[35] Because of this asymmetry, the novel cannot claim to be an extended gloss on it. Though Sanskrit and Arabic are somewhat interchangeable within the novel's scheme of things, it is only the former that the novel can claim fully and make part of its own structure, while the latter is left hanging between different attempts at reading, forever marked as unread. With the Arabic text there is the further suggestion that Raphaël's translation is without any original, and the talisman, after all, is a blank piece of skin. *La Peau de chagrin*, as a confirmation of this translation, turns into a simulation structured around blankness. Its central void is shrouded in its manifold loquacity, as if the novel undertakes its verbal fecundity as its own condition as well as final goal, without having the option of falling back on an external source or a programmatic code. What we read then is a fiction that cites two different texts in Sanskrit and Arabic as its source, but makes the first one invisible and the second unreadable. The novel stands in for both, and asks us to read it as the true representation of the message contained in not one but two oriental texts, but does so within its own order of fictionality. It creates a form of textuality similar to that of orientalism.

Literature as a "System"

This is of course part of the literary sovereign paradigm I have been charting so far. Here I want to concentrate on a particular moment of this history in order to address the problem in Balzac's novel, namely Friedrich Schlegel's *Über die Sprache und Weisheit der Indier* (*On the Language and Philosophy of the Indians*, 1808) and *Geschichte der alten und neueren Literatur* (*Lectures on the History of Literature, Ancient and Modern*, 1815). Across these two texts, I suggest, we can chart a clear trajectory of the new notion of literature as taking shape within and as part of what could only be called early discussions on world literature. The title page of the second text states that it is based on Schlegel's lectures given in Vienna in 1812, but we know from his own correspondence and other sources that he had been offering these lectures in Paris as early as 1803. Schwab has described these early lectures as "private courses on *world literature* [...], coincidentally with his Indic studies."[36] From the published account, however, it becomes clear that Schlegel defines literature in terms of two thematic categories – the "destiny of nations" (*Schicksal der Nationen*) and the "passage of time"

(*Gang der Zeiten*), or nation and history – and visualizes the *world* of world literature through them.[37] This is a reworking of Jones's suggestion in the "Third Anniversary Discourse," and Schlegel extends it not only by joining literature with national communities, but also through his insistence that this intertwining is a recent event in history that makes it necessary to reimagine literature as an object of serious scholarship.

In his opinion, this recent history begins with the rediscovery of the vernaculars, especially of German, that inaugurates a new phase both in literature and in national life. Almost echoing Fichte's sentiments from *Reden an die deutsche Nation* (*Addresses to the German Nation*, 1808), especially his suggestion that the spirit of the German nation is best preserved in the German language, Schlegel states that "the more that patriotic reminiscences and affections were stirred up within the bosom of her sons, the more intense became the love of Germans for their mother-tongue."[38] This new enthusiasm for the vernacular tongue, he insists, has the much-desired effect of bridging the gap between life and literature, between popular usage of a language on the one hand and the alienated artist on the other. With the introduction of the vernacular, this gap has narrowed since the eighteenth century, and literature or its domain has become identical with life, with its organicity and vitality. Schlegel is quite categorical in maintaining that this identity is most conspicuously visible through the historic notion of the nation, and that literary history from this point onward has to consider national literature as its basic operational unit.

Behind this vernacularization-as-nationalization moment, Schlegel identifies two broad currents of history. First, he suggests that the earliest phase of European civilization in Greece was largely borrowed from Asiatic and African nations: "The Greeks, it is true, derived their letters from the Phœnicians, according to their own testimony, whilst they copied the elements of architecture and the mathematics, certain philosophic ideas, and many of the arts of life, from Egypt or other Asiatic nations. Their earlier legends and poesy are in many instances imbued with the spirit of the oldest traditions of Asia."[39] Schlegel's proposal here is part of what Martin Bernal calls the "Ancient Model" of Greek origins that accepted the Afroasiatic contributions.[40] This was to change soon, around the 1840s, when a second narrative, based on what Bernal calls the "Aryan Model," replaced the earlier one, and suggested that Greek civilization was the product of a mixture of local natives around the Aegean basin and Caucasian conquerors from the north, turning Greece not only into the origin point for all of Europe but also into an autonomous and autochthonous one at that.[41] Under the influence of colonial racism and in tandem with the newly discovered Indo-European language family, he argues, a new narrative of racial purity and cultural autonomy was constructed, and this "fabrication" fitted well with hegemonic views of racial superiority and imperial sovereignty. This new narrative also explains why Egypt gradually disappeared from the public imagination as the quintessential ancient civilization, leaving the space open for India and the "Oriental Renaissance" from the late eighteenth century.

Bernal squarely blames the German Romantics, and especially Schlegel, for this new racialized narrative of ancient civilizations.[42] The evidence, however, is much more complex and hardly in accordance with his sweeping accusation. Schlegel uses both these elements – race and comparative philology – to create his literary history, but recalibrates them to produce very different effects. Schlegel's position, as quoted above, is neither a blind repetition of the "Ancient Model" nor a simple narrative of anti-semitism. Rather, this acknowledgment of cultural interaction in ancient times is a prerequisite for the new literary history he is about to propose. His fundamental aim is to narrate a literary history of Europe and to show how popular cultures in different nations had always been in dialogue with each other to keep a non-classical tradition alive. To argue a case like this, he must first establish the primary requirements for a culture to be recognizable as such, and then identify the mechanisms through which a culture can be delimited from within.

As I have suggested above, this mechanism for Schlegel is the nation, and he has few qualms about imposing this essentially modern idea on ancient history. If Greece is to be the quintessential childhood of all of Europe, it follows that it must have a national unity that marks its uniqueness and then allows it to distinguish itself from similarly formed nations outside its borders. In the light of the new developments in comparative philology, which bring together language and nation as historical allies, Schlegel finds it immensely tempting to rethink literary history in terms of national units. Even if it means endorsing the "Ancient Model" or non-European civilizations (after all, the Indo- part of the new nomenclature was all too obvious), he is quite willing to do so; it is the world divided into different as well as discreet nations that has primacy in his scheme of things. His ratification of a race–language continuum is thus designed to establish this national framework as the cornerstone of literary history, and that is why he shows little hesitation in embracing the "Ancient Model" despite the fact that it runs against the prevalent and racialized discourses of culture. He also secures, by the same move, a longer history for his methods and guards himself against any charge of anachronism.

Literary history, in Schlegel's mind, thus is not an inert record of historical events and their literary representation, but an active force that documents literature's participation in and shaping of life. As he argues, if literature is to be understood as the "manifold variety essentially characteristic of the production of the mind," then it has to be evaluated against the possible "beneficial influence either on individuals or the nation," and in either case the national character of popular literature has to be prioritized.[43] This schematization of history through national cultures becomes even more pressing as Schlegel approaches the second historical trend, including more contemporary times and literatures. With his insistence on the vernacularization of literary traditions, he completely overturns the accepted narratives of literary history, and suggests instead that literary history becomes thinkable only when seen through national cultures.

It is not the case that history produces different national literatures and hence they need serious attention; rather, literary history turns out to be a valid category of thinking only as an aggregate of national literatures. Without this underlying structure of nations, and their mutual connectedness, there would be no literary history at all. This is apparent in his frequent lamentation over the absence of national unity in Germany – such an absence not only thwarts the possibility of German national literature, but even prevents Germany from entering into this wider literary history.[44] Schlegel indeed maintains that, unlike England and France, Germany as a nation "divided into a number of petty states" has developed neither philosophical materialism nor abstract rationalism and remains fragmented both nationally and intellectually. It is the absence of a national intellectual narrative that holds back Germany and its literary genius from realizing their full potential.[45]

These two broad events in Schlegel's text – ancient and modern – were inspired by the recent histories of colonial philology, especially in British India. Aamir Mufti argues that Schlegel's *Über die Sprache und Weisheit der Indier* was responsible for "a mode of producing the *canon* of 'Indian literature,' that is, a conception of *the unique tradition* of the vast and complex society of the subcontinent, and grounded it in the notion of the Indo-European family of languages."[46] Schlegel was attracted to the British orientalists' methods and wanted to replicate them for Europe. He admits as much in the final section of the text, and suggests that "Indian records" of India's own antiquity show the stages in Mosaic history which are mostly left out of the Bible. He consciously works within the chronology set by Jones (see Chapter 3), adopts its central thesis that Mosaic history is perfectly capable of explaining Indian antiquity since they are identical, and extends it further as a justificatory framework for his own work.[47]

But what this Mosaic history reveals, he claims, is nothing short of a revolutionary rethinking of literature itself:

> As in popular history, the Europeans and Asiatics form only one great family [*große Familie*], and Asia and Europe one indivisible body [*unzertrennbares Ganzes*], we ought to contemplate the literature of all civilized people as the progressive development of *one entire system*, or as *a single perfect structure* [*die Literatur aller gebildeten Völker als eine fortgehende Entwicklung und ein einziges innig verbundenes Gebäude und Gebilde*]. All prejudiced and narrow ideas will thus consciously disappear, many points will first become intelligible in their general connexion, and every feature thus viewed will appear in a new light.[48]

This is perhaps the earliest systematic statement on world literature as a single system or structure developed from the insights offered by colonial philology. As a precursor to this *system* or *structure*, he proposes both a modified "Ancient Model" and recent developments in comparative philology; but it is the central suggestion that literatures of different nations form "one entire system" that changes both the status of literary history and that of literature itself. It is no longer possible to view literature as an "absolute" category, as the Schlegel brothers and their coterie at Jena had maintained earlier, and it is even more impossible to see literary production in national isolation.[49] Schlegel firmly establishes the possibility of literature in its globality, in its participation in world literature.

At this point we can go back once again to Balzac's novel and Rancière's reading of it. I have argued above that Balzac made the extraordinary point of grounding a French novel in two oriental languages that had unique purchase in his time, and, in effect, attested the point Schlegel made about literature. The prospect of fiction was not restricted to one literary culture or one national tradition, but was distributed across languages and nations. The so-called "Oriental style" of Balzac was a recognition of this global trajectory of fiction, and it was ratified further by the ubiquitous orient Balzac and his readers encountered in their everyday life. *La Peau de chagrin*, in other words, functioned within this unified "system" and "structure," within world literature as a concrete possibility, and was meant to be read as such.

Rancière's argument about readability misses this central point, and restricts the paradigm of literature within national cultural traditions against the very spirit of the novel. This is clear even in the opening sequence as the novel exhorts its readers to "read" signs of individual national cultures, but also makes it clear that these diverse signs can share the same space that is non-hierarchized and homogeneous. The sequence's literariness does not reside in individual objects or signs, but functions through the mutual relationship they share, through their ability to participate in the same system and structure that render them readable. Like Schlegel's global literary history, these objects also conjure a world out of their respective signs, and, just as Schlegel's history eventually needs a world as its logical end, so these objects end up covering the whole breadth of a new world of fiction. That is precisely the point of the "poem" unfolding in front of Raphaël, since its force emerges from what Schlegel calls "general connexion" and its beauty is revealed in the "new light" of a unified system. The ubiquitous orient of *La Peau de chagrin* is the novelistic signal of this new worldly career of literature.

Cuvier and Comparatism

Rancière, however, connects Balzac's novel to a different knowledge paradigm derived from the works of the naturalist Georges Cuvier in the following words:

> Further on in the same book [i.e. *La Peau de chagrin*], Balzac contrasts Byron, the poet who has expressed with words some aspects of spiritual turmoil, to the true poet of the time, a poet of a new kind – Cuvier, the naturalist, who has done "true poetry": he has re-built cities out of some teeth, re-populated forests out of some petrified traces and re-discovered races of giants in a mammoth's foot. The so-called realist novelist acts in the same way. He displays the fossils and hieroglyphs of history and civilization. He unfolds the poeticality, the historicity written on the body of ordinary things.[50]

In his eagerness to establish links between literature, science, and politics, Rancière again fails to acknowledge that, by the time Balzac came to invoke Cuvier, the latter's system of comparative anatomy did not stand in secluded brilliance; it was thoroughly integrated into the other system of knowledge I have charted above through the literary sovereign, and through Schlegel.

Indeed, it is Schlegel who makes this point obvious when, while discussing grammatical structures of the languages belonging to the Indo-European family, he submits the following: "There is, however, one single point, the investigation of which ought to decide every doubt, and elucidate every difficulty; the structure or comparative grammar of languages furnishes as certain a key of their genealogy as the study of comparative anatomy has done to the loftiest branch of natural science."[51]

He offers this analogy not to summon intellectual respectability, but more to uncover what he sees as the deeper structural affinities between the two disciplines. As Konrad Koerner suggests, some of Schlegel's central insights into philology are inspired by "those natural sciences which were making considerable advances during the late 18th and the early 19th century, namely, (taxonomic) botany, comparative anatomy, (evolutionary) biology, and geology."[52] This intertextuality leads to two foundational ideas in Schlegel's text – internal structural coherence of a language, through which it can be distinguished from other languages; and typology of languages under different groups. Foucault suggests that it is this genetic understanding of language largely derived from Cuvier's *Leçons d'anatomie comparée* (1800–5) that allows Schlegel (and later Bopp, Grimm, and Rask) to remove languages from the domain of representation and to delineate them "according to the way in which they link together the properly verbal elements that compose them."[53] This transformation from representation to grammatical rules as genetic codes further implies ways of marking differences between two large groups of languages, represented in Schlegel's text through Chinese and Sanskrit. Between these two extremes, Schlegel maintains, every other language can be located and accounted for.

Schlegel's reliance on Cuvier reveals the architecture of comparative philology, and also its calibration of a historical model to flesh out its central insights. I want to draw attention to a frequent usage in Schlegel's text, his assumed interchangeability between Sanskrit and Indian (*Indisch*). While many other languages immediately imply a national community through their names (Chinese, German, or even Basque), Sanskrit does not, but that hardly deters him from accepting that it is a quintessential representation of India as a nation. My point is that the genetic structure of languages is not an end in itself; in Schlegel's scheme of things, every language has to be related to some innate and immutable racial as well as national characteristics. If Sanskrit represents a highly sophisticated structure of inflections, of "perfect simplicity, combined with the richest artistic construction," it naturally suggests a community capable of "the most profound study and the clearest intelligence."[54] The genetic features of languages are thus building blocks with which he wants to compare different languages, to gather them under specific groups or families, and eventually to map the larger distributions of nations. Balzac's invocation of Cuvier needs to be seen as part of this history where comparative anatomy and comparative philology joined hands and created a model of history that ran parallel to the literary history I have charted above.

Balzac returned to Cuvier to elaborate on this point about history in his 1842 forward to *La Comédie humaine*. This time, however, he did not refer to Cuvier's poeticity, but discussed a dispute between Cuvier and Étienne Geoffroy Saint-Hilaire in 1830 on what the latter termed "philosophical anatomy."[55] What is even more striking is that in this dispute Balzac supported Saint-Hilaire and denounced Cuvier. This is part of Balzac's explanation of his "motives" behind *La Comédie humaine*, and he suggests that the "idea originated in a comparison between humanity and animality" (*WAS*, xli). In a pre-Darwinian era, these two foremost naturalists of France argued against each other on a fundamental point in biological sciences, "whether animal structure ought to be explained primarily by reference to function or by morphological laws."[56] While Cuvier represented the functionalist approach and opposed homologies between broadly separated embranchments, Saint-Hilaire suggested a unified vision based on such homologies. Balzac, against the popular sentiment, decided to align with Saint-Hilaire (*WAS*, xlii).

Balzac notes that the point on which the two naturalists disagree is not restricted to science alone, but has deeper and longer roots in philosophy:

> Unity of structure, under other names, had occupied the greatest minds during the two previous centuries. As we read the extraordinary writings of the mystics who studied the sciences in their relation to infinity, such as Swedenborg, Saint-Martin, and others, and the works of the greatest authors on Natural History Leibnitz, Buffon, Charles Bonnet, etc., we detect in the *monads* of Leibnitz, in the *organic molecules* of Buffon, in the *vegetative force* of Needham, in the correlation of similar organs of Charles Bonnet [...] we detect, I say, the rudiments of the great law of self for self, which lies at the root of *unity of plan*. (*WAS*, xli–xlii; emphasis original)

Saint-Hilaire's theory thus represents the culmination point of a longer trend in intellectual history and, for Balzac the devout Catholic, it is nothing short of a vindication of the doctrine of monogenesis. The "Creator," he argues, "works on a single model for every organized being," and the differences in "zoological species" must be explained with reference to their specific environments (*WAS*, xlii).

Immediately after this, Balzac claims that he was all along familiar with this idea, and was convinced of its veracity even before Saint-Hilaire came along to prove it. This time, however, the proof is furnished not from scriptural texts but from his observation of French society in its totality and from his conviction that "in this respect society resembled nature." Social types or species (*espèces sociales*) are his approximation of zoological species, and he works with the hypothesis that these social types not only constitute the social whole but also impart its typical characteristics. These types, like zoological species, spring from the same source, but display their difference owing to their circumstances. The only distinction, he maintains, is that these social types are much more complex than their zoological counterparts, and hence they are much more inscrutable.

Balzac laments the fact that all the great civilizations of the past – Greek, Roman, Egyptian, or Indian – had such types, but their great writers simply "have forgotten to give us the history of manners" that could have described them. Even modern writers, except Walter Scott, have not fared any better. It is here, Balzac insists, that he conceived the basic structure and purpose of *La Comédie humaine*: "French society would be the real author; I should only be the secretary. By drawing up an inventory of vices and virtues, by collecting the chief facts of the passions, by depicting characters, by choosing the principal incidents of social life, by composing types out of a combination of homogeneous characteristics, I might perhaps succeed in writing the history which so many historians have neglected: that of manners" (*WAS*, xlv). After setting out this initial plan, he goes on to divide the multitude of characters and the varied social contexts they occupy into six distinct classes "Scenes of Private Life, of Provincial Life, of Parisian, Political, Military, and Country Life," with the belief that in their individuality as well as representativeness they more or less exhaust the social domain of the contemporary France of his time (*WAS*, liii). Balzac is keenly aware of the ambitious nature of his project, but, to justify it, he again turns to natural philosophy – "If Buffon could produce a magnificent work by attempting to represent in a book the whole realm of zoology," he asks rather rhetorically, "was there not room for a work of the same kind on society?" (*WAS*, xlii).

In setting up this vast array of characters and types, Balzac uses a striking metaphor – a "gallery" (*WAS*, liii). A gallery, he suggests, offers an organizing principle for this vast material by dividing and classifying individuals into different groups and panels, where they can be observed according to their "doings and movements" as well as their "own sense and meaning" (*WAS*, liii). The chief benefit of this organized view is that it allows one to pay attention to individual pavilions, to *read* their minutiae, while the entire gallery also conjures the space of the all-inclusive nation as filled up by different classes and their types. While the gallery may, initially at least, give a sense of haphazard randomness, it is the larger narrative of the nation that holds it together and gradually imposes a sense of signification as well as purpose. The gallery allows one to see how the social species make up the national space, or how the social and the national become interchangeable spatial configurations. Balzac reinforces this sense of the national organicity by quoting his young admirer Felix Davin, who once described the different parts of *La Comédie humaine* as representing different stages of human life, thus establishing a direct homology between his fiction and the French nation (*WAS*, liii).

At this point, with this gallery of characters and events, we are back to the opening sequence of *La Peau de chagrin* and its unique organization of a horizontal readable space. This space is structured around different racialized disciplines of modern orientalism that needed the nation as the eventual framing; and, as the assortment of objects also testifies, a possible world made up of these discreet objects/nations. But this organization makes visible a very different idea of literature that was fashioned through these new disciplines and their cross-sections, at the cusp of world literature. It is hardly a wonder, then, that in a letter to his lover Mme. Hanska written in 1842 Balzac described his ambitious project in these words: "Thus, man, society, and humanity will be described, judged, and analyzed without repetition, and in a work which will be like the *Thousand and One Nights of the West*."[57]

Objects, Exhibitions, Worlds

What Balzac proposed to do in *La Comédie humaine* had another close parallel, again, in Napoleon and his commission to the Institut de France to produce a tableau *générale* representing the advancement of learning since 1789. Though meant to put on display the progress made in the sciences and arts more broadly over the last decade, the tableau and its report – *Tableau historique de l'érudition française: Ou Rapport sur les progrès de l'histoire et de la littérature ancienne depuis 1789* – took a special interest in the new disciplines studying the orient in its myriad diversity, and made it one of the centerpieces of the whole affair. In effect, as Said notes, the tableau exteriorized the orient with the implication that "[k]nowledge was essentially the *making visible* of material, and the aim of a tableau was the construction of a sort of Benthamite Panopticon" (*O*, 127). The report likewise reproduced copious material on oriental geographies, histories, languages, and literatures, with separate entries on Hebrew, Arabic, Persian, Turkish, and so on. In his prefatory discourse, Bon Joseph Dacier, the noted philologist and the secretary of the Académie des Inscriptions et Belles-Lettres, acknowledged Napoleon's oriental campaigns (especially in Egypt) as providing a critical fillip to the expanding study of the orient – making, therefore, an explicit connection between colonial power and orientalism – and expressed his confidence in philology's ability to shape the contours of the new studies undertaken by future scholars.[58]

However, it was Silvestre de Sacy, Balzac's contemporary and one of the chief architects both of the *Tableau historique* and of its report, who most clearly exemplified the idea of knowledge as governmental technique. As Said has shown, Sacy not only invented modern "Orientalism" as an academic discipline, but, quite literally, put the orient on display through his erudition. His works on Arabic embodied this visual drive, and presented the orient to his European audience as a spectacle with hidden meanings and unexplained aesthetic ideals. This spectacular quality was evident, for instance, in his chosen genre in the field, that of the chrestomathy, that "present[ed] the Orient by a series of representative fragments, fragments republished, explicated, annotated, and surrounded with still more fragments." Once these fragments had been pressed into this representative function, as in his popular *Chrestomathie arabe* (3 Vols., 1806), they acquired a life of their own; over time the orientalist's effort to select, edit, annotate, and display these fragments became invisible, and the chrestomathies functioned as independent representations of the land. Much like the *Tableau historique*, these fragments "Orientalized" the orient by producing the illusion of direct and unmediated access to its core cultural otherness (*O*, 128–30).

Sacy's propinquity to Balzac is even more striking in his plan for an "Asiatic museum" in 1823, as "a vast depot of objects of all kinds, of drawings, of original books, maps, accounts of voyages, all offered to those who wish to give themselves to the study of [the Orient]; in such a way that each of these students would be able to feel himself transported as if by enchantment into the midst of, say, a Mongolian tribe or of the Chinese race, whichever he might have made the object of his studies" (quoted in *O*, 165). For him, recent philological researches in oriental languages and civilizations inevitably led to the museum as the next logical step. What he implied in his chrestomathies – that is, unmediated access to the orient – he now wanted to recreate within the more immediate and tactile experience of the museum, and with more power and clarity of vision.

Equally important to note here is the fact that neither Balzac nor Sacy proposed these galleries or museums in some kind of void. Such museums did materialize in the late eighteenth and nineteenth centuries, especially in the French exhibitions starting from 1798, and then at an even larger scale as the Great Exhibition of 1851 in London and as the Exposition Universelle or World Exhibition from 1855 in Paris.[59] The "world" of these exhibitions incorporated the orient as a special place of curiosity: as the catalogue of

Figure 5.2 "La Rue du Caire," Delort de Gléon, *La Rue du Caire: L'Architecture Arabe des Khalifes d'Égypte à l'Exposition Universelle de Paris en 1889* (Paris: Librairie Plon, 1889), 21, 25.

the 1855 exhibition stated, out of the 20,000 exhibitors at least 9,500 – or roughly half – were drawn from the French empire.[60] The reports for 1855 further noted the presence of oriental exotica and artifacts that created quite a stir among the visitors: "Long oriental pipes: books of yellow amber, glass, ivory, horn, metal, coral, etc., pipes of cherry, jasmine, bamboo, rush, reed, etc."[61] The parallel between such exhibitions and Balzac's curiosity shop is obvious, and Sacy's grand vision of being "transported as if by enchantment" into the world represented by these objects was shared by both.

However, this sense of presenting the orient as spectacle reached its climax in what Timothy Mitchell has described as the "object-world" of the 1889 iteration of the World Exhibition in Paris. One of the central attractions of the exhibition was the recreation of a medieval Cairo street or "La Rue du Caire," in the form of a bazar with twenty-five buildings, mosques, and minarets designed by Ferdinand de Lesseps and built by the businessman Delort de Gléon (Figure 5.2). With a view to representing the quintessential orient, the Cairo street included overhanging buildings, shops and stalls selling "perfumes, pastries, and tarboushes," and French actors and models dressed as Egyptian traders, drivers, and belly-dancers. Furthermore, in an attempt to reinforce the sense of authenticity, de

Gléon even imported fifty Egyptian donkeys with their drivers and grooms as well as a shipload of rubble from Cairo.[62] He in fact declared that his version of "the Rue de Caire on the Champs de Mars was more authentic than the streets of Cairo itself, because [...] it was impossible to find an untouched old street in Cairo."[63]

With enough of a hint of the exoticism and chaos of an oriental bazar, the Cairo street invited the visitors to *read* the spectacle, and to decipher the "mute letters" strewn all over the haphazard assortment of oriental objects. Mitchell argues that the Exposition Universelle of 1889 put on display not just an exhibition of objects, but a very specific European "ordering up of the world itself as an endless exhibition" that required the orient as an "outside" foil or an "external reality" to produce the desired effect.[64] The authenticity of the exhibition, thus, belonged less to the orient it sought to represent, and more to the European search for a reliable method of ordering the truth that would render everything legible, irrespective of provenance and purpose. Just like Schlegel's "one entire system," Saint-Hilaire's unified homology, or Balzac's "unity of structure," the exhibition staged the quest for a "world" that was not only an assortment of objects but also a logic of organization that could possibly extend beyond the limits of the designated exhibition area, into the real world as it were.

Mitchell further argues that the effort to put the unruly oriental objects under some kind of ordering gaze or even the close connection between these objects and their commercial potential cannot be reduced to the familiar idea of commodity fetishism. Though these tableaus and exhibitions strongly suggested parallels with what Walter Benjamin sees as the quintessential representation of nineteenth-century Parisian life – namely the arcades built from the middle of the century[65] – the idea of fetishism would do a disservice to this material because of the way it remains too beholden to the notion of misrepresenting the external reality through commodities. Instead of thinking in terms of misrepresentation, Mitchell submits, this new ordering of the world through exhibitions forces one to consider "the novelty of continuously creating the effect of an 'external reality' as itself a mechanism of power."[66]

It follows that, even when the exhibition space deployed these objects to create an authentic spectacle of the orient, what such displays produced was a version of the world beyond the exhibition, as a text or as a painting that one was already aware of. This is why many Europeans, such as Gustave Flaubert, Edward Lane, or Gérard de Nerval, sought to make sense of the "real East" when they visited Egypt or some other place in the Middle East through what they remembered of such exhibitions or through other forms of pre-circulated representations of the east in books, paintings, photographs, prints, and so on. The corporeal east made little sense to them, and, to discipline its bewildering profusion of objects and visuals, like Raphaël in Balzac's novel, they referred back to reading strategies they were familiar with before they actually landed in the orient; as Flaubert put it, "the attentive European rediscovers here much more than he discovers."[67] The world outside the exhibition – or, in fact, the "real East" – was primarily a place for rediscovery and rereading as a way to face the immanent logic that was supposed to structure the spectacle and its exteriority (or the text and the world) even before one entered either of them.

Across a range of disciplines one notices the gradual consolidation of the insights made available by the colonial paradigm of the literary sovereign. It was the potent combination of an aesthetic idea with an anthropological world that made the paradigm popular. However, it was the same combination that pushed the paradigm toward a broader framework that Schlegel and others identified as literary history. It is this framing that we now need to address.

CHAPTER 6

National Enframing

The eventual destination of the literary sovereign was a discursive field that brought together the disparate elements I have been discussing so far – the singularity of literature, the progressive but incremental time of the empire, the framing of world literature, and various "sciences" around race, ethnicity, and civilization. A field shared by different imperial configurations and disciplinary fields, and also claimed by different actors dispersed across its surface, it was especially equipped to appeal to a range of sensibilities and concerns, producing different kinds of affect or intimacy. The fulcrum of this new discursivity, despite its ability to be multivocal and polysemic, however, was the nation, as both its *raison d'être* and its final framing. Around the nation – and also its autonomy and sovereignty – the literary sovereign found its most coherent counterpart, and its immanent anthropological rationale flourished within the new climate of nationalist imagination.

In literary studies, or in critical engagements with literary texts more broadly, this coming together of the literary sovereign and the nation was signaled most prominently by the genre of literary history. With a curious mix of language, race, and ethnicity, literary history made the nation the inevitable and yet ennobling destination for every literary act. In this narrative, the nation was the framing of literary texts and, at the same time, a mode of legitimation. In this chapter, I use the Heideggerian concept of "enframing" or *Gestell* to explore literary history in England from the late eighteenth century onward and argue that it was the nation that literary history posed as the mechanism through which the true being of the literary expressed itself.[1] Within a century or so, the nation presented literature not only as an organic expression of itself but also as a chronicler of its origin that included critical components such as race and language. In other words, if the nation was what Heidegger calls the "setting forth" of the being of the literary, literary texts in turn furnished a record of the being of the nation over time, of its essential characteristics and forms.

This mutual reinforcement was discernible even in Thomas Warton's *The History of English Poetry*, 3 Vols. (1774–81), described by René Wellek as the "first history of English literature 'in form,'" which made some tentative connections between race and language on the one hand and the nation on the other.[2] Within a Habermasian public sphere bristling with print and public debates, Warton sought to organize his material and then to chronicle the very autonomy of English poetry through the framing of the nation. The crucial philosophical connection between race, language, and the nation, however, did not happen with Warton and his contemporaries in England. Such a proposition took shape in two German publications of the same year – Johann Gottlieb Fichte's *Reden an die deutsche Nation* (*Addresses to the German Nation*, 1808) and Friedrich Schlegel's *Über die Sprache und Weisheit der Indier* (*On the Language and Wisdom of the Indians*, 1808). The early beginnings of the literary sovereign's journey toward the national enframing in England found a solid philosophical as well as philological foundation in these two texts, and eventually became the common currency across Europe. Schlegel is particularly important in this respect as he made a programmatic statement out of the colonial archives of British India and offered a virtual blueprint for literary history at a global scale (see Chapter 5).

As a parallel to this gradual dissemination of comparative philology across Europe as the ground for literary history, England also saw the consolidation of various "race sciences" that sought to provide physiological heft to philological theories. As I have indicated in Chapter 3, from its very inception the Indo-European model harbored a racialized core as it made suggestive connections between language families and races. In the imperial context, and with the growing investment in colonial governance during the nineteenth century, these ideas about race, physiology, language family, civilization, and so on – often collected under the sign of *anthropology* – assumed a new status and informed administrative decisions, scholarly discussions, and popular consciousness with unprecedented penetration. Alongside the colonies, even England and Europe were subjected to these new race sciences, and racial demography became an important point of departure for a number of disciplines. English literary history embraced both these ideas surrounding race – philological and anthropological – as its organizing principles, and soon proposed the nation as an aggregate of different racial identities. In different versions, Celtic, Germanic (or Teutonic), Scandinavian (or Saxon), and Norman races constituted the modern English, and their traces were unearthed in available literature with almost forensic precision.

This aggregate, however, was also underwritten by a common origin, by the suggestion that all these races were of Indo-European descent. Beneath the linguistic and physiological diversity, thus, literary history presumed a common racial prototype, and eventually argued that this commonality expressed itself in the form of the nation. In such a narrative, the nation was not only a political entity but also a cultural unit that offered a coherent expression of what it meant to be English. I read Matthew Arnold and his contemporaries as expressing this version of national literature, with its particular emphasis on literary history as the new form of inquiry that brought the nation and its literature together. In a host of English literary histories, as a result, this tension between language, race, and the nation was what defined the literary; as if it were only by breaking up the literary into smaller units that literature could be brought within the ambit of historical order and its history could be written. English literary history thus proposed a somewhat paradoxical idea – while the grand narrative of national literature was the order of the day, the history of such an idea could be related only in terms of smaller units such as race and language, and that too by referring to a range of concepts and disciplines that resided outside the autonomous realm of the literary.

This paradox marked the final objective of the literary sovereign. The anthropological core of the new paradigm made this confluence with the nation almost inevitable. But the specificities of this new narrative of national literature were settled by an array of histories and ideas with clear colonial origin that came together in unexpected ways over time. What this means is twofold: first, the colonial paradigm of the literary sovereign was now truly a global one, with its unique currency across cultures and nations; and second, it was the paradox of being, simultaneously, autonomous and national, autotelic and racialized, singular and historicized, that provided the purchase for this globalization. This chapter tracks this paradoxical destiny of the literary sovereign through the twists and turns of literary history in England.

History before History

The first volume of *The History of English Poetry* (1774) by Thomas Warton – an Oxford don and the Poet Laureate between 1785 and 1790 – begins with a cautionary note. While he acknowledges the pleasure one can derive from narrating the passage from antiquity to the present age with a "tacit comparison of the infinite disproportion between the feeble efforts of remote ages, and our present improvements in knowledge," he believes that it will be hasty and imprudent to discard the past altogether. He urges his readers first to consider the way the "manners, monuments, customs, and opinions of antiquity" form "so strong a contrast with those of our own times" – and thereby reveal "human nature and human invention in new lights" – and then to reflect further on how this historical distance can appeal to "a feeling imagination." Even if one agrees with the general narrative of "transitions from barbarism to civility," the past nonetheless remains an important resource for curiosity and imagination, eventually leading to a political solidity. Any history of English poetry, in Warton's opinion, must take into account this evocative nature of the past, and turn it into a vital component of its central framework. Only when one is ready to accept this duality of the past, he believes, does it become "interesting and instructive" to "pursue the progress of our national poetry, from a rude origin and obscure beginnings, to its perfection in a polished age." It is only when one accords due importance to past efforts that one can appreciate the role of poetry as an "art" that can offer the "most picturesque and expressive representations of manners" or even can "faithfully [record] the features of the times."[3]

Such a historical consciousness was not unique to Warton. In fact, it is possible to argue that he responded to what Jürgen Habermas has described as the typical development of the eighteenth-century public sphere in Britain, namely the phenomenal proliferation of print in the form of biographies, critical editions, commentaries, magazines and periodicals, miscellanies, marginalia, genre history, and so on that introduced a new critical idiom in the public sphere about literary texts.[4] This is evident in the way Warton's text accommodates an astonishing range of material and sources from contemporary scholarship, a rough catalogue of which is provided by Wellek: "[Warton] refers unmistakably to all the biographical dictionaries, from Bale to Cibber, the anthologies, editions, critical works, and partial histories [...]. They are supplemented by an independent inspection of hundreds of manuscripts and printed books, never before used by any author, except the compilers of catalogues. The great Cottonian and Oxford catalogues, Wanley's list in Hickes, the catalogue of the Harleian manuscripts, the Catalogue of Bennet library and bibliographies, especially Ames' *Typographical Antiquities*, were the guide-books which made Warton's search possible and comparatively easy."[5] Within this thriving public discussion, Warton built on the materials made available by an age that took an increasing interest in literary pasts, and used history as an organizing principle. By the same token, he also sought to distinguish his account from notable predecessors such as Alexander Pope's *Essay on Criticism* (1711), William Collins's *Verses to Sir Thomas Hanmer* (1743), Thomas Gray's *Progress of Poesy* (1754), or even Horace Walpole's *Catalogue of the Royal and Noble Authors of England* (1758).

One of the central outcomes of this public interest in literary history, including Warton's *History*, as James Turner has shown, was the production of "a newly prominent object of philological scrutiny: English literature." Though the "field" remained somewhat uncertain and variegated, and less coherent than "biblical or Anglo-Saxon scholarship," the central emphasis on vernacular literary texts marked it as a distinguished venture in the second half of the eighteenth century.[6] With the labor of such authors as Gerard Langbaine, Zachary Grey, Lewis Theobold, William Oldys, Thomas Birch, John Upton, Thomas Percy, Samuel Johnson, Edward Capell, and many others, English literature made significant inroads in both academic and public discussions. For someone like Warton writing the history of English poetry, the central challenge was to find a method to arrange the unprecedented profusion of material in his contemporary era and then to conceive of a historical narrative that would be commensurate with the enormity of a national literary tradition.

He uses both "nation" and "race" to define the underlying unity of the corpus whose history he sets out to recount, but nevertheless remains committed to finding a historical model that not only incorporates the recent textual/philological scholarship (often put together under the general name of "criticism"), but also appropriately characterizes the manifold ways texts and communities interact with each other. I shall return to this invocation of the nation and race – often in tandem, sometimes as interchangeable – in a moment, but let us first pay attention to the notion of literary history that Warton espouses:

> I have chose to exhibit the history of our poetry in a chronological series: not distributing my matter into detached articles, of periodical divisions, or of general heads. Yet I have not always adhered so scrupulously to the regularity of annals, but that I have often deviated into incidental digressions; and have sometimes stopped in the course of my career, for the sake of recapitulation, for the purpose of collecting scattered notices into a single and uniform point of view, for the more exact inspection, or for a comparative survey of the poetry of other nations.[7]

What stands out in this passage is his eagerness to designate his method as a serial but somewhat qualified chronology that is different both from "periodical divisions" and from simple linear accounts as recorded in traditional "annals."

The point becomes even more noteworthy as he tells his readers that, while choosing this method, he considered and abandoned two other contemporary proposals for literary history prepared by Alexander Pope and Thomas Gray – both described as the "most distinguished ornaments" of English poetry – because they either divided the English poets under "their supposed respective schools" or "sacrificed much useful intelligence to the observance of arrangements." For him, such divisions and artificial periodization are detrimental to literary history because they falsify chronological development and present a distorted picture. His method of uninterrupted yet qualified chronology, depicting the "gradual improvements of our poetry," Warton insists, works better than these ambitious but eventually flawed schemes because it has the advantage of historical progress on its side.[8] In a letter to Gray dated April 20, 1770, he defends his plan of writing chronological history "in sections" and continuing it "as matter successively offer itself." He also adds: "Though I proceed chronologically, yet I often stand still to give some general view, as perhaps a particular species of poetry, etc. and even anticipate sometimes for this purpose. These views often form one section, yet are interwoven with the tenor of the work, without interrupting my historical series."[9]

Quite clearly, Warton is operating with a model of literary history that is different from those proposed by either Pope or Gray. This is how he formulates the usefulness of his method: "My performance [...] exhibits without transposition the gradual improvements of our poetry, at the same time that it uniformly represents the progression of our language."[10] This clubbing together of poetry and language as the groundwork for literary history is a vital point for Warton and also for my argument in this chapter, and hence I want to spend a little more time on this claim. Immediately after this statement, he points out that his decision to omit the "Saxon poetry" from his "annals" will perhaps be a controversial one. As a justification for his choice, he offers various reasons, including the facts that Anglo-Saxon language is confined to a handful of specialists and that Anglo-Saxon poetry offers little more than "religious rhapsodies," but the real cause lies elsewhere. He argues that, linguistically speaking, there is very little that his present era shares with the Anglo-Saxon ancestors. Ironically enough, this rupture in history was occasioned by the Norman conquest of 1066 that shaped both the English race and its language – before it, Warton admits frankly, "we were an unformed and unsettled race." "That mighty revolution," he continues, "obliterated almost all relation to the former inhabitants of this island; and produced that signal change in our policy, constitution, and public manners, the effects of which have reached modern times." It is but natural for him to begin his history "with that era, when our national character began to dawn."[11] His decision to exclude Anglo-Saxon poetry is thus both cultural and chronological, and he believes that any literary history worthy of the name must submit to these two vital axes.

In Warton's account, culture and chronology, as two interdependent lines of historical development, encompassing a people and its time, are accessible first through the fundamental connection between language and literary production and then through the gradual development of a race/nation. The first set of coordinates in this formulation – that is, language and literature – are indeed organic expressions of the second set that combines the nation and race. Warton demonstrates this connection as he begins his history with the "Saxon language." He first divides it into three distinct phases – "British Saxon," "Danish Saxon," and "Norman Saxon" – and then takes up the third as the starting point for his literary history.[12] What arrests our attention is his insistence on a parallel between literary composition and the post-conquest settlement of English history until the reign of Henry II, with a suggestion that the confused tongue of the earlier era achieved a distinct poetic quality with political stability. Of course, this was partly aided by the frequent interaction with French and Latin through the conquerors; but the bulk of Warton's analysis relies on the emergence of a distinct national character. English poetry for him is closely tied to the English identity, both as a race and also as a nation, with distinct cultural markers.

At this point, we can access some of the essential assumptions behind Warton's literary history. His central point is chronological, of course, but this chronology is closely tied to a sense of cultural autonomy. A history of English poetry becomes possible and narratable only when the idea of being "English" could be ascertained with some degree of certitude, and when such a field could be demarcated internally. Warton's transition narrative from the annals of an "unformed and unsettled race" to a recognizable national canon is premised on the fact that it is in the language after conquest, despite its "grossness and absurdity," that one can recognize the "antient manners" of this emerging nation – he is even ready to argue that such manners are reminiscent of the "pictures of manners" in Homer, as both are "founded in truth and reality, and actually painted from the life."[13]

Alongside this emphasis on language and national identity, Warton also feels obliged to reproduce the narrative arc of progress from the Conquest to Restoration, as espoused by many of his contemporaries, with authors such as Dryden and Pope as the pinnacle of English versification. While he does subscribe to such a general view, he also devotes a large part of his *History* to early English poetry. He ends the first volume with Chaucer, but it is equally remarkable for its recuperation of pre-Chaucerian poetry through extensive quotes, critical comments, short biographies, various "digressions," and so on that brought this body of writing to public notice for the first time. This is not an accidental outcome, but a long-standing research project for him. In his early publication *Observations on the Faerie Queene of Spenser* (1754), for instance, he proposed a short and somewhat schematic account of early English poetry, but it is only with his *History* that he is able to flesh it out and give it a definite narrative form.

I suggest that Warton's *History*, along with several other publications, including Edward Capell's *Prolusions or Select Pieces of Antient Poetry* (1760), John Bowle's *Miscellaneous Pieces of Antient Poesie* (1764), Thomas Percy's *Reliques of Ancient English Poetry* (1765), William Duff's *Critical Observations on the Writings of the Most Celebrated Original Geniuses in Poetry* (1770), or even Johnson's *The Lives of the English Poets* (1779–81), created a sense of a literary past that was both unique to the second half of the eighteenth century and essential to the growing nationalist politics. The fact that such a literary past could play an instrumental role in shaping nationalist consciousness had been demonstrated a few years earlier by James Macpherson's controversial "Ossian" poems from the 1760s.[14] Macpherson's claims of "translating" old poems originally composed in the "Gaelic or Erse Language" from the Scottish Highlands sharply divided public opinion – whereas eminent English critics such as Johnson attacked the Ossian poems as a "Scotch conspiracy in national falsehood," the Scottish minister of the church and professor of rhetoric at the university of Edinburgh Hugh Blair wrote a full-fledged defense entitled *A Critical Dissertation on the Poems of Ossian, The Son of Fingal* (1763). As Katie Trumpener has demonstrated, the support for Macpherson soon turned into a wholesale endorsement of Scottish nationalism, while the attack on him was seen as a repudiation of the Scottish cause itself.[15] It was evident across the acrimonious divide that the Ossian poems validated different national prerogatives within the union, by making Scotland a claimant to the shared "British" past and yet signposting its difference through its essentially Gaelic identity.

Macpherson's alleged translations made a direct connection between history, literature, and the nation, and, ironically enough, the following debates actually gave his formulation a stamp of approval while contesting some of its implications. It was clearly evident that one of the most vital resources for the nationalist claim could be literature, or, to be more precise, literary history. Many of the early attempts at English literary history – Percy's *Reliques of Ancient English Poetry*, for instance – were written in the context of the Ossian controversy, and often with an explicit aim to refute Macpherson's claims by proposing an alternative and "authentic" English tradition. Such a close connection between literary scholarship and political configurations, as Lee Morrissey has shown, has a long history in England, at least since the Civil War of the middle of the seventeenth century. The "debate over literacy and democracy," in Morrissey's reckoning, "moves from a 'participatory' model in the 1640s, to a 'republican' idea in the 1650s, to a 'representative' democracy articulated by Addison and Steele, to a 'procedural' approach hinted at by Hume, to the constitutional approach described by Johnson."[16]

Following from this, it is possible to argue that Warton and early English literary history, as yet another development in textual scholarship, represented a further cycle and made a connection between literary history and nationalism. Either one of Macpherson's claim of retrieving an ancient Gaelic past or Warton's attempt to portray "manners, monuments, customs, and opinions of antiquity," when seen through this evolving history of politics and textual scholarship, inevitably directs one to the autonomy of a collective self, poised between the nation and the empire.

What we encounter in early English literary history, in other words, is a paradoxical situation – on the one hand, the new concern with literary history was closely tied to the eventual autonomy of a public sphere that relied heavily on print; on the other, this new history could have been told only within the national frame, as an "authentic" articulation of the people, which was inimical to such an autonomy. In a sense, this new narrative form is indebted to the Habermasian bourgeois public sphere and its heavy premium on public reason. This eighteenth-century public sphere, as Habermas puts it, was a decidedly modern phenomenon as it emerged as a unique discursive space different both from the state and from the market.

In the "model" British case, this phenomenon consolidated itself through a literary public sphere, aided by journals and other print material as also by coffee houses and clubs. During the eighteenth century, the proliferation of journals and weekly or daily newspapers including the *Craftsman*, the *Gentleman's Magazine*, the *London Magazine*, and eventually the *Morning Chronicle* and the *Times* also meant a gradual but decisive entry into the political sphere, where the newly constituted public could also participate in discussions about the monarch or the parliament. In Habermas's account, this transition from the literary to the political remains one of the decisive features of the autonomy of the public sphere and also one of the mechanisms that held together many contradictory forces of the new publicness.[17] In English literary history, however, such a transition was not an external phenomenon but its constitutive force, even its essential *raison d'être*, as it attempted an unprecedented union of the literary and the political by making the latter the precondition of the former. What Habermas describes as the gradual emergence of the autonomous public sphere received a succinct but powerful parallel in the development of literary history.

In another sense, however, this autonomy was undercut by the eagerness to find a historical horizon for the political. In a way, this was the most logical resolution for the growing intimacy between textual criticism and politics, as the autonomy of this transaction had to find an eventual structural unity. In the growing sentiment of the period, which Saree Makdisi has described as "antimodern," this unity was the nation.[18] What is equally important to note is the imperial context of this resolution – first in the case of the British Isles and then within the larger empire more gradually. The literary public sphere was being reshaped with the expansion of the British empire, and the political core of the empire – that is, the nation – began to dominate the scholarship on literary history. Warton's *History* uses the nation as a loose framework for the history he intends to tell, but the text struggles to keep together the resources derived from contemporary scholarship that was decisively modern and the idea of a primordial nation that somehow bestows coherence on this material. Many of his peers pointed out the jumbled nature of this text that seemed somewhat uncertain of its own mission. In fact, most of his contemporaries struggled with the same dilemma, and remained ambivalent about a possible resolution. As I argue in the following pages, this resolution eventually came from colonial histories, through the literary sovereign's double premium on race and language. But, to chart that story, we first need to turn to the texts of Fichte and Schlegel.

German Detour

In his *Addresses to the German Nation*, delivered in a Berlin under Napoleonic occupation in 1807–8, Fichte identifies a peculiar relationship between language, literature, and political sovereignty. He notes the popular opinion that, even if political independence had been lost for the time being, the essential nationhood can still hope to survive the present crisis by being true to its language and literature – by preserving them for posterity – since these are the fundamental resources that define the people. Insofar as German literature is concerned, this is a particularly paradoxical case – on the one hand, Germany, being "split up into several separate States [...] was held together as a common whole almost solely by the instrumentality of the man of letters, by speech and writing." On the other, however, Fichte strongly feels that language and national sovereignty are so entangled with each other that one cannot meaningfully sustain itself without the other. If it is true that "wherever a separate language is found, there a separate nation exists," it naturally follows for him that "where a people has ceased to govern itself, it is equally bound to give up its language and to coalesce with its conquerors, in order that there may be unity and internal peace and complete oblivion of relationships which no longer exist."[19] At a time when the political independence of the German states is threatened by Napoleon and when an uneasy calm prevails across the land following the humiliating Treaties of Tilsit (1807), Fichte finds little comfort in the idea that German language and literature will continue the essence of Germany's nationhood and hand it down to future generations. For him, the other possibility of German culture being overwhelmed by the victorious French one and German literature turning into a pale imitation of the conqueror's literature is far more real and proximate.

Fichte's anxiety frames the idea of the literary sovereign in a number of ways. At one end of his argument is the high premium he places on German as a "living language" that has continued unbroken from its inception. As opposed to the "neo-Latin" or "foreign" languages of other peoples of Teutonic descent, German is a living language because it "has developed continuously out of the actual common life of the people" and it has never entertained any element "that did not express an observation actually experienced by this people" (*AGN*, 61–2). The obvious Herderian core of this formulation acquires further impetus as Fichte proposes an original and universal language of all humanity, and then distinguishes each individual language through a complex interaction of its "sensuous" and "supersensuous" components.[20] For a "living" language like German, he argues, these two components remain organically available to its speakers because both the linguistic symbol and the mental image spring from the "whole previous life of the nation." In fact, the bond between the "idea and its designation" in a living language is so strong that the language functions as the virtual archive of the "whole history of the nation's culture" (*AGN*, 68–9).

For my purpose here, the important point is this unambiguous qualification of the living language as the archive of a national culture. In fact, what distinguishes a "living" language from a "dead" one, in his view, is precisely this archival quality that constitutes the foundation for a national culture and yet remains somewhat detached from it as a parallel resource. This essential doubling of language – as both *arché* and *telos* – is what Fichte takes as the defining relationship between a language and the nation it embodies. It is important to note here that he is quite willing to accept one part of the popular opinion he later notes and rejects, namely the archival quality of German as a language. However, Fichte discards the other part – survival of the nation through language even under political subjugation – since he believes that such archival quality in itself is not a guarantor of nationhood; even for a "living" and continuous language, the crucial question of survival is closely tied to political independence. The all-important issue of "freedom" that underpins both his reflections on the French Revolution and his formulations in the *Wissenschaftslehre* or *The Science of Knowledge* (first published in 1794) as the unfettered autonomy of human spirit reappears here as the precondition for both linguistic and national self-sufficiency.[21] German survives as a living language and a communal archive because it remains free of "foreign" or external influences such as Latin; and, similarly, German nationhood can build on this linguistic resource only if it can achieve political sovereignty.

In a crucial sense, Fichte squarely places history at the heart of his reflections on language and nationhood, as both an animating force and a frame. This is most prominently visible in the justification for his somewhat chauvinistic view that German is the only living language. He does compare German to Greek on the ground that both are "primitive" languages, but for his contemporary world his mother tongue remains the only example of a living language. At one level, this is a political choice – for the future linguistic cohesion of a community that is currently scattered across small states and duchies, the special quality of the language has to be highlighted. Fichte, likewise, argues that it is the *history* of this shared language – continuous and living – that harbors the future promise of the nation. When he qualifies German as "living," the qualification applies equally to the language and the history of sharing that language, and unites all German-speaking people within a hitherto-unattainable organic unity.

But, at another level, this is a point about history itself. Fichte is quite unambiguous in stating that living and dead languages have different historical implications: his central idea is that in a community of living language "mental culture [*Geistesbildung*] influences life," whereas in a community of dead language "mental culture and life go their way independently of each other" (*AGN*, 70). As we shall see soon, this initial idea has further consequences for these respective communities, but the fundamental point remains that the distinction between the two different types of language is derived from history and that language, in turn, shapes national histories in discrete ways. Languages and nations, in other words, are tied in a causal chain, and history is that often-overlooked but inevitable chain.

What Fichte calls the mental culture or *Geistesbildung* of a people, and the way he connects it to language, indeed holds the key to his theory of history. As I have mentioned above, his point about German is its qualification as a *living* language. In such a language, he argues, the central feature is that it preserves something "native" or an element of the local that remains somewhat unchanged over time. While all languages develop according to strict rules that combine vocalic sounds and local influences, living languages are marked by a continuity of these rules. What is striking in Fichte's argument is his eagerness to treat language as a "thing": "Just as things immediately present influence man, so must the words of such a [living] language influence him who understands them; for they, too, are things, and not an arbitrary contrivance" (*AGN*, 61). Such thingness of language covers both the "sensuous" and the "supersensuous" (described as "Thing-without-image") elements, and produces temporal continuity. In such a continuous and living language, he asserts, "all its parts are life and create life" (*AGN*, 61). In a language like German, what is immediately local and also what remains abstractly distilled are two different expressions of the same "native" element, especially through its persistent continuity through history. German is, in fact, first distinguished by the native elements that constitute the sensuous world; and then its quintessential quality is maintained through the gradual development of the supersensuous that grows later but nonetheless remains faithful to the "original people" (*AGN*, 62).

Such a theory of language, with its overpowering emphasis on the "native" elements or the "original people," inevitably leads to the idea of race. Of course, Fichte's *Addresses* begins with the assumption that the Germans form a distinct and "original" race, but once the question of language is introduced, he feels it necessary to spell out the special relationship that these two components share with each other in order to provide the nation with its specific shape and vocation. In the "Fourth Address" he makes the point about "origin" – for both race and language – central to his argument, and suggests a natural continuum between the original people and their language. One of the reasons for German's qualification as the only living language is that its speakers stayed in their original homeland and never accepted the supremacy of a foreign language.

This parallel continuity of race and language, and their intimate ties with whatever is local or native, in Fichte's view, distinguish the Germans from other people of Teutonic descent. And it is this parallel again that allows him to argue that the mental culture produced from such a combination will inevitably find its characteristic expressions in philosophy, science, or poetry. Just as language constitutes an individual or a people (and not the other way around), similarly the same language expresses itself through the mental culture of the people, through its arts and modes of thinking. Race and language are manifestations of the same spirit that defined the Germanness in the first place. In fact, it is possible to argue that they function as the precondition for each other.

Let us look at Fichte's note on poetry to illustrate my point. The first point to note is the divergence he marks of his theory of race, language, and poetry from the existing tradition, including the discussions among English literary historians I have charted above. His primary point is that the original people have access to a living language and its resources in a way that a "new people" with an adopted and "dead" language can never have. Fichte draws a direct connection between sensuous and poetic language, where the latter is a creative extension of the former. "Only a living language," he maintains, "can have such poetry, for only in such a language can the range of sensuous imagery be extended by creative thought, and only in it does what has already been created remain alive and open to the influence of kindred life" (*AGN*, 79). As opposed to this, the dead language adopted by a new people has inadequate scope for poetic creation. Though they may create, for a limited period, what sounds like good poetry by "placing [...] unfamiliar vesture upon the commonplace that gives it a charm akin to that produced by idealization," eventually this will be an incomplete and somewhat futile act (*AGN*, 79–80). The distinction here is the organic progression from the sensuous to the poetic – a process reserved exclusively for the living language – and the absence of such a path means a closure to the poetic genius. Any dead language will eventually grow out of the charm of "idealization" in poetry and will repeat itself in a superficial way. The striking thing about this formulation is Fichte's insistence on poetry being an extension of the race–language combination, almost in the sense of historical destiny, and the invocation of the idea of organic life as the determining force for literary composition.

History – or literary history – in this Fichtean model can only be a chronicle of this organicity that runs across race, language, and poetry and enlivens all three by its sheer force. He says as much when he asks rhetorically: "What does a sensible writer want, and what can he want? Nothing else but to influence public life and the life of all, and to form and reshape it according to his vision; and if he does not want to do this, everything he says is empty sound to tickle the ears of the indolent" (*AGN*, 215). This submission to "public life and the life of all" is also a submission to the "governors" and eventually to the "State," and Fichte holds the view that "every effort in science indirectly serves the State" (*AGN*, 215). What literature as an expression of the original people can do – and *must* do, according to him – is to align itself with the "language of the dominant race" that constitutes the State, and remain alive to a future that will bring this relationship into a perfect union. In a crucial sense, such an alignment is necessary for the "worth and [...] independence" of literature, and without this link literary texts will lapse into the dead superficiality that Fichte abhors. Sovereignty of the state, in the final analysis, is the conclusive destiny of literature and its autonomy (*AGN*, 215–16).

A second line of inquiry around the same set of issues and within the context of literary history is available in Schlegel. As I have argued in Chapter 5, Schlegel's main achievement was to transform the tree of comparative philology into a map for literary history. Jones's conjectures on the connections between philology and ethnology, and the migration of population with their respective languages (see Chapter 3 for details), received an extended treatment in the hands of Schlegel. The combination of race, language, and the nation – as a cultural block of elements that mutually reinforced each other and not as isolated traits of a population – became the groundwork to imagine history. Schlegel first proposes this idea, like Jones and Colebrooke before him, through language and identifies two broad groups on the basis of the following principle: "Modifications of meaning, or different degrees of significations, may be produced either by inflection or internal variations of the primitive word, or by annexing to it certain peculiar particles, which in themselves indicate the past, the future, or any other circumstance."[22]

With a far better grip on philology than Fichte, he then proceeds to offer a typology of different languages. At one end of his table is the "Indian Language" – by which he means Sanskrit – which allows maximum inflection, and on the other is Chinese, which is "almost without inflection." After marking out these two extreme flanks, he groups different languages according to their proximity to the one or the other – while Greek, Latin, Persian, or Germanic languages are docketed toward Sanskrit, others including Arabic, Hebrew, Malay, Basque, Coptic, and the various "dialects" of the Americas are docketed toward Chinese. The first group has one common origin, which will soon be named the Indo-European, while the latter group does not have any shared ancestry. Though Schlegel argues that this distinction is primarily a philological one, it is nonetheless not value-neutral – the first group is the superior one, and, even though he occasionally lauds the rhetorical flourish of Arabic or Hebrew, he has little doubt about their inherent inferiority (*AMW*, 446–8).

As Schlegel relies on comparative philology – a discipline of colonial origin – for his analyses of Indian languages and philosophy, history emerges as his central framework, and he increasingly deploys a form of historical comparatism that is global in ambition. This world historical perspective is anchored in language, and the two groups of languages are identified both in terms of their elementary grammatical structures as well as in relation to their progress in history. It is important to note here that the refinement of a language is not an isolated incident in Schlegel's scheme of things; rather, language is seen as an organic expression of a race or civilization. Thus, for instance, when he describes the fundamental features of these two groups, the language is loaded with phrases that are not restricted to philology alone.

Such sweeping typology allows Schlegel to reflect on a number of issues ranging from the origins of language to the complex structure of Indian philosophy, but it becomes especially useful as he comes to comment on poetry and its history. Like Fichte, he also suggests that languages are individual archives, but his argument is a more historicist one, as he maintains that the ancient past can be understood only when one combines a "comprehensive review of the entire scheme of mythology" with the "historical genealogy of the language" (*AMW*, 496). Poetic diction springs from these ancient mythologies and marks a progress from an original "wild and gigantic power" to later "softer and sweeter impulses," and this development is contained in individual languages (*AMW*, 499). Through a comparative framework of Greek, Egyptian, and Indian mythologies, Schlegel proposes this origin story for poetry as both universal and historically verifiable. He even suggests that "all to which that name [i.e. poetry] has been given in later times, when art had annexed so much to the original germ, becomes so only when it breathes a kindred spirit with those old heathen fictions, or because it springs from them" (*AMW*, 499). Any history of poetry is a history of this gradual progression from an "original ground work" that is "strange and wild" to a later version of "spiritual loveliness" (*AMW*, 500).

This multilingual and comparative frame, however, is undergirded by an elaborate narrative of race, migration, and colonization. As he notes, "the distribution of races of men, like the internal formation of mountains to the geologist, supplies a portion of our lost historical records, laying before us, as it were, a ground-plan of history" (*AMW*, 502). Race in such an imagination is as natural as the geological components of a mountain, and, presumably, just as readable to an expert eye. But Schlegel insists that such signs are evident less in physiological features and more in languages. It is this claim about language that leads him to trace ancient migration of races along the Indo-European tree, and to propose the revolutionary theory that such migrations are all "directly or indirectly of Indian origin." Even when one considers the case of Europe, he describes it as a gradual migration toward the north-west; and, on the other hand, wherever this migration did not happen – as in the Americas or southern Africa – the people remained in their "original necessitous and barbarous condition" with "scarcely any history" (*AMW*, 504–5). Migration, colonization, and history are interrelated in ways that are not immediately visible, but Schlegel feels confident enough to state that even the reach of the Roman empire is but a mere trifling matter when compared with this ancient migration of Indian or Asiatic peoples across Asia, northern Africa, and Europe.

When put together, Schlegel's reflections on the gradual progress of poetry and racial migration form a global scheme of things, and distribute literary history according to racial groups and their gradual refinement over time. His account of literary history is closely connected to a sense of global history where the whole world is divided according to the two philological groups he identifies initially, and then the same world is accessed through the variegated degrees of literary achievement. In a way, this world history model is borrowed from what Thomas Trautmann calls Jones's "Mosaic ethnology."[23] Unlike Jones, however, Schlegel is somewhat ambiguous about a parallel reading of Mosaic and Indian histories. Rather, he is much more interested in tracing a global history by combining the two, by suggesting that the "oriental system in general will [...] furnish a most instructive comment on the Holy Scriptures" (*AMW*, 516). Philology and ethnology are thus redeployed to read such scriptural texts as enlightening each other, and then operationalized as the groundwork for history itself. When he proposes a global scheme of literary history, Schlegel mobilizes all these elements to rethink the literary – its vicissitudes across race, region, and migration/colonization. Unlike Fichte, he does not pose an essential opposition between life and death, but imagines the question of life as gradational and contingent; and, accordingly, proposes literary history as evidence as well as testimony.

This becomes clear as he charts out a literary history for India. In the second part of his text, he divides Indian antiquity into four ages – the periods marked by the Vedas, by *Mahābhārata* and *Rāmāyana*, by Vyasa and Purāṇas, and by Kālidāsa and other poets (*AMW*, 494–5) – and suggests that his proposed literary history must also follow a similar scheme of periodization. For Schlegel, this is an important point, since he believes that "[a] general knowledge of philosophy is indispensable for the investigation of Oriental literature, and particularly for the Indian branch of it" and hence they need to be mapped across each other (*AMW*, 521). Like many colonial officials before him, he describes such literature in the following words: "The chief peculiarities of Oriental literature are supposed to consist in a bold and lavish pomp of imagery, and in the tendency to allegory usually combined with those qualities" (*AMW*, 523). But, unlike his predecessors, he identifies the reason behind this not so much in climate or geography but in the "highly intellectual religion" of India (*AMW*, 523).

This interdependence of philosophy and literature recounts all his previous assumptions about race, language, religion, and so on, but this time he marks a crucial change by suggesting that, within the global historical scheme, Indian literary tradition remains beholden to something external to itself. In its general development, he adds, this literary tradition attains its autonomy only as it offers the expression of an underlying national unity, as is evident in the "Socountalâ of Câlidâs" (*AMW*, 523–4). As against the earlier phases of Indian intellectual history that produced the Vedas and the Purāṇas or even the two epics, he suggests, the period of Kālidāsa demonstrated greater literary freedom as it gravitated more toward a national frame. In other words, with the fourth phase of Indian history, the idea of the nation becomes prominent and also functions as the guarantor of the autonomy of literature.

This peculiar character of Indian literary history, however, is not available in its isolation. On the contrary, the complex interaction between Indian philosophy and literature becomes visible only when it is set against other histories and other nations, especially in Europe, and when Indian literature is judged as a national corpus. In fact, the underlying premise of comparative philology is reinvented as global literary history in Schlegel's thought, and this globe is an aggregate of nations. Literature is not simply added to this mix, but is seen as an essential expression of the nation, comprising its critical components such as race and language. Through Fichte and Schlegel's works, the idea of literary history was irrevocably tied to the nation in the first place and subsequently to its constitutive elements, and in the ensuing decades this would become a ready template for appropriation. The literary sovereign's singularity and autonomy, from this point onward, would be trapped in the complex cultural matrix created by the nation.

Nation, Race, History

By the middle of the nineteenth century, these philological and anthropological insights on race and the nation saturated European public discussions so thoroughly that they in fact became available for commonsensical citation. Such discussions were not fueled by mere ignorance or deep prejudice alone, but decisively sustained by what Maurice Olender calls "erudition" or different branches of knowledge production that deployed race in myriad ways.[24] In many of these usages, the nation emerged as the eventual and also the most logical framing. In England, race and the nation became two of the most dynamic categories to think through both the ever-expanding empire and the exclusivity of English history. As numerous scholars have shown, English cultural thinking was so thoroughly racialized in the nineteenth century that it was almost impossible to find any branch of it that did not adopt race or racialism in some form or other. Even a central text of English culture like Matthew Arnold's *Culture and Anarchy* (1867–8) was completely infused with contemporary race-thinking. His central categories of distinction – Hellenism and Hebraism – were but thinly veiled racialized terms, derived from diverse sources such as the philologist Ernest Renan and the anthropologist W. F. Edwards.[25]

In accordance with this general intellectual climate, literary history in England embraced these arguments as its founding principles. In fact, I argue in the following pages that literary history gave a coherent expression to many of these disparate elements circulating as part of both public discussions and scholarly concerns. W. J. Courthope, in the very first volume of his influential *A History of English Poetry* (1895), for instance, describes his methods in the following words: "In this history I have looked for the unity of the subject precisely where the political historian looks for it, namely, in the life of the nation as a whole: my aim has been to treat poetry as an expression of the imagination, not simply of the individual poet, but of the English people."[26] In his gloss he adds further that the "poet is [...] the epitome of the imaginative life of his age and nation; and, indeed, it may be said that in what may be called his raw materials – his thought, imagination, and sentiment – his countrymen co-operate in his work." Because of this deeply communal nature of poetry, "[a]lmost every great English poet has shown his consciousness of the organic national life" and hence a "great poem is, in fact, an image of national feeling."[27]

Leslie Stephen repeats this sentiment in his *English Literature and Society in the Eighteenth Century* (1904) – delivered as Ford Lectures at Oxford in 1903 – when he observes that "there is a close relation between the literature and the general social condition of a nation." Though he is doubtful of literature's ability to capture the nation in its entirety, he is nonetheless ready to admit that the "growth of new forms is obviously connected not only with the intellectual development but with the social and political state of the nation."[28] Even a popular textbook like Thomas B. Shaw's *Shaw's New History of English Literature* (1874) proposes to conjoin English "nationality" and "language" as the groundwork for its literary history.[29]

Some of the germs of this formulation can be traced back to Henry Hallam's monumental three-volume *Introduction to the Literature of Europe in the Fifteenth, Sixteenth, and Seventeenth Centuries* (1837–9), which imagines Europe as an aggregate of nations and then proceeds to chronicle their national literary genius with some details. For him, Chaucer and Wicliffe (John Wycliffe) signal a "national literature" for England or Gil Vicente represents the "old national style of Spain and Portugal," and he defends the coinage "the Anglo-Norman language" as an agreeable description of the "amalgamation of two different races."[30] He seems convinced of the fact that the nation provides the most persuasive unity to literary history, but less so regarding its constitutive elements. At times, he proposes language as the essential and adequate ground, especially with the rise of modern vernaculars after the decline of Latin across Europe. The development of such vernaculars is often seen as paralleling – and embodying – the progress of respective nations. At other times, however, Hallam also offers additional ideas such as race or an underlying spirit of the age to define national literature, culture, or even style.

His account of English literature is a case in point. Like Warton before him, he spends some time on the problematic issue of determining the difference between languages before and after the Norman conquest, but, unlike his predecessor, he is less certain of a complete break. Even when he subscribes to the general narrative of a transition from Anglo-Saxon to English as a consequence of the conquest, he nevertheless points out the slow and gradual nature of the change and remains somewhat noncommittal regarding the idea of the post-conquest language announcing a completely new beginning for the English nation.

He seems more certain of an English national literature around the beginning of the fifteenth century, after the interventions of gifted authors such as Chaucer and Gower, and suggests that at this point it becomes comparable to its European counterparts: "Thus by the year 1400, we find a national literature subsisting in seven European languages, three spoken in the Spanish peninsula, the French, the Italian, the German, and the English; from which last, the Scots dialect need not be distinguished.

Of these the Italian was the most polished, and had to boast of the greatest writers; the French excelled in their number and variety. Our own tongue, though it had latterly acquired much copiousness in the hands of Chaucer and Wicliffe, both of whom lavishly supplied it with words of French and Latin derivation, was but just growing into a literary existence. The German, as well as that of Valencia, seemed to decline."[31] Insofar as he is concerned, the post-conquest nation stabilized itself only after a considerable period of time, and, even though the new language was heavily infused with "words of French and Latin derivation," it still managed to express a national unity. The question of the origin and purity of the language remained somewhat uncertain and unsettled for some time before the new linguistic flourish could find solid ground to claim a national community of its own.

Hallam's dilemma in defining what constitutes a nation – and, consequently, a national literature – is typical of his time. Although his vision of Europe as an aggregate of discreet nations reminds one of Schlegel's plan for a global literary history, the latter's conceptualization of language as an exclusive repository of national characteristics is somewhat missing. Around this time a new idea of the nation that was based on race – a derivative of the imperial culture – gradually made inroads in England and defined much of its intellectual endeavor. Through successive hands, such as those of Samuel George Morton, Josiah Clark Nott, George Gliddon, Arthur de Gobineau, Robert Knox, John Beddoe, Edwards, Renan, and others, this new idea of racialized history – based on "scientific racialism" – entered the arena of Europe.

One early and close parallel is available in James Prichard's *Researches into the Physical History of Man* (1813), which argues that "all the nations on the earth are descended from a single family, and [...] the varieties which we observe in their aspect and bodily structure [can be attributed] to the action of natural causes on a race originally uniform."[32] In his argument he writes extensively on the "Gothic or German race" and the "Celtic race" (in addition to his remarks on Asia, Africa, and the South Sea islands) with the conclusion that "all the German tribes deduce themselves by a close affiliation from the same origin, among which we reckon the Cimbri, Teutones and Gutes, on the southern side of the Baltic; the Goths, Swedes, and Norweigians, in Scandinavia; the Caledonians or Picts in North Britain, and the Belgæ in Gaul and in South Britain."[33] He also adds that the "western districts of Europe have been the abode of the Celtic tribes from periods of time which reach beyond our earliest account," before they were driven out by various German tribes.[34] Hence, the original Britons in Prichard's account were racially Celtic.

What is remarkable about Prichard's theory is his conscious attempt to align this description of races – or what he calls "physical history" – with comparative philology, as a way of emphasizing his central thesis of monogenesis:

> Now the languages of these races [Sclavonian, German, and Pelasgian] and the Celtic respectively, although differing much from each other and constituting the four principal departments of dialects which prevail in Europe, are yet so far allied in their radical elements, that we may with certainty pronounce them to be branches of the same original stock. The resemblance is remarkable in the general structure of speech and in those parts of the vocabulary which must be supposed to be most ancient, as in words descriptive of common objects and feelings, for which expressive terms existed in the primitive ages of society. We must therefore infer that the nations to whom these languages belonged emigrated from the same quarter.[35]

In other words, the underlying anthropological element in the philological works of Jones or Schlegel was now being exploited fully to understand races, nations, and their mutual relations.

Robert Knox, in his *The Races of Men: A Fragment* (1850), took this innate cultural connotation of race a step further, first by saying that "human character, individual and national, is traceable solely to the nature of that race to which the individual or nation belongs," and then by triumphantly declaring that "[r]ace is everything: literature, science, art, in a word, civilization, depend on it."[36] Notwithstanding the title of his treatise, Knox is primarily concerned with just one race – what he calls the "Saxon" or the "Scandinavian" – and the bulk of the work is devoted to distinguishing this race from the Celts, and to establishing the superiority of the former. In fact, his method of "transcendental anatomy" that is employed to inquire into the history of races has but one purpose and that is a deeply political purpose – to save the Saxon population of England from what he calls its "Norman government," and to get rid of the Celtic population from its various parts: "The really momentous question for England, as a *nation*, is the presence of three sections of the Celtic race still on her soil: the Caledonian, or Gael; the Cymbri, or Welsh; and the Irish, or Erse; and how to dispose of them."[37] He repeats Prichard's thesis that the original inhabitants of Britain and France were Celtic in race, but then turns the subsequent history of the island into a political battleground between different races, with the prediction of the eventual supremacy of the Saxons. The battle between the Celts and the Saxons, he points out repeatedly, will decide the future of both Britain and Europe.

European history is thus reduced to clashes between different races. At the same time, the motor of this history is empires and their colonies, from the ancient Roman empire to the contemporary ones of his time. In Knox's account, races clash with each other, or intermingle, as a consequence of colonization. He describes the "Scandinavian or Saxon" as appearing both in ancient Greece and in ancient Rome, and then spreading elsewhere in Europe, reaching its "greatest colony" of England: "The Saxon of England is deemed a colonist from Jutland, Holstein, and Denmark. [...] He must have occupied eastern Scotland and eastern England as far south as the Humber, long prior to the historic period, when the German Ocean was scarcely a sea. The Saxons of these northern coasts of Scotland and England, resemble very closely the natives of the opposite shores; but the Danes and Angles who attacked South England, already occupied by a Flemish race, did not make the same impression on the population. They merely mingled with it; the country, that is, South England, remains in the hands of the original inhabitants to this day."[38]

After describing the initial arrival of the Saxons in England as an act of colonization, he extends it further through history:

> Following out the geographical position of the Saxon race, we find him in Europe, intersected but not amalgamated with the Sarmatian and Slavonian, in eastern Europe; with the Celtic in Switzerland; deeply with the Slavonian and Flaming in Austria and on the Rhine; thinly spread throughout Wales; in possession, as occupants of the soil, of northern and eastern Ireland; lastly, carrying out the destinies of his race, obeying his physical and moral nature, the Anglo Saxon, aided by his insular position, takes possession of the ocean, becomes the great tyrant at sea; ships, colonies, commerce – these are his wealth, therefore his strength. A nation of shopkeepers grasps at universal power; founds a colony (the States of America) such as the world never saw before; loses it, as a result of the principle of race. Nothing daunted, founds others, to lose them all in succession, and for the same reasons – race: a handful of large-handed spatula-fingered Saxon traders holds military possession of India. Meantime, though divided by nationalities, into different groups, as English, Dutch, German, United States man, cordially hating each other, the race still hopes ultimately to be masters of the world.[39]

Race and colonization form a template for him, and he uses the case of the Saxons to make it a universal story. Every event in history, according to this plan, has to be explained according to racial peculiarities, as manifest, among other things, their ability to colonize other races and their territories.

Literature, art, and the sciences – or "civilization," broadly speaking – according to Knox are manifestations of such innate and immutable racial characteristics. Hence, he has little hesitation in declaring, following his hierarchized racial taxonomy, that the "real Jew has no ear for music as a race, no love of science or literature," or that "[a]s a race, the Celt has no literature, nor any printed books in his original language," and so on.[40] He even proposes a general theory of race and culture by suggesting that the "Saxon and Celtic races did not invent the sciences, nor the arts, nor literature, nor the belles-lettres; [...] neither the 'Iliad' nor 'Odyssey' were written by Saxons or Celts, nor 'The Elements of Euclid'; nor did the Saxons as Saxons discover the theory of eclipses, nor calculate the periodic returns of comets, nor build bridges over the Danube and Euphrates, nor plan and erect the Parthenon, nor carve the Apollo and the Venus."[41] If anything, he argues, the cultural evidence available to us does not necessarily suggest a story of linear racial progress as had been suggested a few years earlier by Robert Chambers in his bestselling *Vestiges of the Natural History of Creation* (1844).

Instead, Knox identifies ancient Greece and Rome as the core of European culture, and suggests further that successive races borrow these original models and merely add qualities that are typical of those races. Hence, Voltaire's *La Pucelle d'Orléans* (*The Maid of Orleans*) reveals its typical Celtic character of being "refined, witty, alarmingly sacrilegious and licentious" and Samuel Butler's *Hudibras* shows its essential Saxon traits of being "[c]oarse, brutal, filthy, but pithy; practical, utilitarian, abounding with common sense."[42] For him, classical Greece remains the highest achievement in civilization, since it combined all the best features of the different races of Europe – such a civilizational state cannot be repeated in contemporary times since those races are broken apart and are antagonistic to each other. As a result, contemporary national literatures can only reflect individual racial characteristics, and can only repeat a fragment of classicism.[43]

Some of these ideas about racial groups in Britain reached their statistical apogee in 1885 in John Beddoe's *The Races of Britain*. Beddoe's central method is simple – he takes the human hair color and iris color as near-permanent racial features and argues that, when such data are related to other sets of data about the human cranium, collected through various techniques associated with phrenology, one may deduce a fairly reliable idea of racial types. He in fact collates such data on a large scale through personal observation and records them on small cards as his raw material.[44] Although he attaches a great deal of importance to the accuracy of such observations made during his daily business, and offers various ways of curbing probable flaws, his central mechanism of dividing people into racial groups is statistical computation. He assures his readers that, although physical observations may, at least occasionally, lead to inexactitude, statistics is capable of bestowing an irrefutable scientific foundation to his conclusions. And hence, armed with these two techniques of physical observation and statistics, he produces copious tables and maps in order to capture the racial profile of Britain (Figure 6.1).

Furthermore, he uses the same set of data to chronicle Britain's history from the Paleolithic age down to his contemporary times, with each age introducing new racial types within the overall population. Thus, his account of "Prehistoric Races" is followed by the racial confusion before the Roman conquest, Roman immigration, the Anglo-Saxon conquest, the Danish period, the Norman conquest and French–Norman immigration, subsequent immigration, and so on. As a result, the same set of data about hair or iris color allows Beddoe to do two things at once – to map racial profiles of his contemporary Britain and to claim that such a distribution of races is the outcome of history, that is, of successive conquests and immigrations. Race is thus proposed as an anthropological phenomenon that is historically determined, and yet capable of explaining contemporary realities such as political choices or cultural predilections.

His confidence in statistical computation as a means of arriving at such a dual role for race is rooted in contemporary events in the colonies, especially in southern Africa and South Asia, where race became a governmental category. Keith Breckenridge has shown the rise of a "biometric state" in South Africa since the nineteenth century, and Nicholas Dirks has chronicled how the colonial state gradually transformed itself into an "ethnographic state" in India.[45] In fact, it is possible to see the emergence of this heady cocktail of biological sciences and statistics around race across the empire, constituting an imperial model of politics that I have elsewhere described as "somapolitics."[46] Beddoe, for his part, took a keen interest in developments in India and applauded the anthropometric work by colonial officials like G. Campbell and H. H. Risley.[47] He even harbored the ambitious plan of conducting a similar anthropological survey for the whole of Europe.[48]

The idea that Britain was constituted through an amalgamation of different races and that such racial types existed as autonomous groups even in the present age developed as a consequence of the empire. From Prichard's early speculations on the Indo-European linguistic family to Knox's emphasis on colonization and eventually to Beddoe's statistical account of British

COLOUR OF HAIR AND EYES IN SEVERAL DISTRICTS OF THE UNITED KINGDOM, FROM PERSONAL OBSERVATION.

SCOTLAND.

Colour of Hair ...	... Number	... Sex	EYES LIGHT. Red	Fair	Brown	Dark	Nig.	Eyes Light.	EYES INTERMEDIATE OR NEUTER. Red	Fair	Brown	Dark	Nig.	Eyes Neuter.	EYES DARK. Red	Fair	Brown	Dark	Nig.	Eyes Dark.	Indices. Gross.	Per Cent.
THE ISLES.																						
1. Shetland (Lerwick, Scalloway, Sound, &c.) per cent.	285	both	3·5	21	35·4	11·9	...	71·8	1	1	2·1	3·8	...	7·9	1	·6	3·8	14·3	?	19·7	...	1·9?
2. Kirkwall (Orkney) per cent.	400	both	3	16·2	37·5	13·5	...	69·2	·5	1·7	5·2	6·7	...	14·3	·5	·5	3·2	11·2	?	16·5	...	9 ?
3. Stromness, Stennis, Hoy, Haray, &c., per cent.	168	both	4·7	13·1	41·7	15·5	...	75·3	...	1·2	4·1	6·5	...	11·8	·6	·6	4·7	5·9	?	12·8	...	7·7?
4. Orkney, total, per cent. ...	568	both	3·5	15·3	38·7	14·1	...	71	·4	1·6	4·9	6·7	...	13·6	·5	·5	3·7	9·7	?	15·4	...	8·7?
5. Sternoway (Lewis), per cent.	125	=	6·8	22·4	21 6	10·8	·8	62 4	...	1·6	5·6	7·2	...	14·2	...	...	9·2	7·6	6·4	23·2	...	9·2
6. Strath, Sconser, Broadford (Skye), per cent.... ...	145	both	4·1	16·5	38·6	13·1	2·1	75·6	·7	...	1·4	5·5	·7	7·7	·7	...	4·8	9	2·7	16·7	...	16·6
7. Portree (Skye), per cent. ...	70	♂m.	3·5	21·4	22·8	18·5	·7	67	...	...	1·4	7·1	4·3	13	1·4	...	2·1	11·4	5	20	..	30·7
8. Skye, total, per cent.	215	both	4	18·1	33·5	14·9	1·6	72	·5	...	1·4	6	1·8	9·7	·9	...	4	9·7	3·5	18·1	...	21
9. Seal and Luing (Argyle), per cent.	68	♂m.	1 5	20	31·5	11	2·2	66·2	...	1·5	5·9	7·3	1·5	16·2	1·5	...	4·4	8·7	3	17·6	...	15·9
CAITHNESS.																						
10. Wick, town, per cent.	300	both	5	14	30·6	12	...	61·9	1·3	1·6	7·6	5·3	...	15·8	·6	1	6·6	14·3	...	22·3	...	8·1+
NORTHERN HIGHLANDS.																						
11. Sutherland, N.E., per cent.	35	both	5·7	12·8	34·2	10	...	62·7	...	...	...	...	...	...	...	2·9	2·9	21·4	10	37·2	...	30
12. Ullapool (Ross), per cent. ...	50	♂m.	10	16	21	22	1	70	2	...	8	6	2	18	...	...	4	6	2	12	...	16
	1	2	3	4	5	6	7	8	9	10	11	12	13	14	15	16	17	18	19	20	21	22

Figure 6.1 John Beddoe, *The Races of Britain* (Bristol: J. W. Arrowsmith 1885), 150.

races in the final decades of the nineteenth century, the imperial connection is writ large on modern race sciences. Variously called physical history, ethnology, or anthropology, this obsession with race and its underlying cultural connotation made popular the idea that Britain, like its colonies, is a racially diverse country. The exact nomenclature changed over time, and acrimonious debates often broke out in public, but the idea of racial diversity was seldom contested. During the second half of the nineteenth century one encountered a broad consensus that Britain was constituted through racial groups such as the Celts, the Saxons, the Normans, and so on, and that the crucial question of national unity depended on the management of such groups. Culture was seen as an unmistakable manifestation of racial characteristics, as an intrinsic expression of a race's moral and intellectual dispositions, and hence an inalienable part of race sciences. In fact, the idea of the autonomy of a cultural realm was decisively underwritten by contemporary speculations on race.

History of the Literary

In his short but influential essay *On the Study of Celtic Literature* (1867), Matthew Arnold gives voice to his contemporary race-thinking when he states at the outset that "[t]o know the Celtic case thoroughly, one must know the Celtic people; and to know them, one must know that by which a people best express themselves, – their literature."[49] Such an inquiry, though intended for general readership, however, cannot "avoid touching on certain points of ethnology and philology," and the trick of the trade is that the "mere literary critic" must choose his authorities in these fields judiciously (*CL*, 25). Likewise, Arnold chooses a set of diverse authorities to support his case – from Lord Strangford and Prichard to Renan, Edwards, Whitley Stokes, and Henri Martin. In this tract, he eventually makes the plea for a chair in Celtic literature at Oxford as an olive branch to Ireland, but, in order to do so, he first has to establish its origin and vicissitudes, and here these authorities become his allies. A Renan or a Stokes, in other words, becomes as important as a literary critic such as Thomas Malory, and together, across disciplinary fields, they give shape to Arnold's putative subject, that is, "Celtic literature" and its history.

It has been noted by Arnold scholars that *On the Study of Celtic Literature* bears a striking resemblance to Renan's essay "Sur la poésie des races celtiques" (1854), included in his *Essais de morale et de critique* (1859). Arnold himself praised Renan's book and especially this piece in glowing terms in a letter to his sister in 1859, and even claimed that "I think we are singularly at one in our ideas."⁵⁰ His reliance on Renan is evident, for instance, in his formulation of the Celtic sentimentality or in some direct references to La Villemarqué's *Les Romans de la Table Ronde et les contes des anciens Bretons* (1841), from which both of them quote. Arnold's more fundamental debt to his contemporary scholarship, including Renan, however, is expressed in his belief that the question of Celtic literature cannot be probed adequately without having recourse to "sciences" such as philology and physiology. He proposes a two-pronged strategy of investigation, through "external" and "internal" evidence – the first of which includes the "language and the physical type of our race," whereas the latter is reliant on "our literature, genius, and spiritual production generally" (*CL*, 89). Celtic literature – or its defining features, at any rate – is distributed across these two groups, and the autonomy of the literary is made conditional on elements that are external to its being.

Of course, this limitation, as also its external qualification, is announced by the very appellation "Celtic literature" by Arnold or "poetry of the Celtic races" by Renan, but Arnold takes it a step further by identifying an exact correspondence between racial types and literary genius – he states with confidence that "[a]s there are for physiology physical marks, such as the square heads of the German, the round head of the Gael, the oval head of the Cymri, which determine the type of a people, so for criticism there are spiritual marks which determine the type, and make us speak of the Greek genius, the Teutonic genius, the Celtic genius, and so on" (*CL*, 95). Race, literary genius, and criticism in such formulations are made part of a cultural continuity, and it is further suggested that, to elaborate on any of these elements, one must also engage with the rest.

Arnold's account differs from Renan's in one crucial point – Renan is interested in finding the essential features of Celtic poetry, whereas Arnold searches for the Celtic element beneath the overwhelming Germanic or Saxon influence on both English literature and race. This is an important point of departure for him, as it allows him to subsequently join race with the nation, as a form of social sublimation that unites the disparate elements of a national literature. Hence, he identifies three different "forces" behind the English genius:

> The Germanic genius has steadiness as its main basis, with commonness and humdrum for its defect, fidelity to nature for its excellence. The Celtic genius, sentiment as its main basis, with love of beauty, charm, and spirituality for its excellence, ineffectualness and self-will for its defect. The Norman genius, talent for affairs as its main basis, with strenuousness and clear rapidity for its excellence, hardness and insolence for its defect. (*CL*, 115–16)

The important point behind this passage is that all these three "forces" or "geniuses" are identified by the twin "sciences" of philology and ethnology (or physiology, as a subset), as if in an attempt to bring together Prichard and Knox, and offered as a map of history.

English history – whether literary or otherwise – is taken to be a hybrid amalgamation of these different racial components but harmonious at the national level; even if history introduces such diversity, the eventual nation offers a way of uniting them. Arnold takes great care in explaining how the English national culture of literature is composed of these three forces but reducible to none of them. He concedes, for instance, the contemporary opinion that the English race is overwhelmingly Germanic or Saxon, but he also painstakingly distinguishes the two in the "habit and gait" of their respective languages, in their rhetorical flourish, in their respective aptitude for the "plastic arts," or in their religious preferences (*CL*, 116–25).

It is with poetry, however, that all these scattered speculations of Arnold come together. He begins the final section of the essay with a curious claim: "If I were asked where English poetry got these three things, its turn for style, its turn for melancholy, and its turn for natural magic, for catching and rendering the charm of nature in a wonderfully near and vivid way, – I should answer, with some doubt, that it got much of its turn for style from a Celtic source; with less doubt, that it got much of its melancholy from a Celtic source; with no doubt at all, that from a Celtic source it got nearly all its natural magic" (*CL*, 135). Each and every claim made on behalf of Celtic/English literature in this passage works against its foil – that is, what he calls the "Germanic genius."

Take the issue of "style" as an example. Arnold struggles a bit to define what he means by style, and, even at his eloquent best, he remains somewhat abstract or even vague. The idea, however, begins to assume conceptual solidity as soon as he relates it to racial types. He first names Pindar, Virgil, Dante, and Milton as exemplars of style and then offers a comparative reading of Milton and Goethe. For him, the "Germanic" Goethe, despite being "lucid, harmonious, earnest, eloquent" remains caught up in a "prosaic" style. The Celtic–English Milton, on the other hand, expresses "a style which seems to have for its cause a certain pressure of emotion, and an ever-surging, yet bridled, excitement in the poet, giving a special intensity to his way of delivering himself" (*CL*, 137). As opposed to Goethe, he suggests, Milton possesses a "poetical" style. And soon this idea of a "poetical" style is connected to an essentialized Celtic core and extended to include Shakespeare, Gray, Byron, Keats, Wordsworth, and other English poets. And, again and again, this English panoply is set against German poets, most notably Goethe, with the final declaration that "[s]tyle, then, the Germans are singularly without" (*CL*, 141).

Arnold's comparative framework, to put it differently, is not only literary but also racialized. This is partly because he is faced with an apparent conundrum – the English race is overwhelmingly Germanic and yet English poetry bristles with style. Since, in his opinion, Germans lack any sense of style, this should not have been the case. His earlier argument (borrowed from Edwards and others) that Celts form a latent foundation to English national culture returns here as a literary argument, and he revises the status of English literature by identifying the Celtic style in the middle of its apparent Germanic robustness. In fact, the history of English literature from Shakespeare to Wordsworth, according to this theory, is replete with instances when this Celtic core bursts forth and creates what he calls "magic": "Magic is just the word for it, – the magic of nature; not merely the beauty of nature, – that the Greeks and Latins had; not merely an honest smack of the soil, a faithful realism, – that the Germans had; but the intimate life of nature, her weird power and her fairy charm" (*CL*, 159). In the final instance, it is this Celtic magic that sets English literature apart from its other European counterparts. Even when he admits the presence of such a magical element in literature produced by other racial types, he nonetheless insists that it sounds more authentic in its native land, amidst its natural surroundings.

English literature for Arnold is an essentially hybrid racialized expression, but that does not necessarily mean that it lacks unity or that its history cannot be written as a single narrative. The underlying unity is provided by the fact that both the Celts and the Saxons, after all, are Indo-European races and hence, despite their antagonistic history, as attested by recent race sciences, they could contribute to a larger English stock. He notes with some details how Irish was gradually accepted as an Indo-European language and cites important landmarks such as Johann Kaspar Zeuss's *Grammatica Celtica* (1853) and Stokes's notes on *Three Irish Glossaries* (1862) in support (*CL*, 72, 83). He even argues, with a note of optimism that clearly is premature, that, with such progress in comparative philology, England is gradually becoming conscious of the fact that "there is no such original chasm between the Celt and the Saxon as we once popularly imagined, that they are not truly, what Lord Lyndhurst called them, *aliens in blood* from us, that they are our brothers in the great Indo-European family." It is the "feeling of Indo-Europeanism," he insists, that supersedes the apparent racial resentment, and it is the same feeling that holds out the possibility of imagining racial diversity within a singular nation (*CL*, 22–3; emphasis original).

Interestingly enough, however, the final confirmation for such a conjecture comes not so much from an independent philological history of Indo-European races as from their opposition to Semitic races. At one point in his essay, Arnold notes the curious fact that both the single-race Germans and the hybrid English are equally deficient in their religious poetry, especially in hymns. For the English case, he compares Roundell Palmer's religious anthology *The Book of Praise: From the Best English Hymn-Writers* (1864) with Francis Turner Palgrave's secular anthology of English poetry *The Golden Treasury of the Best Songs and Lyrical Poems in the English Language* (1861), and declares unhesitatingly that "while the *Golden Treasury* is a monument of a nation's strength, the *Book of Praise* is a monument of a nation's weakness" (*CL*, 148). What is even more surprising is the fact that the quintessential quality of English poetry for him – that is, its *style* – is severely wanting in English hymns. The root of such incongruities, he conjectures, must be sought in racial groups and their predispositions.

His explanation for such an anomalous event once again refers to contemporary scholarship in comparative philology as he makes a sharp distinction between the "Semitic genius [that] placed its highest spiritual life in the religious sentiment, and made that the basis of its poetry" and the "Indo-European genius [that] places its highest spiritual life in the imaginative reason, and makes that the basis of its poetry." The former is capable of producing religious poetry of an exalted order, whereas the latter, because of its different orientation, is not. Such a schematization, derived from the "science" of philology, explains the conundrum he is so eager to resolve. However, this is not just a qualitative difference for Arnold, but a chronological one as well, since he believes that "mankind's Semitic age," which "produced the great incomparable monuments of the pure religious sentiment [like] the books of Job and Isaiah, the Psalms," is over. In contrast, he places "we, the Indo-Europeans," including the English, Celtic, and Germanic races, as occupying the present, and unleashing the new poetry of "imaginative reason" (*CL*, 149–51). It is as much in the unity of the Indo-Europeans as in their opposition to the Semites that Arnold imagines the eventual harmony of English hybridity. Insofar as the English nation and English literature are concerned, the underlying components of Indo-Europeanism, as manifest in both language and race, turn them into historical objects.

On the Study of Celtic Literature, despite its title, proposes a scheme of history for English literature, and makes "Celtic literature" a subterranean and yet incontrovertible part of it. Arnold is eager to elevate the new discipline of literary history to the status of established "sciences" such as philology and ethnology, and hence has little compunction in borrowing their methods and vocabulary. His grand plan for English literary history, as a consequence, repeatedly has recourse to a Celtic–Saxon or Celtic–German structure within the larger Indo-European narrative, and he explicitly cites his sources from contemporary scholarship. However, this formulation has very different implications for the literary – or the literary sovereign – as I have tracked it in previous chapters. When historicized as a concept within the prevalent climate of philology and ethnology, as Arnold does here, the literary can only be thought through other categories and other methods, leaving it devoid of its own being or vocation. It is either held hostage by philological groups of languages, and hence the insistence on the Indo-Europeanism of English literature; or it is made subservient to racial categories, and hence the emphasis on the Celtic–Saxon. In either case, English literature is broken down into components that are neither literary nor autonomous; and it is the process of disintegration that is offered as the history of the literary.

This is especially noteworthy since around the same time Arnold is developing his much-celebrated theory of "culture" as an overriding "social idea" in *Culture and Anarchy* (1869), and suggesting further that it "seeks to do away with classes; to make all live in an atmosphere of sweetness and light, and use ideas, as it uses them itself, freely, – to be nourished and not bound by them." He even adds that the "great men of culture" are the "true apostles of equality" as they "have had a passion for diffusing, for making prevail, for carrying from one end of society to the other, the best knowledge, the best idea of their time."[51] In this argument, culture is bigger than any group or community like what he calls the "Barbarians," the "Philistines," and the "Populace," and hence coincidental with a supra-communal idea like the nation. Culture in this Arnoldian sense is inevitably national culture, and this is borne out in *Culture and Anarchy* by the preponderance of the invocation of the nation every time he attempts to invest it with meaning and purpose. When set against such an expansive idea of culture, literature looks fragmented and desultory, always in need of external support to express itself and forever caught in the debates of the precise "sciences."

Arnold's answer to this crisis, as I have indicated above, is the nation, and, much like culture, this conception of a national literature is a capacious concept. At the same time, the way he combines philology and literature to arrive at this formulation completely refutes Foucault's thesis in *The Order of Things*, if any refutation were ever required, that separates the two and suggests an antagonistic relationship between them. In Foucault's opinion, it is this separation that allows literature a distinct identity of its own. As I have argued in the Introduction and in Chapter 3, however, this proximity of philology and literature was determined by colonial history, with its emphasis on a lettered sovereignty and the eventual literary sovereign, and was part of the new idea of literature from its inception. What Arnold does in *On the Study of Celtic Literature* is that he simply takes this intimacy to its logical conclusion, and suggests literary history as the domain where this coming together can be seen most clearly. Literature as national literature, in other words, is a possibility that was present from the beginning; literary history, with its emphasis on race and language, only quickens such possibilities. Arnold is important for my argument precisely for the way he makes this connection explicit, and makes it popular.

How far such a version of English literary history penetrated the mass consciousness of the second half of the nineteenth century can be gauged from some of the popular texts of the time. Henry Morley's extremely popular *A First Sketch of English Literature* (1873), written as a companion volume to his equally popular *English Writers*, 10 Vols. (1864–94), for example, begins with the standard Indo-European hypothesis and tells its readers that the first Celtic occupants of Britain, and following invaders like the Teutons or Saxons, originally came from the "region that we now call Asia." They came from the plains and valleys "once occupied by the Medes and Persians" or from the "lands watered by those five rivers of the Punjaub which flow into the Indus." Although the exact details of these early migrations to Britain are lost in a hoary past, Morley nonetheless insists that in their "unlike tempers lay some of the elements from which, when generations after generations more had passed away, a Shakespeare was to come."[52]

Very much like Arnold, he describes Shakespeare's genius as an effect of the admixture of Celtic and Teutonic races. And, again like Arnold, he downplays the Celtic element and describes the arrival of the Teutons in Britain as the beginning point for English proper. In an ingenious move, he proposes to drop the term Anglo-Saxon altogether and replace it with "First English": "The First English who are commonly known by the school-name of Anglo-Saxons, but who called themselves, as we call ourselves now, the English people (*Englisc folc*), were formed by a gradual blending of Teutonic tribes." These tribes – identified as Scandinavians, Danes, and Frisians – came "at different times and in different generations" and settled in various parts of the island. They also drove the majority of the existing Celtic races out of England and into the recesses of Scotland, Ireland, and Wales, thus establishing a new racial identity of

Englishness with its Germanic origin. Morley also notes that not only the race but even the language needs to be rethought and suggests that the language commonly known as Anglo-Saxon was indeed the beginning of a modern English that was "mainly Frisian in structure": "They called it English. It was English. Let us call it, then, First English, and avoid the confusion of ideas produced by giving it – as if it were the language of another people – the separate name of Anglo-Saxon."[53]

The first two chapters of Morley are devoted to "The Forming of the People" and are subtitled "Celts" and "First English." Unlike the first part concerning the "Celts," however, the section on the "First English" is much more ambivalent, insofar as it combines both race and language to offer the real foundation for English literature. He argues that the "First English" for four centuries prior to the Norman conquest remained stable and "have come down to us in one language as fixed as that which we now speak." Things changed drastically after 1066, and during the three centuries between the "Conquest and Chaucer there was continuous change." In order to accommodate these two phases of the language, and also the racial profiles behind them, he invokes the efforts of the Early English Text Society (founded in 1864) that included Anglo-Saxon texts in its publication and made it clear that "English before the Conquest has as much right to be called Early as the English after it." Likewise, he first emphasizes the Teutonic credentials of the Normans, and then suggests that Early English literature needs to be divided into two parts – "First English (or Anglo-Saxon) Literature" and the "literature of TRANSITION ENGLISH."[54] The first phase includes works such as *Beowulf*, whereas the second encompasses such authors as Geoffrey of Monmouth.

Morley's strategy here is to exploit the central ambiguity of comparative philology, its simultaneous commitment to language and race, to imagine a national literature. If he can show racial continuity between pre- and post-conquest England with a clear Teutonic origin, and if he can effectively pose both of them as antithetical to the Celts, then he believes he has sufficient ground to claim a national tradition. The Celtic element in his account, as in that of Arnold, remains active at a clandestine level, without disturbing the homogeneity of the Germanic race. The fact that the Indo-European hypothesis allowed a form of historical anthropology, with its insistence that racial histories can be recuperated through successful reconstruction of ancient languages, is at the root of claims like these. What is more, Arnold, Morley, and others – largely following Schlegel – assume that literary history is a natural extension of the Indo-European hypothesis as it offers the possibility of foisting literary texts onto the solid scaffolding of philology and race sciences, thereby securing a continuous history that already enjoys widespread admiration. A Chaucer or a Shakespeare, therefore, is but the inevitable outcome of this history of national genius, displaying the peculiar features of their race and language.

Race, language, and the nation together designate the final destination of the literary sovereign. It is true that these elements were present even at the moment of its inception through colonial history, but it was literary history that brought out this ensemble of ideas in sharp prominence. In fact, I suggest that literary history made the constellation of such ideas prevalent, so much so that they became available across popular discussions and scholarly deliberations. Hippolyte Taine's *Histoire de la littérature anglaise*, 5 Vols. (1863–9) proposed a similar structure of the Saxons and the Normans as forming the national core or "Les origines" for English literature.[55] This pattern is repeated in countless textbooks and popular accounts: George Saintsbury's *A Short History of English Literature* (1898),[56] A. Hamilton Thompson's *A History of English Literature* (1901),[57] William Henry Hudson's *An Outline History of English Literature* (1912),[58] A. S. Mackenzie's *History of English Literature* (1914),[59] Robert Huntington Fletcher's *A History of English Literature* (1916),[60] Edward Albert's *A History of English Literature* (1923),[61] A. J. Wyatt's *The Tutorial History of English Literature* (1928),[62] and so on. And eventually Émile Legouis gave it an organic form by suggesting that English literature is like a river formed by two streams, Anglo-Saxon (or Germanic) literature and the Franco-Latin literature "imported from France by the Normans." "As in a biography," he continued, "the study of any available records of his forebears tends to throw light on the hero's character, so he who would know the river must follow each of these two streams back to its source."[63]

Nation as *Gestell*

From Warton to Arnold, covering roughly a century, the literary went through progressive fragmentation. What was seen as an autonomous and autotelic order of textuality at the end of the eighteenth century, and what marked a clear break in intellectual history at a global scale, was reformulated in smaller units with specific histories. What is important for my argument in this book is that the source for this historicization also emerged through colonial histories in the form of comparative philology and race sciences. The Indo-European hypothesis, suggested by Jones and fleshed out by Schlegel, Bopp, and others, was built around an ambivalent doubling of language and race, often suggesting that these two categories were interchangeable. However, as soon as the two were joined with each other as a seamless continuum or as organic expressions of each other, the hypothesis needed something bigger to accommodate both of them. Schlegel first realized this potential and argued that this larger unit had to be the nation. Once race and language were seen as conjoined, it followed, for him, that every branch of the Indo-European family had to lead to a separate and self-contained nation. If the central achievement of comparative philology was to install historicism in humanistic knowledge systems, then that methodological apparatus found its final goal in the nation. The question of history and literature, as a consequence, was intensely nationalized during the nineteenth century.

How greatly the idea of a national literature appealed to popular consciousness across the nineteenth century can be seen in numerous publications including William Ellery Channing, *The Importance and Means of a National Literature* (1830), M. Keijzer (ed.), *Select Specimens of the National Literature of England* (1856), L. Herrig, *The British Classical Authors: Select Specimens of the National Literature of England* (1860), Joseph F. O'Carroll, *A National Irish Literature* (1876), and many more. In fact, the idea became so popular that the nation and its literature were seen as mutually sustaining each other.

In his pioneering work *Comparative Literature* (1886), Hutcheson Macaulay Posnett thus claims that the modern idea of "literature" attained its definition only with the rise of modern nations such as England and France. The fact that classical civilizations in Greece and Rome did not have a comparable idea is explained by the absence of the nation – the Greeks depended on "city commonwealths" for political organization and the Romans shifted directly from being a "municipality" to establishing a "world-empire" without ever becoming a nation:

> It was only when bodies of national writings, such as those of England and France, had been long enough in existence to attract reflection, it was only when the spread of democratic ideas in the eighteenth century began to make men regard the writings of their countrymen as something more than elegant copies of antique models made under the patronage of courts and princes, as in truth the fruits of the nation's historic past, that the word "literature" became useful to mark an idea peculiar to the nations of modern Europe.[64]

Despite Posnett's emphasis on "modern Europe," however, this is more or less a universal formula. Soon he repeats the same idea to describe Indian and Chinese literatures, suggesting a naturalized relationship between the nation and its literature.

Put another way, Posnett suggests that this proximity of literature and the nation, first made visible in the eighteenth century, can become one of the central analytical frames for literary history, and this frame then can be applied retrospectively. His idea of world literature, as a result, becomes a series of observations on what he claims to be common features across different literary traditions like the Greek, the Hebrew, the Chinese, and the Indian. World literature is not an additive process where one need only add more and more national literatures; rather, it is the job of the literary historian to find out what these separate national literatures share with each other, and then to construe a narrative of world literature. Significantly enough, the unique purchase of national literature remains intact in such a description of world literature. In fact, Posnett interprets Goethe's suggestion of the end of national literature and the beginning of world literature to mean not the annihilation of the former, but its reconstituted afterlife in the latter. National literature is the building block for every other form of literary history, since it is the nation that makes literature a recognizable category.

The arrangement of Posnett's book reveals the historical scheme he has in mind – his chapters progress from "Clan Literature" and "City Commonwealth" to "World Literature" and finally "National Literature." The true being of literature is disclosed only in the final chapter, when it is associated with modern nations such as England and France and embodies a "national life, a spiritual bond of national unity."[65] Other descriptions of literature are either stepping stones toward the full realization of this national model or its further configurations, but by no means a substitute for it. Literary history is the new mode of inquiry responsible for making this connection visible and also for preparing the ground for disciplinary study of literature. It is hardly a wonder that the rise of literary history and the professionalization of literary studies happened around the same time during the nineteenth century in Europe. For such a fate of literature, Posnett, like his contemporaries, brings the twin point of comparative philology and race studies under the broad rubric of the nation.

As I have shown at different points in this chapter, this national enframing of the literary in many ways completed the journey of the literary sovereign. For one thing, the idea of a sovereign order of textuality that defined the new conceptualization of the literary found its ideal match in the notion of national sovereignty. This identification took shape with the mediation of language and race under the disciplinary headings of comparative philology, anthropology, physiology, various branches of the contemporary race sciences, and so on. In a crucial sense, such a historical juncture was a result of imperialism and various events through colonial histories. In Chapters 4 and 5, and in this one, I have tracked how colonial histories saturated different fields ranging across aesthetics, politics, narratology, and others to give shape to the new idea of the literary sovereign and how such histories circulated across texts and territories thanks to imperial networks. However, on the other hand, the underlying anthropological principle of the new paradigm made it especially susceptible to a range of appropriations, repeatedly refashioning its being and scope. This final destination of the nation made sure that the doubling of the textual–anthropological paradigm of colonial histories made itself a global reality for the literary.

Coda: Decolonization after World Literature

Decolonization as a political and intellectual project has gone through three distinct phases. The first one is recuperative in nature as it identifies non-European or precolonial knowledge forms or intellectual traditions and restores them as legitimate disciplines of study. At its core, this phase is primarily concerned with challenging the hegemony of Europe by suggesting other – often forgotten or lost – bodies of knowledge and scholarship. The second phase is meant, in Dipesh Chakrabarty's formulation, to "provincialize" Europe, by showing the genealogy of certain ideas within specific and sectoral histories.[1] This phase also represents an ethical dilemma as it positions the postcolonial intellectual as forever caught between a provincialized Europe and his or her own intellectual terrain. If the first phase is caught up in rejecting Europe and foregrounding other traditions, in order to establish the autonomy of indigeneity, the second is much more concerned with the impossibility of recuperating a pristine precolonial moment. In fact, the second phase proposes this impossibility of returning to a past unsullied by colonialism as an ethical horizon, as a limit to postcolonial thought itself. In contrast, the third phase has been more interested in unraveling the global and connected histories of some of the central categories of thought with which we operate now and which we often take for granted. In painstaking detail and through dusty archives, this phase of decolonizing thinking has concentrated on the multicultural, multilingual, and often intermedial genealogies of thought categories that shape modernity and its intellectual culture.

This book belongs to the third phase of decolonization, though it is not unmindful of the first two. Through parallel and connected histories, through conjoined archives, and through a range of genres and texts, I trace the evolution of the modern culture of letters as entangled with colonial histories. My argument here is that the modern idea of the *literary*, which is traceable to the eighteenth century, is the product of long and connected histories produced by modern empires. In the transition of modern imperialism's center from the Americas to Asia and Africa during the middle of the eighteenth century, I have argued, the fundamental character of sovereignty changed and it became progressively reliant on textuality (as opposed to the territorial model in the Americas). It was here, in colonial governance's search for a new model of sovereignty in South Asia, that the idea of the literary – or the *literary sovereign* – was fashioned. It involved elements from European history (especially discussions surrounding English law), and also components from indigenous cultures, texts, and traditions. What emerged out of this colonial encounter and what had a spectacular life both in the colony and beyond in the subsequent centuries was not simply a new idea of a self-conscious literary language but a complete overhauling of culture across the colonial divide. It was, at the same time, a transcultural and multilingual phenomenon that had little precedent in history.

Once this central tenet of the new literary culture was settled, it soon traveled across borders and boundaries, transforming texts, criticism, and literary landscapes on a global scale. I have outlined three broad fields in German aesthetic theory, French novels, and English literary history from the eighteenth and the nineteenth centuries to follow the global trajectory of the literary sovereign. Whether in Kant and Goethe's reflections on aesthetics, Balzac's novels, or Matthew Arnold's programmatic schema of literary history, I have shown that colonial histories shaped the outcome in significant ways. Such histories functioned at multiple levels, across texts and traditions, and made inroads into areas that have been largely seen as autonomous and also autochthonous to Europe. Instead, this book opens up the insularity of such thinking and restores the global context of modern empires, in a gesture of decolonization. Without this essential plurality of histories, I argue, the modern culture of letters cannot be appreciated in its complexity.

In a crucial way, the methodology of this book is anchored in the intellectual milieu of decolonization. Some of the ideas of this book presented themselves when I was working on my first book, *Postcolonial Writing in the Era of World Literature: Texts, Territories, Globalizations* (2018).[2] As I started exploring the interface between postcolonial and world literature studies, and as I sifted through the archives to see the origins of the concept of *Weltliteratur* in colonial histories, it appeared to me that not only world literature but a whole range of concepts, institutions, and practices associated with modern literary studies could be found strewn across those archival records. Right in front of me, in those yellowed and dusty remnants of a defunct empire, I could recognize the genealogy of a range of ideas I had been taught as part of my training in literary studies. Equally importantly, I could also identify multiple languages, cultures, and histories behind such ideas, attesting to the fact that modern empires were polyglot and multicultural at their core. Though in my first book I primarily wrote about contemporary authors such as V. S. Naipaul, J. M. Coetzee, and Salman Rushdie, I became conscious of a longer history behind these novels, a history that demanded a separate book of its own.

It was here, in the juxtaposition of postcolonial texts and imperial histories, that the methodology of this book took shape. While I was writing about, for instance, certain connections between the fictions of Kipling and Naipaul, I sensed a broader shared ground between the two about what constitutes a literary text. Or, to take another example, when I was exploring Coetzee's complex reflections on race in South Africa, I was struck by the parallel discussions in colonial South Asia. The proximity of race and cultural values – where the former is a physiological equivalent to the latter – developed across colonies, within shared political contexts. As a result, my methodology in exploring the paradigm of the literary sovereign placed both contiguous geography and the connected history of the empire at the center, as a way of constituting a field of investigation. What I follow here is far from being a straightforward repetition either of intellectual history or of Foucauldian genealogy. Rather, my aim is to mobilize the material history of this conjoined field, to segregate a set of practices, discourses, and texts generated through colonial histories, that I believe were responsible for the modern culture of letters. In a method like this, the literary is always and already enmeshed in other discourses and practices, and its genealogy is distributed across domains that are external to itself.

To put it differently, the method is a redeployment of decolonization, but not to assert the inherent autonomy of any one tradition or to upend colonial history *tout court*; rather, the point of this book is to recover the necessarily multilingual and multicultural roots of the literary, and to see colonial histories as decisively shaping its modern being. Decolonization here functions both as a method and as a political orientation, and allows one to pay attention to the inherent heterogeneity of colonial histories while pursuing a set of ideas across texts and territories. When recast like this, decolonization can – and, I believe, *does* – become a material practice or even a form of intellectual pursuit that shares a relationship of critical intimacy with the material one is working with. It is possible to repurpose the ideals of decolonization into working methods.

This recasting of the decolonizing spirit is interdisciplinary and multilingual. One of the central points of postcolonial studies in literature has also been to mobilize interdisciplinary energies to explore texts. In this book, as I activate decolonization as a method, my inquiries necessarily spread beyond literary studies and cover different disciplinary fields including history, politics, philology, anthropology, philosophy, and so on. However, I wish to signpost here that this interdisciplinarity is inspired by the encounter between postcolonial and world literature studies. I have argued elsewhere that the recent past has witnessed an increasingly shared vocation of these two fields, in their common thinking about central categories such as the world and the planet. In all likelihood, this is set to grow further in a context of global crises such as climate change and the coronavirus pandemic.[3] In this book, I want to borrow their shared concern with history and literature, the strategy of placing such categories within longer time frames and diverse geographies, to inaugurate a further phase of decolonization.

This book, then, is situated in the wake of the recent debates on world literature – or what I call *after* world literature – that have reopened different archives and cultures and have made it possible to question some of the received wisdom of literary studies. Instead of treating these debates as signs of literary scholars' somewhat belated and hasty discovery of globalization, I am more interested in seeing in these discussions a profusion of methodological tools and the possibility of renewing our professional commitment to literary studies. My interest more specifically is in the interface of postcolonial and world literary studies – in the promise of renewing the energies of both through this encounter – that I think is capable of generating new research agendas and strategies. If world literature invites us to engage with more languages and literary cultures, and if these engagements can take us through the *longue durée* of literary history, I feel it is possible to recalibrate such moves for a decolonized method. Decolonization, after all, is not about intellectual insularity; it is, if anything, a call to reach beyond accepted tenets and accredited traditions of thought.

Notes

Introduction: Formations of the Literary Sovereign

1 For a history of the Asiatic Society, see O. P. Kejariwal, *The Asiatic Society of Bengal and the Discovery of India's Past, 1784–1838* (Delhi: Oxford University Press, 1988).
2 For Johnson's praise of Jones, see James Boswell, *The Life of Samuel Johnson, LL.D., Including a Journal of His Tour to the Hebrides*, 10 Vols. (London: John Murray, 1835), 9: 169.
3 The standard biography of Jones is Garland Cannon, *The Life and Mind of Oriental Jones: Sir William Jones, The Father of Modern Linguistics* (Cambridge: Cambridge University Press, 1990). See also S. N. Mukherjee, *Sir William Jones: A Study in Eighteenth-Century Attitudes to India* (Cambridge: Cambridge University Press, 1968); and Michael J. Franklin, *"Orientalist Jones": Sir William Jones, Poet, Lawyer, and Linguist, 1746–1794* (Oxford: Oxford University Press, 2011).
4 William Jones, "A Discourse on the Institution of a Society, for Inquiring into the History, Civil and Natural, the Antiquities, Arts, Sciences, and Literature of Asia," in *The Works of Sir William Jones*, 13 Vols. (London: John Stockdale and John Walker, 1807), 3: 1–3. All references to Jones's works, unless otherwise indicated, are from this edition and cited hereafter with volume and page numbers in parentheses. The details of the meeting are from Cannon, *Life and Mind*, 203–4, and Franklin, *"Orientalist Jones,"* 210–12.
5 The enduring appeal of this vision was evident, for instance, when Henry Thomas Colebrooke, Jones's younger colleague in Calcutta and the chief Company Sanskritist after his untimely death in 1794, repeated somewhat similar sentiments in his inaugural speech at the Royal Asiatic Society of Great Britain and Ireland in 1823: "The course of inquiry into the arts, as into the sciences, of Asia, cannot fail of leading to much which is curious and instructive. The inquiry extends over regions, the most anciently and the most numerously peopled on the globe. The range of research is as wide as those regions are vast; and as various as the people who inhabit them are diversified. It embraces their ancient and modern history; their long-enduring institutions; their manners and their customs; their languages and their literatures; their sciences, speculative and practical: in short, the progress of knowledge among them; the pitch

which it has attained; and last, but most important, the means of its existence." He also made the additional point that Britain with its "great Asiatic empire" was in a position not only to acquire "varied information, and correct knowledge of the people and the countr[ies]" under its possession, but even to use such knowledge profitably in "[p]olitical transactions, operations of war, relations of commerce, the pursuits of business, the enterprise of curiosity, the desire of scientific acquirements." H. T. Colebrooke, "A Discourse Read at a Meeting of the Royal Asiatic Society of Great Britain and Ireland, on the 15th of March, 1823," in E. B. Cowell (ed.), *Miscellaneous Essays*, 2 Vols. (London: Trübner, 1873), 1: 2–3, 6. Several such societies to inquire into Asiatic histories came up during the nineteenth century with similar research agendas – in Bombay (1838), Colombo (1845), Tokyo (1875), Kuala Lumpur (1877), and Seoul (1900).

6 For this cartographic revolution, see Christian Jacob, *The Sovereign Map: Theoretical Approaches in Cartography Throughout History*, trans. Tom Conley (Chicago: University of Chicago Press, 2006). For the density of imperial maps in British India, see Matthew H. Edney, *Mapping an Empire: The Geographical Construction of British India, 1765–1843* (Chicago: University of Chicago Press, 1990) and Nilanjana Mukherjee, *Spatial Imaginings in the Age of Colonial Cartographic Reason: Maps, Landscapes, Travelogues in Britain and India* (New York: Routledge, 2021).

7 W. W. Hunter, *Life of Brian Houghton Hodgson: British Resident at the Court of Nepal* (London: John Murray, 1896), 2–3.

8 Maurice Olender, *The Languages of Paradise: Race, Religion, and Philology in the Nineteenth Century*, trans. Arthur Goldhammer (Cambridge, MA: Harvard University Press, 2009); Thomas R. Trautmann, *Aryans and British India* (Berkeley: University of California Press, 1997).

9 Quoted in Raymond Schwab, *Oriental Renaissance: Europe's Rediscovery of India and the East, 1680–1880*, trans. Gene Patterson-Black and Victor Reinking (New York: Columbia University Press, 1984), 60.

10 Friedrich Schlegel, "On the Language and Wisdom of the Indians," in *The Æsthetic and Miscellaneous Works of Frederick von Schlegel*, trans. E. J. Millington (London: Henry G. Bohn 1849), 522–3.

11 Samuel Johnson, *A Dictionary of the English Language: In Which the Words Are Deduced from Their Originals, and Illustrated in Their Different Significations by Examples from the Best Writers*, 2 Vols. (London: W. Strahan, 1755), II: n.p.

12 The point here is not to deny the importance of precolonial histories, but to productively think colonialism as a form and a project, to pay attention to its own claims of newness.

13 Here I partly build on Aamir Mufti's suggestion that "world literature" is essentially an "orientalist" idea. However, my focus is more on colonial governance, and the implications of my argument, as would be evident below, are quite different from those of Mufti's. See Aamir R. Mufti, *Forget English! Orientalisms and World Literatures* (Cambridge, MA: Harvard University Press, 2016).

14 Thomas R. Metcalf, *Ideologies of the Raj* (Cambridge: Cambridge University Press, 1995), 1–27. See also Robert Travers, *Ideology and Empire in Eighteenth-Century India: The British in Bengal* (Cambridge: Cambridge University Press, 2007).
15 G. W. F. Hegel, *Elements of the Philosophy of Right*, trans. H. B. Nisbet (Cambridge: Cambridge University Press, 2003), 316–17.
16 Edmund Burke, "Speech in Opening the Impeachment [of Warren Hastings], First Day: Friday, February 15, 1788," in *The Writings and Speeches of Edmund Burke*, 12 Vols. (Boston: Little, Brown and Company, 1901), 9: 348–50.
17 Adam Smith, *An Inquiry into the Nature and Causes of the Wealth of Nations*, 2 Vols. (London: W. Strahan and T. Cadell, 1776), 2: 251.
18 See Bernard S. Cohn, *Colonialism and Its Forms of Knowledge: The British in India* (Princeton: Princeton University Press, 1996); Philip J. Stern, *The Company-State: Corporate Sovereignty and the Early Modern Foundations of the British Empire in India* (Oxford: Oxford University Press, 2011); Sudipta Sen, *A Distant Sovereignty: National Imperialism and the Origins of British India* (London: Routledge, 2016); William Dalrymple, *The Anarchy: The Relentless Rise of the East India Company* (London: Bloomsbury, 2019).
19 Governor and Council in Bengal, letter to the Court of Directors, 3 November 1772, in House of Commons, *Reports from Committees of the House of Commons*, 15 Vols. (London: House of Commons, 1804), 4: 346.
20 Travers, *Ideology and Empire in Eighteenth-Century India*, 117.
21 On the use of writing and print by the Company, see Miles Ogborn, *Indian Ink: Script and Print in the Making of the English East India Company* (Chicago: Chicago University Press, 2008); Daniel E. White, *From Little London to Little Bengal: Religion, Print, and Modernity in Early British India, 1793–1835* (Baltimore: Johns Hopkins University Press, 2013); and James Mulholland, *Before the Raj: Writing Early Anglophone India* (Baltimore: Johns Hopkins University Press, 2021).
22 For a representative and recent case, see Alexandre Gefen, *L'Idée de littérature: De l'art pour l'art aux écritures d'intervention* (Paris: Corti, 2020).
23 Stern, *The Company-State*, 7.
24 East India Company, George Christopher Molesworth Birdwood, and William Foster, *The Register of Letters, &c., of the Governour and Company of Merchants of London Trading into the East Indies, 1600–1619* (London: B. Quaritch, 1893), xvi–xvii.
25 Stern, *The Company-State*, 14.
26 For historical details on the transition, see P. J. Marshall, *Bengal: The British Bridgehead, Eastern India 1740–1828* (Cambridge: Cambridge University Press, 1987).
27 The Company's monopoly rights, however, were often overstated in contemporary debates. Though the Company enjoyed such rights in England, in the subcontinent it had to compete with other European companies. In addition, the Company's rights were also compromised by private business of its own employees. See Emily Erickson, *Between Monopoly and Free Trade: The English East India Company, 1600–1757* (Princeton: Princeton University Press, 2014).

28 Smith, *An Inquiry*, 2: 252.
29 Smith, *An Inquiry*, 2: 256.
30 On the recurring theme of Indian "despotism" in Europe, see Ranajit Guha, *A Rule of Property for Bengal: An Essay on the Idea of Permanent Settlement* (Delhi: Orient Longman, 1982), 25–31; also see Sudipta Sen, *Empire of Free Trade: The East India Company and the Making of the Colonial Marketplace* (Philadelphia: University of Pennsylvania Press, 1998), 132–4.
31 Manan Ahmed Asif, *The Loss of Hindustan: The Invention of India* (Cambridge, MA: Harvard University Press, 2020), 19–21.
32 On Montesquieu's claims about the connection between climate and despotism, see Montesquieu, *The Spirit of the Laws*, trans. and ed. Anne M. Cohler et al. (Cambridge: Cambridge University Press, 1989 [1748]), Part III, Book XVII, 278–84.
33 Alexander Dow, *The History of Hindostan, from the Death of Akbar, to the Complete Settlement of the Empire under Aurungzebe* (London: T. Becket and P. A. De Hondt, 1772), vii–xxxvii.
34 Dow, *The History of Hindostan*, lii, cxii. For a somewhat similar view, expressed by another Company official around the same time, see William Bolts, *Consideration on Indian Affairs; Particularly Respecting the Present State of Bengal and Its Dependencies* (London: J. Almon et al., 1772).
35 Sankar Muthu, *Enlightenment against Empire* (Princeton: Princeton University Press, 2003); Sunil M. Agnani, *Hating Empire Properly: The Two Indies and the Limits of Enlightenment Anticolonialism* (New York: Fordham University Press, 2013).
36 John H. Zammito, *Kant, Herder, and the Birth of Anthropology* (Chicago: University of Chicago Press, 2002).
37 Zammito, *Kant, Herder, and the Birth of Anthropology*, 250–3; Robert B. Louden, *Kant's Human Being: Essays on His Theory of Human Nature* (Oxford: Oxford University Press, 2011), 79–81.
38 Quoted in Travers, *Ideology and Empire in Eighteenth-Century India*, 103.
39 Travers, *Ideology and Empire in Eighteenth-Century India*, 103–4.
40 Travers, *Ideology and Empire in Eighteenth-Century India*, 106.
41 Radhika Singha, *A Despotism of Law: Crime and Justice in Early Colonial India* (Delhi: Oxford University Press, 1998), 16–32.
42 Quoted in G. R. Gleig, *Memoirs of the Life of the Right Hon. Warren Hastings, First Governor-General of Bengal*, 2 Vols. (London: Richard Bentley, 1841), 1: 400–3.
43 James Fraser, *The History of Nadir Shah, Formerly Called Thamas Kuli Khan, The Present Emperor of Persia* (London: W. Strahan 1742), appendix 1–40. For a detailed account of Fraser in India, and his exploration of local cultures and texts, see Sanjay Subrahmanyam, *Europe's India: Words, People, Empires, 1500–1800* (Cambridge, MA: Harvard University Press, 2017), 144–210.
44 J. Z. Holwell, *Interesting Historical Events, Relative to the Provinces of Bengal, and the Empire of Indostan*, 3 Vols. (London: T. Becket and P. A. De Hondt, 1765), 1: 10.
45 Alexander Dow, "Preface," in *Tales Translated from the Persian of Inatulla of Delhi*, 2 Vols. (London: T. Becket and P. A. De Hondt, 1768), 1: iv–vi.

Notes to pages 18–26

46 Alexander Dow, *History of Hindostan; From the Earliest Account of Time, to the Death of Akbar*, 2 Vols. (London: T. Becket and P. A. De Hondt, 1768), 1: ii–iii. For a critical reading of Dow's translation of Firishtā, see Asif, *The Loss of Hindustan*, 185–201.
47 Nathaniel Brassey Halhed, "The Translator's Preface," in *A Code of Gentoo Laws. Or, Ordinations of the Pundits, from a Persian Translation, Made from the Original, Written in the Shanscrit Language* (London: n.p., 1776), x.
48 Halhed, "The Translator's Preface," x–xii.
49 Halhed, "The Translator's Preface," xxiii–xxvi.
50 On Halhed's influence on Indology, see Rosane Rocher, *Orientalism, Poetry, and the Millennium: The Checkered Life of Nathaniel Brassey Halhed* (Delhi: Motilal Banarsidass, 1983), especially Part II, "The Discovery of India."
51 Nathaniel Brassey Halhed, *A Grammar of the Bengal Language* (Hoogly: n.p., 1778), iii.
52 Halhed, "The Translator's Preface," xxiii.
53 Halhed, *A Grammar of the Bengal Language*, iii–iv.
54 William Jones, *Poems, Consisting Chiefly of Translations from the Asiatick Languages* (Oxford: Clarendon, 1772), 173–91.
55 Jones, *Poems*, 182–3, 189.
56 Governor and Council in Bengal, letter to the Court of Directors, 3 November 1772, in House of Commons, *Reports from Committees of the House of Commons*, 16 Vols. (London: House of Commons, 1803–4), 4: 346.
57 Guha, *A Rule of Property for Bengal*, 20–1.
58 *Reports from Committees of the House of Commons*, 4: 346.
59 *Reports from Committees of the House of Commons*, 4: 346.
60 Warren Hastings, "Letter from Warren Hastings, Esq. Governor-General of Fort-William, in Bengal, to the Court of Directors of the United Company of Merchants of England, Trading to the East-Indies," in Halhed (ed.), *A Code of Gentoo Laws*, iv.
61 Warren Hastings, "To Nathaniel Smith, Esquire," in Charles Wilkins (ed.), *The Bhăgvăt-Gēētā, or Dialogues of Krĕĕshnă and Ărjŏŏn* (London: C. Nourse, 1785), 7.
62 William Jones, *Letters*, 2: 643.
63 Cohn, *Colonialism and Its Form of Knowledge*, 69.
64 H. T. Colebrooke, "On the Sanscrit and Prácrit Languages," *Asiatick Researches*, Vol. 7 (1803), 200.
65 The point was made succinctly by Forster in defense of his grammar: "Our political connexion with the people [of India] as their sovereigns, renders it both an act of duty towards them, as well as of advantage to ourselves, to endeavour to acquire all their languages, and though the philosopher's curiosity may ultimately be disappointed, the legislature's ends must be accomplished. With respect to the Sanskrit, it is almost an indispensable qualification for those who may be called to discharge the functions of a judicial appointment, seeing we continue to administer justice, in a great measure, to the natives, according to their own laws, which are all written in it and few of them have

been translated, nor should translations be recurred to merely to save the trouble of learning the language." H. P. Forster, *An Essay on the Principles of Sanskrit Grammar*, Part 1 (Calcutta: Ferris and Co., 1810), iv.
66 See, for instance, Nasser Hussain, *The Jurisprudence of Emergency: Colonialism and the Rule of Law* (Ann Arbor: University of Michigan Press, 2003).
67 Giorgio Agamben, *State of Exception*, trans. Kevin Attell (Chicago: University of Chicago Press, 2005), 1 and *passim*.
68 William Jones, "The Preface," in *Institutes of Hindu Law: Or, The Ordinances of Menu* (Calcutta: Order of the Government, 1794), iii.
69 The scholarship on literary singularity is vast. For a concise and clear account, see Derek Attridge, *The Singularity of Literature* (London: Routledge, 2004).
70 Jean-Luc Nancy, *Dis-Enclosure: The Deconstruction of Christianity*, trans. Bettina Bergo et al. (New York: Fordham University Press, 2008), 106. The sense of the untranslatable I invoke here is also indebted to Barbara Cassin (ed.), *Dictionary of Untranslatables: A Philosophical Lexicon*, trans. Stephen Rendall et al. and ed. Emily Apter et al. (Princeton: Princeton University Press, 2014).
71 Hastings, "To Nathaniel Smith, Esquire," 12–13.
72 Hastings, "To Nathaniel Smith, Esquire," 7–8.
73 Schwab, *Oriental Renaissance*, 59, 61.
74 William Robertson, *Historical Disquisition Concerning the Knowledge Which the Ancients Had of India* (London: A. Strahan, and T. Cadell, 1791), 227, 274.
75 For a succinct account of Goethe's use of the term *Weltliteratur*, see David Damrosch, *What Is World Literature?* (Princeton: Princeton University Press, 2003), 1–38.
76 Gayatri Chakravorty Spivak, *A Critique of Postcolonial Reason: Toward a History of the Vanishing Present* (Cambridge, MA: Harvard University Press, 1999), 7–8.
77 As accounts of his personal library or of his borrowings from various public libraries confirm, he voraciously read a large amount of translations from various oriental languages, including Sanskrit, Persian, Chinese, Japanese, Arabic, and so on. See B. Venkat Mani, *Recoding World Literature: Libraries, Print Culture, and Germany's Pact with Books* (New York: Fordham University Press, 2016), 53–4.
78 Johann Peter Eckermann, *Conversations of Goethe with Eckermann and Soret*, trans. John Oxenford (London: George Bell & Sons, 1874), 211–12.
79 Eckermann, *Conversations of Goethe*, 213.
80 Pheng Cheah, "What Is a World? On World Literature as World-Making Activity," *Daedalus*, Vol. 137, No. 3 (2008), 26–38.
81 This Goethean vision is reiterated almost in toto in Pascale Casanova, *The World Republic of Letters*, trans. Malcolm DeBevoise (Cambridge, MA: Harvard University Press, 2007).
82 Eckermann, *Conversations of Goethe*, 213.
83 Jacques Rancière, *Dissensus: On Politics and Aesthetics*, trans. Steven Corcoran (London and New York: Continuum, 2010), 155.

84 Rancière, *Dissensus*, 162.
85 Joseph Jacobs, "Introduction," in Thomas North (ed.), *The Earliest English Version of the Fables of Bidpai, "The Morall Philosophie of Doni" by Sir Thomas North*, ed. Joseph Jacobs (London: David Nutt, 1888); I. G. N. Keith-Falconer, *Kalilah and Dimnah or The Fables of Bidpai: Being an Account of Their Literary History, with an English Translation of the Later Syriac Version of the Same* (Cambridge: Cambridge University Press, 1885).
86 Paulo Lemos Horta, *Marvellous Thieves: Secret Authors of the Arabian Nights* (Cambridge, MA: Harvard University Press, 2017).
87 Srinivas Aravamudan, *Enlightenment Orientalism: Resisting the Rise of the Novel* (Chicago: University of Chicago Press, 2012).
88 Michel Foucault, *The Order of Things: An Archaeology of the Human Sciences*, trans. Publisher (London: Routledge, 2002), 327.
89 F. Bopp, "Analytical Comparison of the Sanskrit, Greek, Latin, and Teutonic Languages, Shewing the Original Identity of Their Grammatical Structure," *Annals of Oriental Literature*, Vol. 1, No. 1 (1820), 2.
90 John Borthwick Gilchrist, *The Strangers' East Indian Guide to the Hindoostanee; Or Grand Popular Language of India, (Improperly Called Moors)* (London: Black, Parry, and Kingsbury, 1808), xxviii.
91 Sisir Kumar Das, *Sahibs and Munshis: An Account of the College of Fort William* (New Delhi: Orion, 1978).
92 Schlegel, "On the Language and Wisdom of the Indians," 496, 515.
93 Schlegel, "On the Language and Wisdom of the Indians," 523–6.
94 Schlegel, "On the Language and Wisdom of the Indians," 526; emphasis added.
95 John Guillory, *Cultural Capital: The Problem of Literary Canon Formation* (Chicago: University of Chicago Press, 1993), 85–133.
96 Gauri Viswanathan, *Masks of Conquest: Literary Study and British Rule in India* (New York: Columbia University Press, 1989).
97 On Renan's influence on Arnold, see Robert J. C. Young, *Colonial Desire: Hybridity in Theory, Culture and Race* (London: Routledge, 1995), 65–7, 79–82.
98 Maurice Olender, *Race and Erudition*, trans. Jane Marie Todd (Cambridge, MA: Harvard University Press, 2009).
99 See, for instance, Ronald Inden, *Imagining India* (Oxford: Blackwell, 1990); Cohn, *Colonialism and Its Forms of Knowledge*; Kate Teltscher, *India Inscribed: European and British Writing on India, 1600–1800* (Oxford: Oxford University Press, 1997); Subrahmanyam, *Europe's India*.

1 Ethnographic Recension

1 Horace Hayman Wilson, *Select Specimens of the Theatre of the Hindus, Translated from the Original Sanscrit*, 3 Vols. (Calcutta: Asiatic Press, 1827), 1: 7.
2 See Aamir R. Mufti, *Forget English! Orientalisms and World Literatures* (Cambridge, MA: Harvard University Press, 2016); Siraj Ahmed, *Archaeology of Babel: The Colonial Foundation of the Humanities* (Stanford: Stanford University Press, 2017).

Notes to pages 56–61

3 Nicholas B. Dirks, *Castes of Mind: Colonialism and the Making of Modern India* (Princeton: Princeton University Press, 2001), 44.
4 William Jones, "Preface," in *A Grammar of the Persian Language* (London: W. and J. Richardson, 1771), ii–iii.
5 See Garland Cannon, "Sir William Jones, Persian, Sanskrit and the Asiatic Society," *Histoire Épistémologie Langage*, Vol. 6, No. 2 (1984), 85–6.
6 Jones, "Preface," vi.
7 Jones, "Preface," vii.
8 Jones, "Preface," viii.
9 Jones, "Preface," vii.
10 Jones, "Preface," viii.
11 Nathaniel Brassey Halhed, *A Grammar of the Bengal Language* (Hoogly: n.p., 1778), ix.
12 Srinivas Aravamudan, *Enlightenment Orientalism: Resisting the Rise of the Novel* (Chicago: Chicago University Press, 2012), 4.
13 Thomas R. Trautmann, *Aryans and British India* (Berkeley: California University Press, 1997), 32–6.
14 Jerome J. McGann, *A Critique of Modern Textual Criticism* (Charlottesville: Virginia University Press, 1992), 15.
15 On the connection between colonial officials like Jones and their work on comparative philology and the early developments in stemmatics, see Sebastiano Timpanaro, *The Genesis of Lachmann's Method*, trans. Glenn W. Most (Chicago: Chicago University Press, 2005), 120–1.
16 See Karl Lachmann, "Prefation," in *Nolum Testamentum Graece et Latine*, Vol. 1 (Berlin: Reimer, 1842), v–vi.
17 See L. D. Reynolds and N. G. Wilson, *Scribes and Scholars: A Guide to the Transmission of Greek and Latin Literature* (Oxford: Oxford University Press, 2013), 208–42.
18 Quoted in Timpanaro, *The Genesis of Lachmann's Method*, 71.
19 Quoted in Timpanaro, *The Genesis of Lachmann's Method*, 71.
20 See, for instance, William Jones, "Lettre à Monsieur A***du P***," in William Jones (ed.), *Works of Sir William Jones*, 13 Vols. (London: John Stockdale and John Walker, 1807), 10: 408, 412.
21 For a critical account of the theory of "final intentions," see McGann, *A Critique of Modern Textual Criticism*, 28–36.
22 Aravamudan, *Enlightenment Orientalism*, 4–5. He proposes a long list of these authors from eighteenth-century Europe: "Enlightenment Orientalism had among its practitioners some very significant eighteenth-century French fiction writers, including Galland, Marana, Fontenelle, Pétis, Montesquieu, Hamilton, Crébillon, Prévost, Voltaire, and Diderot; its English wing can be represented by Behn, Defoe, Swift, Haywood, Montagu, Goldsmith, Johnson, Smollett, Sheridan, Beckford, and a host of minor writers who are largely unread today except by eighteenth-century specialists." Arvamudan, *Enlightenment Orientalism*, 5.

23 Zak Sitter, "William Jones, 'Eastern' Poetry, and the Problem of Imitation," *Texas Studies in Literature and Language*, Vol. 50, No. 4 (2008), 404.
24 William Jones, *Poems, Consisting Chiefly of Translations from the Asiatick Languages* (London: Clarendon, 1772), vii; henceforth abbreviated as *Poems* and cited parenthetically with pagination.
25 M. H. Abrams, *The Mirror and the Lamp: Romantic Theory and the Critical Tradition* (New York: Oxford University Press, 1971 [1953]), 87. On Jones's break with the neoclassical tradition, also see René Wellek, *A History of Modern Criticism, 1750–1950*, Vol. 1 (New Haven: Yale University Press, 1955), 123. For a critical assessment of Abrams's reading of Jones, see Mufti, *Forget English!*, 67–8.
26 Abrams, *The Mirror and the Lamp*, 87.
27 Some preliminary ideas in this direction can be seen in another early piece by Jones, namely his *Dissertation sur la littérature orientale* (1771) – see Jones, *The Works of Sir William Jones*, 12: 282–3.
28 Aravamudan, *Enlightenment Orientalism*, 26–8.
29 Mufti, *Forget English!*, 105; emphasis original.
30 See William Jones, "Letter to Lord Althorp, 2nd Earl Spencer, August 17, 1787," in Garland Cannon (ed.), *The Letters of Sir William Jones*, 2 Vols. (Oxford: Clarendon, 1970), 2: 751.
31 For a brief overview of the European engagement with Sanskrit, see Rosane Rocher, "Discovery of Sanskrit by Europeans," in E. F. K. Koerner and R. E. Asher (eds.), *Concise History of the Language Sciences: From the Sumerians to the Cognitivists* (Oxford: Pergamon, 1995), 188–91.
32 Bernard S. Cohn, *Colonialism and Its Forms of Knowledge: The British in India* (Princeton: Princeton University Press, 1996), 29.
33 Cannon (ed.), *The Letters of Sir William Jones*, 2: 747.
34 Cannon (ed.), *The Letters of Sir William Jones*, 2: 756.
35 Warren Hastings, "To Nathaniel Smith, Esquire," in Charles Wilkins (ed.), *The Bhăgvăt-Gēētā, or Dialogues of Krēĕshnă and Ărjŏŏn* (London: C. Nourse, 1785), 7.
36 Hastings, "To Nathaniel Smith, Esquire," 10.
37 Hastings, "To Nathaniel Smith, Esquire," 8–9.
38 Hastings, "To Nathaniel Smith, Esquire," 9.
39 Hastings, "To Nathaniel Smith, Esquire," 13; emphasis added.
40 Hastings, "To Nathaniel Smith, Esquire," 13; emphasis added.
41 Cohn, *Colonialism and Its Forms of Knowledge*, 27.
42 For the details of Halhed's life and his career in India, see Rosane Rocher, *Orientalism, Poetry, and the Millennium: The Checkered Life of Nathaniel Brassey Halhed, 1751–1830* (Delhi: Motilal Banarsidas, 1983).
43 Garland Cannon, *The Life and Mind of Oriental Jones: Sir William Jones, the Father of Modern Linguistics* (Cambridge: Cambridge University Press, 1990), 230–1; Trautmann, *Aryans and British India*, 32.
44 Nathaniel Brassey Halhed, *A Code of Gentoo Laws, Or, Ordinations of the Pundits, from a Persian Translation, Made from the Original, Written in the Shanscrit Language* (London: n.p., 1776), x.

252 Notes to pages 71–80

45 Halhed, *A Code of Gentoo Laws*, xi.
46 Halhed, *A Code of Gentoo Laws*, xxxii.
47 Halhed, *A Code of Gentoo Laws*, xxiii–xxxvi.
48 Nathaniel Brassey Halhed, *A Grammar of the Bengal Language* (Hoogly: n.p., 1778), vi.
49 Halhed, *A Grammar of the Bengal Language*, iii–v.
50 William Jones, "The Third Anniversary Discourse, on the Hindus, delivered 2nd of February, 1786," in *The Works of Sir William Jones*, 3: 29.
51 Jones, "The Third Anniversary Discourse," 3: 28.
52 William Jones, "On the Literature of the Hindus, from the Sanscrit," in *The Works of Sir William Jones*, 13 Vols. (London: John Stockdale and John Walker, 1807), 4: 99–110.
53 Jones, "On the Literature of the Hindus," 4: 112.
54 Jones, "On the Literature of the Hindus," 4: 113.
55 Raymond Schwab, *Oriental Renaissance: Europe's Rediscovery of India and the East, 1680–1880*, trans. Gene Patterson-Black and Victor Reinking (New York: Columbia University Press, 1984), 61. Also see Michael J. Franklin, *Orientalist Jones: Sir William Jones, Poet, Lawyer, and Linguist, 1746–1794* (Oxford: Oxford University Press, 2011), 251–86.
56 William Jones, "The Preface," in *Institutes of Hindu Law: Or, The Ordinances of Menu, According to the Gloss of Cullúka. Comprising the Indian System of Duties, Religious and Civil*, in *The Works of Sir William Jones*, 7: 75.
57 Jones, "The Preface," in *Institutes of Hindu Law*, 75–6.
58 William Jones, "Advertisement," in *The Moallakát, or Seven Arabian Poems, Which Were Suspended on the Temple at Mecca; With a Translation and Argument*, in *The Works of Sir William Jones*, 10: 4.
59 William Jones, "Preface," in *Sacontalá; Or, The Fatal Ring: An Indian Drama by Cálidás* (London: Edwards, 1792), vii.
60 Jones, "Preface," in *Sacontalá*, ix–xi.
61 Romila Thapar, *Śakuntalā: Texts, Readings, Histories* (New York: Columbia University Press, 2011), 197–8.
62 Jones, "Preface," in *Sacontalá*, vii.
63 Wilson, "Preface," 1: iii.
64 Wilson also argues: "Mohammedan literature has ever been a stranger to Theatrical writings […]. There is no record that theatrical entertainments were ever naturalised among the ancient Persians, Arabs, or Egyptians." Wilson, "Preface," 1: iii–iv.
65 Wilson, "Preface," 1: iv.
66 Monier Williams, "Introduction," in *Śakoontalá; Or, The Lost Ring; an Indian Drama*, trans. Monier Williams (Hertford: Stephen Austin, 1856), xii.
67 Monier Williams, "Preface," in *Śakuntalá; Or Śakuntalá Recognized by the Ring* (Hertford: Stephen Austin, 1853), viii.
68 Williams, "Preface," xii–xiii.
69 Wilson, "Dramatic System of the Hindus," in *Select Specimens of the Theatre of the Hindus*, 1: 1–7.
70 Wilson, "Preface," x.

Notes to pages 82–5 253

2 Colonial Untranslatables

1 For an account of how the Company officials, especially Alexander Dow, created this history of Mughal misrule in India, see Manan Ahmed Asif, *The Loss of Hindustan: The Invention of India* (Cambridge, MA: Harvard University Press, 2020).
2 See Bernard S. Cohn, *Colonialism and Its Forms of Knowledge: The British in India* (Princeton: Princeton University Press, 1996); Tejaswini Niranjana, *Siting Translation: History, Post-structuralism, and the Colonial Context* (Berkeley: University of California Press, 1992); Thomas Trautmann, *Aryans and British India* (Berkeley: University of California Press, 1997); Joseph Errington, *Linguistics in a Colonial World: A Story of Language, Meaning, and Power* (Oxford: Blackwell, 2008); and Siraj Ahmed, *Archaeology of Babel: The Colonial Foundation of the Humanities* (Stanford: Stanford University Press, 2018) among others.
3 Emily Apter, "Preface," in Barbara Cassin (ed.), *Dictionary of Untranslatables: A Philosophical Lexicon*, trans. Steven Rendall et al. (Princeton: Princeton University Press, 2014), vii.
4 Lawrence Venuti, "Translation as a Social Practice: Or, The Violence of Translation," *Translation Perspectives*, Vol. 9 (1996), 195–213.
5 See Srinivas Aravamudan, *Enlightenment Orientalism: Resisting the Rise of the Novel* (Chicago: Chicago University Press, 2012).
6 P. J. Marshall, "Introduction," in P. J. Marshall (ed.), *The Writings and Speeches of Edmund Burke*, vol. V: *India: Madras and Bengal, 1774–1785* (Oxford: Clarendon, 2000), 1–2.
7 See Colin Burrow, *Shakespeare and Classical Antiquity* (Oxford: Oxford University Press, 2013), 202–39.
8 Joseph Jacobs, "Introduction," in Thomas North (ed.), *The Earliest English Version of the Fables of Bidpai, "The Morall Philosophie of Doni" by Sir Thomas North* (London: David Nutt, 1888), xi.
9 Jacobs, "Introduction," xii.
10 I. G. N. Keith-Falconer, *Kalīlah and Dimnah or The Fables of Bidpai: Being an Account of Their Literary History, with an English Translation of the Later Syriac Version of the Same* (Cambridge: Cambridge University Press, 1885), ix.
11 The popularity of these tales was evident in the way the fables traveled across cultures and languages and appealed to different religious sensibilities including Buddhism, Hinduism, Zoroastrianism, Judaism, Islam, and Christianity – and also in the way each passage and every cultural milieu added additional layers to the core of these fables. The earliest known translation was done into Pehlevi or Old Persian by Barzōye or Burzoë, the physician of the Sasanian king of Persia Khosrū Nūshīrvān, in the sixth century. In this, and in many subsequent versions, Barzōye's journey to India in search of the famed book, his adventures in the foreign land, and his eventual translation of the book of Indian wisdom for the king back home became part of the story-cycle itself. Barzōye's translation (now lost) led to further translations into old Syriac by Būd or Bōd (in the sixth century) and into Arabic by Abdullah Ibn al-Muqaffa' (in the eighth century),

Notes to pages 86–8

and the latter, in turn, inspired more translations into Syriac, Greek, Persian, Hebrew, and Castilian Spanish between the tenth and the sixteenth centuries. Of the later Persian versions, Ḥosayn Wāʿeẓ Kāšefi's translation *Anwār-e sohaylī* (in the fifteenth century) and Abu'l-Fażl's *Īār-e dāneš* (in the sixteenth century) gained prominence and were translated into other languages. Meanwhile, a second line of translations appeared when al-Muqaffa's version was translated into Hebrew, which in turn was rendered into Latin in the thirteenth century by John of Capua with the title *Directorium humanæ vitæ*. The Latin text became the popular source for further translations into a number of European languages, including German, Spanish, Italian, French, English, Danish, and Dutch. Keith-Falconer, *Kalīlah and Dimnah*, xiii–lxxiii.

12 Janet L. Abu-Lughod, *Before European Hegemony: The World System A.D. 1250–1350* (Oxford: Oxford University Press, 1989), 12.
13 North, *The Earliest English Version*, 13–14.
14 Anonymous, "Avertissement," in *Les Fables de Pilpay, philosophe indien ou la Conduite des rois* (Paris: Florentin et Pierre Delaulne, 1698), n.p.
15 Friedrich Max Müller, "Lecture on the Migration of Fables, Delivered at the Royal Institution, June 3, 1870," in *Chips from a German Workshop*, 4 Vols. (New York: Scribner, Armstrong, and Co., 1876), 4: 145–6.
16 Müller, "Lecture on the Migration of Fables," 4: 145–64.
17 See Walter Benjamin, "The Task of the Translator," in Marcus Bullock and Michael W. Jennings (eds.), *Walter Benjamin: Selected Writings*, vol. I: *1913–1926* (Cambridge, MA: Belknap Press of Harvard University, 2004), 253–63.
18 Jacobs, "Introduction," l.
19 Aravamudan, *Enlightenment Orientalism*, 115–59.
20 David Damrosch, *What Is World Literature?* (Princeton: Princeton University Press, 2003), 4; emphasis original.
21 James Fraser, *A Catalogue of Manuscripts in the Persic, Arabic, and Sanskerrit Languages*, in *The History of Nadir Shah, Formerly Called Thamas Kuli Khan, The Present Emperor of Persia. To which is prefix'd A short History of the Moghol Emperors. At the End is inserted, A Catalogue of about Two Hundred Manuscripts in the Persic and Other Oriental Languages, collected in the East*, 2nd edition (London: A. Millar, 1742), 19–20. For a contemporary translation from *Ayār-e-Dāniš*, a Persian translation of *Pañcatantra* prepared by the Mughal emperor Akbar's courtier and minister Abu'l-Fażl in the late sixteenth century, see "The Fatal Effects of Precipitation – From the Ayar Danish of Abulfazel," in *The Asiatic Miscellany: Consisting of Original Productions, Translations, Figurative Pieces, Imitations, and Extracts from Curious Publications*, Vol. 1 (Calcutta: Daniel Stuart, 1785), 55–9. For similar catalogues in circulation, see Samuel Guise, *A Catalogue of Oriental Manuscripts, Collected in Indoostan* (Calcutta: n.p., 1793).
22 Alexander Dow, *Tales Translated from the Persian of Inatulla of Delhi*, 2 Vols. (London: T. Becket and P. A. de Hondt, 1768) 1: 1–275.
23 William Jones, "The Third Anniversary Discourse," in *The Works of Sir William Jones*, 13 Vols. (London: John Stockdale and John Walker, 1807), 3: 43; subsequent references to this edition are cited with volume and page numbers.

Notes to pages 89–100

24 Jones, "The Third Anniversary Discourse," in *The Works of Sir William Jones*, 3: 43.
25 For the posthumously published translation, see William Jones, "Hito'pode'sa of Vishnusarman," in *The Works of Sir William Jones*, 13: 3–210.
26 Charles Wilkins, "Preface," in *The Hĕĕtōpādēs of Vĕĕshnŏŏ-Sărmā, in a Series of Connected Fables, Interspersed with Moral, Prudential, and Political Maxims; Translated from an Ancient Manuscript in the Sanskreet Language with Explanatory Notes* (Bath and London: R. Cruttwell, 1787), xiv–xv; henceforth abbreviated as *H* and cited parenthetically with pagination.
27 Jacques Derrida, *Dissemination*, trans. Barbara Johnson (London: Continuum, 2004), 1, 63, 372.
28 It would be useful here to remember the philological distinction between "interpretation" and "commentary" as suggested by Hans Gumbrecht. Interpretation is supposed to be a "vertical" movement that is located beyond the text, usually at a "depth" below the "surface." But commentary, in contrast, is a "lateral" and unfinished elaboration that exists at the surface level with the text: "It is this contiguity between the commentator's text and the text on which to comment that explains why the material form of the commentary depends on and has to adapt to the material form of the commented-on text." Hans Ulrich Gumbrecht, *The Powers of Philology: Dynamics of Textual Scholarship* (Urbana: University of Illinois Press, 2003), 43–4.
29 Anonymous, *Les Conseils et les Maximes de Pilpay Philosophe Indien sur les divers Etats de la vie* (Paris: n.p., 1792), 87–8.
30 Joseph Harris, *The Instructive and Entertaining Fables of Pilpay, an Ancient Indian Philosopher. Containing a Number of Excellent Rules for the Conduct of Persons of All Ages, and in All Stations: Under Several Heads*, 6th edition (London: J. F. and C. Rivington et al., 1789), 82–3.
31 Charles Wilkins, *The Bhăgvăt-Gēētā, or Dialogues of Krĕĕshnă and Ărjŏŏn; in Eight Lectures; with Notes* (London: C. Nourse, 1785), 24–5.
32 Charles Hamilton, *The Hedàya, or Guide; A Commentary on the Mussulman Laws*, 4 Vols. (London: T. Bensley, 1791), 1: v–vi.
33 Hamilton, *The Hedàya*, 1: iv–v.
34 Hamilton, *The Hedàya*, 1: xxii–xxxix.
35 Hamilton, *The Hedàya*, 1: xxxiii.
36 Hamilton, *The Hedàya*, 1: xxxiii–xxxix.
37 Hamilton, *The Hedàya*, 1: xlii.
38 Hamilton, *The Hedàya*, 1: xxxix.
39 Hamilton, *The Hedàya*, 1: iii.
40 Hamilton, *The Hedàya*, 1: xliv.
41 William Jones, *Al Shirájiyyah: Or, The Mohammedan Law of Inheritance, with a Commentary* (Calcutta: Joseph Cooper, 1792), iii–iv.
42 Jones, *Al Shirájiyyah*, iv–v.
43 Jones, *Al Shirájiyyah*, iv.
44 Jones, *Al Shirájiyyah*, viii.
45 Jones, *Al Shirájiyyah*, ix.
46 Jones, *Al Shirájiyyah*, vi.

47 Jones, *Al Shirájiyyah*, xi.
48 William Jones, "Charge to the Grand Jury, at Calcutta, December 4, 1783," in *The Works of Sir William Jones*, 7: 3–5.
49 Jones, *Al Shirájiyyah*, xiii.
50 Edmund Burke, *Reflections on the Revolution in France, and on the Proceedings in Certain Societies in London* (London: J. Dodsley, 1790), 28–9.
51 Sunil M. Agnani, *Hating Empire Properly: The Two Indies and the Limits of Enlightenment Anticolonialism* (New York: Fordham University Press, 2013), 69–71; see also Sara Suleri, *The Rhetoric of English India* (Chicago: Chicago University Press, 1992), 26.
52 Burke, *Reflections on the Revolution in France*, 143–4.
53 Burke, *Reflections on the Revolution in France*, 144; Agnani, *Hating Empire Properly*, 72.
54 Nicholas B. Dirks, *The Scandal of Empire: India and the Creation of Imperial Britain* (Cambridge, MA: Belknap Press of Harvard University, 2008).
55 Burke, *Reflections on the Revolution in France*, 66.
56 Hamilton, *The Hedàya*, 1: i–ii.
57 See Edmund Burke, *Article of Charge of High Crime and Misdemeanors, against Warren Hastings, Esq. Late Governor General of Bengal; Presented to the House of Commons, on the 4th Day of April, 1786* (London: J. Debrett, 1786).
58 Writing in 1841, almost half a century after the trial, Thomas Babington Macaulay captured the essence of the trial in the following words: "[O]n the thirteenth of February, 1788, the sitting of the Court commenced. There have been spectacles more dazzling to the eye, more gorgeous with jewellery and cloth of gold, more attractive to grown-up children, than that which was then exhibited at Westminster; but, perhaps, there never was a spectacle so well calculated to strike a highly cultivated, a reflecting, an imaginative mind. [...] Every step in the proceedings carried the mind either backward, through many troubled centuries, to the days when the foundations of our constitution were laid; or far away, over boundless seas and deserts, to dusky nations living under strange stars, worshipping strange gods, and writing strange characters from right to left. The High Court of Parliament was to sit, according to forms handed down from the days of the Plantagenets, on an Englishman accused of exercising tyranny over the lord of the holy city of Benares, and over the ladies of the princely house of Oude." Thomas Babington Macaulay, *Warren Hastings*, ed. K. Deighton (London: Macmillan, 1896), 110.
59 For details on the impeachment trial, see the various documents collected in *The History of the Trial of Warren Hastings, Esq. Late Governor-General of Bengal, before the High Court of Parliament in Westminster-Hall, on an Impeachment by the Commons of Great-Britain, for High Crimes and Misdemeanor* (London: J. Debrett, 1796). The standard scholarly account of the trial is P. J. Marshall, *The Impeachment of Warren Hastings* (Oxford: Oxford University Press, 1965).
60 Edmund Burke, "Speech in Opening the Impeachment," in *The Writings and Speeches of Edmund Burke*, 12 Vols. (Boston: Little, Brown and Company,

1901), 9: 331–2; all references to Burke's speeches during the impeachment are from this edition, and henceforth cited with volume and page numbers.
61 Dirks, *The Scandal of Empire*, 204.
62 Suleri, *The Rhetoric of English India*, 28.
63 Burke, "Speech on Mr. Fox's East India Bill, December 1, 1783," in *The Writings and Speeches of Edmund Burke*, 2: 446.
64 Suleri even suggests that Burke's colonial sublime has a close narrative parallel in the famed Marabar Caves in E. M. Forster's novel *A Passage to India* (1924) – "both tangible and resistant to cognition […] the India sublime is at its most empty at the very point when it is most replete, dissolving the stability of facts and figures into hieroglyphs that signify only the colonizer's pained confrontation with an object to which his cultural and interpretative tools must be inadequate." Suleri, *The Rhetoric of English India*, 31.
65 Hayden White, *The Content of the Form: Narrative Discourse and Historical Representation* (Baltimore: Johns Hopkins University Press, 1987), 68.
66 Burke's choice of Holwell as a credible source to counter Hastings is intriguing. Holwell first gained fame – and later notoriety – through his dubious claims on the Calcutta "black hole" during the siege of the city by the Nawab of Bengal, Siraj-ud-daulah, in 1756; see Partha Chatterjee, *The Black Hole of Empire: History of a Global Practice of Power* (Princeton: Princeton University Press, 2012), 1–32; Dirks, *The Scandal of Empire*, 1–6.
67 For a detailed account of Mill's history and its teleological framework, see Javed Majeed, *Ungoverned Imaginings: James Mill's* The History of British India *and Orientalism* (Oxford: Clarendon Press, 1992).
68 For a genealogy of this unusual arrangement, see Philip J. Stern, *The Company-State: Corporate Sovereignty and the Early Modern Foundations of the British Empire in India* (Oxford: Oxford University Press, 2011).
69 See Jones, *Letters*, 2: 643–4. On the relationship between Burke and Jones, see Garland H. Cannon, "Sir William Jones and Edmund Burke," *Modern Philology*, Vol. 54, No. 3 (February, 1957), 165–86.
70 Warren Hastings, *The Defence of Warren Hastings, Esq. (Late Governor General of Bengal,) at the Bar of the House of Commons* (London: J. Stockdale, 1786), 105–6. Also see Anonymous, *The Answer of Warren Hastings, Esq. to the Articles* (London: J. Debrett, 1788).
71 Hastings, *The Defence of Warren Hastings*, 106.
72 Anonymous, *The History of the Trial of Warren Hastings, Esq. Late Governor-General of Bengal, Before the High Court of Parliament in Westminster-Hall* (London: J. Debrett, 1796), 37–8.
73 Srinivas Aravamudan, *Tropicopolitans: Colonialism and Agency, 1688–1804* (Durham, NC: Duke University Press, 1999), 190–232.
74 Hastings, *The Defence of Warren Hastings*, 105–6.
75 Warren Hastings, "To Lord Mansfield, Fort William, 21st March, 1774," in G. R. Gleig (ed.), *Memoirs of the Life of the Right Hon. Warren Hastings, First Governor-General of Bengal*, 3 Vols. (London: Richard Bentley, 1841), 1: 401.

258   *Notes to pages 116–20*

76 Hastings, "To Lord Mansfield," 1: 400, 403.
77 Hastings, "To Lord Mansfield," 1: 403–4.

3 Comparatism in the Colony

1 Ferdinand de Saussure, *Cours de linguistique générale* (Lausanne: Payot, 1916), 14.
2 Raymond Schwab, *La Renaissance Orientale* (Paris: Payot 1950), English translation *Oriental Renaissance: Europe's Rediscovery of India and the East, 1680–1880*, trans. Gene Patterson-Black and Victor Reinking (New York: Columbia University Press, 1984); David Kopf, *British Orientalism and the Bengal Renaissance: The Dynamics of Indian Modernization, 1773–1835* (Berkeley: University of California Press, 1969).
3 Michel Foucault, *Les Mots et les choses: Une Archéologie des sciences humaines* (Paris: Gallimard, 1966), 233, 247, 253.
4 Edward W. Said, *Orientalism* (New York: Pantheon, 1978), Chapter 2.
5 Bernard S. Cohn, "The Command of Language and the Language of Command," *Colonialism and Its Forms of Knowledge: The British in India* (Princeton: Princeton University Press, 1996), 55.
6 Aamir R. Mufti, "Orientalism and the Institution of World Literatures," *Critical Inquiry* 36 (Spring 2010), 458–93; Aamir R. Mufti, *Forget English! Orientalisms and World Literatures* (Cambridge, MA: Harvard University Press, 2016); Siraj Ahmed, "Notes from Babel: Toward a Colonial History of Comparative Literature," *Critical Inquiry*, Vol. 39, No. 2 (Winter 2013), 306; Siraj Ahmed, *Archaeology of Babel: The Colonial Foundation of the Humanities* (Stanford: Stanford University Press, 2018).
7 Governor and Council in Bengal, letter to the Court of Directors, 3 November 1772, in House of Commons, *Reports from Committees of the House of Commons*, 15 Vols. (London: House of Commons, 1804), 4: 346.
8 William Jones, "Anniversary Discourses," in *The Works of Sir William Jones*, 13 Vols. (London: John Stockdale and John Walker, 1807), 3: 1–252.
9 George Abraham Grierson, *Linguistic Survey of India*, 11 Vols. (Calcutta: Government of India Central Publication Branch, 1903–28). For a detailed reading of the survey, see Javed Majeed, *Colonialism and Knowledge in Grierson's Linguistic Survey of India* (London: Routledge, 2019) and Javed Majeed, *Nation and Region in Grierson's Linguistic Survey of India* (London: Routledge, 2019).
10 Cohn, "Introduction," in *Colonialism and Its Forms of Knowledge*, 5.
11 Michel Foucault, *The Order of Things: An Archaeology of the Human Sciences*, trans. Publisher (London: Routledge, 2002), 326; hereafter abbreviated *OT*. See also Philippe Lacoue-Labarthe and Jean-Luc Nancy, *The Literary Absolute: The Theory of Literature in German Romanticism*, trans. Philip Barnard and Cheryl Lester (Albany, NY: SUNY Press, 1988).
12 Jones's own interest in this regard was partly due to the fact that he became increasingly wary of the pundits and maulvis who translated and interpreted these legal texts for the company officials. Jones complained to a friend: "I

can no longer bear to be at the mercy of our pundits, who deal out Hindu law as they please, and make it at reasonable rates, when they cannot find it ready made." William Jones, "Letter to Charles Chapman, 28 Sept. 1785," in, Garland Cannon (ed.), *The Letters of Sir William Jones*, 2 Vols. (Oxford: Clarendon, 1970), 2: 683–4. And eventually he decided to learn Sanskrit.

13 William Jones, "A Discourse on the Institution of a Society, for Inquiring into the History, Civil and Natural, the Antiquities, Arts, Sciences, and Literature, of Asia," in *The Works of Sir William Jones*, 3: 5, 6, 7.
14 Friedrich Nietzsche, "Notes for 'We Philologists,'" trans. William Arrowsmith, *Arion*, Vol. 1, No. 2 (1973–4), 317.
15 Gauri Viswanathan, *Masks of Conquest: Literary Study and British Rule in India* (New York: Columbia University Press, 1989), 93; hereafter abbreviated *MC*.
16 James Turner, *Philology: The Forgotten Origins of the Modern Humanities* (Princeton: Princeton University Press, 2014), 94–5.
17 Quoted in Michael J. Franklin, *Orientalist Jones: Sir William Jones, Poet, Lawyer, and Linguist, 1746–1794* (New York: Oxford University Press, 2011), 13.
18 Cohn, "The Command of Language and the Language of Command," 21. See also Ahmed, "Notes from Babel," 321–2.
19 Thomas R. Trautmann, *Aryans and British India* (Berkeley: University of California Press, 1997), 42, 41.
20 Trautmann, *Aryans and British India*, 42.
21 George Abraham Grierson, "Preface," in George Abraham Grierson (ed.), *Linguistic Survey of India*, vol. 1: Introductory (Calcutta: Government of India Central Publication Branch, 1903–28), Part 1: i–ii; hereafter abbreviated *I*.
22 See J. A. Baines, *General Report on the Census of India, 1891* (London: Her Majesty's Stationery Office, 1893), 283–8.
23 Javed Majeed, "What's in a (Proper) Name? Particulars, Individuals, and Authorship in the Linguistic Survey of India and Colonial Scholarship," in Indra Sengupta and Daud Ali (eds.), *Knowledge Production, Pedagogy, and Institutions in Colonial India* (New York: Palgrave, 2011), 19.
24 See *The Imperial Gazetteer of India*, 26 Vols. (Oxford: Clarendon, 1907–9), 1: 349–401. By 1911 this model had become the dominant one, and the census conducted that year fully internalized Grierson's survey; see E. A. Gait, *Census of India, 1911*, vol. 1 (Calcutta: Bengal Secretariat Press, 1911–13), Part II: 90–121.
25 William Jones, "On the Chronology of the Hindus," in *The Works of Sir William Jones*, 13 Vols. (London: John Stockdale and John Walker, 1807), 4: 33, 2.
26 Jones, "On the Chronology of the Hindus," 4: 2.
27 See Jones, "On the Chronology of the Hindus," 4: 47.
28 William Jones, "A Supplement to the Essay on Indian Chronology by the President," in *The Works of Sir William Jones*, 13 Vols. (London: John Stockdale and John Walker, 1807), 4: 65–6.
29 William Jones, "On the Literature of the Hindus, from the Sanscrit," in *The Works of Sir William Jones*, 13 Vols. (London: John Stockdale and John Walker, 1807), 4: 109.

30 William Jones, "On the Mystical Poetry of the Persians and Hindus," in *The Works of Sir William Jones*, 13 Vols. (London: John Stockdale and John Walker, 1807), 4: 228.
31 Jones, "On the Mystical Poetry of the Persians and Hindus," 4: 230.
32 William Jones, "Essay on the Poetry of Eastern Nations," in *The Works of Sir William Jones*, 13 Vols. (London: John Stockdale and John Walker, 1807), 10: 359, 355.
33 Grierson did not invent the concept of *apabhraṃśa*; it was already prevalent in Sanskrit grammatical traditions, but his deployment of the term in the survey is quite different from existing sources, as he makes it a cornerstone of linguistic evolution.
34 Grierson developed this theory further by demonstrating the three types of vocabulary – *tatsama* (words used in the same form as in Sanskrit), semi-*tatsama*, and *tadbhava* (words derived from Sanskrit) – which secured ties between Sanskrit and modern vernaculars.
35 Also see George Abraham Grierson, *Linguistic Survey of India*, vol. 1: *Comparative Vocabulary* (Calcutta: Government of India Central Publication Branch, 1903–28), Part II: i.
36 Brian Houghton Hodgson, "Comparative Vocabulary of the Languages of the Broken Tribes of Népál," *Journal of the Asiatic Society of Bengal*, Vol. 26, No. 5 (1857), 318.
37 Brian Houghton Hodgson, "On the Kiránti Tribe of the Central Himalaya," in Brian Houghton Hodgson (ed.), *Miscellaneous Essays Relating to Indian Subjects*, 2 Vols. (London: Trübner, 1880), 1: 399.
38 William Wilson Hunter, *Life of Brian Houghton Hodgson: British Resident at the Court of Nepal* (London: John Murray, 1896), 289.
39 Hunter, *Life of Brian Houghton Hodgson*, 297.
40 Brian Houghton Hodgson, "On the Aborigines of North-Eastern India," in Brian Houghton Hodgson (ed.), *Miscellaneous Essays Relating to Indian Subjects*, 2 Vols. (London: Trübner, 1880), 2: 3.
41 Hodgson, "On the Aborigines of North-Eastern India," 2: 3.
42 Brian Houghton Hodgson, "Aborigines of the North-East Frontier," *Miscellaneous Essays Relating to Indian Subjects*, 2 Vols. (London: Trübner, 1880), 2: 11. In his biography of Hodgson, Hunter summarizes the project in the following words: "He conceived the idea of a complete and systematic survey of the whole non-Aryan races in India, with a view to working out their mutual affinities and of fixing their position among the great families of mankind." Hunter, *Life of Brian Houghton Hodgson*, 295–6.
43 William Wilson Hunter, *A Comparative Dictionary of the Languages of India and High Asia, with a Dissertation* (London: Trübner, 1868), 1; hereafter abbreviated *CD*.
44 See Albrecht Weber, *Akademische Vorlesungen über Indische Literaturgeschichte* (Berlin: F. Dümmler, 1852); Leopold von Schroeder, *Indiens Literatur und Kultur in historischer Entwicklung* (Leipzig: Haessel, 1887); R. W. Frazer, *A Literary History of India* (London: T. F. Unwin, 1898); Victor Henry,

Les Littératures de l'Inde: Sanscrit, pâli, prâcrit (Paris: Hachette, 1904); and Richard Pischel, "Die Indische Literatur," in Erich Schmidt et al. (eds.), *Die orientalischen Literaturen* (Berlin: B. G. Teubner, 1906), 160–213.
45 See George Abraham Grierson, *Linguistic Survey of India*, vol. v: *Indo-Aryan Family, Eastern Group*, Part 1: *Specimens of the Bengali and Assamese Languages* (Calcutta: Government of India Central Publication Branch, 1903–28), 23–4.
46 Grierson, *Linguistic Survey of India*, vol. v, Part 1: 24–7.
47 George Abraham Grierson, *The Modern Vernacular Literature of Hindustan* (Calcutta: Asiatic Society, 1889), viii; hereafter abbreviated *MVL*.
48 See Garcin de Tassy, *Histoire de la littérature hindoui et hindoustani* (Paris: Imprimerie royale, 1839).
49 See Erich Auerbach, "Farinata and Cavalcante," in Erich Auerbach (ed.), *Mimesis: The Representation of Reality in Western Literature*, trans. Willard R. Trask (Princeton: Princeton University Press, 2003), 174–202. See also Erich Auerbach, *Dante, Poet of the Secular World*, trans. Ralph Manheim (Chicago: Chicago University Press, 1961).
50 Stuart Blackburn and Vasudha Dalmia, "Introduction," in Stuart Blackburn and Vasudha Dalmia (eds.), *India's Literary History: Essays on the Nineteenth Century* (Delhi: Permanent Black, 2004), 4.
51 See H. H. Wilson, *Sketch on the Religious Sects of the Hindus* (Calcutta: Bishop's College Press, 1847); James Tod, *Annals and Antiquities of Rajasthan, or the Central and Western Rajput States of India*, 3 Vols., ed. William Crooke (Oxford: Oxford University Press, 1920).
52 Mufti, *Forget English!*, 109.

4 Impure Aesthetics

1 See, for instance, David Damrosch, "Goethe Coins a Phrase," in David Damrosch (ed.), *What Is World Literature?* (Princeton: Princeton University Press, 2003), 2–36.
2 John Pizer, *The Idea of World Literature: History and Pedagogical Practice* (Baton Rouge: Louisiana State University Press, 2006), 1–17.
3 Johann Wolfgang von Goethe, *Conversations with Eckermann: Being Appreciations and Criticisms on Many Subjects*, trans. John Oxenford (Washington and London: M. Walter Dunne, 1901), 175.
4 M. M. Bakhtin, *Speech Genres and Other Late Essays*, trans. Vern W. McGee (Austin: University of Texas Press, 1986), 25.
5 For an account of the connection between Kant's anthropological lectures and his aesthetic theory, see Paul Guyer, "Beauty, Freedom, and Morality: Kant's *Lectures on Anthropology* and the Development of His Aesthetic Theory," in Brian Jacobs and Patrick Kain (eds.), *Essays on Kant's Anthropology* (Cambridge: Cambridge University Press, 2003), 138–9.
6 For a discussion on the "feeling of life" and the "feeling of spirit" in Kant, see John H. Zammito, *The Genesis of Kant's Critique of Judgment* (Chicago: University of Chicago Press, 1992), 292–305.

7 Ernst Cassirer, *The Philosophy of the Enlightenment*, trans. Fritz C. A. Koelln and James P. Pettegrove (Princeton: Princeton University Press, 1951), 278.
8 Ernst Cassirer, *Rousseau, Kant, Goethe: Two Essays*, trans. James Gutmann et al. (Princeton: Princeton University Press, 1947); Géza von Molnár, "Goethe's Reading of Kant's 'Critique of Esthetic Judgment': A Referential Guide for Wilhelm Meister's Esthetic Education," *Eighteenth-Century Studies*, Vol. 15, No. 4 (Summer, 1982), 402–20; see also Fritz-Joachim von Rintelen, "Goethe und Kant," *Wissenschaft und Weltbild*, Vol. 26 (April, 1973), 91–7. For a different view on the relationship between Kant and Goethe, see Georg Simmel, *Kant und Goethe: Zur Geschichte der modernen Weltanschauung* (Leipzig: Kurt Wolff, 1916).
9 Goethe, *Conversations with Eckermann*, 195–6. Goethe's admiration for Kant's third *Critique* is again evident when he says in an earlier essay entitled "The Influence of Modern Philosophy" (1817) that in it he finds his "most disparate concerns brought together" through Kant's unique way of joining "artistic and natural productions" as also through his proposition that aesthetic and teleological judgments mutually enlighten each other. Johann Wolfgang von Goethe, "The Influence of Modern Philosophy," in Johann Wolfgang von Goethe, *Scientific Studies*, trans and ed. Douglas Miller (New York: Suhrkamp Publishers, 1988), 28–30. For a discussion on Goethe's engagement with his contemporary philosophers including Kant, see Hans-Georg Gadamer, "Goethe and Philosophy" and "Goethe and the Moral World," in Hans-Georg Gadamer (ed.), *Literature and Philosophy in Dialogue: Essays in German Literary Theory*, trans. Robert H. Paslick (Albany: SUNY Press, 1994), 1–30.
10 Matthew Bell, *Goethe's Naturalistic Anthropology: Man and Other Plants* (Oxford: Clarendon, 1994); Karl J. Fink, *Goethe's History of Science* (Cambridge: Cambridge University Press, 1991), 11–15; Chad Wellmon, *Becoming Human: Romantic Anthropology and the Embodiment of Freedom* (University Park: Pennsylvania State University, 2010), 246–50.
11 The idea of *impure aesthetics* in Kant is inspired by a somewhat similar project on "impure ethics" by Robert Louden. See Robert B. Louden, *Kant's Impure Ethics: From Rational Beings to Human Beings* (New York: Oxford University Press, 2000). My suggestion also needs to be distinguished from Hugh Grady's reading of Kant through the Frankfurt School, and his subsequent conclusion that "impurity" of aesthetics is a way of suggesting that it stands in for a number of other concerns and hence is always beyond itself. As would be evident during the course of this chapter, my reading prioritizes a constitutive dilemma in Kant's aesthetic theory quite different from Grady's formulation. See Hugh Grady, *Shakespeare and Impure Aesthetics* (Cambridge: Cambridge University Press, 2009), 1–44.
12 Philippe Lacoue-Labarthe and Jean-Luc Nancy, *The Literary Absolute: The Theory of Literature in German Romanticism*, trans. Philip Barnard and Cheryl Lester (Albany, NY: SUNY Press, 1988), 30.
13 Lacoue-Labarthe and Nancy, *The Literary Absolute*, 32.
14 Lacoue-Labarthe and Nancy, *The Literary Absolute*, 54.
15 Lacoue-Labarthe and Nancy, *The Literary Absolute*, 105.

Notes to pages 153–63   263

16 Lacoue-Labarthe and Nancy, *The Literary Absolute*, 119; emphasis original.
17 Immanuel Kant, *Lectures on Logic*, trans. J. Michael Young (Cambridge: Cambridge University Press, 2004), 538.
18 See Immanuel Kant, *Anthropology from a Pragmatic Point of View*, trans. Robert B. Louden (Cambridge: Cambridge University Press, 2006).
19 Jacques Rancière, *The Politics of Aesthetics: The Distribution of the Sensible*, trans. Gabriel Rockhill (London and New York: Continuum, 2004), 13.
20 Rancière, *The Politics of Aesthetics*, 9.
21 Jacques Rancière, *The Philosopher and His Poor*, trans. John Drury et al. (Durham, NC: Duke University Press, 2003), 163, 198; emphasis original.
22 Jacques Rancière, *Dissensus: On Politics and Aesthetics*, trans. Steven Corcoran (London and New York: Continuum, 2010), 155.
23 Rancière, *Dissensus*, 162.
24 Kant, *Lectures on Logic*, 538.
25 Michel Foucault, *The Order of Things: An Archaeology of the Human Sciences*, trans. Publisher (London: Routledge, 2002), 371.
26 Kant, *Lectures on Logic*, 538; emphasis original.
27 Foucault, *The Order of Things*, 372.
28 Foucault's view is partly informed by the fact that Kant often saw anthropology and physical geography as part of a continuous exploration of "man." He also offered seventy-two courses in anthropology and physical geography during his tenure at the University of Königsberg as opposed to fifty-four in logic, forty-nine in metaphysics, twenty-eight in moral philosophy, and twenty in theoretical physics. See J. A. May, *Kant's Concept of Geography and Its Relation to Recent Geographical Thought* (Toronto: University of Toronto Press, 1970), 4.
29 Michel Foucault, *Introduction to Kant's Anthropology*, trans. Roberto Nigro and Kate Briggs (Los Angeles: Semiotext(e), 2008), 33; emphasis added; henceforth abbreviated as *IKA* and cited parenthetically with pagination.
30 Immanuel Kant, *Anthropology from a Pragmatic Point of View*, trans. Robert B. Louden (Cambridge: Cambridge University Press, 2006), 3–4; emphasis original; henceforth abbreviated as *A* and cited parenthetically with pagination.
31 Immanuel Kant, *Opus Postumum*, trans. Eckart Forster and Michael Rosen (Cambridge: Cambridge University Press, 1993), 233.
32 Gayatri Chakravorty Spivak, *A Critique of Postcolonial Reason: Toward a History of the Vanishing Present* (Cambridge, MA: Harvard University Press, 1999), 7.
33 Goethe, *Conversations with Eckermann*, 173.
34 Goethe, *Conversations with Eckermann*, 174.
35 Goethe, *Conversations with Eckermann*, 175; emphasis added.
36 Goethe, *Conversations with Eckermann*, 175.
37 Goethe, *Conversations with Eckermann*, 175–6.
38 In this respect, see Robert Bernasconi, "Who Invented the Concept of Race? Kant's Role in the Enlightenment Construction of Race," in Robert Bernasconi (ed.), *Race* (Malden, MA and Oxford: Blackwell, 2001), 11–36.

39 Immanuel Kant, "Of the Different Human Races," trans. Jon Mark Mikkelsen, in Robert Bernasconi and Tommy Lee Lott (eds.), *The Idea of Race* (Indianapolis: Hackett, 2000), 8.

40 The parallel between Kant's anthropology of race and Jones's almost contemporary "new" philology of languages is conspicuous because of their similar emphasis on monogenesis of race and languages.

41 For a short review of Kant's racist statements from various texts, see Louden, *Kant's Impure Ethics*, 98–100. Louden notes that the "gap between Gobineau and Kant is unfortunately not always as wide as one would like it to be."

42 Emmanuel Chukwudi Eze, "The Color of Reason: The Idea of 'Race' in Kant's Anthropology," in Emmanuel Chukwudi Eze (ed.), *Postcolonial African Philosophy: A Critical Reader* (Cambridge, MA: Blackwell, 1997), 112–13.

43 Immanuel Kant, *Critique of the Power of Judgment*, trans. Paul Guyer and Eric Matthews (Cambridge: Cambridge University Press, 2000), henceforth abbreviated as *CPJ* and cited parenthetically with pagination.

44 As Gilles Deleuze explains, "[a]esthetic common sense does not represent an objective accord of the faculties [...], but a pure subjective harmony where imagination and understanding are exercised spontaneously, each on its own account." Gilles Deleuze, *Kant's Critical Philosophy: The Doctrine of Faculties*, trans. Hugh Tomlinson and Barbara Habberjam (London: Athlone, 1984), 49.

45 Lacoue-Labarthe and Nancy, *The Literary Absolute*, 31.

46 Lacoue-Labarthe and Nancy, *The Literary Absolute*, 32.

47 Poetry is given the highest status among all of the beautiful arts in *Critique of the Power of Judgment* because, through its reliance on imagination, it can elevate "itself aesthetically to the level of ideas," and can thus display in full what Lacoue-Labarthe and Nancy call the analogical function of beautiful art. Poetry, or literature more generally, it seems, holds out a possibility of overcoming the impurity of aesthetic judgment, albeit provisionally (*CPJ*, 203–4).

5 Sanskrit on Shagreen

1 Johann Wolfgang (von) Goethe, "On World Literature," in Theo D'haen et al. (eds.), *World Literature: A Reader* (London: Routledge, 2012), 14.

2 For a somewhat programmatic statement on his project, see Jacques Rancière, *The Politics of Aesthetics: The Distribution of the Sensible*, trans. Gabriel Rockhill (London: Continuum, 2004).

3 Rancière, *The Politics of Aesthetics*, 10. He repeats the point in Jacques Rancière, *The Aesthetic Unconscious*, trans. Debra Keates and James Swenson (Cambridge: Polity, 2009), 4–5.

4 Jacques Rancière, *Dissensus: On Politics and Aesthetics*, trans. Steven Corcoran (London: Continuum, 2010), 152–3. Also see Jacques Rancière, *The Flesh of Words: The Politics of Writing*, trans. Charlotte Mandell (Stanford: Stanford University Press, 2004); Jacques Rancière, *The Politics of Literature*, trans. Julie Rose (Cambridge: Polity, 2011).

5 Rancière, *Dissensus*, 152.
6 Jacques Rancière, *Mute Speech: Literature, Critical Theory, and Politics*, trans. James Swenson (New York: Columbia University Press, 2011).
7 Erich Auerbach, *Mimesis: The Representation of Reality in Western Literature*, trans. Willard R. Trask (Princeton: Princeton University Press, 2003).
8 It is possible to read Rancière as yet another example of French theory's abiding color blindness and "sanctioned ignorance" of colonial histories. A fuller discussion of this problem is beyond the scope of this chapter or, indeed, of this book; for a comprehensive mapping, see the special issue on "Racial France" of *Public Culture*, Vol. 23, No. 1 (2011).
9 Baidik Bhattacharya, "Somapolitics: A Biohermeneutic Paradigm in the Era of Empire," *Boundary 2*, Vol. 45, No. 4 (2018), 127–59.
10 Edward W. Said, *Orientalism* (London: Penguin, 2003 [1978]); Maurice Olender, *Race and Erudition*, trans. Jane Marie Todd (Cambridge, MA: Harvard University Press, 2009).
11 Honoré de Balzac, *The Wild Ass' Skin and Other Stories*, trans. Ellen Marriage (Philadelphia: Gebbie, 1897), 15; further references are abbreviated as *WAS* and cited parenthetically with pagination. All references to the French original are from H. de Balzac, *La Peau de chagrin* (Paris: Charpentier, 1839).
12 Rancière, *Dissensus*, 162. Also see Rancière, *The Politics of Literature*, 15, 66–7.
13 Rancière, *Dissensus*, 163. For a critique of Rancière's chronology, see Bill Brown, *Other Things* (Chicago: Chicago University Press, 2016), 170–1.
14 For a history of the term "civilization" since the eighteenth century, and its genealogical entanglement with colonialism and racism, see Bruce Mazlish, *Civilization and Its Contents* (Stanford: Stanford University Press, 2005).
15 Raymond Schwab, *Oriental Renaissance: Europe's Rediscovery of India and the East, 1680–1880*, trans. Gene Patterson-Black and Victor Reinking (New York: Columbia University Press, 1984).
16 Quoted in Said, *Orientalism*, 77.
17 William Jones, "A Discourse on the Institution of a Society, for Inquiring into the History, Civil and Natural, the Antiquities, Arts, Sciences, and Literature, of Asia," in William Jones (ed.), *The Works of Sir William Jones*, 13 Vols. (London: John Stockdale and John Walker, 1807), 3: 5.
18 Edward Said, "Raymond Schwab and the Romance of Ideas," in Edward Said (ed.), *The World, the Text, and the Critic* (Cambridge, MA: Harvard University Press, 1983), 250.
19 Said, *Orientalism*, 86. Also see, for the continuity of many such projects throughout the nineteenth century, Timothy Mitchell, *Colonising Egypt* (Cambridge: Cambridge University Press, 1988).
20 Said, *Orientalism*, 88.
21 Jonathan Culler, "Anderson and the Novel," *diacritics*, Vol. 29, No. 4 (1999), 30. For a somewhat related argument vis-à-vis nineteenth-century English novels and their "metropolitan autoethnography," see James Buzard, *Disorienting Fiction: The Autoethnographic Work of Nineteenth-Century British Novels* (Princeton: Princeton University Press, 2005).

22 For a definition of this "modern Orientalism" of the eighteenth century, see Said, *Orientalism*, 42.
23 Ruth Bernard Yeazell, *Art of the Everyday: Dutch Painting and the Realist Novel* (Princeton: Princeton University Press, 2008), 5–6.
24 Bernard Weinberg, *French Realism: The Critical Reaction, 1830–1870* (New York: Modern Language Association of America, 1937), 55–6.
25 Yeazell, *Art of the Everyday*, 8.
26 It is equally instructive that "realism" as an aesthetic concept emerged with reference to such paintings in the 1830s. As Ian Watt notes, "The main critical associations of the term 'realism' are with the French school of Realists. 'Réalisme' was apparently first used as an aesthetic description in 1835 to denote the 'vérité humaine' of Rembrandt as opposed to the 'idéalité poétique' of neo-classical painting; it was later consecrated as a specifically literary term by the foundation in 1856 of *Réalisme*, a journal edited by Duranty." Ian Watt, *The Rise of the Novel: Studies in Defoe, Richardson and Fielding* (Berkeley: University of California Press, 1957), 10.
27 Weinberg, *French Realism*, 60.
28 See, for instance, Peter Brooks, *Reading for the Plot: Design and Intention in Narrative* (Cambridge, MA: Harvard University Press, 1992), 60–1; Thomas M. Kemple, *Reading Marx Writing: Melodrama, the Market, and the "Grundrisse"* (Stanford: Stanford University Press, 1995), 239–40. For a broader connection between Balzac's oeuvre and *A Thousand and One Nights*, see E. R. Curtius, *Essays on European Literature*, trans. Michael Kowal (Princeton: Princeton University Press, 1973), 140, 193, 201; Roland Barthes, *S/Z*, trans. Richard Miller (Oxford: Blackwell, 1992), 33, 89, 205; Alex Woolock, *The One vs. the Many: Minor Characters and the Space of the Protagonist in the Novel* (Princeton: Princeton University Press, 2003), 257, 289. For a complex history of the translation of the *Thousand and One Nights* and its eventual journey into world literature, see Paulo Lemos Horta, *Marvelous Thieves: Secret Authors of the Arabian Nights* (Cambridge, MA: Harvard University Press, 2017).
29 Balzac is by no means exceptional. Similar presence of the Orient in European cultural texts, especially in novels, during the nineteenth century was quite abundant, and has been documented by several critics. See, for instance, Elaine Freedgood, *The Ideas in Things: Fugitive Meaning in the Victorian Novel* (Chicago: Chicago University Press, 2010); Christie McDonald and Susan Rubin Suleiman (eds.), *French Global: A New Approach* (New York: Columbia University Press, 2010), especially "Part II: Mobilities"; Suzanne Daly, *The Empire Inside: Indian Commodities in Victorian Domestic Novels* (Ann Arbor: Michigan University Press, 2011); Jennifer Yee, *The Colonial Comedy: Imperialism in the French Realist Novel* (Oxford: Oxford University Press, 2016).
30 On the complexity of inheritance in the novel, and its connection with India, see Yee, *The Colonial Comedy*, 33–4.
31 See, Rancière, *Mute Speech*, 173.
32 This has been suggested by a number of critics; see, for instance, Geoffrey Baker, *Realism's Empire: Empiricism and Enchantment in the Nineteenth-Century*

Novel (Columbus: Ohio State University Press, 2009), 43–4; Patrick M. Bray, "Balzac and the Chagrin of Theory," *L'Esprit Créateur*, Vol. 54, No. 3 (Fall 2014), 75–6; Yee, *The Colonial Comedy*, 34.
33 Said, *Orientalism*, 139.
34 See, for instance, Samuel Weber, *Unwrapping Balzac: A Reading of 'La Peau de Chagrin'* (Toronto: University of Toronto Press, 1979), 162; Michal Peled Ginsburg, *Economies of Change: Form and Transformation in the Nineteenth-Century Novel* (Stanford: Stanford University Press, 1996), 26.
35 For a detailed comparison between the Arabic text and its French translation, see Alois Richard Nykl, "The Talisman in Balzac's *La Peau de chagrin*," *Modern Language Notes*, Vol. 34, No. 8 (1919), 481.
36 Schwab, *Oriental Renaissance*, 69; emphasis added.
37 Frederick Schlegel, *Lectures on the History of Literature, Ancient and Modern*, trans. Publisher (London: George Bell, 1889), 1. All references to the German original are from Friedrich von Schlegel, *Geschichte der alten und neuen Literatur* (Berlin: M. Simion, 1841).
38 Schlegel, *Lectures on the History of Literature*, 4. Fichte argued that, "even if our political independence were lost [in the wake of Napoleonic invasion] we should still keep our language and our literature, and thereby always remain a nation." Johann Gottlieb Fichte, *Addresses to the German Nation*, trans. R. F. Jones and G. H. Turnbull (Chicago: Open Court, 1922), 213. For more on this connection between Schlegel and Fichte, see Chapter 6.
39 Schlegel, *Lectures on the History of Literature*, 12.
40 Martin Bernal, *Black Athena: The Afroasiatic Roots of Classical Civilization*, vol. 1: *The Fabrication of Greece 1785–1985* (New Brunswick: Rutgers University Press, 1987), 1 and *passim*.
41 Bernal, *Black Athena*, 2.
42 Bernal, *Black Athena*, 204–6, 230–33.
43 Schlegel, *Lectures on the History of Literature*, 4.
44 Schlegel, *Lectures on the History of Literature*, 359–61.
45 Schlegel, *Lectures on the History of Literature*, 330–2.
46 Aamir R. Mufti, *Forget English! Orientalisms and World Literatures* (Cambridge, MA: Harvard University Press, 2016), 107–8; emphasis original.
47 Friedrich von Schlegel, "On the Language and Philosophy of the Indians," in *The Aesthetic and Miscellaneous Works of Frederick von Schlegel*, trans. E J. Millington (London: Henry G. Bohn, 1849), 515–17. All references to the German original are from Friedrich von Schlegel, *Über die Sprache und Weisheit der Indier: Ein Beitrag zur Begründung der Alterthumskunde* (Heidelberg: Mohr und Zimmer, 1808).
48 Schlegel, "On the Language and Philosophy of the Indians," 526; emphasis added.
49 For a theory of literature as an "absolute" category in German Romanticism, see Philippe Lacoue-Labarthe and Jean-Luc Nancy, *The Literary Absolute: The Theory of Literature in German Romanticism*, trans. Philip Barnard and Cheryl Lester (Albany, NY: SUNY Press, 1988).

50 Rancière, *Dissensus*, 162–3.
51 Schlegel, "On the Language and Philosophy of the Indians," 439.
52 Konrad Koerner, *Practicing Linguistic Historiography: Selected Essays* (Amsterdam: John Benjamins, 1989), 275.
53 Foucault, *The Order of Things*, 308.
54 Schlegel, "On the Language and Philosophy of the Indians," 445, 454.
55 For a review of this debate, see Toby A. Appel, *The Cuvier–Geoffroy Debate: French Biology in the Decades before Darwin* (New York: Oxford University Press, 1987); Hervé Le Guyader, *Étienne Geoffroy Saint-Hilaire, 1772–1844: A Visionary Naturalist*, trans. Marjorie Grene (Chicago: Chicago University Press, 2004), 96–224.
56 Appel, *The Cuvier–Geoffroy Debate*, 2.
57 Quoted in Kemple, *Reading Marx Writing*, 239.
58 Bon Joseph Dacier, "Discours de M. Dacier," in *Tableau historique de l'érudition française: Ou Rapport sur les progrès de l'histoire et de la littérature ancienne depuis 1789* (Paris: Imprimerie impériale, 1810), 23–5.
59 For a chronology of these exhibitions since 1798, see Anonymous, *Catalogue général: Exposition Universelle de 1867 à Paris*, Œuvres d'art: Groupe I, Classes 1 à 5, Vol. 1 (Paris: E. Dentu, 1867), 25–34. For the international trend of such exhibitions since the nineteenth century, see Marta Filipová (ed.), *Cultures of International Exhibitions 1840–1940: Great Exhibitions in the Margins* (London: Routledge, 2017).
60 Anonymous, *Exposition universelle, 1855: Catalogue des objets exposés dans la section britannique de l'exposition, en anglais et français* (London: Chapman, 1855), 3.
61 Anonymous, *Exposition universelle de 1855: Rapports du jury mixte international*, vol. 11 (Paris: Imprimerie impériale, 1856), 338.
62 Timothy Mitchell, "The World as Exhibition," *Comparative Studies in Society and History*, Vol. 31, No. 2 (1989), 217; Roger Luckhurst, *The Mummy's Curse: The True History of a Dark Fantasy* (Oxford: Oxford University Press, 2012), 131.
63 Quoted in Luckhurst, *The Mummy's Curse*, 131.
64 Mitchell, "The World as Exhibition," 218–19.
65 See Walter Benjamin, *The Arcades Project*, trans. Howard Eiland and Kevin McLaughlin (Cambridge, MA: Belknap Press of Harvard University, 2002).
66 Mitchell, "The World as Exhibition," 225.
67 Quoted in Mitchell, "The World as Exhibition," 227–30.

6 National Enframing

1 For a definition of *Gestell*, see Martin Heidegger, *The Question Concerning Technology and Other Essays*, trans. William Lovitt (New York: Harper, 1977), 20.
2 René Wellek, *The Rise of English Literary History* (Chapel Hill: University of North Carolina Press, 1941), vi.
3 Thomas Warton, *The History of English Poetry*, Vol. 1 (London: J. Dodsley et al., 1774), i–iii.

Notes to pages 204–17

4 For a general bibliographical overview of this profusion of print on literary subjects, see George Watson (ed.), *The New Cambridge Bibliography of English Literature*, vol. II: *1660–1800* (Cambridge: Cambridge University Press, 1971). For a survey of Warton's own reading habits in his formative years, with special bearing on his *History*, see David Fairer, "The Origins of Warton's *History of English Poetry*," *The Review of English Studies*, Vol. 32, No. 125 (1981), 37–63.
5 Wellek, *The Rise of English Literary History*, 174.
6 James Turner, *Philology: The Forgotten Origins of the Modern Humanities* (Princeton: Princeton University Press, 2014), 108.
7 Warton, *The History of English Poetry*, vol I, iii–iv.
8 Warton, *The History of English Poetry*, vol I, iv–v.
9 Quoted in Wellek, *The Rise of English Literary History*, 172.
10 Warton, *The History of English Poetry*, vol I, v.
11 Warton, *The History of English Poetry*, vol I, vi.
12 Warton, *The History of English Poetry*, vol I, 1–3.
13 Warton, *The History of English Poetry*, vol I, 42.
14 For a brief overview of the Ossian controversy, see Kenneth McNeil, *Scotland, Britain, Empire: Writing the Highlands, 1760–1860* (Columbus: Ohio University Press, 2007), 25–50.
15 Katie Trumpener, *Bardic Nationalism: The Romantic Novel and the British Empire* (Princeton: Princeton University Press, 2021), 77–9.
16 Lee Morrissey, *The Constitution of Literature: Literacy, Democracy, and Early English Literary Criticism* (Stanford: Stanford University Press, 2007), 24.
17 Jürgen Habermas, *The Structural Transformation of the Public Sphere: An Inquiry into a Category of Bourgeois Society*, trans. Thomas Burger (Cambridge, MA: MIT Press, 1991), 57–67.
18 Saree Makdisi, *Romantic Imperialism: Universal Empire and the Culture of Modernity* (Cambridge: Cambridge University Press, 1998), 10. Makdisi, of course, uses it to describe the romantics primarily, but the idea was widespread and common among others as well.
19 Johann Gottlieb Fichte, *Addresses to the German Nation*, trans. R. F. Jones and G. H. Turnbull (Chicago and London: Open Court, 1922), 216–17. Further references are abbreviated as *AGN* with pagination.
20 For somewhat similar ideas about language, see Johann Gottfried von Herder, "Treatise on the Origin of Language," in Johann Gottfried von Herder, *Philosophical Writings*, trans. and ed. Michael N. Forster (Cambridge: Cambridge University Press, 2002), 68.
21 For a concise discussion on "freedom" in Fichte's early writing, see Wayne Martin, "Fichte on Freedom," in Steven Hoeltzel (ed.), *The Palgrave Fichte Handbook* (London: Palgrave Macmillan, 2019), 285–306.
22 Frederick von Schlegel, *The Aesthetic and Miscellaneous Works of Frederick von Schlegel*, trans. E. J. Millington (London: Henry G. Bohn, 1849), 446; further references are abbreviated as *AMW* and cited with pagination.
23 Thomas R. Trautmann, *Aryans and British India* (Berkeley: University of California Press, 1997), 28.

24 Maurice Olender, *Race and Erudition*, trans. Jane Marie Todd (Cambridge, MA: Harvard University Press, 2009).
25 Robert J. C. Young, *Colonial Desire: Hybridity in Theory, Culture and Race* (London: Routledge, 1995), 53–84.
26 W. J. Courthope, *A History of English Poetry*, Vol. 1 (New York: Macmillan, 1895), xv.
27 Courthope, *A History of English Poetry*, 2–3.
28 Leslie Stephens, *English Literature and Society in the Eighteenth Century* (London: Duckworth, 1904), 21–4.
29 Thomas B. Shaw, *Shaw's New History of English Literature*, ed. Truman J. Backus (New York: Sheldon, 1874), 5.
30 Henry Hallam, *Introduction to the Literature of Europe in the Fifteenth, Sixteenth, and Seventeenth Centuries*, 3 Vols. (London: John Murray, 1837–9), 1: 65, 361, 59.
31 Hallam, *Introduction to the Literature of Europe*, 1: 65.
32 James Cowles Prichard, *Researches into the Physical History of Man* (London: John and Arthur Arch, 1813), 2.
33 Prichard, *Researches into the Physical History of Man*, 502.
34 Prichard, *Researches into the Physical History of Man*, 526.
35 Prichard, *Researches into the Physical History of Man*, 534.
36 Robert Knox, *The Races of Men: A Fragment* (Philadelphia: Lea and Blanchard, 1850), 7.
37 Knox, *The Races of Men*, 253; emphasis original.
38 Knox, *The Races of Men*, 41–2.
39 Knox, *The Races of Men*, 42.
40 Knox, *The Races of Men*, 131, 217.
41 Knox, *The Races of Men*, 128.
42 Knox, *The Races of Men*, 218.
43 Knox, *The Races of Men*, 270–80.
44 John Beddoe, *The Races of Britain: A Contribution to the Anthropology of Western Europe* (Bristol: J. W. Arrowsmith, 1885), 4.
45 Keith Breckenridge, *Biometric State: The Global Politics of Identification and Surveillance in South Africa, 1850 to the Present* (Cambridge: Cambridge University Press, 2014); Nicholas B. Dirks, *Castes of Mind: Colonialism and the Making of Modern India* (Princeton: Princeton University Press, 2001).
46 Baidik Bhattacharya, "Somapolitics: A Biohermeneutic Paradigm in the Era of Empire," *Boundary 2*, Vol. 45, No. 4 (2018), 127–59.
47 John Beddoe, "Anthropometry in India," *Science Progress*, Vol. 4, No. 21 (November, 1895), 188–203.
48 John Beddoe, *The Anthropological History of Europe* (London: Alexander Gardner, 1893).
49 Matthew Arnold, *On the Study of Celtic Literature* (London: Smith, Elder and Co., 1867), 24; henceforth abbreviated as *CL* and cited with pagination.
50 Quoted in Lewis F. Mott, "Renan and Matthew Arnold," *Modern Language Notes*, Vol. 33, No. 2 (1918), 66.

51 Matthew Arnold, *Culture and Anarchy: An Essay in Political and Social Criticism* (London: Smith, Elder and Co., 1869), 49.
52 Henry Morley, *A First Sketch of English Literature* (London: Cassell, Petter, & Galpin, 1873), 2.
53 Morley, *A First Sketch of English Literature*, 11–12.
54 Morley, *A First Sketch of English Literature*, 39–41.
55 Hippolyte Taine, *Histoire de la littérature anglaise*, 5 Vols. (Paris: Librairie de L. Hachette, 1863–9), 1: 3–170.
56 George Saintsbury, *A Short History of English Literature* (London: Macmillan, 1898), 1–47.
57 A. Hamilton Thompson, *A History of English Literature* (London: John Murray, 1901), 1–37.
58 William Henry Hudson, *An Outline History of English Literature* (London: G. Bell, 1912), 11–19.
59 A. S. Mackenzie, *History of English Literature* (New York: Macmillan, 1914), 1–51.
60 Robert Huntington Fletcher, *A History of English Literature* (Boston: Richard G. Badger, 1916), 27–58.
61 Edward Albert, *A History of English Literature* (London: George A Harrap, 1923), 9–19.
62 A. J. Wyatt, *The Tutorial History of English Literature* (London: University Tutorial Press, 1928), 1–25.
63 Émile Legouis, *A Short History of English Literature*, trans. V. F. Boyson and J. Coulson (Oxford: Clarendon, 1934), 1.
64 Hutcheson Macaulay Posnett, *Comparative Literature* (New York: D. Appleton and Company, 1886), 6.
65 Posnett, *Comparative Literature*, 341.

Coda: Decolonization after World Literature

1 Dipesh Chakrabarty, *Provincializing Europe: Postcolonial Thought and Historical Difference* (Princeton: Princeton University Press, 2000).
2 Baidik Bhattacharya, *Postcolonial Writing in the Era of World Literature: Texts, Territories, Globalizations* (London and Delhi: Routledge, 2018).
3 Baidik Bhattacharya, "Postcolonialism and World Literature," in Theo D'haen, David Damrosch, and Djelal Kadir (eds.), *The Routledge Companion to World Literature*, 2nd edition (New York and London: Routledge, 2022), 165–75.

Bibliography

Abrams, M. H. *The Mirror and the Lamp: Romantic Theory and the Critical Tradition* (New York: Oxford University Press, 1971).
Abu-Lughod, Janet L. *Before European Hegemony: The World System A.D. 1250–1350* (Oxford: Oxford University Press, 1989).
Agamben, Giorgio. *State of Exception*, trans. Kevin Attell (Chicago: University of Chicago Press, 2005).
Agnani, Sunil M. *Hating Empire Properly: The Two Indies and the Limits of Enlightenment Anticolonialism* (New York: Fordham University Press, 2013).
Ahmed, Siraj. "Notes from Babel: Toward a Colonial History of Comparative Literature," *Critical Inquiry*, Vol. 39 (Winter 2013), 296–326.
Ahmed, Siraj. *Archaeology of Babel: The Colonial Foundation of the Humanities* (Stanford: Stanford University Press, 2017).
Albert, Edward. *A History of English Literature* (London: George A. Harrap, 1923).
Anonymous. *Les Fables de Pilpay, philosophe indien ou la Conduite des rois* (Paris: Florentin et Pierre Delaulne, 1698).
Anonymous. "The Fatal Effects of Precipitation – From the Ayar Danish of Abulfazel," in *The Asiatic Miscellany: Consisting of Original Productions, Translations, Figurative Pieces, Imitations, and Extracts from Curious Publications*, Vol. 1 (Calcutta: Daniel Stuart, 1785).
Anonymous. *The Answer of Warren Hastings, Esq. to the Articles* (London: J. Debrett, 1788).
Anonymous. *Les Conseils et les Maximes de Pilpay Philosophe Indien sur les divers États de la vie* (Paris: n.p., 1792).
Anonymous. *The History of the Trial of Warren Hastings, Esq. Late Governor-General of Bengal, before the High Court of Parliament in Westminster-Hall, on an Impeachment by the Commons of Great-Britain, for High Crimes and Misdemeanor* (London: J. Debrett, 1796).
Anonymous. *Exposition universelle, 1855: Catalogue des objets exposés dans la section britannique de l'exposition, en anglais et français* (London: Chapman, 1855).
Anonymous. *Exposition universelle de 1855: Rapports du jury mixte international*, 2 Vols. (Paris: Imprimerie impériale, 1856).
Anonymous. *Catalogue général: Exposition Universelle de 1867 à Paris*, Œuvres d'art: Groupe I, Classes 1 à 5, Vol. 1 (Paris: E. Dentu, 1867).
Appel, Toby A. *The Cuvier–Geoffroy Debate: French Biology in the Decades before Darwin* (New York: Oxford University Press, 1987).

Aravamudan, Srinivas. *Enlightenment Orientalism: Resisting the Rise of the Novel* (Chicago: University of Chicago Press, 2012).
Arnold, Matthew. *On the Study of Celtic Literature* (London: Smith, Elder and Co., 1867).
Arnold, Matthew. *Culture and Anarchy: An Essay in Political and Social Criticism* (London: Smith, Elder and Co., 1869).
Asif, Manan Ahmed. *The Loss of Hindustan: The Invention of India* (Cambridge, MA: Harvard University Press, 2020).
Attridge, Derek. *The Singularity of Literature* (London: Routledge, 2004).
Auerbach, Erich. *Dante, Poet of the Secular World*, trans. Ralph Manheim (Chicago: Chicago University Press, 1961).
Auerbach, Erich. *Mimesis: The Representation of Reality in Western Literature*, trans. Willard R. Trask (Princeton: Princeton University Press, 2003).
Baines, J. A. *General Report on the Census of India, 1891* (London: Her Majesty's Stationery Office, 1893).
Baker, Geoffrey. *Realism's Empire: Empiricism and Enchantment in the Nineteenth-Century Novel* (Columbus: Ohio State University Press, 2009).
Bakhtin, M. M. *Speech Genres and Other Late Essays*, trans. Vern W. McGee (Austin: University of Texas Press, 1986).
Balzac, Honoré de. *La Peau de chagrin* (Paris: Charpentier, 1839).
Balzac, Honoré de. *The Wild Ass' Skin and Other Stories*, trans. Ellen Marriage (Philadelphia: Gebbie, 1897).
Barthes, Roland. *S/Z*, trans. Richard Miller (Oxford: Blackwell, 1992).
Beddoe, John. *The Races of Britain: A Contribution to the Anthropology of Western Europe* (Bristol: J. W. Arrowsmith, 1885).
Beddoe, John. *The Anthropological History of Europe* (London: Alexander Gardner, 1893).
Beddoe, John. "Anthropometry in India," *Science Progress*, Vol. 4, No. 21 (November, 1895), 188–203.
Bell, Matthew. *Goethe's Naturalistic Anthropology: Man and Other Plants* (Oxford: Clarendon, 1994).
Benjamin, Walter. *The Arcades Project*, trans. Howard Eiland and Kevin McLaughlin (Cambridge, MA: Belknap Press of Harvard University, 2002).
Benjamin, Walter. *Walter Benjamin: Selected Writings*, vol. 1: *1913–1926*, eds. Marcus Bullock and Michael W. Jennings (Cambridge, MA: Belknap Press of Harvard University, 2004).
Bernal, Martin. *Black Athena: The Afroasiatic Roots of Classical Civilization*, vol. 1: *The Fabrication of Greece 1785–1985* (New Brunswick: Rutgers University Press, 1987).
Bernasconi, Robert. "Who Invented the Concept of Race? Kant's Role in the Enlightenment Construction of Race," in Robert Bernasconi (ed.), *Race* (Malden, MA and Oxford: Blackwell, 2001), 11–36.
Bhattacharya, Baidik. *Postcolonial Writing in the Era of World Literature: Texts, Territories, Globalizations* (London and Delhi: Routledge, 2018).
Bhattacharya, Baidik. "Somapolitics: A Biohermeneutic Paradigm in the Era of Empire," *Boundary 2*, Vol. 45, No. 4 (2018), 127–59.

Bhattacharya, Baidik. "Postcolonialism and World Literature," in Theo D'haen, David Damrosch, and Djelal Kadir (eds.), *The Routledge Companion to World Literature*, 2nd edition (New York and London: Routledge, 2022), 165–75.

Blackburn, Stuart and Vasudha Dalmia (eds.). *India's Literary History: Essays on the Nineteenth Century* (Delhi: Permanent Black, 2004).

Bolts, William. *Consideration on Indian Affairs; Particularly Respecting the Present State of Bengal and Its Dependencies* (London: J. Almon et al., 1772).

Bopp, F. "Analytical Comparison of the Sanskrit, Greek, Latin, and Teutonic Languages, Shewing the Original Identity of Their Grammatical Structure," *Annals of Oriental Literature*, Vol. 1, No. 1 (1820), 1–64.

Boswell, James. *The Life of Samuel Johnson, LL.D., Including a Journal of His Tour to the Hebrides*, 10 Vols. (London: John Murray, 1835).

Bray, Patrick M. "Balzac and the Chagrin of Theory," *L'Esprit Créateur*, Vol. 54, No. 3 (Fall 2014), 66–77.

Breckenridge, Keith. *Biometric State: The Global Politics of Identification and Surveillance in South Africa, 1850 to the Present* (Cambridge: Cambridge University Press, 2014).

Brooks, Peter. *Reading for the Plot: Design and Intention in Narrative* (Cambridge, MA: Harvard University Press, 1992).

Brown, Bill. *Other Things* (Chicago: Chicago University Press, 2016).

Burke, Edmund. *Article of Charge of High Crime and Misdemeanors, against Warren Hastings, Esq. Late Governor General of Bengal; Presented to the House of Commons, on the 4th Day of April, 1786* (London: J. Debrett, 1786).

Burke, Edmund. *Reflections on the Revolution in France, and on the Proceedings in Certain Societies in London* (London: J. Dodsley, 1790).

Burke, Edmund. *The Writings and Speeches of Edmund Burke*, 12 Vols. (Boston: Little, Brown and Company, 1901).

Burrow, Colin. *Shakespeare and Classical Antiquity* (Oxford: Oxford University Press, 2013).

Buzard, James. *Disorienting Fiction: The Autoethnographic Work of Nineteenth-Century British Novels* (Princeton: Princeton University Press, 2005).

Cannon, Garland H. "Sir William Jones and Edmund Burke," *Modern Philology*, Vol. 54, No. 3 (February, 1957), 165–86.

Cannon, Garland (ed.). *The Letters of Sir William Jones*, 2 Vols. (Oxford: Clarendon, 1970).

Cannon, Garland. "Sir William Jones, Persian, Sanskrit and the Asiatic Society," *Histoire Épistémologie Langage*, Vol. 6, No. 2 (1984), 83–94.

Cannon, Garland. *The Life and Mind of Oriental Jones: Sir William Jones, The Father of Modern Linguistics* (Cambridge: Cambridge University Press, 1990).

Casanova, Pascale. *The World Republic of Letters*, trans. Malcolm DeBevoise (Cambridge, MA: Harvard University Press, 2007).

Cassin, Barbara (ed.). *Dictionary of Untranslatables: A Philosophical Lexicon*, trans. Stephen Rendall et al. and ed. Emily Apter et al. (Princeton: Princeton University Press, 2014).

Cassirer, Ernst. *Rousseau, Kant, Goethe: Two Essays*, trans. James Gutmann et al. (Princeton: Princeton University Press, 1947).
Cassirer, Ernst. *The Philosophy of the Enlightenment*, trans. Fritz C. A. Koelln and James P. Pettegrove (Princeton: Princeton University Press, 1951).
Chakrabarty, Dipesh. *Provincializing Europe: Postcolonial Thought and Historical Difference* (Princeton: Princeton University Press, 2000).
Chatterjee, Partha. *The Black Hole of Empire: History of a Global Practice of Power* (Princeton: Princeton University Press, 2012).
Cheah, Pheng. "What Is a World? On World Literature as World-Making Activity," *Daedalus*, Vol. 137, No. 3 (2008), 26–38.
Cohn, Bernard S. *Colonialism and Its Forms of Knowledge: The British in India* (Princeton: Princeton University Press, 1996).
Colebrooke, H. T. "On the Sanscrit and Prácrit Languages," *Asiatick Researches*, Vol. 7 (1803), 199–231.
Colebrooke, H. T. *Miscellaneous Essays*, 2 Vols., ed. E. B. Cowell (London: Trübner, 1873).
Courthope, W. J. *A History of English Poetry*, 3 Vols. (New York: Macmillan, 1895).
Culler, Jonathan. "Anderson and the Novel," *diacritics*, Vol. 29, No. 4 (1999), 19–39.
Curtius, E. R. *Essays on European Literature*, trans. Michael Kowal (Princeton: Princeton University Press, 1973).
Dacier, Bon Joseph. "Discours de M. Dacier," in *Tableau historique de l'érudition française: Ou Rapport sur les progrès de l'histoire et de la littérature ancienne depuis 1789* (Paris: Imprimerie impériale, 1810).
Dalrymple, William. *The Anarchy: The Relentless Rise of the East India Company* (London: Bloomsbury, 2019).
Daly, Suzanne. *The Empire Inside: Indian Commodities in Victorian Domestic Novels* (Ann Arbor: Michigan University Press, 2011).
Damrosch, David. *What Is World Literature?* (Princeton: Princeton University Press, 2003).
Das, Sisir Kumar. *Sahibs and Munshis: An Account of the College of Fort William* (New Delhi: Orion, 1978).
Deleuze, Gilles. *Kant's Critical Philosophy: The Doctrine of Faculties*, trans. Hugh Tomlinson and Barbara Habberjam (London: Athlone, 1984).
Derrida, Jacques. *Dissemination*, trans. Barbara Johnson (London: Continuum, 2004).
Dirks, Nicholas B. *Castes of Mind: Colonialism and the Making of Modern India* (Princeton: Princeton University Press, 2001).
Dirks, Nicholas B. *The Scandal of Empire: India and the Creation of Imperial Britain* (Cambridge, MA: Belknap Press of Harvard University, 2008).
Dow, Alexander. *History of Hindostan; From the Earliest Account of Time, to the Death of Akbar*, 2 Vols. (London: T. Becket and P. A. De Hondt, 1768).
Dow, Alexander. *Tales Translated from the Persian of Inatulla of Delhi*, 2 Vols. (London: T. Becket and P. A. De Hondt, 1768).
Dow, Alexander. *The History of Hindostan, from the Death of Akbar, to the Complete Settlement of the Empire under Aurungzebe* (London: T. Becket and P. A. De Hondt, 1772).

East India Company, George Christopher Molesworth Birdwood, and William Foster. *The Register of Letters, &c., of the Governour and Company of Merchants of London Trading into the East Indies, 1600–1619* (London: B. Quaritch, 1893).
Eckermann, Johann Peter. *Conversations of Goethe with Eckermann and Soret*, trans. John Oxenford (London: George Bell & Sons, 1874).
Edney, Matthew H. *Mapping an Empire: The Geographical Construction of British India, 1765–1843* (Chicago: University of Chicago Press, 1990).
Erickson, Emily. *Between Monopoly and Free Trade: The English East India Company, 1600–1757* (Princeton: Princeton University Press, 2014).
Errington, Joseph. *Linguistics in a Colonial World: A Story of Language, Meaning, and Power* (Oxford: Blackwell, 2008).
Eze, Emmanuel Chukwudi. "The Color of Reason: The Idea of 'Race' in Kant's Anthropology," in Emmanuel Chukwudi Eze (ed.), *Postcolonial African Philosophy: A Critical Reader* (Cambridge, MA: Blackwell, 1997), 103–40.
Fairer, David. "The Origins of Warton's *History of English Poetry*," *The Review of English Studies*, Vol. 32, No. 125 (1981), 37–63.
Fichte, Johann Gottlieb. *Addresses to the German Nation*, trans. R. F. Jones and G. H. Turnbull (Chicago: Open Court, 1922).
Filipová, Marta (ed.). *Cultures of International Exhibitions 1840–1940: Great Exhibitions in the Margins* (London: Routledge, 2017).
Fink, Karl J. *Goethe's History of Science* (Cambridge: Cambridge University Press, 1991).
Fletcher, Robert Huntington. *A History of English Literature* (Boston: Richard G. Badger, 1916).
Forster, H. P. *An Essay on the Principles of Sanskṛit Grammar*, Part 1 (Calcutta: Ferris and Co., 1810).
Foucault, Michel. *The Order of Things: An Archaeology of the Human Sciences*, trans. Publisher (London: Routledge, 2002).
Foucault, Michel. *Introduction to Kant's Anthropology*, trans. Roberto Nigro and Kate Briggs (Los Angeles: Semiotext(e), 2008).
Franklin, Michael J. *"Orientalist Jones": Sir William Jones, Poet, Lawyer, and Linguist, 1746–1794* (Oxford: Oxford University Press, 2011).
Fraser, James. *The History of Nadir Shah, Formerly Called Thamas Kuli Khan, The Present Emperor of Persia* (London: W. Strahan, 1742).
Frazer, R. W. *A Literary History of India* (London: T. F. Unwin, 1898).
Freedgood, Elaine. *The Ideas in Things: Fugitive Meaning in the Victorian Novel* (Chicago: Chicago University Press, 2010).
Gadamer, Hans-Georg. *Literature and Philosophy in Dialogue: Essays in German Literary Theory*, trans. Robert H. Paslick (Albany: SUNY Press, 1994).
Gait, E. A. *Census of India, 1911*, 23 Vols. (Calcutta: Bengal Secretariat Press, 1911–13).
Gefen, Alexandre. *L'Idée de littérature: De l'art pour l'art aux écritures d'intervention* (Paris: Corti, 2020).
Gilchrist, John Borthwick. *The Strangers' East Indian Guide to the Hindoostanee; Or Grand Popular Language of India, (Improperly Called Moors)* (London: Black, Parry, and Kingsbury, 1808).

Ginsburg, Michal Peled. *Economies of Change: Form and Transformation in the Nineteenth-Century Novel* (Stanford: Stanford University Press, 1996).
Gleig, G. R. *Memoirs of the Life of the Right Hon. Warren Hastings, First Governor-General of Bengal*, 2 Vols. (London: Richard Bentley, 1841).
Goethe, Johann Wolfgang von. *Conversations with Eckermann: Being Appreciations and Criticisms on Many Subjects*, trans. John Oxenford (Washington and London: M. Walter Dunne, 1901).
Goethe, Johann Wolfgang von. "The Influence of Modern Philosophy," in *Scientific Studies*, trans and ed. Douglas Miller (New York: Suhrkamp Publishers, 1988), 28–30.
Goethe, Johann Wolfgang von. "On World Literature," in Theo D'haen et al. (eds.), *World Literature: A Reader* (London: Routledge, 2012), 9–15.
Grady, Hugh. *Shakespeare and Impure Aesthetics* (Cambridge: Cambridge University Press, 2009).
Grierson, George Abraham. *The Modern Vernacular Literature of Hindustan* (Calcutta: Asiatic Society, 1889).
Grierson, George Abraham. *Linguistic Survey of India*, 11 Vols. (Calcutta: Government of India Central Publication Branch, 1903–28).
Guha, Ranajit. *A Rule of Property for Bengal: An Essay on the Idea of Permanent Settlement* (Delhi: Orient Longman, 1982).
Guillory, John. *Cultural Capital: The Problem of Literary Canon Formation* (Chicago: University of Chicago Press, 1993).
Guise, Samuel. *A Catalogue of Oriental Manuscripts, Collected in Indoostan* (Calcutta: n.p., 1793).
Gumbrecht, Hans Ulrich. *The Powers of Philology: Dynamics of Textual Scholarship* (Urbana: University of Illinois Press, 2003).
Guyader, Hervé Le. *Étienne Geoffroy Saint-Hilaire, 1772–1844: A Visionary Naturalist*, trans. Marjorie Grene (Chicago: Chicago University Press, 2004).
Guyer, Paul. "Beauty, Freedom, and Morality: Kant's *Lectures on Anthropology* and the Development of His Aesthetic Theory," in Brian Jacobs and Patrick Kain (eds.), *Essays on Kant's Anthropology* (Cambridge: Cambridge University Press, 2003), 135–63.
Habermas, Jürgen. *The Structural Transformation of the Public Sphere: An Inquiry into a Category of Bourgeois Society*, trans. Thomas Burger (Cambridge, MA: MIT Press, 1991).
Halhed, Nathaniel Brassey. *A Code of Gentoo Laws, Or, Ordinations of the Pundits, from a Persian Translation, Made from the Original, Written in the Shanscrit Language* (London: n.p., 1776).
Halhed, Nathaniel Brassey. *A Grammar of the Bengal Language* (Hoogly: n.p., 1778).
Hallam, Henry. *Introduction to the Literature of Europe in the Fifteenth, Sixteenth, and Seventeenth Centuries*, 3 Vols. (London: John Murray, 1837–9).
Hamilton, Charles. *The Hedàya, or Guide; A Commentary on the Mussulman Laws*, 4 Vols. (London: T. Bensley, 1791).
Harris, Joseph. *The Instructive and Entertaining Fables of Pilpay, an Ancient Indian Philosopher. Containing a Number of Excellent Rules for the Conduct of*

Persons of All Ages, and in All Stations: Under Several Heads (London: J. F. and C. Rivington et al., 1789).

Hastings, Warren. *The Defence of Warren Hastings, Esq. (Late Governor General of Bengal,) at the Bar of the House of Commons* (London: J. Stockdale, 1786).

Hegel, G. W. F. *Elements of the Philosophy of Right*, trans. H. B. Nisbet (Cambridge: Cambridge University Press, 2003).

Heidegger, Martin. *The Question Concerning Technology and Other Essays*, trans. William Lovitt (New York: Harper, 1977).

Henry, Victor. *Les Littératures de l'Inde: Sanscrit, pâli, prâcrit* (Paris: Hachette, 1904).

Herder, Johann Gottfried von. *Philosophical Writings*, trans. and ed. Michael N. Forster (Cambridge: Cambridge University Press, 2002).

Hodgson, Brian Houghton. "Comparative Vocabulary of the Languages of the Broken Tribes of Népál," *Journal of the Asiatic Society of Bengal*, Vol. 26, No. 5 (1857), 333–71.

Hodgson, Brian Houghton. *Miscellaneous Essays Relating to Indian Subjects*, 2 Vols. (London: Trübner, 1880).

Holwell, J. Z. *Interesting Historical Events, Relative to the Provinces of Bengal, and the Empire of Indostan*, 3 Vols. (London: T. Becket and P. A. De Hondt, 1765).

Horta, Paulo Lemos. *Marvellous Thieves: Secret Authors of the Arabian Nights* (Cambridge, MA: Harvard University Press, 2017).

House of Commons. *Reports from Committees of the House of Commons*, 15 Vols. (London: House of Commons, 1804).

Hudson, William Henry. *An Outline History of English Literature* (London: G. Bell, 1912).

Hunter, W. W. *A Comparative Dictionary of the Languages of India and High Asia, with a Dissertation* (London: Trübner, 1868).

Hunter, W. W. *Life of Brian Houghton Hodgson: British Resident at the Court of Nepal* (London: John Murray, 1896).

Hunter, W. W. (ed.). *The Imperial Gazetteer of India*, 26 Vols. (Oxford: Clarendon, 1907–9).

Hussain, Nasser. *The Jurisprudence of Emergency: Colonialism and the Rule of Law* (Ann Arbor: University of Michigan Press, 2003).

Inden, Ronald. *Imagining India* (Oxford: Blackwell, 1990).

Jacob, Christian. *The Sovereign Map: Theoretical Approaches in Cartography throughout History*, trans. Tom Conley (Chicago: University of Chicago Press, 2006).

Johnson, Samuel. *A Dictionary of the English Language: In Which the Words Are Deduced from Their Originals, and Illustrated in Their Different Significations by Examples from the Best Writers*, 2 Vols. (London: W. Strahan, 1755).

Jones, William. *A Grammar of the Persian Language* (London: W. and J. Richardson, 1771).

Jones, William. *Poems, Consisting Chiefly of Translations from the Asiatick Languages* (Oxford: Clarendon, 1772).

Jones, William. *Al Shirájiyyah: Or, The Mohammedan Law of Inheritance, with a Commentary* (Calcutta: Joseph Cooper, 1792).

Jones, William. *Sacontalá; Or, The Fatal Ring: An Indian Drama by Cálidás* (London: Edwards, 1792).
Jones, William. *Institutes of Hindu Law: Or, The Ordinances of Menu* (Calcutta: Order of the Government, 1794).
Jones, William. *The Works of Sir William Jones*, 13 Vols. (London: John Stockdale and John Walker, 1807)
Kant, Immanuel. *Opus Postumum*, trans. Eckart Forster and Michael Rosen (Cambridge: Cambridge University Press, 1993).
Kant, Immanuel. *Critique of the Power of Judgment*, trans. Paul Guyer and Eric Matthews (Cambridge: Cambridge University Press, 2000).
Kant, Immanuel. "Of the Different Human Races," trans. Jon Mark Mikkelsen in Robert Barnasconi and Tommy Lee Lott (eds.) *The Idea of Race* (Indianapolis: Hackett, 2000), 8–22.
Kant, Immanuel. *Lectures on Logic*, trans. J. Michael Young (Cambridge: Cambridge University Press, 2004).
Kant, Immanuel. *Anthropology from a Pragmatic Point of View*, trans. Robert B. Louden (Cambridge: Cambridge University Press, 2006).
Keith-Falconer, I. G. N. *Kalilah and Dimnah or The Fables of Bidpai: Being an Account of Their Literary History, with an English Translation of the Later Syriac Version of the Same* (Cambridge: Cambridge University Press, 1885).
Kejariwal, O. P. *The Asiatic Society of Bengal and the Discovery of India's Past, 1784–1838* (Delhi: Oxford University Press, 1988).
Kemple, Thomas M. *Reading Marx Writing: Melodrama, the Market, and the "Grundrisse"* (Stanford: Stanford University Press, 1995).
Knox, Robert. *The Races of Men: A Fragment* (Philadelphia: Lea and Blanchard, 1850).
Koerner, Konrad. *Practicing Linguistic Historiography: Selected Essays* (Amsterdam: John Benjamins, 1989).
Kopf, David. *British Orientalism and the Bengal Renaissance: The Dynamics of Indian Modernization, 1773–1835* (Berkeley: University of California Press, 1969).
Lachmann, Karl. *Nolum Testamentum Graece et Latine*, Vol. 1 (Berlin: Reimer, 1842).
Lacoue-Labarthe, Philippe and Jean-Luc Nancy. *The Literary Absolute: The Theory of Literature in German Romanticism*, trans. Philip Barnard and Cheryl Lester (Albany, NY: SUNY Press, 1988).
Legouis, Émile. *A Short History of English Literature*, trans. V. F. Boyson and J. Coulson (Oxford: Clarendon, 1934).
Louden, Robert B. *Kant's Impure Ethics: From Rational Beings to Human Beings* (New York: Oxford University Press, 2000).
Louden, Robert B. *Kant's Human Being: Essays on His Theory of Human Nature* (Oxford: Oxford University Press, 2011).
Luckhurst, Roger. *The Mummy's Curse: The True History of a Dark Fantasy* (Oxford: Oxford University Press, 2012).
Macaulay, Thomas Babington. *Warren Hastings*, ed. K. Deighton (London: Macmillan, 1896).

Mackenzie, A. S. *History of English Literature* (New York: Macmillan, 1914).
Majeed, Javed. *Ungoverned Imaginings: James Mill's The History of British India and Orientalism* (Oxford: Clarendon Press, 1992).
Majeed, Javed. "What's in a (Proper) Name? Particulars, Individuals, and Authorship in the Linguistic Survey of India and Colonial Scholarship," in Indra Sengupta and Daud Ali (eds.), *Knowledge Production, Pedagogy, and Institutions in Colonial India* (New York: Palgrave, 2011), 19–39.
Majeed, Javed. *Colonialism and Knowledge in Grierson's Linguistic Survey of India* (London: Routledge, 2019).
Majeed, Javed. *Nation and Region in Grierson's Linguistic Survey of India* (London: Routledge, 2019).
Makdisi, Saree. *Romantic Imperialism: Universal Empire and the Culture of Modernity* (Cambridge: Cambridge University Press, 1998).
Mani, B. Venkat. *Recoding World Literature: Libraries, Print Culture, and Germany's Pact with Books* (New York: Fordham University Press, 2016).
Marshall, P. J. *The Impeachment of Warren Hastings* (Oxford: Oxford University Press, 1965).
Marshall, P. J. *Bengal: The British Bridgehead, Eastern India 1740–1828* (Cambridge: Cambridge University Press, 1987).
Martin, Wayne. "Fichte on Freedom," in Steven Hoeltzel (ed.), *The Palgrave Fichte Handbook* (London: Palgrave Macmillan, 2019), 285–306.
May, J. A. *Kant's Concept of Geography and Its Relation to Recent Geographical Thought* (Toronto: University of Toronto Press, 1970).
Mazlish, Bruce. *Civilization and Its Contents* (Stanford: Stanford University Press, 2005).
McDonald, Christie and Susan Rubin Suleiman (eds.). *French Global: A New Approach* (New York: Columbia University Press, 2010).
McGann, Jerome J. *A Critique of Modern Textual Criticism* (Charlottesville: Virginia University Press, 1992).
McNeil, Kenneth. *Scotland, Britain, Empire: Writing the Highlands, 1760–1860* (Columbus: Ohio University Press, 2007).
Metcalf, Thomas R. *Ideologies of the Raj* (Cambridge: Cambridge University Press, 1995).
Mitchell, Timothy. *Colonising Egypt* (Cambridge: Cambridge University Press, 1988).
Mitchell, Timothy. "The World as Exhibition," *Comparative Studies in Society and History*, Vol. 31, No. 2 (1989), 217–36.
Molnár, Géza von. "Goethe's Reading of Kant's 'Critique of Esthetic Judgment': A Referential Guide for Wilhelm Meister's Esthetic Education," *Eighteenth-Century Studies*, Vol. 15, No. 4 (Summer, 1982), 402–20.
Montesquieu, *The Spirit of the Laws*, trans. and ed. Anne M. Cohler et al. (Cambridge: Cambridge University Press, 1989).
Morley, Henry. *A First Sketch of English Literature* (London: Cassell, Petter, & Galpin, 1873).
Morrissey, Lee. *The Constitution of Literature: Literacy, Democracy, and Early English Literary Criticism* (Stanford: Stanford University Press, 2007).

Mott, Lewis F. "Renan and Matthew Arnold," *Modern Language Notes*, Vol. 33, No. 2 (1918), 65–73.
Mufti, Aamir R. "Orientalism and the Institution of World Literatures," *Critical Inquiry*, Vol. 36, No. 3 (Spring 2010), 458–93.
Mufti, Aamir R. *Forget English! Orientalisms and World Literatures* (Cambridge, MA: Harvard University Press, 2016).
Mukherjee, Nilanjana. *Spatial Imaginings in the Age of Colonial Cartographic Reason: Maps, Landscapes, Travelogues in Britain and India* (New York: Routledge, 2021).
Mukherjee, S. N. *Sir William Jones: A Study in Eighteenth-Century Attitudes to India* (Cambridge: Cambridge University Press, 1968).
Mulholland, James. *Before the Raj: Writing Early Anglophone India* (Baltimore: Johns Hopkins University Press, 2021).
Müller, Friedrich Max. *Chips from a German Workshop*, 4 Vols. (New York: Scribner, Armstrong, and Co., 1876).
Muthu, Sankar. *Enlightenment against Empire* (Princeton: Princeton University Press, 2003).
Nancy, Jean-Luc. *Dis-Enclosure: The Deconstruction of Christianity*, trans. Bettina Bergo et al. (New York: Fordham University Press, 2008).
Nietzsche, Friedrich. "Notes for 'We Philologists,'" trans. William Arrowsmith, *Arion*, Vol. 1, No. 2 (1973–4), 279–380.
Niranjana, Tejaswini, *Siting Translation: History, Post-structuralism, and the Colonial Context* (Berkeley: University of California Press, 1992).
North, Thomas. *The Earliest English Version of the Fables of Bidpai, "The Morall Philosophie of Doni" by Sir Thomas North*, ed. Joseph Jacobs (London: David Nutt, 1888).
Nykl, Alois Richard. "The Talisman in Balzac's *La Peau de chagrin*," *Modern Language Notes*, Vol. 34, No. 8 (1919), 479–81.
Ogborn, Miles. *Indian Ink: Script and Print in the Making of the English East India Company* (Chicago: Chicago University Press, 2008).
Olender, Maurice. *The Languages of Paradise: Race, Religion, and Philology in the Nineteenth Century*, trans. Arthur Goldhammer (Cambridge, MA: Harvard University Press, 2009).
Olender, Maurice. *Race and Erudition*, trans. Jane Marie Todd (Cambridge, MA: Harvard University Press, 2009).
Pischel, Richard. "Die Indische Literatur," in Erich Schmidt et al. (eds.), *Die orientalischen Literaturen* (Berlin: B. G. Teubner, 1906), 160–213.
Pizer, John. *The Idea of World Literature: History and Pedagogical Practice* (Baton Rouge: Louisiana State University Press, 2006).
Posnett, Hutcheson Macaulay. *Comparative Literature* (New York: D. Appleton and Company, 1886).
Prichard, James Cowles. *Researches into the Physical History of Man* (London: John and Arthur Arch, 1813).
Rancière, Jacques. *The Philosopher and His Poor*, trans. John Drury et al. (Durham, NC: Duke University Press, 2003).

Rancière, Jacques. *The Flesh of Words: The Politics of Writing*, trans. Charlotte Mandell (Stanford: Stanford University Press, 2004).
Rancière, Jacques. *The Politics of Aesthetics: The Distribution of the Sensible*, trans. Gabriel Rockhill (London and New York: Continuum, 2004).
Rancière, Jacques. *The Aesthetic Unconscious*, trans. Debra Keates and James Swenson (Cambridge: Polity, 2009).
Rancière, Jacques. *Dissensus: On Politics and Aesthetics*, trans. Steven Corcoran (London and New York: Continuum, 2010).
Rancière, Jacques. *Mute Speech: Literature, Critical Theory, and Politics*, trans. James Swenson (New York: Columbia University Press, 2011).
Rancière, Jacques. *The Politics of Literature*, trans. Julie Rose (Cambridge: Polity, 2011).
Reynolds, L. D. and N. G. Wilson. *Scribes and Scholars: A Guide to the Transmission of Greek and Latin Literature* (Oxford: Oxford University Press, 2013).
Rintelen, Fritz-Joachim von. "Goethe und Kant," *Wissenschaft und Weltbild*, Vol. 26 (April, 1973), 91–7.
Robertson, William. *Historical Disquisition Concerning the Knowledge Which the Ancients Had of India* (London: A. Strahan, and T. Cadell, 1791).
Rocher, Rosane. *Orientalism, Poetry, and the Millennium: The Checkered Life of Nathaniel Brassey Halhed* (Delhi: Motilal Banarsidass, 1983).
Rocher, Rosane. "Discovery of Sanskrit by Europeans," in E. F. K. Koerner and R. E. Asher (eds.), *Concise History of the Language Sciences: From the Sumerians to the Cognitivists* (Oxford: Pergamon, 1995), 188–91.
Said, Edward W. *Orientalism* (New York: Pantheon, 1978).
Said, Edward W. *The World, the Text, and the Critic* (Cambridge, MA: Harvard University Press, 1983).
Saintsbury, George. *A Short History of English Literature* (London: Macmillan, 1898).
Saussure, Ferdinand de. *Cours de linguistique générale* (Lausanne: Payot, 1916).
Schlegel, Friedrich. *Über die Sprache und Weisheit der Indier: Ein Beitrag zur Begründung der Alterthumskunde* (Heidelberg: Mohr und Zimmer, 1808).
Schlegel, Friedrich. *Geschichte der alten und neuen Literatur* (Berlin: M. Simion, 1841).
Schlegel, Friedrich. *The Æsthetic and Miscellaneous Works of Frederick von Schlegel*, trans. E. J. Millington (London: Henry G. Bohn 1849).
Schlegel, Friedrich. *Lectures on the History of Literature, Ancient and Modern*, trans. Publisher (London: George Bell, 1889).
Schroeder, Leopold von. *Indiens Literatur und Kultur in historischer Entwicklung* (Leipzig: Haessel, 1887).
Schwab, Raymond. *La Renaissance Orientale* (Paris: Payot 1950).
Schwab, Raymond. *Oriental Renaissance: Europe's Rediscovery of India and the East, 1680–1880*, trans. Gene Patterson-Black and Victor Reinking (New York: Columbia University Press, 1984).
Sen, Sudipta. *Empire of Free Trade: The East India Company and the Making of the Colonial Marketplace* (Philadelphia: University of Pennsylvania Press, 1998).

Sen, Sudipta. *A Distant Sovereignty: National Imperialism and the Origins of British India* (London: Routledge, 2016).
Shaw, Thomas B. *Shaw's New History of English Literature*, ed. Truman J. Backus (New York: Sheldon, 1874).
Simmel, Georg. *Kant und Goethe: Zur Geschichte der modernen Weltanschauung* (Leipzig: Kurt Wolff, 1916).
Singha, Radhika. *A Despotism of Law: Crime and Justice in Early Colonial India* (Delhi: Oxford University Press, 1998).
Sitter, Zak. "William Jones, 'Eastern' Poetry, and the Problem of Imitation," *Texas Studies in Literature and Language*, Vol. 50, No. 4 (2008), 385–407.
Smith, Adam. *An Inquiry into the Nature and Causes of the Wealth of Nations*, 2 Vols. (London: W. Strahan and T. Cadell, 1776).
Spivak, Gayatri Chakravorty. *A Critique of Postcolonial Reason: Toward a History of the Vanishing Present* (Cambridge, MA: Harvard University Press, 1999).
Stephens, Leslie. *English Literature and Society in the Eighteenth Century* (London: Duckworth, 1904).
Stern, Philip J. *The Company-State: Corporate Sovereignty and the Early Modern Foundations of the British Empire in India* (Oxford: Oxford University Press, 2011).
Subrahmanyam, Sanjay. *Europe's India: Words, People, Empires, 1500–1800* (Cambridge, MA: Harvard University Press, 2017).
Suleri, Sara. *The Rhetoric of English India* (Chicago: Chicago University Press, 1992).
Taine, H. *Histoire de la littérature anglaise*, 5 Vols. (Paris: Librairie de L. Hachette, 1863–9).
Tassy, Garcin de. *Histoire de la littérature hindoui et hindoustani* (Paris: Imprimerie royale, 1839).
Teltscher, Kate. *India Inscribed: European and British Writing on India, 1600–1800* (Oxford: Oxford University Press, 1997).
Thapar, Romila. *Śakuntalā: Texts, Readings, Histories* (New York: Columbia University Press, 2011).
Thompson, A. Hamilton. *A History of English Literature* (London: John Murray, 1901).
Timpanaro, Sebastiano. *The Genesis of Lachmann's Method*, trans. Glenn W. Most (Chicago: Chicago University Press, 2005).
Tod, James. *Annals and Antiquities of Rajasthan, or the Central and Western Rajput States of India*, 3 Vols., ed. William Crooke (Oxford: Oxford University Press, 1920).
Travers, Robert. *Ideology and Empire in Eighteenth-Century India: The British in Bengal* (Cambridge: Cambridge University Press, 2007).
Trautmann, Thomas R. *Aryans and British India* (Berkeley: University of California Press, 1997).
Trumpener, Katie. *Bardic Nationalism: The Romantic Novel and the British Empire* (Princeton: Princeton University Press, 2021).
Turner, James. *Philology: The Forgotten Origins of the Modern Humanities* (Princeton: Princeton University Press, 2014).

Venuti, Lawrence. "Translation as a Social Practice: Or, The Violence of Translation," *Translation Perspectives*, Vol. 9 (1996), 195–213.
Viswanathan, Gauri. *Masks of Conquest: Literary Study and British Rule in India* (New York: Columbia University Press, 1989).
Warton, Thomas. *The History of English Poetry*, 3 Vols. (London: J. Dodsley et al., 1774).
Watson, George (ed.). *The New Cambridge Bibliography of English Literature*, vol. II: *1660–1800* (Cambridge: Cambridge University Press, 1971).
Watt, Ian. *The Rise of the Novel: Studies in Defoe, Richardson and Fielding* (Berkeley: University of California Press, 1957).
Weber, Albrecht. *Akademische Vorlesungen über Indische Literaturgeschichte* (Berlin: F. Dümmler, 1852).
Weber, Samuel. *Unwrapping Balzac: A Reading of "La Peau de Chagrin"* (Toronto: University of Toronto Press, 1979).
Weinberg, Bernard. *French Realism: The Critical Reaction, 1830–1870* (New York: Modern Language Association of America, 1937).
Wellek, René. *The Rise of English Literary History* (Chapel Hill: University of North Carolina Press, 1941).
Wellek, René. *A History of Modern Criticism, 1750–1950*, vol. 1 (New Haven: Yale University Press, 1955).
Wellmon, Chad. *Becoming Human: Romantic Anthropology and the Embodiment of Freedom* (University Park: Pennsylvania State University, 2010).
White, Daniel E. *From Little London to Little Bengal: Religion, Print, and Modernity in Early British India, 1793–1835* (Baltimore: Johns Hopkins University Press, 2013).
White, Hayden. *The Content of the Form: Narrative Discourse and Historical Representation* (Baltimore: Johns Hopkins University Press, 1987).
Wilkins, Charles. *The Bhăgvăt-Gēētā, or Dialogues of Krĕĕshnă and Ărjŏŏn* (London: C. Nourse, 1785).
Wilkins, Charles. *The Hĕĕtōpădēs of Vĕĕshnŏŏ-Sărmā, in a Series of Connected Fables, Interspersed with Moral, Prudential, and Political Maxims; Translated from an Ancient Manuscript in the Sanskreet Language with Explanatory Notes* (Bath and London: R. Cruttwell, 1787).
Williams, Monier. *Śakuntalá; Or Śakuntalá Recognized by the Ring* (Hertford: Stephen Austin, 1853).
Williams, Monier (trans.). *Śakoontalá; Or, The Lost Ring; an Indian Drama* (Hertford: Stephen Austin, 1856).
Wilson, Horace Hayman. *Select Specimens of the Theatre of the Hindus, Translated from the Original Sanscrit*, 3 Vols. (Calcutta: Asiatic Press, 1827).
Wilson, Horace Hayman. *Sketch on the Religious Sects of the Hindus* (Calcutta: Bishop's College Press, 1847).
Wooloch, Alex. *The One vs. the Many: Minor Characters and the Space of the Protagonist in the Novel* (Princeton: Princeton University Press, 2003).
Wyatt, A. J. *The Tutorial History of English Literature* (London: University Tutorial Press, 1928).

Yeazell, Ruth Bernard. *Art of the Everyday: Dutch Painting and the Realist Novel* (Princeton: Princeton University Press, 2008).
Yee, Jennifer. *The Colonial Comedy: Imperialism in the French Realist Novel* (Oxford: Oxford University Press, 2016).
Young, Robert J. C. *Colonial Desire: Hybridity in Theory, Culture and Race* (London: Routledge, 1995).
Zammito, John H. *The Genesis of Kant's Critique of Judgment* (Chicago: University of Chicago Press, 1992).
Zammito, John H. *Kant, Herder, and the Birth of Anthropology* (Chicago: University of Chicago Press, 2002).

Index

Abhijñānaśākuntalam, 31, 75
Abrams, M. H., 62, 63, 251
Ābu Ḥānifā, 100
Abu-Lughod, Janet, 85, 87, 254
Addison, Joseph, 209
aesthetic judgment, ix, 34, 47, 150, 151, 165, 168, 169, 171–3, 264
aesthetics, 5, 24, 34, 36, 44, 47, 149–54, 162, 163, 170–3, 175, 176, 238, 240, 262
Agamben, Giorgio, 27
Ahmed, Siraj, xi, 118, 246, 249, 253, 258, 259
allegory, 8, 25
Anderson, Benedict, 180, 265
Angelo, Michael, 182
Anglo-Saxon, 205, 206, 220, 225, 233–5
animal fables, 66, 79, 83–9, 127, 253
Anquetil-Duperron, Abraham-Hyacinthe, 22, 60, 178
anthropology, 3, 7, 9, 14, 15, 23, 29, 44, 45, 63, 150, 151, 153, 155, 156, 158, 159, 163–5, 170–3, 176, 202, 227, 234, 237, 242, 263, 264
Anthropology from a Pragmatic Point of View, 34, 47, 150, 156, 263
Apter, Emily, x, 83, 248, 253
Arabian Nights, 37, 38, 87, 88, 183, 249, 266
Arabic, 3, 5, 10, 18, 20–2, 37, 39, 41, 44, 55, 64, 70, 84–6, 88, 91, 97–9, 103, 104, 185, 186, 196, 197, 215, 248, 253, 254, 267
Aravamudan, Srinivas, 37, 61, 67, 87, 114, 249, 250, 253, 254, 257
Arnold, Matthew, 43, 44, 48, 203, 219, 227–35, 240, 249, 270, 271
Asiatic Society of Bengal, 1, 33, 88, 118, 120, 143, 243, 260
Asiatick Researches, 33, 47, 73, 119, 179, 247
Athenaeum (1798–1800), 9
Auerbach, Erich, 119, 144, 175, 261, 265

Balzac, Honoré de, 36, 38, 48, 67, 154, 155, 176–8, 180–3, 185–7, 191–7, 199, 200, 240, 265–7
Baumgarten, Alexander, 34, 150, 151
Beddoe, John, 221, 224, 225, 270

Benfey, Theodor, 86
Benjamin, Walter, 26, 86, 199, 254, 268
Beowulf, 234
Bernal, Martin, 188, 189, 267
Bhattacharya, Baidik, xi, 265, 270, 271
Bidpāi, 37, 83–5, 87, 88, 90
Birth of Tragedy, The, 118
Blackburn, Stuart, 144, 261
Blair, Hugh, 208
Boccaccio, Giovanni, 37, 87
Böhtlingk, Otto von, 79
Bopp, Franz, 38, 39, 122, 193, 235, 249
Boswell, James, 1
Breckenridge, Keith, 225, 270
Burke, Edmund, 1, 6, 14, 24, 84, 101–16, 245, 253, 256, 257
Burton, Richard, 37, 180
Butler, Samuel, 224
Byron, Lord, 182, 192, 229

Carey, William, 26, 122, 130
Carter, Elizabeth, 1
Cassin, Barbara, 83, 248, 253
caste system, the, 74, 109, 110
census reports, 119, 123, 124, 129, 140, 141, 259
Chakrabarty, Dipesh, 239, 271
Chambers, Robert, 224
Chateaubriand, 32, 75, 179
Chaucer, Geoffrey, 87, 208, 220, 234, 235
Code of Gentoo Laws, or, Ordinations of the Pundits, A, 3, 18, 70, 128, 247, 251
Coetzee, J. M., 241
Cohn, Bernard, 24, 68, 70, 117, 119, 121, 245, 247, 249, 251, 253, 258, 259
Coke, Edward, 98
Colebrooke, H. T., 25, 26, 31, 39, 70, 215, 243, 244, 247
Collins, William, 61, 205
colonial governance, ix, 3, 6, 7, 9, 15, 16, 26, 28, 44, 46, 53, 55, 57, 58, 68, 79, 81, 84, 94, 105, 115, 117–19, 122, 131, 134, 145, 146, 176, 179, 180, 202, 240, 244

286

colonial sovereignty, 5, 7
common law, 5, 16, 98, 99, 101–3
company-state, 7, 11
comparatism, 46, 70, 117–19, 121, 122, 124, 128, 129, 131, 136, 142–4, 159, 161, 163, 168–70, 192, 216
Comparative Dictionary of the Languages of India and High Asia, 47, 130, 260
cosmopolitanism, 34
Courthope, W. J., 219, 270
Critique of Pure Reason, 152, 155, 163
Critique of the Power of Judgment, 34, 47, 150, 162, 165, 168, 169, 171, 172, 264
Culler, Jonathan, 180, 265
Culture and Anarchy, 43, 219, 232, 271
customary law, 99
customs and manners, 53, 97, 103, 110–12, 116
Cuvier, Georges, 36, 38, 175, 192–4, 268

Dalmia, Vasudha, 144, 261
Damrosch, David, x, xi, 87, 248, 254, 261, 271
de Buffon, Comte, 14
De la littérature dans ses rapports avec les institutions sociales, 2 Vols. (1799), 9
de Staël, Germaine, 9
decolonization, x, 10, 49, 239–42
Deleuze, Gilles, 264
democratic petrification, 36–8, 48, 154, 155, 175, 176, 183
Derrida, Jacques, 90, 255
Description de l'Égypte, 38
despotism, 13
Dharmaśāstra, 7
Dictionary of the English Language, A, 5
Diderot, Denis, 14
Dirks, Nicholas, 56, 104, 108, 225, 250, 256, 257, 270
Dou, Gerrit, 181, 182
Dow, Alexander, 3, 13–15, 17–19, 22, 41, 62, 88, 110, 182, 246, 247, 253, 254
Dryden, John, 207

East India Company, 1, 3, 6–9, 11–17, 21–3, 25–7, 40, 46, 56, 68, 69, 76, 82, 84, 88, 95–8, 101–3, 105, 106, 109–16, 120, 144, 145, 243, 245–7, 253, 256, 257, 271
Eckermann, Johann Peter, 32, 33, 35, 149–51, 159–61, 248, 261–3
Edwards, W. F., xi, 219, 221, 227, 230, 252
Egypt, 4, 73, 119, 126, 178–80, 188, 196, 199, 265
Elements of the Philosophy of Right (1821), 6
empire, 16, 18, 26, 31, 33, 49, 57, 77, 79, 95, 97, 100, 102, 104, 106, 107, 108, 111, 115, 118, 119, 130, 159, 198, 201, 209, 210, 217, 219, 223, 225, 236, 240, 241, 244

English East India Company, 11
English literature, 120, 137–9, 202, 205, 220, 228–31, 234, 235
English poetry, 202, 204–8, 229, 231
Enlightenment anti-imperialism, 14
Erasmus, Desiderius, 46, 58
Errington, Joseph, 253
ethnographic recension, 46, 54, 55, 81, 82, 103, 117
ethnology, 46, 121, 126, 180, 181, 215, 217, 227, 229, 232
Eze, Emmanuel, 164, 165, 168, 264

Fichte, Johann Gottlieb, 48, 188, 202, 210–18, 267, 269
Firishtā, Muḥammad Qāsim, 18
Flaubert, Gustave, 48, 154, 179, 199, 200
Fort William College, 21, 40, 146, 249, 257
Foucault, Michel, 38–41, 45, 55, 117, 119, 121, 130, 155–8, 160, 172, 193, 232, 249, 258, 263, 268
Fox, Charles James, 84, 105, 108, 257
Fraser, James, 3, 17, 22, 88, 89, 246, 254

Galland, Antoine, 37, 83
General Grammar, 57
Gibbon, Edward, 1
Gilchrist, John Borthwick, 40, 249
Girtanner, Christoph, 163
Gobineau, Arthur de, 221, 264
Goethe, Johann Wolfgang von, 4, 32–6, 42, 44, 47, 48, 64, 75, 118, 119, 149–51, 158–62, 165, 168, 172–4, 229, 230, 237, 240, 248, 261–4
Goldsmith, Oliver, 66
grammar, 26
Grammar of the Bengal Language, A, 3, 20, 57, 72, 247, 250, 252
Grammar of the Persian Language, A, 22, 56
Gray, Thomas, 205, 206, 229
Grierson, George Abraham, 47, 118, 119, 121–4, 127–32, 136–46, 258–61
Grimm, Jacob, 38, 193
Guha, Ranajit, 22

Habermas, Jürgen, 204, 209, 210, 269
Ḥāfiẓ, 4, 25
Halhed, Nathaniel Brassey, 3, 18, 19, 23, 24, 30, 32, 40, 57, 70–5, 77, 112, 114, 115, 128, 139, 247, 250–2
Hallam, Henry, 220, 221, 270
Hamilton, Charles, 46, 95–8, 103–6, 116, 235, 250, 255, 256, 271
Hastings, Warren, 7, 15–18, 21–4, 29, 30, 33, 37, 43, 45, 46, 55, 57, 68–70, 74, 80, 84, 100, 102, 105–7, 109, 110, 112–16, 120, 121, 245–8, 251, 256–8

Hēētōpādēs of Vēēshnōō-Sārmā, 89
Hegel, Georg Wilhelm Friedrich, 6, 13
Heidegger, Martin, 201, 268
Herder, Johann Gottfried, 13
Hindu, 3, 7, 17–19, 24, 26, 28, 31, 53, 68, 70, 73, 75, 76, 78–80, 84, 92, 94, 106, 110, 112, 113, 115, 116, 125, 126, 248, 252, 259
Histoire philosophique et politique des établissements et du commerce des Européens dans les deux Indes (1770), 14
historicism, 38, 55, 59, 60, 139, 236
History of British India, The, 110
History of Hindostan, The, 3, 13
Hitopadeśa, 89, 91
Hobbes, Thomas 108, 112
Hodgson, Brian Houghton, 47, 118, 129–32, 134, 136, 141, 145, 244, 260
Holwell, John Zephaniah, 3, 17, 19, 22, 110, 112, 246, 257
Homer, 21, 32, 66, 68, 75, 171, 207
Hume, David, 13, 151, 209
Hunter, William Wilson, 3, 47, 118, 123, 130–2, 134, 136, 141, 145, 244, 260

Iliad, 66, 69, 224
impeachment, 46, 84, 105–10, 113–16, 256, 257
Imperial Gazetteer of India, The, 123, 259
imperialism, 5, 14, 27, 33, 43, 101, 106, 150, 238, 240
India, ix, 1–7, 11–13, 15–19, 21–9, 31, 32, 35, 37, 40, 43–5, 47, 48, 53, 54, 56, 62, 65–9, 73, 74, 76–84, 86, 88, 94, 95, 98, 102–20, 122–4, 126, 129–32, 134, 136, 137, 139–46, 149, 178, 183, 189, 190, 193, 202, 217, 223, 225, 243–53, 256–61, 265, 266, 269, 270
indigenous cultural world, 14
Indo-European hypothesis, 4, 20, 38, 40, 42, 86, 89, 117, 118, 179, 189, 190, 192, 202, 203, 215, 217, 225, 230–6
Inquiry into the Nature and Causes of the Wealth of Nations, An (1776), 6
Institutes of Hindu Law: Or, The Ordinances of Menu, 70
Interesting Historical Events, Relative to the Provinces of Bengal, and the Empire of Indostan, 3, 110, 246
Introduction to the Literature of Europe in the Fifteenth, Sixteenth, and Seventeenth Centuries, 220
Islam, 13, 65, 66, 73, 96, 139, 253

Jacobinism, 102
Jacobs, Joseph, 85, 87, 249, 253, 254, 261
James, Henry, 1, 3, 17, 57, 84, 88, 105, 110, 138, 144, 181, 205, 208, 221, 243, 245, 246, 254, 257, 259, 261, 262, 264, 265, 269, 270

Jayadeva, 25
Jena Romantics, 9, 75, 119, 152, 153
Johnson, Samuel, 1, 5, 42, 57, 205, 208, 209, 243, 244, 250, 255
Jones, Sir William, 1–5, 7, 10, 20–2, 24, 25, 28, 29, 31–3, 35, 37–41, 43, 44, 46, 47, 55–68, 70, 72–80, 88–90, 94, 98–101, 103–6, 112, 116–28, 130–2, 136, 141, 142, 144, 145, 151, 178, 188, 190, 215, 217, 222, 235, 243, 247, 248, 250–2, 254–60, 264, 265, 267, 269
"Third Anniversary Discourse" (1786), 4
Journal of the Asiatic Society, 47, 130, 143, 260

Kālidāsa, 4, 31, 32, 75, 77–80, 119, 178
Kant, Immanuel, 13–15, 34, 35, 47, 48, 150–73, 240, 246, 261–4
Keats, John, 229
Kipling, Rudyard, 241
Knox, Robert, 221–5, 229, 270
Koerner, Konrad, 193, 251, 268
Kopf, David, 117, 258

La Comédie humaine, 177, 183, 194–6
La Fontaine, Jean de 37, 86, 87
La Peau de chagrin, 36, 38, 155, 176, 177, 181, 183, 186, 187, 191, 192, 196, 265, 267
Lachmann, Karl, 46, 59, 250
Lacoue-Labarthe, Philippe, 119, 152–4, 171, 258, 262–4, 267
Lamartine, Alphonse de, 75
Lane, Edward, 37, 179, 199
Lebrun, Jean Baptiste Pierre, 182
Legouis, Émile, 235, 271
Linguistic Survey of India, 47, 118, 122, 258–61
literary history, ix, 9, 40–2, 44, 47, 48, 143, 145, 188–93, 200–3, 205–7, 209, 210, 214, 215, 217–21, 231, 233–5, 237, 240, 242
literary singularity, 5, 8, 28, 30, 43, 248
literary sovereign, 1, 5, 6, 8–10, 19–21, 25, 27, 29, 30, 32, 35–40, 43–9, 53, 55, 57, 75, 80, 81, 117–19, 149, 150, 173, 174, 176, 177, 187, 192, 200–3, 210, 211, 218, 232, 233, 235, 237, 240, 241
Littleton, Thomas de, 98
Locke, John 108

Macaulay, Thomas Babington, 236, 256, 271
Macpherson, James, 208, 209
Makdisi, Saree, 210, 269
Malory, Thomas, 227
manners and customs, 7, 8, 14
Marshall, P. J., 84, 245, 253, 256
Marx, Karl, 42, 119, 266, 268
Mill, James, 110, 138, 257
Milton, John, 69, 143, 144, 229

mimesis, 8, 9
Mitchell, Timothy, 198, 199, 265, 268
Molnár, Géza von, 150, 158, 262
Montesquieu, 13, 66, 246, 250
The Morall Philosophie of Doni: Drawne out of the ancient writers, 85
More, Hannah, 1
Morley, Henry, 233, 234, 271
Morrissey, Lee, 209, 269
Mosaic history, 125, 126, 190, 191
Muʿallaqāt, 76, 119, 178
Mufti, Aamir R., x, 68, 117, 145, 190, 244, 249, 251, 258, 261, 267
Mughal, 12, 15, 16, 100, 106, 115, 145, 146, 253, 254
Muhammad, Sirāj al-Dīn, 99
Müller, Friedrich Max, 86, 122, 254

Naipaul, V. S., 241
Nancy, Jean-Luc, 30, 119, 152–4, 171, 248, 258, 262–4, 267
Napoleon Bonaparte, 177, 179, 196, 211
nation, 9, 10, 21, 24, 34, 35, 39, 44, 48, 54, 55, 65, 74, 75, 78, 107, 111, 136, 188–90, 193, 195, 196, 201–3, 205, 207–13, 215, 218–23, 228–32, 235–8, 267
national literature, 21, 34, 120, 136–8, 149, 188, 190, 203, 220, 221, 228, 232, 234, 236, 237
Nerval, Gérard de, 199
New Testament, 53, 59
Nietzsche, Friedrich, 118, 120, 259
Niranjana, Tejaswini, 253
Norman conquest, 206, 220, 225, 234
North, Sir Thomas, 6, 85, 86, 94, 95, 102, 144, 145, 221, 249, 253, 254, 260, 268

Odyssey, 69, 224
Olender, Maurice, 43, 176, 219, 244, 249, 265, 270
On the Study of Celtic Literature, 48, 227, 231, 233, 270
Oriental Renaissance, 4
orientalism, 37, 58, 67, 70, 71, 106, 121, 131, 181, 183, 185, 187, 196
Ossian, 32, 208, 209, 269

Pañcatantra, 37, 85, 87, 88, 91, 254
Pāṇini, 26
paradigm, 32, 34, 35, 44, 45, 47, 48, 55, 75, 80, 81, 117, 119, 130, 144, 149, 156, 159, 165, 173–6, 182, 183, 187, 191, 192, 200, 203, 238, 241
performative language, 8
Persian, 1, 3–5, 10, 17–22, 24, 30, 37, 39, 40, 41, 44, 55–7, 61, 62, 64, 66, 68, 70–2, 75, 84, 85, 88, 91, 98, 100, 103, 119, 126, 196, 215, 246–8, 250, 251, 253, 254

philology, 4, 7, 21, 24, 26, 38–43, 45, 46, 72, 117–23, 126–8, 134, 154, 189–91, 193, 197, 202, 215, 216, 218, 222, 227–32, 234, 235, 237, 242, 250, 264
comparative philology, 39, 72, 117, 118, 122, 126, 191, 193, 236
Philosophical Enquiry into the Origin of Our Ideas of the Sublime and Beautiful, A, 108
phrenology, 224
Pilpay, 37, 83, 85–8, 90, 91, 254, 255
Plutarch, 85
Poems, Consisting Chiefly of Translations from the Asiatick Languages, 20, 60, 247, 251
Politian, 46, 58
political sovereignty, 8
Pope, Alexander, 205–7
Posnett, Hutcheson Macaulay, 236, 237, 271
postcolonial, ix, x, 49, 239–42
Postcolonial Writing in the Era of World Literature: Texts, Territories, Globalizations, 240
Power of the Critique of Judgment, 152
Prichard, James, 221, 222, 225, 227, 229, 270

race, 14, 15, 32, 42, 43, 48, 108, 134, 136, 151, 163–5, 167, 169, 170, 176, 189, 197, 201–3, 205–7, 210, 213–25, 227–31, 233–5, 237, 241, 264
Races of Britain, The, 224
Races of Men: A Fragment, The, 222
Rancière, Jacques, 36, 38, 48, 154, 155, 174–8, 180–5, 191, 192, 248, 249, 263–6, 268
Rask, Rasmus, 38, 193
recensio, 59–62, 66–71, 76, 77, 79, 80
Reflections on the Revolution in France, 101, 102, 104, 105, 256
Reiske, Johann Jacob, 59
Rembrandt, 182, 266
Renan, Ernest, 43, 219, 221, 227, 228, 249, 270
Reynolds, Joshua, 1
Rousseau, Jean-Jacques, 151, 164, 262
Royal Society of England, 2
rule of law, 16
Rushdie, Salman, 241

Sacontalá; Or, The Fatal Ring, 28, 31, 32, 75, 77, 252
Sacy, Silvestre de, 38, 197, 198
Said, Edward, 117, 176, 179, 181, 185, 196, 197, 258, 265–7
Saint-Hilaire, Étienne Geoffroy, 194, 199, 268
Śakoontalá; Or, The Lost Ring; an Indian Drama, 78
Sanskrit, 3–5, 10, 16–20, 22, 24–6, 30, 37, 39, 40, 44, 55, 68–75, 77, 78, 80, 84, 85, 88, 90–3, 97, 117, 119, 120, 124, 126–9, 143, 144, 174, 184–7, 193, 215, 248–51, 259, 260
Sanzio, Raphael, 182

Saussure, Ferdinand de, 117, 132, 258
Scaliger, Joseph, 46, 58
Schlegel, Friedrich, 4, 13, 32, 38–42, 44, 48, 75, 187–93, 199, 200, 202, 210, 215–18, 221, 222, 234–6, 244, 249, 267–9
Schwab, Raymond, 4, 31–3, 75, 117, 178, 187, 244, 248, 252, 258, 265, 267
Select Specimens of the Theatre of the Hindus, Translated from the Original Sanscrit, 78, 249
Shakespeare, William, 33–5, 53, 66, 77, 78, 85, 229, 230, 233, 235, 253, 262
Shariʿa, 7
Sharīf, Sayyid, 99
Sheridan, Richard B., 19, 84, 250
singularity, 27, 28
Sirāj-ud-Daulāh, 12
Smith, Adam, 6, 12
somapolitics, 176, 225
sovereignty, ix, 5, 6, 8, 9, 12–15, 17, 25–30, 33, 35, 44–6, 53, 82, 84, 92, 94, 95, 100–4, 106–8, 111–13, 115, 116, 189, 201, 210, 212, 233, 237, 240
Spitzer, Leo, 119
Spivak, Gayatri Chakravorty, x, 33, 159, 248, 263
state of exception, 27
Steele, Richard, 209
stemmatics, 59, 250
Stephen, Leslie, 219, 248, 252
Stern, Philip, 11
sublime, 47, 62, 65, 68, 108–11, 114, 115, 152, 162, 257
Suleri, Sara, 108, 110, 256, 257
Supreme Court of Judicature of Bengal, 1
Swift, Jonathan, 87, 250

Tales Translated from the Persian of Inatulla of Delhi, 3, 17, 62, 246
Tasso, 32, 75
Tassy, Garcin de, 143–5, 261
textual criticism, 53–5, 57, 58, 61, 67, 70, 76, 79, 210
Thapar, Romila, 77
Theocritus, 32, 75
Tod, James, 144, 261

translation, 1, 3, 9, 11, 18, 19, 22, 23, 25, 29, 31, 36, 37, 46, 56, 58, 60, 61, 69, 70, 73, 75, 76, 78–94, 96–101, 103–6, 114, 115, 117, 119, 123, 124, 160, 178, 184, 186, 187, 247, 253–5, 266, 267
Trautmann, Thomas, 121, 217, 244, 250, 251, 253, 259, 269
Trumpener, Katie, 208, 269

untranslatability, 11, 29, 31, 84, 94, 115, 117
untranslatables, 29, 46, 82–4, 90, 91, 94, 98, 104, 106, 114

Vedas, 20, 71, 74, 217, 218
Venuti, Lawrence, 83, 253
vernacular, 42, 124, 127, 142–6, 188, 205
Viswanathan, Gauri, 137–9, 249, 259
Voltaire, 13, 87, 178, 224, 250

Walpole, Horace, 205
Warton, Thomas, 42, 48, 202–10, 220, 235, 269
Weinberg, Bernard, 181, 266
Wellek, René, 202, 204, 251, 268, 269
Weltliteratur, 6, 32, 47, 64, 121, 149, 156, 158, 160, 168, 174, 240, 248
White, Hayden, 109
Wilkins, Charles, 23, 26, 28, 30, 32, 37–9, 46, 69, 70, 74, 75, 89–94, 97, 98, 100, 104, 116, 139, 151, 247, 251, 255
Williams, Monier, 78–80, 122, 252
Wilson, Horace Hayman, 3, 47, 54, 78–80, 118, 144, 249, 250, 252, 260, 261
Wolf, Friedrich August, 59
Wordsworth, William, 42, 229, 230
World Exhibition, 197, 198
world literature, ix, 6, 9, 21, 32, 34–7, 42, 44, 48, 87, 117, 149–51, 158–63, 165, 172–4, 177, 187, 191, 196, 201, 237, 239, 240, 242, 244, 266

Yeazell, Ruth, 181, 182, 266

Zend-Āvestā, 22, 60, 178